MAJOR LEWIS W. McKEE (1854-1930)

A HISTORY

Of

Anderson County

Begun in 1884 by

Major Lewis W. McKee

Concluded in 1936 by

Mrs. Lydia K. Bond

1780-1936

"Those who live in history only seem to walk the earth again."
—Longfellow.

"I like to see a man proud of the place in which he lives. I like to to see a man who lives in it so live that his place will be proud of him."
—Abraham Lincoln.

CLEARFIELD COMPANY

Originally Published
Frankfort, Kentucky
[1937]

Reprinted
Regional Publishing Company
Baltimore, 1975

In Cooperation with
Anderson County Historical Society
Lawrenceburg, Kentucky

Library of Congress Catalogue Card Number 75-15200
International Standard Book Number 0-8063-8004-7

CONTENTS

CHAPTER I

	Page
The First White Man	7
Wilderness Trails	9
The First White Men	9
Early Settlement of Anderson, Franklin and Mercer	12
Descriptions of the Large Stations	14
Jacob Coffman, First Anderson County Pioneer	15
Captain Arnold and Samuel Hutton	17
Daniel Boone	18

CHAPTER II

Early Land Entries	21
Samuel Arbuckle, Pioneer Builder	24
The Town of Lawrence	25
Early Sales of Lots in Lawrence (Afterwards Lawrenceburg)	28
Alleys in Lawrenceburg	30-31
History of the Pierian Club Building	32
The Erection of Anderson County	33
Early Settlement of Lawrenceburg	37

CHAPTER III

Names of Men in Anderson County in 1827	40
First Court House	42
First County Court	50
First Jail	53
Pillory, Stocks and Whipping Post	55
First Circuit Court in Anderson County	55
Second Term of County Court	57

CHAPTER IV

Old Court Records	59
Turn Pikes in Anderson County	61
Slavery in Anderson County	62
Guerrillas in Anderson County	64
Asiatic Cholera	66

CHAPTER V

Bonds Mill Established by J. F. Hudgins	67
Covered Bridges	68
Early Factories in Lawrenceburg	69
Early Industries Reviewed	70
Old Fields	73
Noted Springs in Anderson County	74
Unknown Confederate Soldiers	76

CHAPTER VI

	Page
Reminiscences	78
Confederate Soldiers in Anderson County	79
Mexican War Volunteers	82
Revolutionary Soldiers	83
Disasterous Fires	84
Early Churches	85-89
Marriages in Anderson County, 1830-1835	90-91

CHAPTER VII

First Anderson County Schools	92-94
Personal Sketches—Capt. James Gustavus Dedman, Major Draffen	95
Nathan Hammond, The Utterbacks	96
Matthew Galt	97
Capt. W. E. Bell, James F. Witherspoon	98
Capt. E. Scott Dawson	98
Ephrim Lillard and Family	100
Rev. John Penny	101
Dr. Richard Randolph Stephenson	101
Grandison Utterback	103
Memucan Allin	103
Richard Clough Anderson	104
William B. Wallace	106
Jordon H. Walker	107
Wilsons, Ripys and Others, Naturalized	107

CHAPTER VIII

Anderson County Officers	109
Common School Commissioners	110
Coroners	111
Clerks	111
Representatives	111
County Attorneys	112
Judges	113
Sheriffs	113

BOOK II

CHAPTER I

Resume of Early History	119
Lawrenceburg Today	120
Towns of Anderson County	123-129
Lawrenceburg Cemetery	129
Mounds	130

CHAPTER II

	Page
Banks of Lawrenceburg	131
Anderson County Fair Association	132
Great Fires in Lawrenceburg	133
The Fire Department	133
Schools of Anderson County	134-139
Churches	140-147

CHAPTER III

Industries—Thread, Broom and Cheese Factories	148
Distilleries, Newspapers and Flour Mills	149-154
Walnut Grove Stock Farm and Hatcheries	154
Electric Light and Ice Plant	154-155
First Railroad and Tyrone Bridges	155-159

CHAPTER IV

The Confederate Monument	160
Clubs—Commercial, Magazine, Rotary, Scouts and Book Club	160-163
Masonic Lodge, D. A. R., U. D. C. and Pierian Club	164-167
Montrose	167
Anderson County in the World War	168
Sons of Anderson County Pioneers	170-178

CHAPTER V

Kentucky's First Settlers	179
Family Sketches	180-212
Yesteryears in Anderson County	213
Old Records	217
Black Mammys	218
Finale	218

Foreword

Major Lewis W. McKee over a period of many years compiled historic data, narrative and information which he had planned to incorporate into a history of Anderson County. The work was begun in 1884 when he was a member of the State Senate at Frankfort, Ky. At his death in 1930, the large portfolio of his manuscript was entrusted to his son, Andrew Irwin McKee, Lieutenant Commander in the United States Navy, stationed at the Navy yards in Philadelphia. This young man had no time to assemble and prepare for publication his father's history of the county, nor did he have recourse to our courthouse records for research in completing the work. It was a kindly honor when the son brought the manuscript back to Kentucky in 1934 and requested me, an old neighbor of his parents, to assemble the scattered pages, decipher the faint handwriting, fill in the gaps and give it to the public that had requested the history from Major McKee's pen.

The work shows much preliminary labor, for, prior to 1827 Anderson had been a part of Franklin County for thirty-three years, and Major McKee had to search old records in the Franklin County Court for much of our early history. He made his first notes from 1884 to '89, and he has "linked our present and the future with the living 18th century," whose decades are of historic significance to the people of Anderson County.

Sir Walter Raleigh said, "It is not the least debt we owe unto history that it has made us acquainted with our dead ancestors; and out of the depth and darkness of the earth delivered us their memory and fame." In the history of Anderson County, we find the people of this community perpetuating the names of our early settlers. Major McKee made sketches of some of the pioneer families. He observed there were some gaps in the narration of events, some of the history shadowy and some "hear-say," but he has taken meager known facts, and as a scientist reconstructs a dinosaur from a few bones, he has brought to life something of real value for the people of this locality who appreciate the work of their forebears. I have delved into the records of the court house for information suggested in Major McKee's notes, have gleaned additional facts and gathered later history and inserted it into the original. Other citizens of the county interested in the romance of our beginnings, have been consulted and lent valuable assistance.

I cannot arrange the early history of the county as Major McKee would have done it, but have tried to put it in proper sequence according to dates and historical setting of events. Major McKee was a deep student of history. He had an alert mind, a retentive memory, a keen intellect, and kept in touch with public affairs, which endowed him with ability to give the historic events embraced in this book. He was a successful lawyer and took an active interest in the political life of the country. He was an honored and respected citizen, and just what he was without pretense. In supplementing and arranging this history of Anderson County, we have but tried to

"Hold high the torch, you did not light its glow,
'Twas given you by other hands you know;
'Tis only yours to keep burning bright
And pass to others when you no more need light."

—Lydia Kennedy Bond.

BOOK I

Young's High Bridge and the Joe Blackburn Bridge over Kentucky River at Tyrone.

CHAPTER I

THE FIRST WHITE MAN IN ANDERSON COUNTY

The probability is that the first white man in Anderson county was Christopher Gist. The following account is taken by Judge Kerr, or a writer for the History of Kentucky which he edited, from the diary of Christopher Gist, an account of which occurs in Vol. 1. The Ohio company was formed in the Colony of Virginia in 1748. One of the members of that company was John Hanberry, a merchant of London. The other eighteen members were inhabitants of the Province of Maryland, and all were prominent in the affairs of their time. The company was granted 200,000 acres of land. It was to be located on the south side of the Ohio river, between Kiskiminitis creek and Buffalo creek, and on the north side of the Ohio between Buffalo creek and Cross creek. This manner of grant would place an English settlement on the north side of the Ohio river, and at that time there was a very unfriendly rivalry between the English and the French for the possession of all the land west of the Alleghaney mountains, and in making this grant of land to this Ohio company, the Colony of Virginia was binding its efforts to colonize the territory with English settlers. The French were equally as strenuous in their efforts for possession of this territory. The land was given with the condition that the company would settle 100 families thereon, within seven years, and also erect and maintain an adequate fort. If these conditions were complied with, the company was to become entitled to 300,000 acres of additional adjoining land.

In preparation for the compliance with the terms of the grant, the company erected a large storehouse, and perhaps other buildings opposite what is now the city of Cumberland, Maryland. From this point it caused a road to be opened to the Turkey Foot, as the point of the three forks of the Yonghiogheny was called. This road was completed in 1751. A large quantity of merchandise suitable for this particular trade was sent over from England in 1749 and '50, and placed in the storehouse; and in further pursuance of its engagements, the company employed Christopher Gist to make an exploration of the country in which the operation of its enterprise was to be conducted. Gist was a surveyor, a native of Maryland, of excellent character, energetic, fearless and a thorough woodsman. The instructions to Gist were brief and mandated September 11, 1750: "You are to go out as soon as possible, to the westward of the great mountains and carry with you such a number of men as you think necessary, in order to search out and discover the lands upon the Ohio river and other adjoining branches of the Mississippi down as low as The Great Falls thereof. You are particularly to observe the ways and passes through all the mountains you cross, and take an exact account of the soil, quality and product of the land, and the wideness and deepness of the rivers and several falls belonging to them, together with the courses and bearings of the rivers and mountains as near as you conveniently can. You are also to observe what nations of Indians inhabit there, their strength and numbers, who they trade with and in what commodities they deal. When you find a large quantity of good, level land as you think will suit the company, you are to measure the bredth of it in three or four places, and take the courses of the rivers and mountains on which it binds in order to judge the quantity. You are to fix the beginnings and bounds in such a manner that they may easily be found again by your description; the nearer in the land lies the better, provided it be good and level, but we had rather go down the Mississippi than take mean broken land." He was to go to the Falls of the Ohio. The above part of Gist's instructions are not given as a part of interesting data, but with an entirely different purpose. As to the number of assistants Gist took with him does not matter. He probably had light equipment. He set out from the house of Col. Thomas Cresab, on the 31st of October, 1750, at Old Town, a former Indian village on the north side of the Potomac, fifteen miles southeast of Cumberland, in Alleghaney county, Maryland. He followed "an old Indian path" and made eleven miles the first day. This "old Indian path" was the warrior's path up the Potomac to the Ohio county. It followed the east base of Warrior mountain. At Badford, Pennsylvania, it branched into two roads, one leading northeast to Vernango, the other to Shannopinstown, now Pittsburg. The latter was followed by Gist. He remained several days and went to Loggstown November 25th on the north bank of the Ohio, eighteen miles below Pittsburg. There were hostile or French Indians, and to protect himself he gave out that he was on the King's business. After days of numerous meanderings, he was notified that if he went down the Ohio he would meet French Indians who would kill him. But he determined to go to the Falls. He crossed to Kentucky and was there for the first time. He remained in the Shawnee town on the Kentucky side until the 13th, and started for the Falls of the Ohio. He went through Boone county and got a mastodon tooth and took it to the Ohio county. He continued on in the direction of The Falls until the 18th when he was on a stream he calls Lower Salt Lick creek (probably Floyd's Fork of Salt river), which had been described to him by Robert Smith as being about fifteen miles above The Falls. He heard several guns fired in the woods, and saw newly set traps and feared French Indians. He was compelled to change his course and disregard his instructions to visit The Falls.

* * * * * * * * * * * * * * * *

Gist's explorations carried him through Greenup, Lewis, Mason, Scott, Harrison, Nicholas, Bourbon, Franklin, Shelby, Woodford, Fayette, Estill, Lee, Breathitt, Perry, Knott and Letcher. If the course is as set out that on the 16th he reached the Kentucky river near Frankfort, "the Salt Lick" which he found on the 18th was that called Bullett's Lick later, on Floyd's Fork of Salt river, in the present Bullitt county near Shepherdsville, and about eighteen miles from Louisville, and on the 19th he crossed a number of creeks, flowing to the southwest * * * tributaries of Basahear's creek * * * he must have deviated very much to the north, or he must have passed through Anderson county, and his fast progress from Bullitt's Lick on the 18th must have taken him a straight line or he could not have reached Kentucky river as quickly as he did, and if he continued a straight course, he would necessarily have crossed Anderson county.

WILDERNESS TRAILS

The wilderness was penetrated by trails. Such roads were followed by all persons going into the west from the Atlantic seaboard. No one struck into the wilderness at random. For ages animals, especially buffalo and the deer family, migrated from one locality to another in search of grazing of grass, cane, or for salt at the licks. Even with animals these were highways. As grazing was exhausted in one locality, these herds followed the trails of countless generations of animals before them, and moved on to new pastures and licks. Nor did they follow the lowlands or creeks, because of high or low water, except in crossing from one divide to another, but they followed the high ground. They crossed at the passes in the mountains and fords in the rivers. In winter it was impossible to follow rivers on account of high water and back water in the creeks. They followed the divides, where were the springs or shallow creeks. One of the ford crossings was at Leestown below Frankfort where the trail is crossed by the Frankfort and Georgetown railroad, and to this day holds its own, more than a hundred yards wide, and reminding the observer of an old worn dirt road used by a numerous traveling public. (Keer's History, Vol. 1). These old trails did not follow the streams but at the head waters of the creeks supplying them. Over some of these trails came Gist, Boone, Sevier, the Long Hunters, Kenton and George Rogers Clark. "One of these old ways was called Nemicolon's Path, because pointed out by Nemicolon, a Delaware Indian. It became Braddock's Trail. At Fort Pitt it branched off to all points of the compass. One of these branches followed through the country south of the Ohio to the point where Charleston, West Virginia, now stands. Passing over the Kenawha, here it plunged into the heavy woods in a course almost due west. This course continued until the forks of Great Sandy Creek (Big Sandy River) were reached. Here again a number of branches were encountered. One followed up each fork of the Great Sandy on to the mouth of the stream, and one continued on to the westward. At each principal branch of any stream, a road left the main way to follow the subordinate stream up to its head waters, there to clamber through a 'gap' and descend another subordinate stream down to a larger one. This process was repeated everywhere and the forest was threaded with roads. The main roads did not keep down the streams but held to the ridges, the divides and watersheds, crossing the streams where they were small. The means for transportations for explorers and pioneers were pack horses." Thus came the early settlers to Kentucky, and an intrepid pioneer from the back woods of Pennslyvania pushed on until he located his settlement and built his cabin in, what today is Lawrenceburg. This was Jacob Coffman who took up his claim here in February, 1780. In a few of the records his name is spelled Kaufman.

THE FIRST WHITE MEN*

On July 18, 1773, according to the most trustworthy accounts, the first white men set foot on the territory of what is now Anderson county. A party of adventurers, consisting of James, George and Robert McAfee, James McCoun, Jr., and Samuel Adams, on the 10th of May of that year left their

---

*In this chapter Major McKee reviews the McAfee explorations from two writers of Kentucky History.

homes in Botetourt county, Virginia, and crossing the Alleghaney mountains to the northwest, struck the Kanawha river near the mouth of Elk river. They commenced a voyage down the Kanawha and Ohio rivers, and in their descent meeting with Hancock Taylor and two parties of surveyors, and also Captain Bullitt and his company. The three parties proceeded together till they arrived at the mouth of Kentucky river. Here Capt. Bullitt's company continued their voyage to the falls of the Ohio, while the MAcfee and Hancock Taylor companies, proceeded up the Kentucky river, arriving at the mouth of Drennons Lick creek on the 9th of July. They left the Lick and canoes and proceeding southward on foot, crossed the Kentucky river below where the city of Frankfort now stands, where Robert McAfee had two surveys made embracing 600 acres, and including the Frankfort bottom. From here the McAfee party continued their course up the river, and landing on the west bank, they arrived at the Cave spring on the 18th of July, in the present territory of Anderson county. This spring was afterwards known as Lillard's spring, now as McCalls, and it is five miles south of Lawrenceburg, on the road leading to Harrodsburg. They continued here two days, when proceeding on their journey in a westerly direction they came to Salt river, which they called Crooked creek, and went down it to the mouth of Hammonds creek. They then returned up the river to a point two miles above where Harrodsburg now stands. They remained on the waters of Salt river but ten or twelve days, when on July 31st they turned their faces homeward through the mountains of eastern Kentucky, suffering many privations and hardships by reason of the scarcity of food and roughness of the tractless mountain way. Such is the simple story of the first visitation of the white man to the soil of what is now Anderson county. Kentucky was then a vast wilderness, and there was not to be found in all its borders a single white settlement. The territory was not then known as Kentucky, but as forming a part of Fincastle county, Virginia. By act of the Virginia Legislature, Fincastle county after December 31, 1776, was divided into three counties and all that part lying south and west of a line beginning on the Ohio river at the mouth of the Great Sandy river, running up the same to the main northeasterly branch thereof to the great Laurel ridge, or Cumberland mountains—thence southwesterly along said mountain to the North Carolina line, was designated as Kentucky county. Kentucky county was divided, and formed into three counties, Jefferson, Fayette and Lincoln, by the Virginia Legislature in 1780, and the territory of Anderson was included in Lincoln. Mercer county was the first county formed out of Lincoln and was erected into a county by the Virginia Legislature in 1785, and Anderson was included in Mercer. Franklin county was carved out of Mercer, Woodford and Shelby by the Kentucky Legislature in 1794.

Anderson was formed into a county by the Kentucky Legislature in 1827, out of parts of Franklin, Mercer and Washington, mostly, however, from Franklin, and was named for Richard Clough Anderson, Jr., who died the year before, while United States Minister to one of the states of South America. It lies in the central portion of the state and contains about 175 square miles, and is bounded on the north by Franklin, on the west by Spencer, on the south by Mercer and Washington, and on the east by Woodford. The surface is rolling and in some parts hilly. The soil is rich and productive and when properly cared for, produces hemp, tobacco and corn, and all the cereals and grapes to great perfection, and is susceptible of a high state of cultivation. In the early years of the county, hemp was produced in considerable quanti-

McCall's Spring.

ties, and Lawrenceburg could boast of two or three hemp factories, or, as they were then called, rope-walks. The county is well watered, having the Kentucky river on its eastern borders, and Salt river entering from the south and passing out westwardly through the central portion of the county; while in the northern part the three Benson creeks, Big, Little and South Benson, have their sources in the county, besides other creek tributaries of Kentucky and Salt rivers. That portion of the county east and south of Salt river, with Lawrenceburg as a center, was settled at a much earlier period, than the portion north and west of that river, which remained an almost unbroken forest to within the memory of the present generation, but is now filled by a sturdy and industrious population. Some of the reminiscences of the early settlement and principal pioneers may be interesting: Richard Benson, Nathan Hammond, and William McBrayer were among those who spent sometime at Harrodsburg after March 11, 1775, the date of the arrival and re-occupancy of the cabins built in 1774, by Capt. James Harrod's company. The Revolutionary War was commencing at this period, together with the Indian hostilities till the close of the war, and some time after, made it extremely hazardous for the few sturdy pioneers to live outside of forts or block houses and stations. After the close of the war, however, emigration began in earnest, and as early as 1784 settlers began to spread out over the country. Richard Benson at an early period made a settlement claim of 400 acres on the Kentucky river, including the mouth of Little Benson creek, and built his cabin above the mouth of the creek in what is now the northeastern corner of this county, though most of the claim lies in Franklin. Benson impressed his name on the four creeks—Big, Little, North and South Benson, three of them having their sources in the northern portion of the county, and flowing into the Kentucky river. His settlement claim of 400 acres, fell into the hands of Robert McKee of Woodford, by assignment, who obtained a patent for it. Nathan Hammond was of the company of Capt. James Harrod of 1775. From him, Hammonds creek, a tributary of Salt river, took its name. Jacob Coffman, a Dutchman, located the land in and around Lawrenceburg at a very early date. His cabin stood to the northeast of town, near where the residence of the late John M. Walker stands. He was said to have been killed by hostile Indians about one mile north of his residence, and when his good wife heard of his death, she said, "I always told my old man that these savage Ingens would kill him,—I'd rather lost my best cow at the pail than my old man." His family afterwards lived in a house two or three hundred yards northwest of the court house, near where the Presbyterian church now stands.

William, son of James McBrayer, was of the company of Captain Harrod in 1775 at Harrodstown. He went back to Virginia for his parents, and returned with his father and mother and three younger brothers, James, Hugh and Andrew. The family settled on the farm now owned by Bailey Roach, two miles west of town, and near neighbors to John Penny, Sr., Philip White and Robert Blackwell. On the death of the parents, the place fell to Andrew, the youngest son, who married a daughter of Robert Blackwell. Andrew McBrayer was a member of the Legislature in 1829 and '38. He raised up a large family of sons and daughters, only two of whom are now living, Judge W. H. McBrayer and Mrs. Curry.*

---

*This record was written about the year 1885. Judge McBrayer died in 1888.—L. K. Bond.

William McBrayer, who was the pioneer of the family in Anderson county, was a surveyor and made a number of surveys to the north and east of town. He settled near Lawrenceburg and built the stone house which now stands near the Clifton pike about two miles from town. His first cabin stood between the present house and the creek. The property afterwards fell to his son James, who built a brick house on the opposite side of the creek, but this has since been destroyed. This son represented the county, then Franklin, in the Legislature in 1824. William McBrayer had eight sons and two daughters, and a number of his grandchildren now reside in the county. The farm is now owned by Dr. J. A. Witherspoon. James McBrayer, the next younger brother of William, settled near to the place where Providence church (near Ninevah) was built, and Hugh settled on the south side of Little Benson, opposite what was known in early times, as Hogsheads church, and is said to have given the land on which the church was built. He was never married. Thomas Baker, ancestor of Reuben Baker, settled the Wash farm lying between that of William and James McBrayer, in 1782. Among other pioneers of an early date may be mentioned William Nelson, who settled on the place where his son, Benoni Nelson, now resides. Peter Carr owned the farm now occupied by J. P. Reddin; George Marrs, Mountjoys and Lynch on the Bush place, afterwards, Meux. The Providence church in this neighborhood was built about 1825 under the auspices of Rev. Wm. Hickman, by Thomas Oliver, John Mothershead, Jerry Buckley and others.

EARLY SETTLEMENT OF ANDERSON, FRANKLIN AND MERCER

The history of the early settlement of Anderson county is the history of Franklin and Mercer, for this county is a part of the original boundaries. One of the first expeditions ever made to this state, passed through the eastern part of this county. Butler writes in his history of Kentucky, "This party consisting of James, George and Robert McAfee, James McCoun, Jr., and Samuel Adams, left Sinking creek in Bottetourt County, Virginia, on the 1st of June, 1773, they struck across the county to New river, where having sent back their horses by John McCoun and James Pawling, they descended the river in canoes. The party continued in company with Bullitt and his companions until they came to the mouth of the Kentucky river; at this point the company separated, Capt. Bullitt proceeding to The Falls, and the McAfees with Hancock Taylor ascending the Kentucky river to Drennon's Lick creek, which they went up as high as the lick. Here they found a white man by the name of Drennon, who had crossed the country from Big Bone Lick, and got before the McAfees one day. The same appearances presented themselves here as at all the licks of the western country; a profusion of every sort of game struggling for the salt all in sight at once, and the roads about the lick as trodden and wide as in the neighborhood of a populous city. They are spoken of as streets by the old hunters. The party took one of these roads, or traces as they were called, so fortunately made by the buffalo and other game through almost impenetrable canebreaks, and crossed the Kentucky river at the ford below Frankfort opposite to what has been since called Leestown. Here they turned up the river and surveyed the bottom in which Frankfort now stands, being the first survey made on the Kentucky river. They went up the ridge along the Lexington road until they again crossed the Kentucky river seven

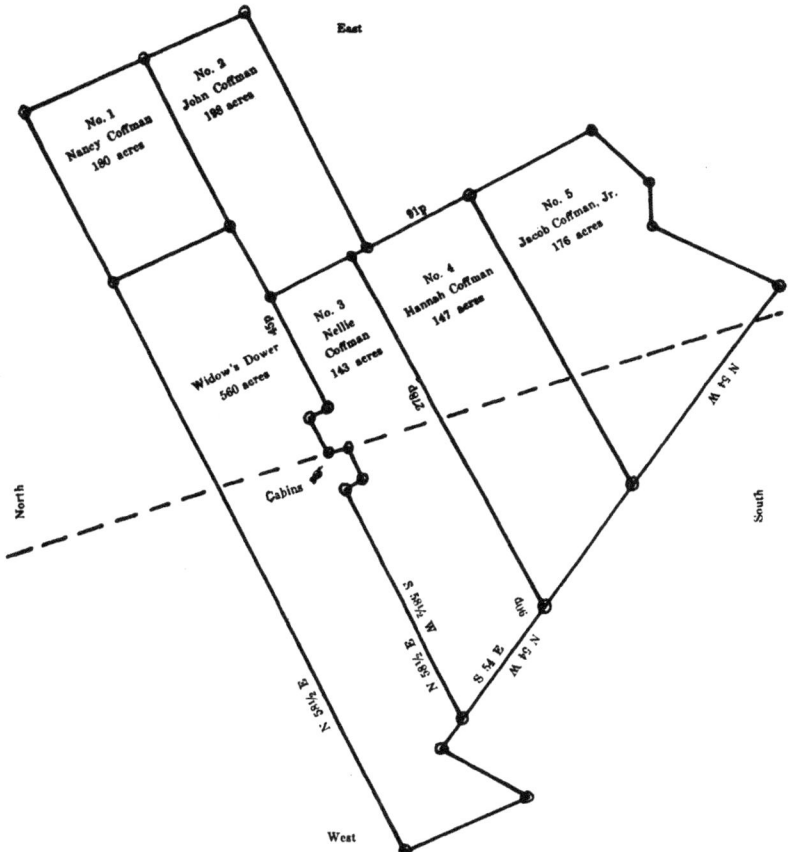

A copy of the division of the land of Jacob Coffman, pioneer, in Franklin County Court, Inventory and Wills Book, page 104 (1804). The dotted line running north and south, indicates the State highway today. This is the present site of Lawrenceburg.

miles above Frankfort, and passed a little east of the present Lawrenceburg and encamped near the remarkable spring which is situated under a rock on the road between Frankfort and Harrodsburg, then called the Cave spring, now known as McCalls." The above quotations have been made full for the reason that some discrepancy seems to exist as to the location of the spring mentioned. Some claiming that it is the Cave spring about three-fourths of a mile southeast of Lawrenceburg. This cannot be true when it is remembered that the McAfee from whose notes Collins and Butler obtained their information, afterwards lived for many years near Salt river in Mercer county, and fully identified the spring, which is located on the Louisville and Crab Orchard road, five miles south of Lawrenceburg, between the houses of John and James McCall and now known as the McCalls spring. It was at one time known as Lillard spring by reason of Thomas Lillard, Esq., owning all the land about it, when the turnpike that is now built was unknown and Harrodsburg and other places to the north were connected only by a dirt road which ran over almost the same ground. This spring has changed some in appearance since then owing to the fact that so many people travelling the road, have stopped there, but as before observed, one among the first parties who ever made an expedition of survey and discovery passed through what is now Anderson county, and near its present county seat, Lawrenceburg.

In the year 1780 no settlement had been made where Frankfort now stands, although there was a stopping place at Leestown, a mile or more below Frankfort, where Lock No. 4 has been built. At this place there was situated a ripple, or low water place, an animal crossing used by animals, and a crossing for men who followed the animal trails. Animal trails converged here from almost all directions for this crossing. So wide was this animal trail and worn so deep, that it can be seen today where the Frankfort and Georgetown railroad crosses it. It being necessary to trestle the railroad at this point. In the year 1780 a party of men going for salt camped on the site where Frankfort is now situated and were attacked by Indians, and one of them, a man named Frank, was killed. It is said that when Frankfort was settled it was named for him. Another noted crossing of Kentucky river was where Shryock's ferry is now located. An animal trail crossed there, a ripple was there and that meant shallow water. There are traces of this trail now, showing conclusively that it existed, and in places, its location. People were out hunting the best land. They tramped all over central Kentucky. Harrodsburg was five years old. Boonesboro slightly younger. A settlement had been made near where Shelbyville is located, and a settlement at "The Falls" at Louisville. There were no roads. Land hunters took the shortest route and of the least resistance. They did not follow river bottom, but went in ways toward the heads of deep tributaries. Land hunters from the east came by Cumberland Gap through Logan's fort, Harrodstown, and from Boonesboro by Boones' settlement in Shelby to the settlement on Bear Grass creek to "The Falls." People coming from east of Kentucky river crossed at the ripple, now at Shyrocks ferry. These two trails passed where Lawrenceburg now is, to Nelson and Washington counties, and it was only a question of time until a settlement would be made at this crossing. In January of 1780 Jacob Coffman entered 400 acres where Lawrenceburg now is, and made his settlement, and in June of that year he entered an additional 1,000 acres adjoining his settlement, and that was the beginning of Lawrenceburg.

In writing of facts relative to a sketch or sketches of events in a county, it is found to be impossible without some repetition of facts concerning other facts as to people and property.

DESCRIPTIONS OF THE LARGE STATIONS OF KENTUCKY

Since the large stations played such an important part in the defense of Kentucky during the War of the Revolution and following it, until the last incursion of Indians into central and northern Kentucky in 1793, it will be of interest to give a description of these large stations—the stations at Harrodsburg, Boonesboro, St. Asaphs (Logans Fort). There were many smaller stations situated throughout central Kentucky. It will be remembered that the first settlements in Kentucky were made south of the Kentucky river. This was probably due to the fact that the principal crossing places of the Indians over the Ohio river were near the city of Maysville, at the mouth of the Big Sandy and near the mouth of the Licking, opposite the city of Cincinnati, although there were crossings at "The Falls" (Louisville), and at the mouth of Salt river, but the most generally used of these crossings were further east than the mouth of Salt river or The Falls. There were several reasons for crossing at these places; they were nearer to the Indian towns which were principally in central Ohio and on the Great Lakes. They had been used for generations as being near to the Blue Licks and Big Bone Lick where they obtained their supply of salt. The following description is given in Kerr's History of Kentucky: "The frontiersmen now organized their activities to the smallest detail on a war basis. The lives of men, women and children were all regulated by the exigencies of war and defence. All were grouped in a fort or barricaded settlement within one inclosure, with cabins, stockades and block houses. The cabins formed the walls of at least one side of the fort, or in some instances, all sides. Stockade walls of strong timbers completed the inclosure where there were no cabins. The outer walls of the cabins extended perpendicularly to the top, and the roof sloped down inward. The cabins were separated from one another by log partitions, and consisted generally of one room with the ground as a floor, or sometime puncheon floors. At each angle of the fort (and they were generally quadrilateral), there was a stockhouse with the upper story protruding from one to two feet in every direction. Portholes were cut at convenient places in all the outer walls of the fort; a large folding gate was made on the side nearest the water supply. The wilderness was cleared back for a way on all sides, both to secure protection against sudden Indian surprises as well as to provide fields for corn, pumpkins, melons and garden products. The men cultivated the fields, carried out hunting expeditions into the surrounding forests and fought the Indians. The women and children busied themselves with the many tasks in and about the fort; helped in planting and harvesting and always stood ready to aid in repelling the Indian attacks. The simple furnishings of the cabins were, for the most part, the handiwork of the frontiersmen themselves, with now and then a few articles brought out from the eastern settlements. Their dress was simple, but substantial; the hunting shirt was a distinctive part of their clothing. The restricted lives of the people were not wholly uninteresting, nor without their pleasures. The ever present Indian dangers provided excitement enough of its kind, and the manners and customs in the forts were so shaped as to minister to many a want and craving for social outlets. Games and sports were indulged, and marriages were made and celebrated. The children were taught in a rudimentary way to read and write."

"Warefare raged around these forts as centers, they were constantly the object of attack by crafty bands of Indians who lurked in the forests waiting to cut off some one who ventured too far out. At times they were besieged in force. The hunters in the forests to replenish the meat supply, were frequently killed or captured, and at all times were required to exercise the utmost vigilance. Yet, in spite of all this, these pioneers would build their isolated cabins in the forests, move their families to them and live there until they would hear of some family being murdered by Indians, when there would be a general rush for the large stations. They were willing to take any risks to live on the land they had entered. There was little danger from the Indians in the winter season. These fortified places were called, indiscriminately, Stations, Forts, Fortified Villages, Blockaded Hamlets—probably Fortified Village would be most appropriate. Trails led through the forests from villages, following the line of least resistance."

JACOB COFFMAN, FIRST ANDERSON COUNTY PIONEER

Jacob Coffman was one of the first, if not the first, to build his cabin or fort, in what is now Anderson county. His fort, or strong cabin (it was not one of the large stations or forts), stood on the corner lot made by what is now Woodford and Main streets, the lot now (1928) occupied by the Presbyterian church. This cabin was put up between February 3, 1780 and June 23, 1780, the time he made his 1,000 acre entry, the second entry using the term, "adjoining his settlement and around the same." Here Coffman lived from 1780 until his death by Indians in 1792. As to where he came from the records of Anderson and Franklin counties are silent. Quite a number of Dutch settlers came to Kentucky at a very early date, and he may have been one of these. There was a Revolutionary soldier named Jacob Coffman, eighty-four years old, living in Casey county, Kentucky, in 1840. This may have been the son of the pioneer. He had a son who sold the land laid off to him in his father's estate. It is known that he sold his part of the land to Samuel Arbuckle on January 17, 1805, and he does not appear again in the records of Franklin or Anderson county. The land of Jacob Coffman was divided amongst his widow and heirs in 1804.* (Inventory and will book Franklin county court). There was laid off to his widow 565 acres for her dower; to Nancy Coffman (lot No. 1) 108 acres; to John Coffman (lot No. 2) 198 acres; to Eleanor (Nellie) Coffman (lot No. 3) 143 acres; to Hannah Coffman (lot No. 4) 147 acres and to Jacob Coffman, Jr. (lot No. 5) 176 acres. This land covered the whole of what is now Lawrenceburg, except the part lying north of Ballard street, and a line crossing main, running west as Ballard street extended. Roughly speaking, the widow's dower ran from an east and west line, crossing Main street at Ballard street to a line parallel with it crossing Main at White's alley (by Baptist church), but it dipped into a square running to Woodford street and this dip was made to include the Presbyterian property. Following Main street south, Eleanor's (Nellie's) line crossed at Brook's alley (now Chatauqua). Her land included the court house and the central part of the town. Hannah Coffman's lot extended to a

---

*See drawing of division of Coffman land.

line crossing at the Fox Creek pike, and Jacob Coffman's lot extended to the Bond and Lillard pike, cutting out what is now the Lawrenceburg cemetery, that part of his line running with the entrance, to the entrance of the old McKee fair grounds, the north side of the cemetery. The Nancy Coffman lot, 180 acres, laid on the east side of the dower, and comprised the old John M. Walker land and the old distillery property. The John Coffman lot, 198 acres, laid east of Eleanor's lot and a part of Hannah's. It was what was later the old Driskell farm. Prior to the division of the Jacob Coffman land in 1804, every one of these lots had been built on by the heirs. A house had been built on lot No. 1, where the Jno. M. Walker brick residence stands, and has stood for many years. The John Coffman lot had been built where the old Driskell-Mizner house stood, now the intersection of Court street and Gatewood Ave. The old Coffman house was where the Presbyterian church stands and was Nellie's lot. A house also on the dower, in the yard of T. J. Ballard; one on Hannah's lot, just back of Stites Milton's home, and the Jacob Coffman lot where J. M. Johnson lived down town for a number of years now occupied by Service Garage. After the sale of the dower and the sale of the Nelly Coffman lot, or that part of her lot where the Presbyterian church is the widow and Nellie moved to a house in the woods, on Nellie's land, now the property of Stanley Trent. They continued to live there until they moved to Clay County, Missouri, where they were living on June 2, 1830, when Nellie sold the residue of her land to Samuel Arbuckle for $1,200. Unless Jacob Coffman, Jr., moved to Casey County, Kentucky, as suggested heretofore, this removal of the widow and Nellie to Clay County, Missouri, is the only known fact as to where any of the Coffman family went after the division and sale of their lands.

Jacob Coffman, Sr., was killed in 1792, and there were several versions of his death, how it occurred and where. Mr. W. S. McBrayer gave the writer the version that many old people thought the Indians did not kill him, but that Samuel Arbuckle killed him in order to get his land, and that he was killed near the brick residence of John C. McBrayer on the Clifton pike. Samuel Arbuckle did finally get the title to the lots of Jacob, Jr., and Hannah, and the greater part of Nellie's, but the records show that he got it many years after the death of Jacob, Sr., and that he paid prices for it that compared with prices paid for other similar land in the community. The most reasonable version of Jacob, Sr.'s, death heard by the writer, and it was heard many times years ago, was that he and his wife were walking not far from Coffman's Station one Sunday afternoon when they discovered two Indians not far away and apparently approaching them. Coffman sent his wife to the station to bar the doors, as he thought the Indians did not intend harm and he could get rid of them. He walked to where they were and some talk occurred, but suddenly the Indians clubbed him to death and scalped him. The alarm was given and a number of people got together under the command of Major Herman Bowmar living in Woodford county, and a deputy sheriff living in that county, came and tried to track the Indians, but could find no trace of them. (Collin's History, Vol. 2.)

The summer and fall of 1792 saw the last incursion into any part of central Kentucky, and the killing of Coffman here, and of a Mr. Todd in South Frankfort, were the last killings by Indians.

The land laws enacted in 1779 by the Legislature of Virginia were partly the cause, and partly the result of increased immigration into Kentucky, and in the fall of 1779 a land office was opened at St. Asaph's (near Standford).

Tracts of land were reserved as bounties for Virginia troops. Each family of actual settlers was allowed a settlement right of 400 acres for the sum of $9.00, and every such settler acquired a pre-emption right to purchase 1,000 acres adjoining. (Roosevelt's Winning of the West.) Jacob Coffman by his settlement of his 400 acres on February 3, 1780, and entering his pre-emption of 1,000 acres adjoining on June 23rd of the same year, clearly shows the fact that he was a Revolutionary soldier, either Continental or Militia, and as Kentucky and Tennessee, prior to 1780, were settled exclusively by backwoodsmen—backwoodsmen from the backwoods of Pennsylvania and Virginia and North Carolina, his name would almost entirely indicate that he came from the backwoods of Pennsylvania. Coffman built his home on what afterwards became lot 26 on the town plot, now partly occupied by the Presbyterian church.

ARNOLD'S STATION, CAPT. JOHN ARNOLD AND SAMUEL HUTTON

Prior to the year 1780, there was no great flood of immigration into Kentucky. That commenced in 1780. Up to that time the settlements were at Harrodsburg in 1774; Boonesboro, 1775; McClellands (Georgetown), 1776; St. Asaphs (Logan's, Stanford), 1775; Louisville, 1778; Bryans, 1779 (Fayette county); Squire Boones, near Shelbyville, 1779, and one station just above the mouth of Little Benson creek, on Kentucky river, in 1783. This station was set up by Capt. John Arnold, who commanded a company of spies, and was in what is now Anderson county. These spies, or most of them, took up land and built their cabins in the country or vicinity of this fort, and depended on the spies to give notice of Indian invasions. They patrolled the county on the south and west of the Kentucky river, and the banks of the Ohio below the mouth of the Kentucky, and usually were able to give notice of Indian invasions in time for the settlers to go into the big stations for safety, but not always; so there were many battles with the Indians at these cabins. In numerous instances the men of a cabin would all be killed in the first surprise attack, and the women would make a successful defense. Among these spies in Capt. Arnold's company, was one Samuel Hutton, who took up a body of land and built his cabin near Clifton, in what is now Anderson county. His cabin was built over a spring near the present residence (1928) of W. Y. Spencer, or on his farm. Nancy Hutton, the wife of Samuel, was, one day, surprised by the appearance of an Indian, and succeeded in getting to the room above the spring, and as the Indian followed her up the ladder, she killed him with the blow of an axe. This is legendary, and is the version given by Dr. R. I. McQuiddy, whose father afterwards owned and occupied the farm. Another version is, that there were several Indians in the attack on the cabin and after killing the one, she successfully defended the cabin against the others. Samuel Hutton afterwards sold the farm and bought land where Lawrenceburg now is, 107½ acres, from Thomas Prather and wife. The residence on this land was located where the brick building stands, now owned by the County Board of Education (1928), known as the Witherspoon property. Samuel Hutton was one of the most active of the spies, under the command of Capt. John Arnold, but he seems not to have been as successful as a family man as he was a spy, for as reported in Johnson's History of Franklin county, his wife went before the Franklin county court on the 25th of November, 1800, and demanded that the court make her husband support her baby. The court hummed and hawed and wound up by doing nothing, whereupon Mrs. Hutton laid the infant down on the table and walked out. The court then got action quick, and this order is entered on the order book: "It is ordered that the sheriff do bring immediately before this court, Nancy Hutton, to answer the contempt offered this court by leaving a young infant on the clerk's table." The sheriff returned and reported that "Nancy Hutton could not be found," and it was thereupon ordered that "Samuel Hutton be summoned to appear before the next court to show cause, if any, why he should not support the infant left by said Samuel's wife on the clerk's table."

DANIEL BOONE

The writer makes no attempt to write a biography of Daniel Boone, but there is such a paucity of descriptions of his personal appearance, that it is thought that such a description will not be out of place. Col. John Johnson, who was an Indian agent for the northwestern Indians, principally those of Ohio, wrote autobiography for his children, and John H. Patterson's mother, of Dayton, Ohio, being a daughter, numerous extracts were made from it in a book prepared by Charlotte Reeve Conover for John H. Patterson, called, "Concerning the Forefathers, Col. Robert Patterson and Col. John Johnson." This description of Daniel Boone is copied from Col. Johnson's book: "I spent the winter of 1795 at Bourbon court house (Paris, Kentucky), having an uncle at that time a resident of that county. William Garrard, son of Gov. Garrard, an early friend and acquaintance who had received his education at Dickinson College, Carlisle, Pennsylvania, resided a few miles from the court house. This made my sojourn there agreeable. I there made the acquaintance of the celebrated Daniel Boone, who was brought to the place by a Mr. Ewings, as well as I can recollect, for the purpose of tracing up some land lines and titles. I slept four or five nights in the same room with Boone. He was a modest, retiring person of medium size, few words, scarcely speaking unless spoken to. His age at that time might have been fifty years, although in mid-winter, he was poorly attired, his garments all, or nearly all, being linen. In the earlier period of his life he was a prisoner among my Shawonoise Indians, and as such often trod the ground of Nepper Piqua, for so many years my home, and seat of my agency for Indian affairs in the northwest." In 1847 Col. Johnson wrote the following impression of Daniel Boone: "It is now fifty-four years since I first saw Daniel Boone. He was then about sixty years of age, of medium size, about five feet, ten, not given to corpulency, retired, unobtrusive, and a man of few words. My acquaintance was made with him in the winter season, and I well remember his dress was of toro cloth, and not a woolen garment on his body, unless his stockings were of that material. Home-made was the common wear of the people of Kentucky at that time, sheep were not yet introduced into the country. I spent four nights in the house of one West, with Boone. There were a number of strangers and he was constantly occupied in answering questions." From Appleton's Encyclopaedia, American Biography: "Daniel Boone's name is familiar to every boy who reads the romantic history of the great west. He is called the Robin Hood of American pioneer life; an ignorant man if we judge him only by the standard of books, but versed in his craft. As the true education is that one which best enables a man to cope with the difficulties of life, it will be granted that Daniel Boone was, after all, a very well educated man. He could barely read and write, but he knew every thing relating to the forests, the fields and the streams. As a hunter he was a genius, and as an Indian fighter, a terror; strong, brave, lithe, inured to hardship and privation, he traced his steps through the pathless forests, sought out the hiding places of the panther, the bear and the wolf, and was the match of the Indian in the sagacity with which he detected the footsteps of the red man. Daniel Boone was allied with the Quakers in Philadelphia in his youth, but moved to North Carolina, and then to Kentucky, establishing the fort called Boonesboro on the Kentucky river. It is much too long a story to tell here of his capture by the Indians, his flight and journey of 160 miles with only one meal; his adoption into an Indian tribe, after pulling out all his hair excepting one lock. His escape by throwing tobacco dust into the eyes of his captors; his fight at the battle of the Blue Licks, carrying his wounded son on his back to safety; his death in Missouri in 1820, and his burial in the coffin he made for himself and had kept under his bed for years. If one wants romance, fairy tale, and epic all in one, let him read the life of Daniel Boone." The following description is taken from Collin's History of Kentucky: "His manners were simple and unobtrusive—except from the rudeness characteristic of the backwoodsman. In his person there was nothing remarkably striking. His countenance was mild and contemplative, indicating a frame of mind altogether different from the restlessness and activity that distinguished him. His ordinary habiliments were those of a hunter—a hunting shirt and moccasins uniformly composing a part of them. When he emigrated to Louisiana, he omitted to secure title to a princely estate on the Missouri because it would have cost him the trouble of a trip to New Orleans. He would have traveled a much greater distance to indulge his cherished propensities as an adventurer and a hunter. He died as he had lived, in a cabin, and perhaps his trusty rifle was the most valuable of his chattles." In Collin's History we have a detailed account of Daniel Boone passing through Harrodsburg in 1774, when he was on his way to "The Falls" (Louisville), sent by Gov. Dinsmore to warn surveyors and settlers that the northern Indians had become hostile, which eventuated in the Battle of Point Pleasant, October 10, 1774. Boone's course was, naturally, through where Lawrenceburg now is, for reason that it was the nearest and most direct course, following the divide between the Kentucky and Salt rivers, to head of Hammonds creek, then straight to Louisville. To go any other way he would have had to go through the Salt river hills to the west and south.

In 1773 Boone having disposed of all his property, except what he intended to carry with him, he and his family took leave of his friends and started to Kentucky, being joined by five other families, all well armed, in Powell's valley, they proceeded, but when near the Cumberland mountains they were attacked by a large body of Indians. They were beaten off after a severe engagement, but the whites had sustained a loss of six men killed and wounded. Among the killed, Boone's oldest son. They were so discouraged that they retreated to Clinch river, forty miles from the battle. Here they remained until 1775. It was then that Boone was employed by Gov. Dinsmore, of Virginia, to conduct a party of surveyors through the wilderness to the falls of the Ohio, a distance of 800 miles. In going to The Falls he had passed through Harrodsburg, and where Lawrenceburg now is, and it was natural for him to have come back the same way, for any other would have been a much longer and more difficult route. It was the natural way and best way, because Capt. James Harrod afterwards built his "Big Road" to The Falls the same way, and Daniel Boone's acts all show that he took the most direct way, always, unless it was to avoid insurmountable obstructions.

CHAPTER II

EARLY LAND ENTRIES

Amongst the earliest, ablest and most energetic pioneers of Kentucky was Captain James Harrod who, with his party, settled Harrodsburg in 1774. In 1773 four parties from Virginia passed the mouth of Licking river on their way to "The Falls" (Louisville) of the Ohio river, going to points in the interior of Kentucky. One of these parties was led by Capt. James Harrod. The histories of Kentucky refer to his having been at "The Falls" numerous times, from 1773 until the time of his death in 1793. In the early days there were two routes by which immigrants came to Kentucky. One through Cumberland Gap, and the other by the Ohio river by boat. On the Ohio river route, the principal landing places were the mouth of Cabin creek, near Maysville, and the mouth of Licking river opposite Cincinnati. But the territory south of the Kentucky river having been settled first, and for a few years having the greater part of the population, "The Falls" of the Ohio was the principal landing and shipping point for those coming to Kentucky by the river route. For the territory lying between The Falls and as far as Crab Orchard, it remained the principal shipping point for many years. Many of the early deeds to Anderson county land, mentioned as local marks, "Harrod's Big Road to The Falls," and "Harrod's Big Trace to The Falls." As near as the location of this Big Road, or Big Trace can be fixed by these deeds, and by other marks, such as "Stations" or small forts, it passed from Harrod's Station down Salt river by McAfee's Station and continuing down a few miles; then its course changed until it followed the pike now known as the Hardinsville and Crab Orchard to where Lawrenceburg now is, then followed Hammonds creek for about two miles, then left it and continued a straight general direction to "The Falls," now Louisville. It passed what was Squire Boone's Station, now Shelbyville. Gradually as time passed, this road ceased to be referred to in the deeds as "Harrod's Big Road to The Falls," and that part of it west of Lawrenceburg was referred to as the "Shelbyville Road" until it ceased to be a road at all, except in mere patches. It ended as a through road when the Hardinsville and Crab Orchard turnpike was built in 1835-36, and has never been used as a through road since that time.

In 1779 the celebrated Land Law of Virginia was enacted by the Virginia Legislature. There will be no pretense of a discussion of this law here. It was no doubt well intended, but there was no provision of a general survey of the land in Kentucky at the general expense, and its subdivision into sections, sub-sections and quarters. Instead of this, each person possessing a warrant was permitted to locate his land wherever he pleased, and to have it surveyed at his own expense. But his entry had to recognize land already taken up and had to be made somewhere else. To make a good entry required an accuracy of description that ignorant men could not be expected to possess. It had the effect of cutting out such men as Boone, Kenton and others of their class, who had been chiefly instrumental in winning Kentucky from the wilderness, finally causing them to leave the state; the former to Missouri and the latter to Ohio, Kenton to keep out of jail for debt. Another and immediate consequence of this law was a flood of immigration (Collin's History) into Kentucky, in 1779-80. The year 1780 was particularly remarkable for the number of people locating land warrants. While many were located in Anderson county, the following are of interest to people of this county and town: "Jacob Coffman enters 400 acres in Kentucky by virtue of certificate, lying on a branch of Hammonds creek, joining the land said to be claimed by one Bailey on the S. W. side, February 3, 1780."

Jacob Coffman enters a pre-emption warrant of 1,000 acres adjoining his settlement, and around the same on a branch of Hammonds creek, joining the lands claimed by one Bailey, June 23, 1780.

Peter Asturgus enters 400 acres in Kentucky by virtue of a certificate, lying on Hammonds creek waters of Salt river, joining Jacob Coffman on the south and east, in February 11, 1780. Also a pre-emption warrant of 1,000 acres on the head waters of the east branch of Hammonds creek, joining the lands of Coffman on the west side, and adjoining his settlement was William McBrayer, June 1, 1783.

Thos. Madison enters 1,000 acres on T. W. (Treasury Warrant) No. 7202, on the waters of Hammonds creek, to adjoin a survey of Col. S. Trigg's of 900 acres on the lower side, to begin at his S. W. corner and running with the land of S. Trigg's line east, passing the other corner 690 poles, thence at right angles south for quantity. Entered June 13, 1782.

James Crockett enters 1,000 acres upon T. W. No. 6014, to adjoin the above entry of 1,000 acres, the east to extend eastwardly, and southwardly for the quantity, June 13, 1782.

Thos. Madison enters 1,000 acres on the east of Peter Asturgus' grant, issued May 6, 1793, beginning at the most southeastwardly corner, two sugar trees and ash, N. 30, W. 693 poles, to three white oaks (passing the settlement corner at 380 poles), N. 60, E. 231 to an ash and white oak, S. 30, E. 693 poles to a walnut, ash and dogwood, thence to the beginning. Surveyed December 15, 1785. The beginning corner stands 54 poles N. 60 E. of Coffman's west corner and runs the course of Payne's line.

John Harvie and Lewis Clark 1,000 acres, joining Coffman on the N. E. to include an improvement made by J. Bailey and to run down said creek on both sides for quantity, May 15, 1786.

These few entries are selected for the reason that they are all in the immediate vicinity of Lawrenceburg, and for the additional reason that very few others had been made of Anderson county land. Wm. McBrayer's entry on the main Hammonds creek of 1,500 acres having been one of the few early entries. It will be seen from the foregoing entries that Jacob Coffman entered 400 acres on the 3rd of February, 1780, and on June 23rd following of the same year, he entered 1,000 acres "adjoining his settlement and around the same," which would lead to the belief that he erected his station or fort, between February 3rd and June 23, 1780, and except, possibly, for the cabin of William McBrayer on the Clifton pike, where the old stone house now stands, was probably the first building of any kind in the county. It will also be noticed that almost all these entries refer to Coffman's entries, and as binding on one or the other of them, and particularly of his settlement entry, causing the deduction that his building or station, was erected early in 1780, probably following his first entry. Whether this station was erected before or after the clearing out of Harrod's Big Road to The Falls is not known, but it was erected at the place where this road started down Hammonds creek on its way to The Falls. At the time of these entries, Hammonds creek had already received its name from Nathan Hammond, one of the men who was in Harrodsburg as early as 1775. At the time Coffman made his land entries as many as seven stations had been established on Bear Grass creek, near Louisville, and there was a considerable population in and around "The Falls." Squire Boone had established his station at what he called, "The Painted Stone," where as many as twenty families lived in 1780. (Collin's History, Vol. 2.) These cabins, or small stations, some of them such as Coffman's, radiated from the large stations, such as Harrod's, Squire Boone's, near where Shelbyville is, and "The Falls" at Louisville. Gradually cabins and small stations were built out Bear Grass creek in the direction of the interior, and of course, in the direction of Squire Boone's station, until there was a line of these small stations and cabins from "The Falls" to Harrod's Station, so that a road communicating with the Ohio river at The Falls, became an early necessity. It must be remembered that in the year 1780, the territory from Harrodsburg to The Falls was an unbroken wilderness except for the stations and isolated cabins built here and there on land that had been entered in the early entries, the cabins being abandoned, usually in the summer and fall on account of Indian depredations. Leestown, a mile below Frankfort, had been settled as early as 1775, and became a sort of stopping place for those who came to Kentucky by way of the Ohio and up the Kentucky in their hunt for desirable land, and at some very early day a road or way through the wilderness was blazed to Harrod's Big Road to intersect it near Coffmans. This became a part of the first regular post road to Kentucky. It started from Pittsburg, ran by Washington, Pennsylvania, West Liberty in Virginia and Wheeling on the Ohio, to Limestone (Maysville) on the Ohio and Fort Washington. From Limestone by Bourbontown (Paris), Lexington, Frankfort and Harrodsburg to Danville in Kentucky; from Danville by Bardstown to Louisville. This post road was established in 1794. (Kerr's History of Kentucky). Previous to its establishment, a road existed from Frankfort to Coffman's Station. In the meantime a road had been cut to Springfield from Coffmans, and a road, called the "Woodford road," across Kentucky river at Shyrock's ferry to Lexington and other points.

Within a few years after Coffman had entered his land and built his station at what is now Lawrenceburg, quite a network of roads centered at this station; the big road to "The Falls," which became the Harrodsburg road, the Shelbyville road, the Frankfort road, and the Springfield road.

In the meantime others had built their cabins in and around Coffman's station and on Coffman's land. Ephrim Lillard bought land from Coffman heirs in 1807. Other pioneer settlers were, Thomas Prather and wife Polly, John Mizner, Woodford Payne, Zach White, Philip White, Thomas Phillips, Memucan Allin, John Whip, Nelson Johnson, John Moore, John Routt, Jordon Walker, William Wallace and others, among whom were John and William Lawrence, William and John F. Hudgins, Samuel Arbuckle and others who lived on Coffman's land but did not have title or deed.

Jacob Coffman was killed by Indians in 1792, but his land was not divided between his widow and heirs until January 4, 1804, when Col. Anthony Crockett and John Arnold, commissioners, and William McBrayer, surveyor, made the division between his widow and children. The widow and children, except Jacob Coffman, Jr., continued to occupy the land until the first day of August, 1807, when they all joined in two deeds, by which they conveyed the widow's dower, 560¾ acres, to Ephrim Lillard, and 136 acres and forty square poles to Thomas Prather. A reference to the plot will show that all of what is now Lawrenceburg south of a line running S 58 W with Ballard street, and on in same direction westerly from Ballard street, is on Coffman land. Up to the time of the deeds to Lillard and Prather of the widow's dower, no Coffman land had been sold except that Jacob Coffman, Jr., had sold his part of the land, 176 acres, to Samuel Arbuckle on the 17th of January, 1805. His land was located south of a line running east and west with the present Fox Creek pike, extending east with this line about seventy rods, and comprising land from the Fox Creek pike line to the Bond and Lillard distillery pike in front of the residence of W. T. Bond. This is the first mention of the name of Samuel Arbuckle, who will be frequently referred to hereafter. Next, north of the land sold by Jacob Coffman, Jr., to Samuel Arbuckle, lay the land allotted to Hannah Coffman. Her north line ran N 58½, E through a point in the lot now owned by Mrs. Jennie Kinkton, just south of her house. This lot comprised 147 acres, and was sold by Hannah, who in the meantime had married John Moore, to Samuel Arbuckle November 9, 1814. Next, north of Hannah, lay the land allotted to Eleanor (Nellie) Coffman, 143 acres. Her north line ran with the Springfield road near the Glensborough pike N 58½, E to the Lawrenceburg Roller Mill property, then N 31½, W 15 poles, then N 58½, E 48 poles, then S 31½, E 15 poles, then east with Woodford street to her east boundary line. This is the land where Coffman's fort was situated. This line deviating from the Glensboro pike at the mill pond, running north 15 poles then east 48 poles, then south again to Woodford street, is the residence property of Jacob Coffman, Sr., and his station stood on the lot where the Presbyterian church now stands, and his family spring was the spring where the mill pond is now located. Another house stood on this lot, located in the yard of T. J. Ballard's residence, but it had not been conveyed by deed until long after Coffman's land was divided.

SAMUEL ARBUCKLE, PIONEER

The name of Samuel Arbuckle first occurs as to ownership in land in what is now Anderson county, in his purchase of land allotted to Jacob Coffman, Jr., in the division of the land of Jacob Coffman, Sr., 175 acres. This land was afterwards known as the Silas Myers land, and afterwards owned in its entirety by Wm. F. Bond. A part of the land was conveyed by W. F. Bond to his son, C. E. Bond and a part to his daughter, Mrs. Jessie M. Johnson and the rest divided among his children after his death in 1910. C. E. Bond built his large brick residence on the corner of Main and Broadway, and after the death of his wife in 1890, sold this residence to C. C. Lillard. J. M. Johnson built the large brick residence near the C. E. Bond home. Samuel Arbuckle built his home on this land and lived there until he sold it to Benjamin Duncan. Samuel Arbuckle owned this land while he had no deed to it, and did not get a deed until the 17th of January, 1805. He had purchased the undivided interest of Jacob Coffman, Jr., some years before the date of his deed. When the land was divided, then Jacob Coffman, Jr., conveyed the land to him. He sold this land to Benj. Duncan for $1,100 October 21, 1805, although his wife, Barsheba, did not acknowledge the deed until the 11th of December, 1809. By the sale of the land to Benj. Duncan for $1,100, the price he paid Jacob Coffman, Jr., for it indicates that Jacob had built the house and lived in it to the time he conveyed it to Arbuckle. On the 9th of November, 1814, Samuel Arbuckle bought the Hannah Coffman lot from Hannah and her husband, John Moore. This Moore home was almost on the spot where D. L. Moore, Jr., built, lived and died (now owned by Stites Milton). Samuel Arbuckle lived here until a year before he removed to Missouri. He sold the place to John Routt, September 27, 1830. He built a two-story brick house on this same land and on the lot where T. B. Ripy, Jr., now lives. He conveyed his house and lot to Jordon H. Walker and John T. Daviess, trustees for his daughter, Fannie Richardson, and this house and lot was sold by Fannie Richardson's heirs (who had removed from the county in 1831), to John Draffen in 1853. On March 9, 1821, Arbuckle bought lot No. 23, the northeast corner of Main and Woodford Road, from the trustees of Lawrence, for $150. (Deed Book K, Franklin county court.) He built a brick store there with residence above. He sold this building to Dr. Lewis J. Witherspoon in August, 1827, for $850. Dr. Witherspoon established a drug store on the first floor and his residence above it. It was a drug store in 1827 and has been so ever since. Dr. L. J. Witherspoon lived in the second story until 1833.

Importance is given Samuel Arbuckle for the reason he was one of the town builders of Lawrence, now Lawrenceburg. Where he came from does not, so far, appear, but with his son-in-law, William Lawrence, he was the moving factor in establishing the town called Lawrence, renamed Lawrenceburg in 1827. He and his wife, Barsheba, were the parents of six daughters. They were: Annie, the wife of William Lawrence; Winnie, the wife of Thomas Phillips; Fannie, the wife of John C. Richardson; Elizabeth, the wife of Jacob Gudgel, and Hannah, the wife of William Pollard. The Arbuckles had no sons. February 17, 1818, Arbuckle bought from Nellie Coffman land described in the deed as seven town lots and three alleys. This land was an oblong square on the west side of Main street, running from Brooks alley where the Christian church is now located (corner Main and Chautauqua), to Woodford street. On the next day, February 18, 1818, he conveyed it to the trustees of the town and it became the west side of Main street between the points indicated. Samuel Arbuckle bought many tracts in the vicinity of Lawrenceburg which he sold or conveyed to trustees for his daughters. He was a large slave owner for the time and place, and did not divest himself of all his holdings until after his removal to the state of Missouri.

THE TOWN OF LAWRENCE

Hon. L. F. Johnson, in his excellent history of Franklin county, refers to the order of the Franklin county court establishing the town of Lawrenceburg in 1820. Such an order was made by that court in that year, but that was not the date of the establishment of Lawrenceburg, then called Lawrence. On the 24th of February, 1814, Nellie Coffman conveyed 29¼ acres of her land to Wm. Lawrence. This conveyance embraced all of her land on the east of the Harrodsburg road (Main street), beginning six poles north of Mrs. Mary Dowling's north line, and running somewhat beyond Woodford street. On the 15th of March, 1816, she conveyed to Lawrence four and one-half acres and seven square poles, beginning at a stake on west side of Harrodsburg road (corner of Main and Woodford streets), in the forks of the lane, thence N 31½, west 16 poles, to a stake nigh Brown's crib; thence S 58, W 48½ poles to the corner white oak and sugar trees; thence S 31½ E 14 poles to another corner at two honey locusts; thence to the beginning. This latter parcel of land was just north of Woodford street—called Woodford road—on both sides of Main and comprised the Coffman residence property. On the 17th of February, 1818, Nellie Coffman conveyed to Samuel Arbuckle six acres and 88½ square poles, "including seven lots and three alleys of the town of Lawrence." Beginning in Samuel Arbuckle's field at a stake (28 poles and 13 feet west of the division line between the residences of C. D. Lyen and T. B. Ripy); thence N 21, W 138 poles to a stake (Woodford street); thence N 69, E 28 poles and 13 feet to a stake (Main street); thence to the beginning. One line was left out, and that is the division line between Lyen and Ripy on Main street, S 69, W 28 poles and 13 feet to the beginning. It is seen by an examination of the above three deeds that Nellie Coffman had conveyed to Lawrence and Arbuckle all her land that lies on both sides of Main street from a point six rods north of Mrs. Mary Dowling's north line to a point north of Woodford street. The agitation for a town at Lawrence had been going on for two or three years before 1818, and the residents did not wait for a county court order erecting the town of Lawrence. Two men seem to have been instrumental in organizing the town—William Lawrence and his father-in-law, Samuel Arbuckle. On the 18th of February, 1818, William Lawrence and his wife, Annie, conveyed to the trustees of Lawrence two tracts of land. One of these tracts contained six acres and 88½ square poles, beginning at an apple tree in Lawrences' orchard and running thence S 69, W 28 poles and 13 feet to a stake in Main street; thence with Main street N 21, W 138 poles to a stake; thence N 69, E 28 poles and 13 feet to a stake; thence S 21, E 138 poles to the beginning. This tract lay on the east side of Main street to Whites alley. The other tract conveyed to the trustees of Lawrence on the same day consisted of three acres and 123 square poles, and is described as beginning at a stake on the south side of Main street, on the corner of Main and Woodford streets, running parallel with Woodford street.

On the same day Samuel Arbuckle and his wife, Barsheba, conveyed to the town of Lawrence a tract of land beginning at a stake in Samuel Arbuckles' field; thence N 21, W 138 poles to a stake N 69, E 28 poles and 13 feet to a stake; thence S 21, E 138 poles to the beginning. This boundary contained all the land on the west side of Main street from the division line between C. D. Lyen and T. B. Ripy, Jr., to Woodford street, and gives the identical boundary given in the deed of Nellie Coffman to Samuel Arbuckle dated February 17, 1818, the day before this deed. The town had been laid off in half-acre lots before the 18th of February, 1818, but the writer has been unable to find any record of any plot of the town, but when the town was laid off the lots were not laid of 28 poles and 13 feet, but 104 feet, 4 inches front by 208 feet and 8 inches deep, with noprovision for an alley in rear of them, although an alley was gradually opened in rear of the lots and taken off the rear ends of the lots.

The trustees at this time, and who had been appointed and elected before February 18, 1818, as shown by deeds made to town lots, were William B. Wallace, John C. Richardson, William Hudgins, Samuel Russell and Joel Medley, and when the town lots which had been laid off out of the land conveyed to them by Lawrence and Arbuckle were sold, this preamble to the deeds was used: "Whereas, the Legislature of Kentucky did authorize the establishment of a town in said county and state to be named Lawrence, and did nominate and appoint said William B. Wallace, Jno. C. Richardson, Wm. Hudgins, Samuel Russell and Joel Medley to dispose of the lots, and for other purposes usual in such cases. Now this indenture," etc., etc. These

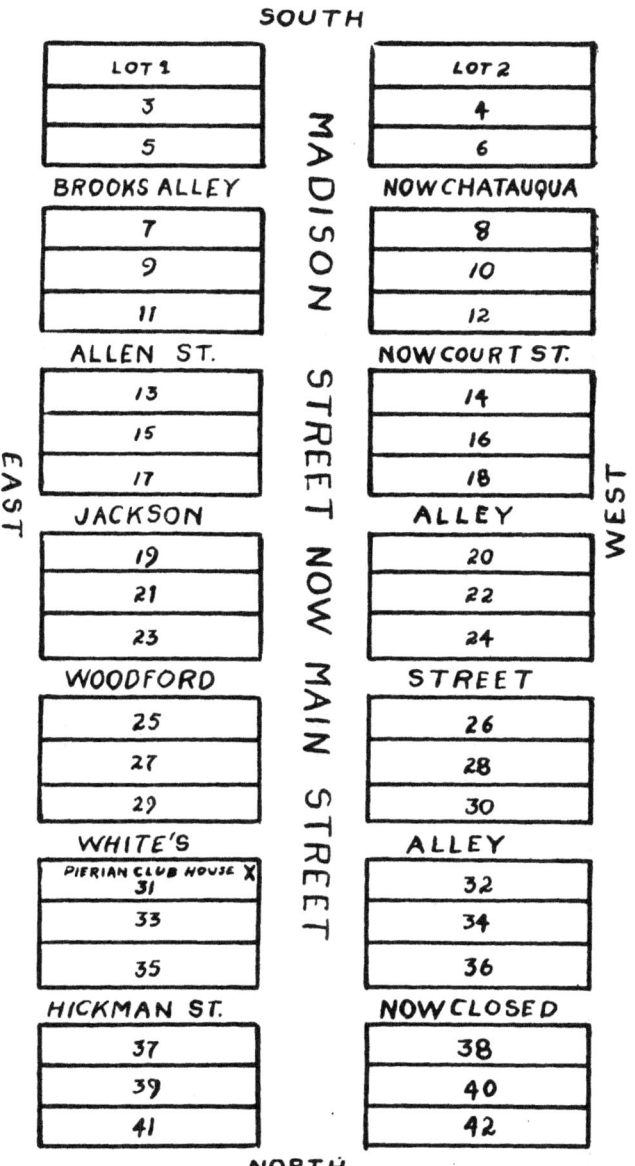

Original plat of Lawrence, now Lawrenceburg, laid off and incorporated in 1818. Lots were 104⅓ feet by 208⅔ and contained ½ an acre. First court was held in Wm. Hudgins' home in 1827. (Lot 17.)

trustees sold several lots out of the land which had been conveyed to them before the town was again incorporated by the Franklin county court. Notably, to-wit:

Wm. B. Wallace, Jno. C. Richardson, Wm. Hudgins, Samuel Russell and Joel Medley, Trustees of the town of Lawrence, to

Joseph Minzner, 17th of May, 1818, lot No. 5.
Same to Ambrose Medley, July 3, 1818, part of lot 32.
Same to Samuel Russell, 3rd of July, 1818, lots 1 and 3.
Same to John Rochester, August 1, 1818, lot 30.
Same to William Hudgins, July 3, 1819, lot No. 18.
Same to Joel Medley, July 3, 1819, lots 32 and 34.
Same to Joshua McMichael, July 16, 1819, lot 20.
Same to Samuel Arbuckle, March 9, 1821, lot 23.
Same to W. W. Penney, April 11, 1821, lot 8.
Same to William Lawrence, May 21, 1821, lot No. 25.
Same to David Griffy, August 4, 1821, lot No. 17.

This incorporation of the town of Lawrence by the Franklin county court occurred at the September term, 1820, and the following trustees were appointed in this order: Wm. B. Wallace, Jno. C. Richardson, Wm. Hudgins, Joshua McMichael, Dixon G. Dedman, and William Lawrence, with full power to act as such trustees agreeable to the Acts of Assembly in such case made and provided. The town retained the name of Lawrence from the first incorporation, until the name was changed by Act of the Legislature approved January 16, 1827, to Lawrenceburg.

William Lawrence kept a tavern at the point in the south part of Lawrenceburg which occupied the ground of the present residence of Mr. Lucien B. McBrayer and a part of Mrs. Jennie Kinkton's lot and also a part of Bush Avenue. Lawrence is the first person known to have kept a tavern here. He had painted on his tavern sign, "Don't give up the Ship;" this sign was put up after the sinking of the Chesapeake, and the death of Captain Lawrence, her commander, who used those immortal words. William Lawrence had kept this tavern for years before and his place was known as Lawrence tavern, and the town was named for him. After he ceased to keep the Lawrence tavern, and after he had bought the Nellie Coffman land, he had brick made at his brick yard, located on the lot owned by the Dowling Cooper Shop on Court street. He also built a brick residence opposite the present Southern railway depot, which stood until the railroad was built in 1888. Lawrence also built a brick hotel on the northeast corner of Main and Woodford streets, which he rented to Matthew Galt who conducted a hotel there, which was named "The Galt House," and stood until it was torn down to make way for the present postoffice. It was occupied as a hotel from its building until about 1910 when it was destroyed by fire, and the walls were taken down for the new Government building. It had been destroyed by fire on two former occasions, but the walls were left in good condition. Before the erection of Anderson County, some of its citizens had been conspicuous in the affairs of Franklin County. Philip White represented Franklin County in the Legislature in 1816; James McBrayer in 1824; David White in 1826. Sheriffs of Franklin County from that part now Anderson, were Robert Blackwell in 1805; he was again the eighth sheriff in 1808; Wm. McBrayer the ninth sheriff in 1909; Philip White, in 1820; John Walker, in 1824; Jordon H. Walker, deputy sheriff, and he held office from that time continuously until his death in 1860.

On account of the densely wooded areas and stock running at large to fatten on acorns, the early farmers had "ear-marks" for their stock recorded, as follows: Jesse Guess, a swallow fork on the right ear; James McBrayer, a split in each ear; Christopher Lillard, a crop and half crop off the right ear; John Hackley, a crop off the left ear and an upper bit off the right ear; James M. Hawkins, a crop and under bit in the right ear and a crop and split in the left ear; James Paxton, a crop off the right ear and a swallow fork in the left ear.

EARLY SALE OF LOTS IN LAWRENCEBURG

A few of the early sales made in Lawrence are given because it is interesting to note that the boundaries are marked by trees. These transactions are recorded in deed books in the Franklin county court:

Aug. 1st. 1807. 560¾ Acres for 362 pounds.

Eleanor Coffman, widow and others, to Ephrim Lillard, (Lillard occupied this land during his life): In Franklin county (now Anderson) Kentucky, being part of the land Jacob Coffman, deceased, seized and possessed of, bounded as follows: Beginning at an ironwood and white oak corner to Thomas Prather; running thence S 58½ W 24 poles to a sugar tree; thence S 31 E 15 poles to a honeylocust; S 58½ W 52 poles to two sugar trees; N 30½ W 15 poles to a redbud; S 58½ W 512 poles to a hickory; N 54 W 26 poles to a red oak; S 44 W 72 poles to a stake in the original line; N 31½ W 116 poles to a hickory; N 58½ E 345 poles to settlement at a Run and corner to Thomas Prather; thence down the Run with its meanders to a buckeye corner to Thomas Prather; S 8 E 85 poles to the beginning." This tract of land representing 560¾ acres in the Coffman settlement, now the town of Lawrenceburg, sold for 362 pounds, which was less than $1,800. On February the 24th, 1814, Nellie Coffman, daughter of Jacob, sold to William Lawrence 29¼ acres: includes the eastern part of her land east of Harrodsburg road, from south part of Lawrence (burg) to Woodford road, for the consideration of $330 for the 29¼ acres. William Lawrence built his tavern on the portion of this land now occupied by the homes of Mrs. Kinkton and Mrs. Lucien McBrayer. On Sept. 25th, 1826, Nellie Coffman sold to William Hudgins, 2 acres and 137 square poles "on the west side of a branch and south side of the Springfield road," which is a part of Stanley Trent's land today. Nellie and her mother Eleanor, lived in a cabin on this place, and after this sale they moved to Clay county, Missouri, and were living there when Nellie sold the residue of her land in Lawrenceburg, June 2, 1830, to Samuel Arbuckle, which consisted of 138 acres for $1,200.

Lots in Lawrenceburg began to advance in price after the erection of the county. On Oct. 1st, 1832, William Hudgins and wife Nancy sold to Delaney Egbert, a lot containing ¼ acre for $500. This lot on the corner of Madison (Main) street and Jackson alley.

Jan. 22nd, 1934, a certain brick meeting house adjoining the town of Lawrenceburg containing ¼ of an acre of land, on which the Presbyterian church now stands, was sold by F. L. Connor to Dixon G. Dedman, James Wallace, and Robert McMichael, trustees for the benefit of the Presbyterian church, for $600. On June 13th, 1835, John T. Daviess to Dedman and McGinnis, Crib lot, known as brick yard. On 11th of Jan., 1830, Wm. Lawrence sold to John and Susannah Whip, his hotel property (Lawrence Tavern) and on Sept. 10th, 1831, gave to his son, Samuel Lawrence, and Randall Walker, Jr., power to convey the property to the Whips when paid for, as he was going to Missouri.

On Jan. 2nd, 1837, Seneca Gregory sold to Elisha Beasley the south half of lot No. 8, containing ¼ acre, for $374. (Mrs. Rose Searcy and Mitt Leathers own homes on this lot today (1936). Dixon G. Dedman and wife sold to William Hickman on the 8th of January, 1837, lot No. 16, for $1,000. This was in the heart of town and today is occupied by the J. W. Shouse dry goods store* and Spencer grocery. William Hickman had a residence and his store on this lot, and his family burial ground in the rear of his property. About the year 1890 the members of his family interred there, were removed to the Lawrenceburg cemetery.

On May 17th, 1841, Wm. Hickman and wife, Frances, sold to James Ripy, "a certain lot and houses thereon, known as lot No. 19, for $630."

On Nov. 2nd, 1837, John F. Hudgins and Fannie sold to Wm. Todd, "a certain house and lot on Main street, immediately in the angle formed by Main street and Jackson Alley on the west side of Main street, known as part of lot No. 20 for $250."

On July 10th, 1844, Albert Linney and wife, sold to James Ripy, "one certain house and lots, known as lot No. 22 on the plat of the town for the sum of $525."

On Feb. 24th Nellie Coffman sold to William Lawrence, 29½ acres on land east of the Harrodsburg road to Woodford road (street), for $330. William Lawrence had a brick kiln about 200 yards east of the railroad on Court street. He built several brick houses in town before moving to Missouri in 1831.

On Nov. 30th, 1830, Thomas Phillips and wife sold to Matthew Galt the brick tavern on corner of Woodford and Madison (Main) street, for $1,600. Today the post office stands on this site.

Whip's livery stable built about 1830, stood on the lot owned today by Mrs. Davis Lyen, on which the cottage occupied by Edward Taylor stands. This is known as lot No. 6 on the plat of the town, and it embraces two houses and the new Christian church. It was sold Feb. 22nd, 1833, by George Morris to Joseph S. Benham of Louisville for $1,212. The stable was still standing and was run by W. H. Searcy from 1887 to about 1892. Part of this lot No. 6 was purchased by Chas. E. Bond, the old stable torn away and the home of C. D. Lyen and the Christian church parsonage and Earl Spencer home erected on the site. In 1920 the corner of the lot next to Chatauqua street was purchased from J. W. Shouse for $8,000 including parsonage, and on this was built the Christian church.

Part of lot No. 6 was sold Aug. 30th, 1831, by William Lawrence to George Morris and the consideration was a house and lot occupied by Lawrence "in the angle opposite and adjoining Brook's alley, and $300 paid; $100 cash paper; $100 on individuals and a negro girl, Melinda."

John Story and wife sold to Jefferson Searcy on May 22nd, 1832, a fraction of lot No. 32 for $60.

F. L. Connor sold to John F. Hudgins the Steam Mill and Carding factory

---

*Now owned by S. V. Gordon.—L. K. B.

on Dec. 7th, 1835. (Today this is the Eagle Roller Mills.) "Beginning at the corner of Robert W. Sea and Tarleton Railey, and F. L. Connor; thence with the post and rail fence, including it to the corner thereof; thence north with the post and rail fence and ending at a point so that a line drawn at right angles with the first line at the beginning will include one acre. From the first day of April, 1834, for the full term of 28 years."

The lot on which the Ford garage stands today, was sold to W. W. Penny on April 11th, 1821, for $100. Penny built a house on this lot and sold it to Wm. Patterson in 1829 for $400. Patterson sold half his lot to Senacca Gregory, who as the best wagon maker in this part of the county at that time. He maintained his house and shop on this lot. Patterson sold half the original lot in 1832, for $350 to John F. Hudgins. The latter disposed of this property to Fielding Connor for $750 in 1835. Later it passed into the hands of L. W. Chambers, who sold the house and lot to James Saffell in 1865. In 1866 it was bought by John Leathers, and at a later period, purchased by Mrs. Sarah Boston for $1,965. Mrs. Boston sold it to Charles E. Bond who erected the brick buildings as they stand today, which brings the history of this property down to the present time.

In Feb., 1819, William Bond (Revolutionary soldier, born 1740), and his wife, Sarah, sold to their son, John Bond, a hundred acres of land on Bailey's Run for 90 pounds. The same year the Hoomes heirs sold to John Bond on Bailey's Run, 53 acres for $75. The first Bond distillery was built on this land. John Bond's son, W. F. Bond, acquired many more acres adjoining this land which runs up to the boundaries of Lawrenceburg, and today, a great granddaughter and great grandson of William Bond 1st, Miss Mollie Bond and W. T. Bond, own this estate and live on the ancestral acres.

ALLEYS IN LAWRENCEBURG

When the town was laid off in 1818, Jackson alley (between Taylor's and courthouse square) was one of the alleys named. It is supposed to have been sixteen feet wide, as all of the alleys are supposed to have been, since wherever the width of an alley is mentioned it is sixteen feet. Jackson alley was not an important alley in 1818, as it afterward became, and not as important as Whites alley was then, nor for some years. But in 1828 the buildings on Main street north and south of Jackson alley had been considerably improved, and the trustees of the town concluded to widen it. On the 15th of August, 1828, the trustees purchased from Anthony C. Miller a strip of ground six feet wide on north side of Jackson alley, and west side Main street, running back 208 and two-thirds feet, and for this strip the trustees paid Miller $20. And at the same time they purchased from James Carter, a strip on the north side of Jackson alley seven feet wide running back the distance of town lots, 208 and two-thirds feet, now from Main to College street, for the sole object of widening Jackson alley. The trustees at the time were Wm. Hudgins, Wm. Patterson, David Bullock, Woodford Payne, Thomas Phillips. For the seven feet on the east side the trustees paid Carter $21.

ALLEY EAST OF LAWRENCEBURG, OCTOBER 23RD, 1840 (NOW COLLEGE STREET)

The alley east of town in 1840, was a part of the land conveyed by Wm. Lawrence to Wm. Hudgins, which is now the Lawrenceburg Graded School property. When Hudgins sold this property to L. J. Whitherspoon, Ephrim Lillard and John Penny, trustees of the Baptist church, he left a space sixteen feet wide running from Woodford street to Jackson alley, nex to the town, the town running back only 208 and two-thirds feet from M n street. The trustees bought this land from Hudgins at the above date, to be kept open for the benefit of the town. The trustees of the town paid Hudgins $25 for this alley. This alley being sixteen feet wide and the alley west of town being sixteen feet wide, impresses the idea that all of the alleys of the town were sixteen feet wide.

When the town was laid off in lots in 1818, no alleys were provided for back of the lots. The alley back of the lots 25, 27 and 29, was opened by Mathew Galt, from whom the old Galt House in town took its name, and after Mathew Galt's death, when his heirs conveyed the Galt House and other property, the following description appears as to the alley and Galt's grave yard: (Deed book "H") W. S. Galt and others, to James Saffell, Aug. 30th, 1852: Beginning at a stake 16 feet from the corner of a plank stable, on the Woodford Road (now Woodford street), and running with said road until it strikes Samuel Hutton's old line, now L. J. Witherspoon's heirs line till you get within 16 feet of the boundary line of said town, thence running in a parallel direction with said boundary line to the beginning reserving an alley 16 feet in width, be the quantity what it may. And also reserving and excepting out of the aforesaid boundary, the following portion thereof, and bounded as follows: beginning at a point 20 feet this side of the southeast corner, and running thence eastwardly, with the Woodford Road to said southeast corner, thence northwardly with said Witherspoon's line 35 feet. Thence westwardly and parallel with the Woodford Road line 20 feet; thence southwardly 35 feet to the beginning, including the grave yard. This alley is a continuation of College street on the north. Many years ago, in the early seventies, and after the part of the lot on which the grave yard was located had been sold, and after a house was built on it, some of the Galt heirs, all of whom had removed from Lawrenceburg for many years, came back, or some of them came back, and claimed the grave yard.

Allen street, now Court, was a narrow street, two small buildings were situated on the south side of the court house square until the court house was destroyed by fire in 1859. Afterwards the street was slightly widened, as new fences were constructed or repaired. There was no sidewalk on either side of Allen street, until the Christian church was built opposite the old jail in 1847-48, when a very narrow brick sidewalk was built along the side of Allen from Main to the church.

White's alley is the alley running by the Baptist church across by the Pierian Club building.

Brooks alley was near Bush avenue, and a part of it is the present Chatauqua street.

HISTORY OF ANDERSON COUNTY

HISTORY OF THE PIERIAN CLUB PROPERTY

The Pierian Club lot was a part of the widow Coffman's dower, and the dower was laid off to her by the commissioners of the Franklin County Court in 1804. One hundred thirty-six acres and 40 square poles of this dower was sold by the widow, Eleanor Coffman, and all of Jacob Coffman's children, on the 1st of August, 1807, to Thomas Prather, and Prather sold to Samuel Hutton 107½ acres of this 136 acres and 40 poles, on the 27th of December, 1813, but reserved one acre from his deed to Hutton by Thos. Prather. (Deed book "D," page 409 Franklin County Court). This one acre contained the Pierian Club lot. This one acre was sold by Thos. Prather to Phillip White on the 26th of July, 1815. Before it was sold again, the town (in 1818) was laid off into town lots and Phillip White had died. A part of this lot became lot 31 of the town, and embraced a half acre, and was sold by Zachariah White, a son of Phillip White, and executor of his will, to Susannah B. Pearson, on the 19th of January, 1835, for the sum of $750. (Deed book "C," Anderson County Court), as follows: Zachariah White and Agnes White, his wife, to Susannah B. Pearson, in Anderson County, Ky., being a lot of ground in the town of Lawrenceburg, on the east side of Main street, known by the lot No 31, and bounded as follows: beginning at a corner on Main street and Whites alley, running east thence with said alley 208 2-3 feet to the town limits; thence running north with said limits to lot 33; thence west with lot 33 to Main street to the beginning, $750 cash. The "Little Brick House" was on this lot when Susannah B. Pearson bought it from White in 1835, and history does not record when it was built, but it was prior to 1825. In February, 1852, Susannah B. Pearson sold the same house and lot to Dr. L. J. Witherspoon for $394 cash. One year later on February, 1853, Dr. L. J. Witherspoon sold the same property to Dr. John A. Witherspoon who owned the property until his death in 1899. It was then inherited by his daughter, Mrs. Emma Witherspoon Sanlin, who sold it to R. S. Collins, April, 1913. On October 15th, 1915, R. S. Collins sold this lot containing the little brick house to the Pierian Club and the deed in part reads as follows: This indenture made and entered into on the 28th of October, 1915, by and between R. S. Collins and wife, Lela Collins, of Lawrenceburg, Anderson County, Ky., parties of the first part and hereafter known as grantors, and Mrs. Mary Dowling, Mrs. R. H. Lillard and Mrs. W. T. Bond, Trustees of the Pierian Club, known as grantees; witnesseth, that for and in consideration of the sum of $350 cash in hand paid the said grantors by the said grantees, and further consideration of $500 each payable in one and two years, drawing interest at rate of 6 per cent per annum after date until paid * * * * conveyed to said grantees a certain house and lot situated on the southwest corner of Main and alley (once known as Whites alley) running back to intersect College street, then in a northerly direction 53 feet to a stone corner to the said R. S. Collins; thence in an easterly direction 214 feet to a stone corner to said Collins, and 49 feet from the said alley; thence in a southerly direction 49 feet to corner of said alley and College street; thence in westerly direction 214 feet with said alley to the beginning.

This being a portion of the lot conveyed to Collins by Emma Witherspoon Sanlin by deed on April 30, 1913.

There was a brick yard in Lawrenceburg in 1818 and Wm. Lawrence was the builder of several brick houses here about that time and as the Pierian

Club house is the oldest house in the town, it is supposed that it was built at that early date.

THE ERECTION OF ANDERSON COUNTY

By an Act of the Legislature approved January 16, 1827, Anderson County was erected and established. By a supplemental Act approved January 18, 1827, the county was to go into effect and operation on the 20th of January, 1827. Willis Blanton and Peter R. Dunn were two of the Commissioners appointed by acts of General Assembly, January 16, 1827, to lay off by metes and bounds, the county. Up to this time the county had been a part of Washington, Mercer and Franklin counties.

By the original Act all that part of the counties of Franklin, Mercer, and Washington included in a boundary, beginning at the mouth of Little Benson creek on Kentucky river in Franklin County; thence with the meanders of said creek, to Brooks spring, near the Harrodsburg road; thence on a straight line to Caleb Tinsley's, leaving him in Franklin County; thence by a line due west to the line of Shelby County; thence along the same to the mouth of Crooked creek on Salt river; thence along the dividing line of Washington and Nelson to the mouth of Beaver creek, on Chaplin's fork on Salt river; thence up said creek to where the road from Springfield to Frankfort crosses the same; thence with a line east so as to leave Vincent Morgan in Washington County, to the dividing line between Washington and Mercer; thence with the Washington and Mercer line to a point from which a line due east will include the house of James Downy; thence a straight line to include the house of Thomas Hardesty on the Harrodsburg road: thence a straight line to the Kentucky river at the ferry of Costello Dawson, Sr.; thence down the river to the beginning. By the same Act, the county was to be called and known by the name of Anderson, in honor of the late Richard C. Anderson, Jr. The date of the county courts were fixed for the first Monday in every month, except the months when the circuit courts were held. The county was attached to the Fourth Judicial District, and the terms of the circuit courts were fixed on the fourth Mondays of January, July and November, with six-day terms. Ten Justices of the Peace were allowed the county, and it was enacted that they should meet at the house of William Hudgins in the town of Lawrence (which name was changed to Lawrenceburg by the Act) on the first court day after the Act went into effect, at which time they were to appoint a clerk. The Governor was authorized to commission a sheriff.

William Trotter of Franklin County, R. D. Shipp of Woodford County, Joel P. Williams of Mercer County, Stephen Lee of Washington County, Wm. T. Webber, of Shelby County and Elias Kinchelo of Nelson County were appointed commissioners, any five of whom might act, to locate the county seat. They were ordered to assemble at the home of Wm. Hudgins in the mouth of March or April (1827) after the Act went into effect, and after being sworn, to select the seat of justice for the county, and make their report of their actions to the county court, for which they were allowed two dollars per day. The court was allowed five constables to be appointed by the court.

Arrangement was made for the levy and collection of taxes, and until the erection of public buildings, it was ordered that circuit and county courts be held at the house of Wm. Hudgins in Lawrenceburg. It was further enacted that Wm. Blanton, of Franklin County; Wm. M. Bell, of Washington County, and Peter R. Dunn, of Mercer County, be appointed commissioners, any two of whom might act, to proceed as soon as practicable to run and mark the boundary lines of the county; and when run and marked, to make out four fair plats of the boundary and transmit one to the county court of Anderson, and one each to the county courts of Franklin, Mercer and Washington; and they were to receive, each, two dollars and a half per day, to be paid by Anderson County. It was also enacted that the free voters of the county shall vote as heretofore in their several counties and precincts as though the Act had not passed, until the next appointment of representatives. On the 28th day of March, 1827, the commissioners, Wm. Trotter, R. D. Shipp, Joel P. Williams, Stephen Lee, Wm. Webber and Elias Kinchelo, who had been appointed by the Act erecting the county, to select the seat of justice for the county, met at the house of Wm. Hudgins, and after taking the oath, proceeded to view the several sites proposed by different citizens. They proceeded on the 28th and 29th, and "after deliberate examination and taking into consideration all the conveniences and inconveniences, are of the opinion that the seat of justice should be located in the town of Lawrenceburg." On the 30th of March, they proceeded to select the most suitable ground for the "public square" and selected the "lots on which George Morris now lives, together with a lot belonging to Messrs. Hudgins." Their report is dated March 30, 1827, and was submitted to the county court on April 2, 1827. They submitted with their report also the bounds of Morris and Hudgins for title, and for removal of all obstructions. This report of the commissioners was respectfully received and filed, but was not adopted at that time. On the contrary the court showed that it knew the ways of justices of the peace, and running true to form, it commenced jockeying for terms. The commissioners were thanked and paid, but the court on its own behalf appointed Esquires John Busey and Reuben Boston, with umpire in case of disagreement, to contract conditionally for the county with Geo. Morris and Wm. and John Hudgins for their lots as fixed by the commissioners, and also to ascertain what other lots in the town suitable for public buildings can be had, and at what price and to report their findings. The first county court had been held before the commissioners appointed by the Act establishing, to select the county seat and to survey the county.

In 1827 when Anderson County was created and the Act creating the county changed the name of the town of Lawrence to Lawrenceburg, it was natural that the creation of a new county with Lawrenceburg a good prospect for the county seat, that a fresh boom occurred in town lots. Quite a number of the lots that had been laid off by the trustees out of the land conveyed to them by William Lawrence and Samuel Arbuckle in 1818, were sold by the trustees in 1827, '28 and '29; and there was quite a sale of the lots sold by the trustees in 1818 and built upon by the purchasers, in fact there had been more than forty transfers of town lots made in those years. However the growth of the town did not meet the anticipation of those who laid out the village in 1818. In 1830 the population of the town had increased to only 320, and of the county, to 4,520. In 1830, and for some years previous, there had been as many as four tanyards, and three rope-walks and bagging factories. There was also one carding mill. One of these ropewalks and bagging factories was working more than forty slaves, and yet, the growth of the town had not met the anticipations of the founders of the town. Before the year 1830 a number of the leading citizens had sold out their properties and left; the Coffmans, or a number of them, to Clay County, Missouri; William Hudgins, Samuel Arbuckle and William Lawrence, to Ray County, Missouri; Fielding L. Conner back to Franklin County where he came from. Many good people remained, but the principal builders of the town left, nor did the town grow for many years. The county, with very few changes, has remained situated as at the time of its erection, except that its population was considerably enhanced by the cutting off from Mercer of a large territory including a population of about four hundred. Immediately upon the establishment of the county, the Governor appointed ten Justices of the Peace and a sheriff, who at once entered upon the discharge of their duties. They secured order books for the courts of the county, and immediately commenced county business. The following are some of the first orders entered upon the records: February term, 1827. Commonwealth of Kentucky, Anderson County, to-wit: Be it remembered that by virtue of an Act of the General Assembly of the Commonwealth aforesaid, entitled, "An Act to erect and establish the county of Anderson out of parts of the counties of Franklin, Washington and Mercer, approved the 16th of January, one thousand eight hundred and twenty-seven; and also another Act of the General Assembly, supplemental thereto, approved January 18th, one thousand eight hundred and twenty-seven. There was begun and held a county court for the said town of Lawrenceburg in the county aforesaid, on the 5th day of February in the year of our Lord, one thousand eight hundred and twenty-seven when and where the following gentlemen, Justices of the county court aforesaid appeared, and having produced, severally, commissions from the Executive of this Commonwealth appointing the Justices of the Peace for the said county, together with certificates, that each of them before the proper authority had taken oath to support the Constitution of the United States of America, and that he will be true and faithful to the Commonwealh of Kenucky so long as he shall continue to be a citizen thereof, and also the oath of office as well as the oath against Duelling, as prescribed by the Constitution and laws of this state. Severally took their seats according to senority as follows, to-wit: Jesse Guess, Presiding Justice; James McBrayer, Dixon G. Dedman, John Wash, Andrew McBrayer, John Busey, Christopher Lillard, Reuben Boston, John C. Richardson and Thomas Phillips, Esquires." The reason for naming the Justices of the Peace by senority, was, that under the Constitution when the senior justice's time expired, he was recommended to the executive for the appointment to the office of sheriff for two years, and unless there was some good and substantial reason for not so doing, he was invariably appointed sheriff. He also had the privilege of selling out his right to be sheriff, and sales were very frequently made by men who did not care to assume the responsibilities of the office. The following is the order of appointing a clerk of the county court: "David White, Jr., produced in court the following certificate, to-wit, State of Kentucky Sct., we do certify that David White, Jr., hath been examined by our clerk in our presence and under our direction, and that we judge him well qualified to discharge the duties of clerk, to any county court, circuit court or court of equal dignity within this Commonwealth. Given under our hands as judges of the Court of Appeals for the state aforesaid at Frankfort this 20th day of January, 1827. George M. Bibb, William Ousley, B. Mills. Attest J. Sweigert, C. C. A. Wherefore it is considered and ordered by the court, that David White, Jr., be, and he is appointed clerk of this court and for the county of Anderson, and thereupon the said David White, Jr., in open court by the presiding Justice thereof took the oath that he will support the Constitution of the United States, and the Commonwealth of Kentucky so long as he shall continue to be a citizen thereof, as prescribed by the Constitution and laws of this state, likewise the oath of office and the oath against Duelling as prescribed by the several Acts of the General Assembly in such cases made and provided." Another order immediately following contains the bond of David White, Jr., with his securities. John F. Blackwell then produced his commission from the executive as sheriff, and immediately executed bond with securities, and took the oath of office. Ephrim Lillard who had been appointed Coroner, came into court and refused to undertake the duties of his office, no matter how light they might be. Everet White was then recommended to the Governor for appointment and was afterwards appointed. George Morris, upon his own motion was appointed jailer, and six gentlemen then produced their several licenses and immediately qualified to practice the law. Thus it is seen that within less than a month after the county was established, Justices of the Peace, a clerk, a sheriff, coroner and constables had all qualified and were then in the discharge of their duties. Another small empire had been established in what was then almost a wilderness, with no roads, except state roads, and no turnpikes whatever, except what nature had built, and while all of this was going on, no site had been selected for a Seat of Justice, but commissions had been appointed for that purpose, and the new county, anxious for some settled location for its county seat, immediately requested them to act and act at once. They came on the 28th day of March, 1827, made a selection of a site and presented their report: "The Commissioners appointed by an Act of the General Assembly to locate the seat of Justice of Anderson County made their report which is in the words and figures following, to-wit: In obedience to an Act of the General Assembly of the Commonwealth of Kentucky, passed on the 16th day of January in the year eighteen hundred and twenty-seven, we, William Trotter, Richard D. Shipp, Stephen Lee, Wm. T. Webber, Joel P. Williams and Elias Kinchelo, Commissioners, do report to the Worshipful the County Court of Anderson County, as follows, to-wit: On the 20th day of March we did meet at the house of William Hudgins in the town of Lawrenceburg and severally took the oath prescribed by law and thereupon on the 29th of March, we proceeded to view the several sites proposed by the different citizens of Anderson County, and after due deliberation and examination, taking into consideration all the conveniences and inconveniences resulting to the citizens of said county, we are of the opinion that the Seat of Justice for Anderson County should be located in the town of Lawrenceburg, and thereupon the 3t0h day of March we proceeded to select the most suitable piece of ground for the public square, and we have agreed in selecting the lots whereupon Geo. Morris now lives, together with a lot belonging to the Messrs Hudgins in the said town, and we herewith submit to the county court of said county, Mr. Morris' and Messrs Hudgins' bond for the removing of all obstructions off of said lots as well also, as for the titles of said lots. Given under our hands this 30th day of March, 1827; William Trotter, R. D. Shipp, Joel P. Williams, Stephen Lee, William T. Webber and Elias Kinchelo." The site is the same upon which the present court house and old jail are situated, and both lots cost not exceeding $450 which was, at that time, considered an exorbitant price, and was sold for really more than its market value. The reason for this increase in price is self evident. A new county had been established, a site for the Seat of Justice selected, and it was very fair to presume this would very much enhance the value of all property in the new county, particularly in the neighborhood of the new county seat. The 14th of January, 1850, saw a

Hebron Presbyterian Church, Built 1827

forming of the street north of the court house, and W. S. Galt, who kept a tavern in the house north of the court house made an application to the county court to move the court house fence back ten feet, and he agreed "to pave the same at his own expense subject at all times to the order of this court," and "it is expressly understood that the court in granting this order, have not and do not, intend to relinquish any right they have in the ten feet of ground which is to extend the whole length of said alley back to the town limits" (208 and two-thirds feet).

In 1852, William F. Leathers, who succeeded W. S. Galt as Tavern keeper, was granted permission to move the fence back eight feet further upon the same conditions binding W. S. Galt. This made a width of eighteen feet for the alley. All additional widening of this street has been done by the county, which finally made a concrete sidewalk, as at present.

From 1850, when the place was opened as an alley, and from that time until the concrete sidewalk was built, there was a row of posts used for hitching horses. The county had gradually widened Allen street (now Court street), and constructed a new fence on the south side of the court house, then finally the concrete sidewalk on the same side.

EARLY SETTLEMENT OF LAWRENCEBURG

(The following notes were made by Mr. McKee about the year 1885. He refers to the corner being occupied by Ottenheimer's grocery; today, 1936, the building is occupied by the Kroger Grocery Co. L. K. B.)

Thomas Prather built the first house in what is now the town of Lawrenceburg. Capt. Wallace, the grandfather of Mrs. W. H. McBrayer, built a house where Dr. J. A. Witherspoon now resides. He sold to a man by name of Philips who sold to Dr. L. J. Witherspoon. William Lawrence built the Galt House about the year 1815 (postoffice site). He afterward built the older part of the Anderson House, and kept a tavern here. On his sign board were the last words of Capt. James Lawrence of the Chesapeake, "Don't give up the ship." Lawrence afterward built the brickhouse in which Capt. J. H. McBrayer resides.* In 1816, Wm. Hudgins built a house where Ottenheimer's grocery stands (now Kroger grocery), and this was afterwards used as the first court house. Hudgins built his residence about the same time on the corner opposite, where the Lawrenceburg Bank is now located. About the same time John G. Daviess lived on the corner where Bell's grocery is.† John Searcy had a gun shop and Collins a blacksmith shop north of the Presbyterian church. Lewis Hyatt built a house on the corner next to the court house. In the vicinity of the town were some pioneer settlers. Wm. Robinson settled just north of town in about 1794, on the place owned by Mrs. Lizzie Witherspoon.‡ Other old settlers of the town we may mention George Morris, Cabel Fenwick, Samuel Lawrence, Dr. L. J. Witherspoon, Dr. Dixon G. Dedman, David White, Wm. McGinnis, Ned Miller, Jerry Beasley, Stoot and Egbert. Ashford established a cabinet shop, Blue established a hat shop, and the first store was owned and conducted by Thorn and Hudgins, and afterwards, Charles Miles. In looking back over the names and character of the early pioneers of the county, the present generation may feel a just sense of pride. They were a brave, industrious and hospitable people.

*Now the Christian Church site.
† Now Anderson News office.
‡ Now Vowels home.

HISTORY OF ANDERSON COUNTY

The earlier pioneers who exercised much influence in the formation of society in the county were John Penny, Sr., Philip White and Robert Blackwell, who were brothers-in-law, and settled in the same neighborhood, and whose farms adjoined; also adjoining that of Andrew McBrayer, two miles west of town. John Penny, Sr., had six sons, Eli, W. W., Thomas, Philip, John and James. The old gentleman was a Baptist preacher, as were his two sons, Eli and W. W. Penny. Under his ministrations the churches at Salt river, Fox Creek, Old Goshen and Little Flock, were built up. Many representatives of this family are now living. Philip White represented Franklin County (now Anderson) in the Legislature in 1816. He raised up six sons and two daughters—John B., Joseph, Everett, Philip, Zachariah and Thomas J. White, Mrs. J. M. Foster, and Mrs. James McBrayer. Joseph and Everett settled in Florida, the former was the first Congressman from that territory, the latter was killed in Florida in a duel. Philip was an eminent lawyer of Philadelphia, and a temperance lecturer of great distinction. Zachariah was a farmer of Woodford County and served as sheriff of the county, and as Representative in the Legislature in 1840. Thomas J. White was a physician and served in the Legislature from Anderson in 1833; he removed to St. Louis and afterward to California and was a member of the first Constitutional Convention of that state, in 1849. Robert Blackwell first settled in Woodford County, but in consequence of the fine range of cane and pea vine, good hunting and fishing in Anderson, he sold out in that county and settled neighbor to his brother-in-law, John Penny, and reared a large family of sons and daughters. Among others of the early pioneers of this neighborhood may be mentioned Archibold Elliott, who lived on Hammonds creek, north of Robert Blackwell's. He built what is thought to have been the first mill and distillery in the county. His son, Robert Elliott, afterwards bought the Philip White place and lived there until his death; Joshua Cummings, Memucan Allen, who first settled where Mrs. Hawkins lives on Hammonds creek at the crossing of the Camdenville pike. Memucan Allen built a mill here, but sold out and settled on the place occupied by J. H. D. McKee, near town. Charles Allen settled on the G. B. Taylor place. George Jordon settled the farm adjoining the John Penny place, on which his son, John G. Jordon, resided for many years. Joshua Saffell built a little to the west. Others were Samuel Marrs, James McClure, Jacob Gudgel and Joseph Griffy; the brothers, Daniel and Authur McGauhey—James McGauhey, now 82 years of age, son of Arthur, now resides on the farm, was a soldier under Gen. Taylor in the Florida war, and served in the Mexican war, was in the Battle of Buena Vista in the company of Capt. John H. McBrayer. Randolph and John Walker settled in the county in 1796. The first on the place now occupied by Monroe Walker, and the latter where Jordon H. Walker resided for many years; both were prominent men in their time, and raised up large families. John was sheriff of Franklin County in 1826, and his son, Jordon H. Walker, was deputy, and officiated at the execution of Jeriboam Beauchamp at Frankfort for the murder of Soloman P. Sharp. Jordan H. Walker became a Baptist preacher of the old school, and for many years clerk of the Anderson County Court and presiding Judge of the county. His brother, Randolph, was sheriff of the county many years, and represented the county in the Legislature in 1845. Of the old pioneers of the Walker neighborhood east of town, may be mentioned Jeremiah, Joseph and James Mizner, Vincent Boggess, Robert Frazier, Edward Wall, Nick Leathers and the Parker family, and further to the southeast of town, on Bailey's run, John and Anthony

Bond, Turner and Chichester Hanks. The farms opened up by these latter pioneers are, for the most part, still held by some of their descendants. Berry Searcy settled the place on Bailey's run on which Judge W. H. McBrayer's distillery is now (1890) located. About the close of the last century, three brothers, Thomas, John and Ephraim Lillard, settled in the county. Thomas settled at the Cave spring—the stopping place in 1773 of the first white men known to have set foot on the soil of Anderson. He had four sons whom he named Matthew, Mark, Luke and John. His brother settled on Salt river at the place known as Rice's ford. He had two sons, Thomas and Christopher. The third brother, Ephraim settled near town on the place lately owned by Dr. John A. Witherspoon. He married a daughter of Thomas Prather, who is said to have built the first house in the present limits of Lawrenceburg, and which is now standing. By this marriage he had three sons, Thomas, Stephen and Ephraim, and seven daughters, Mary, Margaret, Elizabeth, Ellen, Susan, Nancy and Martha. This family is largely represented in the county at the present day.

David Egbert, John Odell, George Freeman, Samuel Butts, William Kavanaugh, ——— Castleman, Jacob Miller, Archie Parker, Joel Thacker, John Crossfield, Hackley, Brown, Hochersmith, Paxton, Bell, Wheat, Gillis and Murphy were names familiar on Salt river south and west of town as of the early pioneers of the county. In 1798 Benjamin Wash made a settlement on Salt river opposite the mouth of Hammonds creek. He had two sons, John and Benjamin, and several daughters. John resided on this place for many years after the death of his father, and then settled on Beaver creek, while his brother, Benjamin, settled the place below town on the Frankfort road, known afterwards as the Eddy Mountjoy, now the Rinehart place. Selling this place to Mountjoy he bought the Baker place, a mile to the eastward, on which he died. His son, Allen Wash, now in his 83rd year, lives on part of the farm. Martin Baker owned a survey of 1,200 acres above the mouth of Hammonds creek, in the neighborhood of Jordon and Griffy. Below the mouth of Hammonds creek we find the pioneers, Roadham Petty and his son, Samuel B. Petty, Daniel Oliver, Wm. Jewell, John Busey, John Morgan, Sr., and his son, John, who has many descendants living in the west end of the county at the present day; below Morgan was the Franklins.

In 1831, John C. Richardson and Thomas Phillips, Justices of the Peace, removed to another state.

CHAPTER III

NAMES OF MEN IN ANDERSON COUNTY IN 1827

Samuel Arbuckle
James Alexander
Joseph Allen
Memucan Allin
Charles Allin
Robert Blackwell
John Blackwell
William Burford
James Breckinridge
Jeremiah Buckley
 (Ferryman)
James Baker
James Buntain
John Buntain
John Busey
Reuben Baker
Joseph Boggess
Matthais Bush
William Bond
 (Died 1829)
James S. Bond
 (Died 1831)
Anthony Bond
John Bond
John B. Bell
Thomas Burgin
Henry H. Buntain
Newman Barnes
 (Died 1833)
John Cardwell
 (Died 1827)
John Cummins
Basil Carlisle
 (Died 1836)
Pat Coontz
Benj. Case
John Crossfield
Walter Cunningham
Felix Coombs
John T. Daviess
J. G. Dedman
D. G. Dedman
Richard Dawson
Jacob Ellison
Robert Elliott
Archibald Elliott

Jacob Ellison
David Egbert
Henry Frazier
James Frazier
John Fidler
George Freeman
Stephen Franklin
Yancy Freeman
Jeremiah Ford
Wealthy Ferguson
Charles Freeman
Dandridge Freeman
Thomas Gaines
David Griffy
Jesse Guess
Elijah Gudgel
Jacob Gudgel
Wm. Gilpin
Joseph Griffy
Richard Gaines
Mathew Galt
 (Died 1833)
Ketan C. Gaines
Thos. Grace
Alvin Herndon
Jas. M. Hawkins
Turner Hanks
Wm. Hudgins
Jno. F. Hudgins
Jno. Hackley
James Hackley
Charles Harris
Webb Harris
Thos. Hedger
Jeremiah Hanks
J. H. Hickman
W. S. Hickman
Jas Hutton
Thos. Hardesty
Jno. Holman
Jno. Hancock
Jno. W. Hutton
Wm. Hill
Thos. Jordon
Cave Johnson
Geo. Jordon

Case Johnson
R. M. Kercheval
John Lillard
Laurence Long
Ephraim Lillard
Christopher Lillard
Mark Lillard
 (Died 1833)
Luke Lillard
Garland Lillard
 (Died 1837)
Jas. S. Littlepage, Sr.
Jno. London
Jno. Lawrence
 (Died 1832)
James Leathers
Clement Lillard
Chas. Lawrence
James McGuire
Samuel McGuire
Woodson Munday
Henry Munday
Joseph Moore
Nimrod Martin
Lewis Madison
James Mizner
Robert Morton
Jno. Mothershead
Jas. McClure
Alex. W. McBrayer
Andrew McBrayer
David Mullins
D. W. Kavanaugh
G. W. Kavanaugh
Allen A. Miller
Thos. Major
Littleton Major
Jos. Mizner
 (Died 1833)
Edward Mountjoy
Wm. Mountjoy
Jas. McBrayer
Jno. S. McBrayer
Jas. Alex. McBrayer
Jas. McQuiddy
Sanford McBrayer

HISTORY OF ANDERSON COUNTY 41

NAMES OF MEN IN ANDERSON COUNTY IN 1827—Continued

Robt. McBrayer
Hiram McBrayer
 (Died 1831)
Jas. G. McCoun
Samuel McCoun
Johnson McCoun
Joel Medley
H. H. Maddox
Smallwood Maddox
Arthur Moore
Elijah Mothershead
James Madison
Benj. Nelson
Pleasant Oliver
 (Died 1833)
Augustus O'Brien
John O'Dell
David Rigg
David J. Roach
Stephen Robin
Jno. C. Richardson
Wm. Robinson
 (Died 1831)
George Rose
Hankerson Reed
Richard Rigg
Winston C. Ryan
Eli Penny
Rodham Petty

Richard Philips
Wm. Philips
Wm. W. Penney
John Penney
 (Died 1833)
Thos. Prather
John Phillips
James Petty
James Paxton
Philip Penney
Jeremiah B. Posey
James Posey
Thos. Q. Roberts
Abram Sharp
Woodford Payne
Turner Satterwhite
Wafer Satterwhite
John Satterwhite
Joshua Saffell
 (Died 1860)
J. D. Street
Daniel Plough
Daniel Slaughter
Edward Sherwood
Henry Searcy
Howard Sutherland
Francis S. Slaughter
 (Died 1832)
Samuel P. Thacker

James Twyman
Joel Thacker
Lewis Thacker
Tekil Taylor
Thompson Thomas
Grayson B. Taylor
W. C. Twyman
Corbin Utterback
William Utterback
Lewis J. Witherspoon
Edward White
Zachariah White
Presley White
Edward Wall
David Woods
Samuel Woods
Joseph Woods
Jordon H. Walker
Randal Walker
John Wash
Benjamin Wash
Lewis Wilson
John Walker
Samuel H. Wills
John Whip
Wm. B. Wallace
Wm. M. Withers
Benj. Young
Leonard Young

The first court house was partly built by popular subscription, and the names of the early contributors are recorded in the Anderson County Circuit Clerk's office: "We, the undersigned citizens of Anderson County are desirous that the Seat of Justice for said Anderson County be fixed at the town of Lawrenceburg and we obligate ourselves to our representatives, to pay to the trustees of the county of Anderson, the amount annexed to our names for the purpose of defraying expense of building a court house in said county which shall be established in the town of Lawrenceburg, payable in installments of one, two and three years: John Dawson, $5.00; John Boggess, $5.00; Hankerson Reid, $5.00; Job Sharp, $20.00; Samuel McGuire, $5.00; William Gilpin, $5.00; Jeremiah Posey, $5.00; Grayson Taylor, $10.00; Thomas Phillips, $10.00; Wm. Hudgins, $25.00; Wm. Lawrence, $50.00; Dr. L. J. Witherspoon, $25.00; F. L. Connor, $25.00; David Bullock, $25.00; James McMichael, $25.00; J. Mizner, $25.00; Lewis Heitt, $25.00; J. H. McCall, $5.00; W. Robinson, $10.00; Wm. Vance, $10.00; John F. Hudgins, $25.00; Robert Doles (to be paid in work), $50.00; Wm. B. Smith, $25.00; Morton Zimmerman, $5.00; A. Zimmerman, $20.00; S. Harberson, $5.00; Mathias Carter, $6.00 and 36 gallons of whiskey; James D. Parker, $5.00; John Story, $6.00; John Penney, $50.00; J. H. Walker, $5.00; O. H. Coslet, $10.00; Chichester Hanks,

$5.00; Martin Parker, $10.00; John Bond, $10.00; Joseph Boggess, $25.00; Edward Wall, $10.00; Berry Searcy, $3.00; John Cummings, $30.00; William H. Penny, $10.00; Jacob Elliston, $25.00; William Utterback, $5.00; James Connor, $50.00; William Allin, $50.00 (on plastering on the !aid building).

COURT HOUSES OF ANDERSON COUNTY

The commissioners who were appointed at the May term of court in 1827 to contract for land and build the jail, were also directed by the same court order "to procure suitable plans for a court house for the county." At the June term, the commissioners not having adopted plans and specifications for a court house were allowed further time to procure and report on them. The October term of court having convened and the commissioners appointed to secure plans for a court house not having done so, a new committee composed of John F. Hudgins, David White and John C. Richardson was appointed "to draft a plan for a court house for this county and make a report of a plan and the probable cost to this court at the next December term."

At the December term of court the commissioners who were appointed at the October term to draft and report a plan for the court house for this county and the probable cost, made their report in writing accompanied by a plan or draft. It was ordered that Ephraim Lillard, Jno. F. Hudgins, William Lawrence and David White, be appointed to let out to the lowest bidder at public auction, the contract for the building of the court house according to the foregoing plans, subject to such alterations as the said commissioners may think proper to make.

The foundation to be of stone, the body thereof to be of good and substantial brick, and the commissioners after giving six weeks notice thereof in some public newspapers, are directed to let out the said building upon the following terms: The foundation, brick work and roof thereof to be completed by the 1st day of December, 1828, and the balance of said building to be completed by the 1st of October, 1829. The undertaker or undertakers giving bond in a sufficient penalty with good security for the performance of his or their contract; and the said commissioners are further directed to contract for the payment of said work (on behalf of this court) to be made in three equal, annual installments, but in letting out the said building they are not to exceed the sum of three thousand dollars."

There was no further order made by the court for the building of the court house, nor to any contractor for the building until the 8th of September, 1828. That the court house was in process of construction, however, is shown by an order entered upon motion made at the court by Nelson C. Johnson on 14th of July, 1828, that "leave be given to the Masonic fraternity in Lawrenceburg to finish off a room, or rooms, in the garret of the court house about to be erected, they paying all additional expenses accruing thereby, and that they have leave to occupy the same room or rooms, as a Masonic Lodge."

On the 8th of September, 1828, the court met and entered an order authorizing William Lawrence, David White, John F. Hudgins and Ephraim Lillard, "the commissioners who were appointed by this court to let out the contract for the building of the court house, be vested with power to contract with the undertaker of said building, for raising the main body of said building,

Court House and Monuments of three Wars.

not exceeding two feet above the height originally contracted for, and to contract for painting the cupalo of said building, (complete) when erected, and for priming with paint the window frames of the building, and the said commissioners are not to exceed the sum of $140 in addition to their present contract."

On November 10, 1828, Robert Logan was allowed the sum of one thousand dollars on his contract of building the court house. At the same time the court again entered an order directing the court house commissioners to have the court house and the clerk's offices painted, not to exceed $100, thirty of which was allowed.

The commissioners appointed by the court had contracted with Robert Logan to build the court house at a cost not exceeding three thousand dollars, payable in one, two and three years, out of a special levy, the levy made by the court in 1828 for the purpose of paying this one thousand dollars per year fell short, and when the first payment was to be made, it fell short more than $300. Logan, of course, was anxious for his money. He went before the court at its February term, 1829, and proposed to the court that if it would arrange to pay the balance on the first payment, and the whole of the second payment due in November, 1829, he would deduct twelve per cent from the second payment when it fell due. The court immediately accepted the proposition, and appointed a committee composed of James McBrayer, John Wash, Andrew McBrayer, Thomas Phillips, and Christopher Lillard, and authorized them to negotiate a loan, or loans, with the Bank of the United States, or any of its branches, or any other bank of the State, for the first installment of his contract, and also the amount that would be due on the second installment, and pay the amount to the said Logan, after deducting the twelve per cent. The commissioners evidently failed to secure all of the money from the banks which was due Logan. On the 9th of March, 1829, Christopher Lillard produced a receipt from Logan, acknowledging payment of $306.68, due on the first payment of the court house, making in all one thousand and thirty dollars, also $409.66 and one-half cents on the second payment. On the 13th of April, 1829, at a regular term of court, Robert Logan, the undertaker of the public building, was allowed $25 to be paid out of the levy of 1829, and $74.66 to be paid out of the levy of 1830, being the amount in full of the additional contract made with him by the commissioners for the erection of two false chimneys to the court house, and for raising the walls two feet above the plan originally contracted for. At the June term, Robert Logan and John F. Hudgins were appointed commissioners, to purchase and put up lightening rods to the court house, and present their account at the next term. At the September term of court, 1829, John C. Richardson was appointed to make all necessary repairs on the house of John and William Hudgins (the house used for the court house), and as soon as they were made to deliver it to the said Hudgins. This was on the 14th of September, 1829, and "it is further ordered that all future courts of this county be held at the new court house upon the public square, the court being informed by the undertaker thereof, that said house will be ready for the reception of the circuit and county courts at the next term."

The next term, October 12, 1829, the first county court was held in the new court house. There were present, composing the court, James McBrayer, Thompson Thomas, Andrew McBrayer and John C. Richardson. Later in the day two more Justices, Thos. Q. Roberts and John Morgan, appeared and also Thomas Phillips.

At the November term, 1829, Robert Logan was allowed $35 in addition to the former $30, for painting the outside of the court house. Twenty-four dollars allowed Robert Logan for two presses erected in the clerk's offices. On the 14th of June, 1830, Ephraim Lillard, David White, William Lawrence and John F. Hudgins were "appointed commissioners to receive the public buildings from those who undertook the building of the same, and when received that they deliver possession thereof to George Morris, the jailer of the county of Anderson, who is hereby appointed keeper of the public grounds and public buildings, and that commissioners make report to the court at next term."

At this term of court a motion was made and adopted that permission be given to all religions to use the court house at any time during the day after the court house is received. While the court house had been used by the county and circuit courts from the 12th of October, 1829, it had not been completed. At the July term of court, July 12, 1830, the commissioners to receive the public buildings made their report, which is of considerable interest: "The commissioners who were appointed by an order of this court at the last term, to receive the public buildings from those who undertook the erection of the same, and when received to be by them delivered to the jailer, this day made to the court the following report, to-wit: In obedience to an order of the Worshipful county court of Anderson County made at the June term of said court 1830, appointing the undersigned commissioners to examine whether the public buildings are completed by the undertakers according to contracts, and if they be finished, then to receive the same from the undertakers, have performed that duty; we are of opinion that after full examination, that the court house and clerk's offices are completed by Robert Logan the undertaker according to his several contracts in a manner which give general satisfaction. Accordingly we have receipted to him for the same. The keys to the clerk's offices are delivered over to the clerk, but owing to some misunderstanding with the keeper of the public buildings, the commissioners have retained the key of the court house which they now deliver up to the court. We have also examined the jail, and we think that the doorway and the upper story is insufficient to confine prisoners; the cheeking and door facings are insufficient, and some of the logs of the upper story may be easily prized out. But as there is no county jail until received by the court, and adopted as the public jail, we have received it as it is. The work on the jail has already been received from the several undertakers of it, which forbids the commissioners from making any further suggestions concerning the insufficient workmanship on the jail, and for as much as the court will order other commissioners to contract for such amendments as they shall direct to that building, we forbear making any other report, all of which is respectfully reported.
(Signed) David White, Wm. Lawrence, E. Lillard.

And it is ordered by the court that the buildings in the said report named be received by the court as the court house, clerks' offices and public jail of the court and the key of the said court house is delivered by the court to George Morris, the keeper of the public buildings. At the same time leave was given to the Lawrenceburg Debating Society to hold their meetings at any time during the day until further order, they being responsible for all damages done by them during the time of their several meetings.

An order was also entered appointing Nelson C. Johnson commissioner to cause the front of the public square to be inclosed "with a neat plank railing and gate." An order was also made appointing commissioners Dixon G. Dedman, Basil O. Carlisle, William Hudgins and Nelson C. Johnson to settle the accounts of the county, and Robert Logan on account of the public buildings. The court also entered an order upon the application of N. J. Hockersmith, permitting him to occupy the lower room of the court house as a school house. James McBrayer and Thompson Thomas objected and required their objections to be noted on the record.

The commissioners appointed by the court at its September term, to settle the accounts between the county and Robert Logan, made their report, finding that the county was indebted to Logan $1,090. This was allowed by the court and ordered to be paid out of the levy of 1831, the next year. The court by a subsequent order however, cut the amount allowed Logan, by $50. It also allowed him twelve per cent on this amount until paid. On the report of the subsequent commissioners, the jail was again received by the court at its October term. It is thus seen that the court house and jail and other public buildings had been completed, and that in building a court house, the court had turned it into a Masonic Lodge, a debating society and a school house, and other probable uses not considered of sufficient importance to be noted.

This court house was destroyed by fire on midnight of October 26, 1859. The October term of the circuit court was being held, and the last order was entered October 26th.

Few records were destroyed by this fire, and the facts seem more surprising when it is realized that the building was in no sense fireproof. Order book "D" and mortgage book "B" were destroyed and never replaced, although the court entered an order requiring the clerk to make a new order book from the minute book, and record all the mortgages he could find in a new book. This was only partially done.

The building of the court house had been commenced in 1827 and the completed structure accepted on the 12th of July, 1830, two and a half years after the work started, although the lower room and the clerks' offices were occupied after the 14th of October, 1829. The court house was of brick, two stories high with a cupalo at the front. The clerks' offices were about as they are now, except that between them there was a recess or vacant covered space paved with brick, extending from one to the other in front of the central or court room. There were two doors of entrance, one at either side of the front. There was an entrance to the clerks' offices from the front, and a door entering the court room from the inside. The upper room was used as a Masonic Lodge and as jury rooms, and had only such finishings as the Masonic fraternity had given it. There were two two-room, one-story frame buildings on the square, one fronting on Allin (Court) street, and one or two fronting on Madison (Main) street. These were used as county attorney, sheriff and law offices. From the time of the selection of Lawrenceburg as the county seat, down to the time of the destruction of the court house by fire, the question of removal of the county seat to some more central location had been agitated at times, with great force, and there were times when some candidates made their campaigns for office on this issue. The destruction of the court house gave these people their long sought opportunity for the change. The question of removal became a burning issue. It was realized that unless the removal could be accomplished before a new court house could be built, it could probably never be. The justices of the peace were holding their offices, and it was not a question of a pull to select those favorable to any particular locality. They were already selected and the question was before them; they must decide. Looking back at the matter from this time, it all seemed very simple; the court orders do not show anything but the cold facts, but there was great excitement about the matter. People were bitterly partisan and epithets were hurled back and forth. The cry of corruption was started, and each side believed, or claimed to believe, that money was being used to influence the votes of the justices. Any man against his locality "sold out," as is a too frequent cry, even to this day.

The last order of the county court was on October 26, 1859, and it was an order granting tavern license to Ephraim Jenkins at the "Fifty Mile" house in Rough and Ready, for the term of one year from date, reciting that Jenkins took the oath required by law, and executed bond with Samuel R. Baker his surety.

The county judge, who was Rev. Jordon H. Walker, called a term of the county court on Wednesday, November 22, 1859, and on motion of the county attorney, ordered that the Justices of the Peace appear at the county judge's office in Lawrenceburg on Thursday the 3rd of November to consider the burning of the court house, and appointed L. J. Mountjoy, Monroe Walker and G. W. Mathews a committee to execute the summons on the justices. At the time the court house was burned, H. Etherington, M. Easley, L. Carter, H. L. Fidler, J. W. Hollis, C. N. Kavanaugh, G. W. Catlett, H. H. Maddox, W. B. Petty and Reuben Morton were the justices. They met at the county judge's office on November 3rd. Reuben Morton was absent, but sent his written request and vote in favor of rebuilding the court house upon the present site. His request was filed. At this session of court a committee consisting of K. C. Gaines, L. J. Mountjoy and C. N. Kavanaugh was appointed to secure a house for the use of court, etc., and after a time returned and reported that they had rented the house of Mrs. Kathrine Ransdall at the rate of $80 per annum, and the court accepted the report and directed the county attorney to prepare the contract with her, which was done and the contract filed. H. H. Maddox, one of the justices, was directed to put this house in condition for use. At this same term of court (November 3rd) the justices with a roll call so far as the record shows, entered this order: "Ordered that the court house and the clerks' offices be rebuilt upon the public square, and that M. Searcy, J. W. Brookie, J. D. Parker, W. W. Penny and C. H. Fenwick be, and they are hereby, appointed a building committee to report at their earliest convenience the plan, etc., for rebuilding a new court house and clerks' offices, and are directed to value the brick and rubbish, except the foundation, and make report thereof at the next term, when they will sell the same to the highest bidder, upon the condition that the purchaser remove them from the public square, provided they bring the estimated value." At a meeting of the justices held on the 14th of November, 1859, the Building Committee appeared and obtained further time until the next term to report on plans for the court house and clerks' offices, and also on the brick and rubbish. At a court held December 12th the Building Committee reported plans for the court house and clerks' offices. The plans were made by a Mr. Haley and a Mr. Shryock, and they were each allowed $30 for these plans, nine of the justices being present. They at once adopted the plans of Mr. Haley—Dennis Haley, as it afterwards appeared, and he built the new court house. The Building Committee was directed to let out the building of the court house to the lowest bidder on the 2nd of January, 1860, according to the plan. The building on the outside to be made of stone, if it can be done as cheap as brick, and the cost to be paid in three equal, annual installments, and that the committee report to the court the lowest bid for ratification or rejection.

At a court held January 9, 1860, H. H. Maddox reported that the house of Mrs. Kathrine Ransdall had been prepared as a court house, and he was allowed $20 for his work, and Leathers and Maddox were allowed $8.75 for chairs, a stove and other items. The house of Mrs. Ransdall was situated on the east side of Main (or Madison) street, and was a part of lot 21 on the plat of the town. It stood where the Kentucky Utilities' place of business (1928) now stands, and consisted of a store room, stairway to the upper story, and residence on the second floor. So far all of sentiment in favor of the removal of the county seat from Lawrenceburg had been "all talk." At this term, January 9th, the sentiment chrystalized into a petition. "The petition of divers citizens of this county to postpone the building of the court house and clerks' offices was this day filed, and thereupon a motion to postpone the building of a court house, etc., being made, and the yeas and nays being called, the vote being taken, resulted as follows: Yeas, H. Etherington, W. B. Petty, H. L. Fidler and M. Easley; nays, H. H. Maddox, Reuben Morton, G. W. Catlett and L. Carter, and thereupon it is ordered that said motion be overruled." Justice C. N. Kavanaugh was absent and he does not appear to have been present at any subsequent time, which would lead to the belief that he was ill or had vacated his office. This vote seems to have disposed of the matter of the removal of the county seat to some point in the county outside of Lawrenceburg. Dr. Landon Carter, who was a physician at Camdenville, now Glensboro, was the deciding factor. It was believed that he would favor his part of the county, and it was said he had not expressed himself either way and both sides expected his vote. He was very severely criticised at the time for voting against the removal, for that was what his vote meant, and there was a great deal of loose talk as to his motives. He lived an honored life after this vote, was regarded very highly by all who knew him well, and served Anderson County in the House of Representatives at Frankfort for the term of 1869-71. At a meeting of the court held on the 10th of January, 1860, the nine justices, L. Carter, M. Easley, J. W. Hollis, W. B. Petty, H. Ethrington, H. L. Fidler, G. W. Catlett, R. Morton and H. H. Maddox, were present. The Building Committee made its report and the court entered this order: "This day the Building Committee reported the bid of John (brother to Dennis Haley) Haley to rebuild the court house and offices according to the specifications and plan on file, for the sum of fourteen thousand dollars, payable in two equal annual installments, at the end of the years 1860 and 1861. The old material of the court house and offices to belong to said Haley, which bid is received and adopted by the court, and said committee is directed and hereby authorized to enter into contract with said Haley, with good security for the construction and completion of the work according to said plan and specifications, and report the same to court for its approval."

At this same term of court a levy was made on all taxable property of the county sufficient to raise seven thousand dollars for each of the years 1860 and 1861, and the sheriff was directed to collect it, although the rate was not fixed. This levy was made by authority of the Legislature then in session for court house purposes.

On the 23rd of April, 1860, the Methodist church was designated to be used by the court as the court house for Circuit Courts, and on the 5th day of

May the house of Mrs. Kathrine Ransdall was again designated for county courts and clerk's offices until completion of new court house.

On the 11th of June, 1860, J. W. Lanes and others, trustees of the church, were allowed ten dollars for the use of the church during the April term of court, and on the 10th day of September the same parties were allowed ten dollars for the use of the church for the July term. J. D. Parker was appointed to superintend the building of the court house, and on the 9th of October, 1860, he was allowed $525 for his services.

On the 22nd of October, 1860, the Methodist church was again designated as the court house, and on November 12, 1860, Jeff Searcy was allowed ten dollars for the use of the church, and on this same day J. M. Hanks, sheriff of the county, was ordered to pay to John Haley, seven thousand dollars, the first installment on the contract for building the court house. On the 3rd of January, 1861, the Building Committee reported the completion of the court house, and the court entered this order relative to the subject: "This day the committee appointed by this court to superintend the building of the court house and offices in Lawrenceburg, Ky., returned their report showing its erection and completion according to contract and specifications which is ordered to be filed. It is further ordered that said house and offices be received by the court, and the same be used until the further order of this court, and thereupon the contractor delivered the keys of said house," etc.

This court house was built of stone, the roof covered with slate. The clerks, sheriff's and judge's offices were built two stories as wings to the court house. There was a front entrance to the lower offices, and a door leading from them to the court room. The court room was down stairs and occupied the whole lower floor, and was bare of ornamentation. In fact there was no ornamentation of any kind except the four pillars in front and the ornamental cupelo. The latter was so tall that it was believed each hard wind would blow it off, but it was so well constructed and braced that it remained until the court house was remodeled in 1905. The second story was the same size as he first and it was bare of ornamentation. The Order of Masons cut off about two-thirds of the back part for a Masonic Lodge, the other third was used as an ante-room for the lodge and as a grand jury room.

During the War Between the States, after the Confederates evacuated Kentucky, this court house was used as quarters for a company of soldiers. The cost of the court house payable in two equal installments, one in 1860 and one in 1861, was $14,000. The cost of superintending (J. D. Parker) was $525. The court house bell was $220, and cost of the two plans, one of which was accepted, was $60, making a total of $14,805. Completed and accepted January 3, 1861. The appearance of this court house was impressive and the people of the county were very proud of it. So far as known there was no court house in the state more sightly, while only a few were larger. It was used for all public purposes; school exhibitions, ameteur theatrical performances as well as professional, conventions, public speakings and things generally. As records accumulated, more room became necessary, and agitation for removal of the court room from the first to the second story, and utilizing the first story for office room became so persistent, that in 1905 the fiscal court ordered the improvement. C. E. Bond was awarded the contract at the sum of five thousand dollars. Under his plans, the wall in front was moved forward a number of feet, that being the only change made in the outside appearance. The cupelo was cut down, and the outside entrances to the clerks' offices were walled up; the old outside iron stairway leading to the second story was removed. A hall through the center of the first floor, from front to rear, was constructed, and the offices on each side made, were entered from this hall. The old bell which had been installed in the court house in 1860 was installed in the court house as changed.

This remodeled court house was destroyed by fire on midnight of April 13, 1915. The jail in rear of the court house was not destroyed. All inside work, windows, floors, partitions, desks and tables were destroyed. A deputy county clerk went into the county clerk's office and opened the vault door and threw all record books and official papers into the vault and locked the door. It was believed at the time he had saved all the records, but as time has gone on it is found that a valuable record is missing and can't be found. These losses are attributed to the fire. The circuit court clerk's office did not fare so well. All records in the vault of this office remained secure but order book "V", and two or three hundred suits and a number of record books in the outer office were destroyed. All pending suits, except a few which lawyers had carried to their offices, were destroyed. The stone walls erected in 1860, stood the test of the fire, and were not damaged except here and there over a window or door, and these were easily replaced. The columns in front were damaged to such an extent as to be unsafe, and those that had not fallen were thrown down.

On April 15th the fiscal court met and rented the whole lower floor and two rooms of the second story of the Masonic building, for a court room and clerks' offices, until such time as a new court house could be constructed. This building is situated just south of the Baptist church on Main street and was used as a court house until the completion of the new court house. At this time J. S. Odell was county judge. In the meantime the court advertised for plans and specifications for a new court house. On April 24th the plans submitted by Joseph and Joseph, architects and engineers of Louisville, were accepted, and that firm was employed to superintend the building.

By these plans the old walls were to be used as far as possible, except the front wall was to be built further forward toward Main street. These plans also provided for wiring and for a separate building for heating. On June 22nd numerous bids for building the court house were received, ranging in price from $34,722 to $47,945; bids for wiring from $327 to $896, and for heating, from $1,894 to $2,075. Awarding of the contracts was deferred until the 28th of June, and on that day the contract for building the court house was awarded to A. J. Stair of Knoxville, Tenn., at his bid of $34,722. A. J. Anderson & Co. was awarded the contract for heating at the bid of $2,177, and the contract for wiring was awarded the F. A. Clegg Co. at their bid of $420. The contract for the clock was awarded Herman C. Korfees for $750; Capital Lumber Co., of Frankfort, for stationary furniture, at $451; Steel furniture to the Art Metal Co., Cincinnati, for $1,077; chairs for court room, $2. each, balcony chairs $1.55 each to American Seating Co., Cincinnati, totaling, without chairs, $39,146.

[The following is copied from the Anderson News of March 26, 1936: The county court house is now paid for. This is great news for a lot of people, and then again there are some who are surprised, thinking it was paid for a long time ago. In reality it was paid for a good while ago, but there was an issue of bonds on April 15, 1916, amounting to $20,000 for the rebuilding of the structure after it had burned in 1915. This money, together with insurance money collected at the time, paid the cost of the present building, and since that time the county has paid on the bonds at the rate of $1,000 a year, plus a five per cent interest.

The last payment was made this week by O. C. McKay, county treasurer, and was for $2,000. The bonds were payable to the Hanover National Bank of New York City. L. K. B.]

THE FIRST COUNTY COURT

The Act erecting Anderson County was approved January 16, 1827. By the 13th section of the Act, it was provided that "this Act shall not take effect until the 20th day of January next, except that the sheriff and justices of said county may be commissioned from and after the passage thereof." This provision, if left alone, prevented any action as a county until the 20th of January, 1828, so that a supplemental Act was necessary in order that the county should function at once. This supplemental Act was approved on the 18th day of January, 1827, and provided merely "that the said county shall go into effect and operation on the 20th day of January next."

The original Act provided that the courts of said county should be held on the first Monday in every month, except the months when circuit courts were held. The Act also provided that courts should be held at the house of William Hudgins in the town of Lawrence ("which shall hereafter be called and known as Lawrenceburg"), on the first court day after this Act takes effect. That day came on Monday the 5th day of February, 1827. On this day there appeared Jesse Guess, Presiding Justice; James W. McBrayer, Dixon G. Dedman, John Wash, Andrew McBrayer, John Busey, Christopher Lillard, Reuben Boston, John C. Richardson and Thomas Phillips, and produced their commissions from the Governor, appointing them Justices of the Peace, with certificates that they had taken the oath, and took their seats. Jesse Guess was Justice of the Peace of Washington County at the time of the erection of Anderson County, and he was commissioned Presiding Justice, there being no such office as County Judge provided for in the Constitution of Kentucky then in form. Immediately upon the call to order of the court, constituted of these Justices of the Peace, David White, Jr., produced a certificate from judges of the Court of Appeals, George M. Bibb, William Owsley and Benjamin Mills, as to his qualifications to discharge the duties of clerk. He was at once appointed clerk of the county court, and immediately executed bond of ten thousand dollars, with John T. Daviess, William Hudgins, Thos. Triplett and William Robinson his sureties, and took the prescribed oath and entered upon the discharge of his duties. Next in order was the qualification of a sheriff. John F. Blackwell produced a commission from the Governor dated January 18, 1827, appointing him sheriff, and with Robert Blackwell, Andrew McBrayer, Thos. Phillips and William Lawrence, his sureties, executed the required bond and entered on his duties as sheriff. One clause of this bond may be of interest at this time. It is, "and pay and satisfy all sums of money or tobacco by him or them received, or which ought to have been received."

The County Court being thus organized proceeded to tranact the business of the county. John F. Blackwell, sheriff, was appointed collector of the county revenue, and executed the revenue bond, with the same surties in the sum of five thousand dollars. Of course little business could be done without the aid of lawyers, and the first lawyers to qualify to practice were,

Lewis Sanders, Jr., Nelson Cole Johnson, Washington Dorrell, John Stutt Greathouse, Thomas Triplett and Preston Samuel Longborough, all of whom produced license and took the required oath. On motion of David White, Jr., the clerk, John T. Daviess, was appointed his deputy, and on motion of John F. Blackwell, sheriff, Sanford McBrayer was appointed his deputy. George Morris was appointed first jailer. Lewis J. Witherspoon was recommended to the Governor for commission as county surveyor, and was shortly commissioned as the first surveyor of the county. Ephraim Lillard to whom a commission was issued by the Governor for coroner, refused to qualify, and it was ordered that the name of Everard White be sent to the Governor for the office of coroner, which was done and he was commissioned. This, with the appointment of Edward Harris, administrator of the estate of Archibald Murphy, was all of the business done by the court until next morning. The court met on the next day, February 6th, and continued with its February term. It laid the county into five constable districts, and appointed James Hackley, James J. Morgan, Joshua McMichael, Randall Walker and Joel Boston, constables in the respective districts.

It appointed and commissioned Dixon G. Dedman, Thomas Phillips and Andrew McBrayer three of the justices to grant injunctions and award writs of ne exeat and habeas corpus, during vacations of the circuit court. It made recommendation to the Governor of the name of Alvin Herndon for appointment to the office of Escheator. He was afterwards appointed. The court fixed the tavern rates for the county for the ensuing year, as follows: Payable in specie, lodging 12½ cents, bedding 12½ cents, supper and breakfast each 25 cents, dinner 25c, horse for night 37½ cents, horse feed 12½ cents, whiskey per half pint 12½ cents, French brandy, peach brandy, rum and wine, each per half pint 25 cents, whiskey toddy, per quart 25 cents, brandy and rum toddy each per quart, 50 cents. Tavern license were granted to Thomas Phillips, Wm. Lawrence and Lewis Hyatt upon their execution of their required bonds. Thomas Phillips' tavern was situated on lot 25, where the Government post office is now located. It was of brick, had been built by Wm. Lawrence and sold by him to Phillips. William Lawrence's tavern was situated on lots one and two, in the south end of town. It was a double two-story log house with large rooms, a wide hall below and above, two rooms deep on the first floor, dining room adjoining back, kitchen back of dining room; a wide porch below and above full length of the house, a negro cabin with three rooms in the back yard. At a later date and after this tavern had been sold by Lawrence to John Whip, a building at each end of the porch was added, and these were entered from the porch, both above and below. They were two rooms in length and two stories. Lewis Hiatt's tavern was the north part of lot 15, and just north of the court house, was of frame, two stories and probably ten rooms. All of the justices who held this first county court, are shown by the records of Anderson County, and before Anderson, by the records of Franklin County, to have been men of affairs, and such men as should have organized the county. The name of Jesse Guess, long since has disappeared from the county; the McBrayer is still a prominent and numerous family; Dr. Dixon G. Dedman practiced his profession in the county for many years. He was the father of Capt. Gus Dedman, who was killed at the battle of Chicamauga; of Dr. W. W. Dedman, who removed to Missouri, and after practicing his profession for many years, died there; and of Henry Dedman who removed to St. Louis and died there, and also of Charles M. Dedman, a prominent druggist for many years in Harrodsburg.

The Wash family is still prominent in the county. The Buseys were at one time a rather numerous family, but have disappeared from the county. The Lillards became a very numerous family and has always been conspicuous. Whether there are descendants of Reuben Boston in the county is not definitely known, but Reuben Boston himself was one of the leading men of his day in county affairs, and had been a soldier of the Revolutionary War. John C. Richardson resided and had a boat landing and warehouse on Kentucky river just above the mouth of Bailey's Run. He was a son-in-law of Samuel Arbuckle. Thos. Phillips owned quite a number of town lots and houses at different times and was quite active in boosting the town and county. He removed to Clay County, Missouri. He also was a son-in-law of Samuel Arbuckle. This is the character of the men who composed the first county court.

The first grand jury in Anderson County was composed of the following men: Richard Phillips, foreman; William Pollard, Thomas Jordon, Lewis Dale, Samuel Butts, Mathias Carter, James Hackley, John Bond, Andrew Gudgel, Garland Lillard, Phillip Penny, Henry Searcy, Martin Parker, Lawrence Long, William Utterback, John Elliott, Edward Hale, James McClure, Winston Ryan, Robert McBrayer, Wm. H. Cosby, Benjamin Wash and George Morris. The first case in the Anderson County Circuit Court was that of the Commonwealth against Robert Allen for lunacy. He was adjudged insane and ordered to the lunatic asylum at Lexington.

JUSTICES OF THE FIRST COUNTY COURT

The justices of the first county court in Anderson County were men of fairly good education and general information for that day. The Presiding Justice, Jesse Guess, wrote the wills and deeds for his neighbors. In 1838 he ran for the Legislature against John Draffen, and an anecdote connected with that election has come down to us from Jeremiah Posey who told it to his son, the late Judge Posey: That election lasted three days and on the last day when Esquire Guess was leaving home his wife called to him, "Oh, Jesse, do you think you will be elected today?"—to which he replied: "I don't know, Nellie, but I hope so." Then she interrogated, "Well, if you are elected to the Legislature, what will I be?"—to which he made the brusque reply: "You'll be the same damned old fool you always were." John Draffen won the election and Esquire Guess removed to Illinois where he lived and died.

John Wash was a prominent justice of the court when the county was erected. He was a man of limited education, but of strong common sense and sound judgment. He was an original abolitionist and had the courage of his convictions, as was evidenced when he took his seat on the rostrum of the old court house when Cassius M. Clay spoke in Lawrenceburg in favor of the gradual emancipation of slavery.

John Busey, another justice of the first county court, was a man of fairly good education, and one of the most influential men of his day. He was the grandfather of Judge I. C. Oliver.

Christopher Lillard was a soldier of the War of 1812, and participated in the battle of the Thames. It was in this conflict that he killed an Indian and secured his tomahawk. This tomahawk is in the possession of his son, Judge C. M. Lillard. General Lillard, as he was called in later life, was an educated man of fine physique and soldierly bearing. The other justices of that court, Reuben Boston, John C. Richardson and Thomas Phillips, were honorable and intelligent officials. The above information of the first justices of the court was furnished by Judge J. M. Posey.

THE FIRST JAIL IN LAWRENCEBURG

From the records the first jail was completed and accepted before the December term of court, 1827. This jail was erected on the lot conveyed to the county by William Lawrence, and not on the land which the commissioners were authorized to purchase. This jail was of smooth surfaced stone and two stories high. A door entered the second story on the north end. There was no door of entrance to the first story. This story was called the dungeon, and was entered by a trap door in the floor of the second story. For many years prisoners charged with felony were confined in the dungeon, and those with misdemeanors in the second story. There was a small window in the south end of each story with iron grating. These windows were twelve by twenty-four inches, and there was no other ventilation except the iron door to the second story at the north end. A wooden stairway outside led to this door. The floor of this second story was composed of thick logs, fitted edge to edge. In after years the dungeon was abandoned on account of water seeping in, and making the floor muddy, as well as bad ventilation, and large iron cages were built in the second story room. No jailer's residence had been built when this jail was completed. This first jail stood on the site occupied by the City Hall today.

LAWRENCEBURG JAIL

As has been said, the old jail was built of stone and George Morris was the first jailer, having been appointed February 6, 1827, but there was no jail until December. The jailer was made keeper of the stray pen. The lot purchased from William Lawrence was purchased for the special purpose of a jail, jailer's residence, yard, etc. It was adjoining the lots purchased from John F. Hudgins and William Hudgins (lot 13), and from George Morris (a part of lot 15) and extended north and south of the full width of those lots sixty feet wide. There was no street or public alley between the court house lots and this lot which was purchased for jail purposes, except a very narrow alley, called Lawrence's alley, and opened by him for convenience. This alley was a part of the sixty foot lot purchased from Lawrence. On the 7th day of May, 1827, John F. Hudgins, Wm. Hudgins, Wm. Lawrence and Ephraim Lillard were appointed commissioners, empowered to contract on the best possible terms, for lot to build a jail, and form a place for a jail building, and contract for the building and completion of a jail by the fourth Monday in July. The work to be paid for, one-half out of the levy of 1827, one-half out of the levy of 1828. These commissioners made their report on the jail at the June term. The report was confirmed and the bond of the contractor, and plans were ordered filed in the clerk's office at the October term. David White, Ephraim Lillard and Wm. Lawrence were appointed commissioners to examine the jail, which was reported completed. These commissioners examined the jail and reported it incomplete, and the commissioners formerly appointed for building it, were ordered to have it completed forthwith, and David White, Ephraim Lillard and David Lawrence were directed to receive it when completed, and deliver it to the jailer. At this same December term, 1827, the court began paying for the jail; $32.50 was paid to J. D. Parker for stone work out of levy 1827, same amount out of levy 1828. John F. and Wm. Hudgins were allowed $45 for woodwork out of the levy 1827, same amount out of levy 1828. Wm. Vance, the contractor, was allowed $159 out of levy 1827, same amount out of levy 1828 for constructing the body of the jail.

As a small relaxation from the duties of building the jail, and other routine matters, on November 28, 1828, the court entered this order: "Ordered that Edward McElvany be forthwith confined in jail, there to remain six hours, for a contempt of the court in cursing, swearing and abusing the court."

The jail had hardly been completed until it was found that it would not hold prisoners. It was only a short time until iron was found necessary, and finally iron cages were built on the inside of the second story. First and last it was a constant and growing expense, and was never satisfactory at any time. The old jail having become too small, and believed to be unsanitary, the inmates becoming sick, one having died, there was quite a demand for a new jail. In 1883, at the January term an order was entered by the fiscal court requiring a new jail to be built. It being winter time, no immediate steps were taken toward building it, or letting a contract. At the following April term the court had changed its mind and passed a resolution that it would not build a new jail, after a committee to consider the matter reported. This committee was composed of Hon. R. H. Crossfield, Dr. J. C. Gibbs and George A. Cohen, the county attorney. Mr. Crossfield and Dr. Gibbs filed a majority report setting out their conviction that the old jail could be repaired at a cost of from two thousand to twenty-five hundred dollars. Cohen filed a minority report stating that the old jail could not be repaired. The court adopted the majority report by a vote of six to four. The matter passed through several terms of court. Cohen, as County Attorney, gave notice that at the October term, 1883, he would go into the county court and move the court to divide the Lawrenceburg Magisterial District into two magisterial districts. The consequence of this move on the county attorney's part, the fiscal court changed its mind again, and set aside the former order to repair the old jail, and ordered a new jail built. It appointed George C. Cohen to advertise for bids. At the November term the plans and specifications of McDonald brothers of Louisville were accepted, and the contract for building the new jail was awarded to them at a cost of eight thousand dollars. The new jail was built and completed in 1884, and at the October term of the fiscal court, G. C. Cohen and L. W. McKee were appointed a committee to receive the jail from the contractors, which was done. In May, 1885, the court ordered the old jail, the residence and all the buildings on the old lot to be sold, and they were sold. The new jail was not built on the old jail lot, but was built on the court house lot, just back of the court house, the first story devoted to the jail and the second story to the jailer's residence. A passage led from the jail to the court room. This jail was not destroyed nor injured when the court house was destroyed by fire in 1915. In May, 1892, the fiscal court ordered vaults to be built for the records of the two clerk's offices, and after bids the contract was awarded McDonald Bros., of Louisville, the contract at $1,815. These vaults were completed and received in 1892. One was built back of, and one east of the clerks' offices, and when the fire occurerd in 1915, no records which were in these vaults were damaged or injured, and only those which were in the main clerk's office were destroyed.

PILLORY AND STOCKS AND WHIPPING POST IN LAWRENCEBURG

The court was evidently determined to prepare things for punishment of law breakers, for with this idea in view, it erected a pillory and stocks on the northwest corner of the lot 15, at the stray pen, thus taking care of stray animals as well as men. So that nothing in the way of convenience should be lacking for the enforcement of the law, a whipping post was established by order of the court, and it was ordered that the post at the southeast corner of the stray pen be designated as the whipping post. The pillory and stocks were erected on the 15th of March, 1831, and the whipping post established on the 12th of November, 1833. Evidently the court concluded that the pillory and stocks did not furnish a sufficient punishment after a trial of two years. The whipping post was used for many years, and at times the punishment was severe. The most severe punishment being 250 lashes, laid on at the rate of twenty-five at the interval of five days. The whipping post punishment was finally abandoned, however, before the whipping post law was repealed. In Order Book A, page 32, we find the following: May term of court, 1827. By order of the court, that the enclosure on the east side of the lot deeded by George Morris to the county court of Anderson County be, and the same is appropriated and set apart for a stray pen for the use of the county. Ordered that George Morris be, and is appointed keeper of the stray pen of Anderson County. Ordered that he give his attendance thereto accordingly. March term of court, 1831. Ordered that Thomas Phillips, a member of this court, be appointed to cause to be erected on the public ground, a good and sufficient pillory and stocks for this county, and that he make report to court. Stocks is an apparatus formerly used for the punishment of petty offenders, as vagrants, trespassers and the like. It usually consisted of a frame of timber in which the legs of the offenders were confined. The pillory was likewise a frame of wood erected on posts with movable boards and holes through which are put the head and hands of the culprit for punishment; a form of punishment formerly widely used and still existent in some countries.

In one of the early court records we read that Leonidas Walker was allowed seven dollars for arresting and whipping seven slaves, and the same date G. W. Sparrow was allowed one dollar for awarding the same punishment to one obstreperous slave.

FIRST CIRCUIT COURT IN ANDERSON COUNTY

The first circuit court convened in Lawrenceburg January 22, 1827, at the house of William Hudgins, where Ottenheimer's grocery* now stands, Henry Davidge being the judge. David White was appointed clerk. Charles S. Bibb appeared as Commonwealth's Attorney. The following grand jurors were impanneled and sworn: Ephraim Lillard, foreman; Mathias Bush, Samuel S. Marrs, Anthony Bond, Samuel B. Petty, Wm. C. Pollard, Archibald Elliott, Moses Duncan, Edward Harris, Joseph Griffy, Wm. McGinnis,

*Today (1936) Kroger Grocery.—L. K. B.

Samuel Burrus, Hankerson Reid, David Bullock, Joseph Boggess, Reuben Holman, Littleton Major, David Egbert, James McClure and John Elliott. During the term the following attorneys were admitted to the bar of this court: Nelson C. Johnson, Patrick H. Darby, Washington Dorrell, Thomas B. Monroe, Thomas P. Wilson, Preston S. Longborough, Southey Whittington, John J. Julian, John G. Simrell, Lewis Sanders, John S. Greathouse and Singleton W. Wilson.

The first petty jury empanneled and sworn were, Edmond P. Gaines, Preston Blackwell, Clark McBrayer, William Abbott, James Waddell, Joshua Towsend, Nathaniel Mothershead, Jack Hockersmith, John Bond, Constantine Rigg, George Sharp and Garland Lillard. The first county court was held at the same place, February 5, 1827, when the following justices of the peace, having been commissioned by the Governor, took their seats: Jesse Guess, Presiding Justice, James McBrayer, Dixon D. Dedman, John Wash, Andrew McBrayer, John Busey, Christopher Lillard, Ruben Boston, John C. Richardson and Thomas Phillips. David White was made clerk of the court; John F. Blackwell, sheriff; Lewis J. Witherspoon, surveyor; Ephraim Lillard, coroner, and George Morris, jailer.

At the April term of court Lewis J. Witherspoon produced a commission of the Governor appointing him surveyor, and qualified. A levy of seventy-five cents on each tithable was ordered for the purpose of erecting public buildings. At its May term, the court took up the matter of its purchase of the lots on which public buildings of the county were to be erected. At this time George Morris tendered his deed to lot 15 and a part of lot 13 as shown on the plot of the town. He had sold, but not conveyed six feet off the north part of lot 15 to Lewis Hyatt. He tendered this deed with the relinquishment by Lewis Hyatt to this six feet at the price of $200, the release by the county of his subscription of $50 toward the erection of public buildings, and sufficient money to remove the woodwork of his house on lot 15 to the opposite side of the street, and the reservation to remove the plank fence between lot 15 and the lot of Lewis Hyatt. The court accepted the deed.

At the same time John F. Hudgins and William Hudgins tendered their deed to the county, conveying the part of lot 13 owned by them for the consideration of 150, and their deed was accepted by the court. These two lots extended from Allen street, now Court street, to the building now owned and occupied by Taylor Bros. There was no street immediately north of the court house. That street now existing, is a part of lot 15 conveyed to the county by George Morris. Back of lot 13 and 15 purchased by the county from Morris and Hudgins there was an alley running north and south, called Lawrence alley; that and the adjoining land east of it was owned by William Lawrence. On the same day the deeds of Morris and Hudgins were executed.

William Lawrence tendered his deed to the county, a strip of land sixty feet wide, including this alley and running the full length of lots 13 and 15, the consideration being that the court release him of his subscription of $25 towards the erection of public buildings. The court accepted this deed. These three deeds comprise all the land which the court purchased for the erection of public buildings. College street as now located immediately east of the court house as it now exists, and the City Hall are on a part of the Lawrence land. The street north of the court house is a part of lot 15, and came to be a street through a great number of years. The title to all of this street is in the county, and the street was first opened as an alley eight feet wide at the request of W. S. Galt on January 14, 1850. Before that time and ever since the lots had been conveyed to the county, first Lewis Hyatt then his successors in the ownership of the hotel, had been permitted to use a four-foot passway on the north end of lot 15 as a passageway to the back premises of the hotel. This order of January 14th gave W. S. Galt the privilege of moving the post and rail fence back towards the court house ten feet, including the little alley, and to pave on the north side at his own expense, but the order expressly stipulated, in the order granting this right, the county did not relinquish the title or control of this part of the county property.

In November, 1852, William F. Leathers was permitted by an order of the court to further widen this alley, or passway, by moving the fence eight feet further in. And so the street, or alley, remained until after the destruction of the court house by fire in 1915, when the street was widened and the concrete sidewalk constructed as it now appears.

SECOND TERM OF THE COUNTY COURT

The second term of the Anderson County Court was held at the house of William Hudgins on the 5th day of March, 1827, with all the members of the court present. At the first court no record steps were taken toward locating the county seat, which, by the Act erecting the county, had been assigned to William Trotter of Franklin County, R. D. Shipp of Woodford County, Joel P. Williams of Mercer County, Stephen Lee of Washington County, William T. Webber of Shelby County and Elias Kinchelo of Nelson County, as commissioners, any five of whom could act. They were directed by the Act to assemble at the house of Wm. Hudgins in the month of March or April, take the oath and proceed to select a sight for the court. At this March term an order was entered inviting these commissioners to meet on Wednesday, the 28th day of March, and perform this duty, and that a copy of the order be sent to each of them. At this same term another order was entered, inviting and requesting Willis Blanton of Franklin County, William M. Bell of Washington County and Peter R. Dunn of Mercer County, who, by the Act had been appointed commissioners, any two of whom might act, to run and mark the boundary lines of the county, and make four plats, one each for Anderson, Mercer, Franklin and Washington. No special time was fixed by the Act for them to meet, but the order of the county court invited them to meet on the third Monday in March, and run and mark the boundary. After having entered these orders, the court proceeded to concern itself to the general routine of county business. It appointed John Story, Captain of Patrol for the town of Lawrenceburg and county, with James Mizner and James S. Hackley to assist him. These patrol appointments were equivalent to police authority, for the district for which they were appointed, and this law remains on the statutes to this time, although it has, in many counties, gone into disuse. Alvin Herndon was appointed commissioner of the Revenue and County Levy for the year 1827. This office corresponded with county assessor or tax commissioner, now in force. The same Alvin Herndon produced his commission from the Governor as Eschator, and qualified. The will of Thos. Harris was probated. Edward White produced a commission from the Governor for the office of coroner, and qualified by giving bond for a thousand pounds, with Alvin Herndon and James McBrayer surities. Allen Moore, an infant, was bound as an apprentice to Woodford Payne to be taught the art and mystery of a cabinet maker. After hearing the reports of viewers of roads, who had been appointed at the former term, the court adjourned.

THE THIRD COUNTY COURT

April 2, 1827. On this day the commissioners appointed by the Act creating the county to select the county seat, filed their report: "The commissioners appointed by an Act of the General Assembly to locate the seat of justice in Anderson County, made their report, which is in words and figures as follows, to-wit: In obedience to an Act of the General Assembly of the Commonwealth of Kentucky passed on the 16th day of January, 1827, we, William Trotter, Richard D. Shipp, Stephen Lee, Wm. T. Webber, Joel P. Williams and Elias Kinchelo, commissioners, do report to the Worshipful, the county court of Anderson County, as follows, to-wit: On the 28th day of March we did meet at the house of William Hudgins in the town of Lawrenceburg, and severally took the oath prescribed by law, and thereupon, on the 29th of March, we proceeded to view the several sites proposed by the different citizens of Anderson County, and after due deliberation and examination, taking into consideration all the conveniences and inconveniences resulting to the citizens of said county, we are of the opinion that the seat of Justice for Anderson County should be located in the town of Lawrenceburg; and thereupon on the 30th day of March we proceeded to select the most suitable piece of ground for the public square, and we have agreed in selecting the lots whereon George Morris now lives, together with the lot belonging to the Messrs Hudgins in the said town, and we have herewith submitted to the county court of said county, Mr. Morris and Messrs Hudgins bonds for the removing of all obstructions off the said lots, as well, also, as for the titles of said lots. Given under our hands this 30th day of March, 1827. William Trotter, R. D. Shipp, William T. Webber, Joel P. Williams, Stephen Lee, Elias Kinchelo."

This was approved and confirmed by the court.

CHAPTER IV

OLD COURT RECORDS

The record on March, 1832, in the Anderson County Court is as follows: "On motion of Jeremiah Mizner it is ordered that John Bond, Joseph Allin, Joseph Woods and Johnson Malone be commissioned to view the way from Madison (Main) street at Mathias Galt's house (now the post office site) on to Wallace's ware houses to Sublett's Ferry, through lands of Joseph Mizner, George Harlan, George Stott, George Walker, Dixon Dedman and down Bailey's Run creek to said ferry and report." This road to Sublett's Ferry (Shryock's) was opened the next year. From 1831 to '33 Anderson County was laid off in roads.

In May, 1833, on motion of Andrew Hawkins and James Dawson, it was ordered that Luke Lillard, Joel Boston, Wm. Burford and Reuben Boston be appointed viewers to view and make a new road by way of Hawkins' mill on Gilbert's creek to Dawson ferry on Kentucky river.

The following is the form to which the first Justices of the Peace had to subscribe: January 18, 1827; I, Henry Davidge, presiding Judge of Anderson County, certify that James McBrayer, Esquire, this day personally appeared before me at the town of Lawrence in Anderson County and made oath on the Holy Evangely of Almighty God that he will support the Constitution of the United States, and that he will be faithful and true to the Commonwealth of Kentucky so long as he shall be a citizen thereof; and also the office of a Justice of the Peace prescribed by the Constitution of the United States, and also the oath prescribed against duelling. In testimony whereof I, Henry Davidge, presiding Judge aforesaid, have set my hand and seal this 23rd of January, 1827, in the 35th year of the Commonwealth." After this oath, a certificate signed by Joseph Desha, Governor of Kentucky, testified that James McBrayer was a qualified Justice of the Peace of Anderson County.

On May, 1830, the court ordered "that Joseph Moore, infant orphan of Sarah Moore, deceased, who will be eleven years of age the 13th of this month, be bound apprentice to Howard Sutherland, until he arrive at age of 21 years to learn the trade of blacksmith." (Signed) N. C. Johnson, Clerk of Court.

In March, 1831, it was "ordered that Thomas Montgomery be bound as an apprentice to Reuben Boston to learn the art of a farmer; said Thomas being nine years of age to be bound until he arrives at the age of 21 years, Sallie Montgomery, mother of Thomas, consenting thereunto in open court." (Signed) John Busey, Clerk.

Another indenture made January 4, 1833, shows that Nelson C. Johnson, Clerk of Anderson County Court, convenented with Thomas Mountjoy that Thomas Slaughter "shall serve Thomas Mountjoy as an apprentice to the tanning business until he arrive at the age of 21, and the said Thomas Mountjoy covenent on his part to learn the said Thomas Slaughter the art, mystery and business of a tanner and to furnish the boy with good board during the term of his apprenticeship, and to school said Thomas as to reading, writing any cyphering to the Rule of Three, and at the end of his term of service to furnish him a good suit of clothes and pay him the sum of three pounds and ten shillings."

In November, 1834, the court ordered that John Busey, Wesley Browning, Andrew McBrayer and John Bond be appointed a committee on behalf of the county (any three of whom may act), to select a situation proper to locate a Poor House for the use of the county; and that said commissioners be authorized to lay out and expend in the purchase the sum of $200 payable out of the county levy of 1835, and the balance of $100 payable out of the county levy of 1836. At this meeting the court ordered a road opened to Hudgin's Mill on Salt river. This became Bond's Mill in 1850, and was in possession of the Bonds for over half a century.

[The first location of the Poor House was on the old Frazier farm, near Rice's Road, back of the J. B. Morris farm. Today it is six miles from Lawrenceburg on the Glensborough pike on Hammond's creek; 105 acres are embraced in this tract, and John Oliver is the present keeper.—L. K. B.]

OLD COURT RECORDS

February 22, 1834: "At the instance of the Judge and members of the Bar and officers of this court it is ordered that they will, as a mark of respect for the memory of John Breathitt, deceased, late Governor of the Commonwealth, attend in procession his corpse as it passes through the county, and the court will adjourn for that purpose." In the old Order Book "A," of an earlier period is found the following: May 28th, 1828; Commonwealth vs. George Stott who "did swear five times and was fined 25 shillings." Also the same against Stephen Neal, Garland Lane and Woodford Watts, each were fined 5 shillings for swearing.

November term, 1855: Commonwealth against Mose, a slave, for felony, 150 stripes; the first to be inflicted on the 26th of November and every five successive days until completed. It is adjudged that he receive the 150 lashes upon his bare back, to be inflicted by a cowhide, by the sheriff or one of his deputies at the public whipping post, if there be one, or in the jail room. Upon the completion of the sentence, it is ordered that said slave be delivered by the jailer to his master.

May 14th, 1860, it is ordered by the Court that the Jailer of the county obey the following rules in reference to the jail: That it shall be his duty to keep the jail clean and clear of filth; second, to provide good and wholesome diet for the prisoners; third, that he shall visit said jail at least three times a day while prisoners are in the same, and examine every thing on the inside; fourth, and make his report monthly to this Court.

February 10th, 1860: Commonwealth against Jim, a slave, charged with burglary. It is ordered that James Posey be appointed attorney to defend the defendant, and the defendant being informed of the nature of the indictment, plea and verdict was asked if he had any legal cause to show why judgment should not be pronounced against him, and none being shown, the Court adjudged that the defendant receive 200 lashes laid upon his bare back, to be inflicted 50 at a time at intervals of five days. The sheriff is directed to execute the order.

Covered bridge over Salt River at Bonds Mill. Erected 1847.

TURNPIKES IN ANDERSON COUNTY

At a session in 1834-'35, the Legislature passed an Act creating a Board of Internal Improvement of Anderson County, and appointed William McGinnis, Jacob Elliston, Dudley George, John B. White, William M. Withers, Thomas McCall, and John B. Higgins members of the Board. They were empowered to build that part of the Hardinsville and Crab Orchard turnpike which passes through Anderson County. To do this they were empowered by this Act to procure relinquishment of sufficient land through which the road was to pass; to condemn land where it was not voluntarially relinquished. There was an earlier Act, (1833-'34), to provide for the improvement of the road from Franklin County. They were directed to procure a right of way not less than 50, nor more than 60 feet wide, and by this last Act, the above members of the Board were named.

On February 22, 1834, petition for tax to build Hardinsville turnpike, according to Act of General Assembly; fifty shares of stock subscribed for. In November, 1834, ordered 25 cents silver, or 80 cents in Commonwealth paper money.

April term for 1835. Jacob Elliston, president Board of Internal Improvement for Anderson County, ordered to call on county for $500 on first of next May, and for $500 every forty days thereafter until the whole amount subscribed by the county is paid. Ordered that Jacob Elliston apply to the Court and get said allowance due in March last. In July, 1835, the sheriff was ordered to pay all balance of turnpike money due on turnpikes to the Treasurer of the Board of Internal Improvement. In January, 1836, Jacob Elliston was ordered by the Board to arrange for free passage of foot and horseback passengers over Hardinsville and Crab Orchard pike. That year Elliston was given use of a hundred hands for three days each year to work on Hardinsville and Crab Orchard pike "for which they are to pass free afoot and horseback over this pike for one year." In March, 1836, Jacob Elliston, president of B. of I. I., moved court to subscribe $1,250 more to the H. and C. O. turnpike, payable one-half March, 1837; balance in March, 1838. It was subscribed by the following vote: Ayes, James G. White, Christopher Lillard, John Morgan, John Hackley, John Sampson, Johnson Malone, John F. Hudgins and Alvin Herndon; nays, John Wash, John G. Jordon, Robert C. McBrayer, James M. Wash, John Busey, and Thompson Thomas. April, 1836, motion that Jacob Elliston, sheriff, pay over to Board of Internal Improvement $1,500 which is all of the balance of the stock subscribed by the county to the Hardinsville and Crab Orchard turnpike. December 12, 1859, five miles of the Lawrenceburg and Camdenville turnpike was completed and ordered to be paid for; this pike was finished in 1860. In 1860 five miles of the Lawrenceburg and Freeman's bridge turnpike road was built and the county authorized to erect toll gates. In May, 1860, the County Court subscribed $500 per mile to the Versailles and Anderson County turnpike. In January, 1864, the Versailles and Anderson road was completed to within one mile of the Louisville and Crab Orchard road. On March 2, 1860, the Lawrenceburg and Camdenville turnpike was completed. The road was received and established and the committee authorized to erect a toll gate. The site of said gate to be erected on the west side of the house of Grayson B. Taylor. On April, 1851, it was ordered that $3,000 be subscribed to build a road from Frankfort to Lawrenceburg, payable after sufficient amount is subscribed; payable out of levies of 1852-'53.

In 1923-'24, turnpike to Shryock's Ferry (State Aid, under recent law), was completed and paid for. The Fiscal Court did not feel that the county was able from a financial standpoint, and concluded it could not pay its 50 per cent required by the State Highway Commission. The people along this road then suggested that they would supplement the county's part so as to bring the amount to be paid by the county to a sum it could afford to pay. The Ripys (the Kentucky River Stone and Sand Co.), and the owners of Shryock's Ferry, who were the principal subscribers, raised a certain amount of funds, and the road from Lawrenceburg to Shryock's Ferry is a part of Road Project 20, and was made so by the Acts of 1920. Under the arrangement for the building this piece of road with the State Highway Commission, and under the law the State Highway Commission immediately took charge of this road and is keeping it in repair at the expense of the State. In 1895-'96, petition for a vote for free turnpikes was filed in County Court and resulted in 1351 for, and 556 against. The matter of payment for other pikes was considered and different propositions made. (Order Book "H"). Commissioners were appointed to assess damages. The county accepted many of them without payment. Following are the amounts paid for some of them: Hardinsville and Crab Orchard, $8,000; Lawrenceburg and Tyrone, $1,800; Lawrenceburg and Fox Creek, $3,375.

In 1860, the three "Justices of the Peace," G. W. Catlett, W. B. Petty, H. H. Maddox and the Civil Engineer, John B. Carpenter, examined the Lawrenceburg and Freeman's Bridge turnpike and declared it was ready to travel. Then it was ordered by the Court that a toll gate be erected on said road, and collect such tolls for travel as prescribed by law; said gate to be erected on land of William Frazier at northeast corner on the turnpike road; the Court reserving power to change its location at any future period.

SLAVERY IN ANDERSON COUNTY

Anderson County was not a large slave holding county, and in looking over the records it is rare indeed to find any owner who had over twenty-five, and the great majority of slave owners possessed less than ten. But they were increasing rapidly for a slave was rarely "sold down the river," as selling to the South was called. Being so few slaves to the householder in this county, the relation between the family and the slave was so intimate that there was a real affection between them, and none but an unruly slave, or for the purpose of settling an estate, was "sold down the river." Many a slave was emancipated by the owner. In some instances a woman and all her children would be freed at the same time. And, while they probably could not make a living while the children were small, they continued to live about the old home, as they did before being emancipated. Free negroes hired themselves out and a majority of them saved their money. Nathan Turner and his wife, Esther (freed slaves) bought their son born in slavery and emancipated him when he was twenty-one years old. When general emancipation came, many farms had suffered on account of over-cultivation to furnish food. Many, while slaves, were permitted to hire themselves out by their masters, and in many instances were given a part of their wages. There were carpenters, blacksmiths, shoemakers, all excellent in their calling. Masters did not allow mistreatment of their slaves as a rule. Only in one instance was a master indicted for cruelty to a slave woman. The following is taken from the court record of October 27, 1853: Slave: Commonwealth against G. Taylor. Commonwealth appeared by Attorney and Defendant ordered to show cause why his female slave, Nilsy, should not be taken from his possession, and hired out in manner and form directed by law. After witnesses were heard, the sheriff was ordered to "take possession of said slave instanter, and hire her out to some citizen of the county, who will treat her humanely, take bond from the hirer that he will have her forthcoming at the next term of the court on April 3, 1854, and that he will not take said slave nor permit others to take her out of the county. The sheriff is directed not to permit the said Taylor to hire nor control said slave, or any else for his use, and to report to this court." At the April term of court in 1854, all the parties appeared by their attorneys and the defendant confessed that he was guilty of the offense charged against him in the indictment; therefore the sheriff was ordered to take the slave, Nilsy, and sell her for the benefit of the defendant either publicly or privately; said Taylor consenting to the sale. The sale to be one-half cash in hand to be paid to Taylor, the balance in six months with good security payable to the defendant. The court records show only this one extreme case. Numerous people in the county were opposed to slavery in varying degrees, but no bitter agitators. They were quiet about the matter and exerted little or no influence. There was little traffic in slaves in the county, slaves being generally sold to neighboring people. The law did not allow slaves to be brought into the state for traffic, but only by those moving into the state for permanent residence. Of course there was "bootlegging" where the temptation was great. Slavery was not as profitable in Kentucky as further south. In consequence of the division of the people in the state on the question, it could never take a stand for or against secession and finally declared for neutrality, which it could not enforce, and was invaded from both sides, the North and the South. Many slaves were emancipated in the county as shown by the following record: Dec. 12th, 1831, Memucan Allin emancipated negro, James Allin, 42 years of age; July, 1832, N. B. Meux emancipated Rachel, mulatto woman 25, and her female child 5 years old; Sept., 1834, emancipated slave Nathaniel by will of James B. Wallace; Dennis Hedgeman, a free man of color, bought his daughter, Rosetta, for $500 cash and emancipated her on March, 1836. In 1839, Easter Mizner was emancipated by Jeremiah Mizner for $300, paid by her to him, and for dutiful service. "For identification said negro is a dark mulatto, about 45 years of age, full in form and five feet high."

In 1844, by Arthur Slaydon's will, Beverly, a black man, about 48 years old, six feet tall, and Cain, about 40 years old and near six feet, were emancipated. August, 1831, Samuel Harrison by deed emancipated his slave Joshua, black in color, ordinary in size. Certificate granted him. September, 1849, George J. Marshall emancipated his slaves (late the slaves of Wm. Marshall), Ellen and her children, bright mulattoes, Ellen 28 years old, her children Frances 10, Jane 8, John 5, Claiborn 3 and Susan Maria 8 months. June, 1850, Deed of emancipation from Nathan Turner and his wife to their slave, Will Turner age about 21, color dark, about 5 feet 8 inches tall.

The court record of April 30th, 1861, ordered that S. E. Bratton and John B. Parker be authorized and directed to examine all free negroes, their quarters and other persons of color in this county, getting permission of the owners of slaves, in case of refusal report to this court those refusing, and deliver all arms and munitions of any kind found in possession of said persons.

HISTORY OF ANDERSON COUNTY

GUERILLAS IN ANDERSON COUNTY

There were many guerillas operating in central Kentucky, principally in Anderson County and Nelson, and counties west of them. Amongst the most prominent of these was Albert McClure, a son of John McClure and Elizabeth Lillard McClure, living at the farm now owned by Allie B. McAfee on the Glensborough pike. Albert McClure had enlisted in Scott Dawson's company of Confederate cavalry in the 5th Kentucky Cavalry which formed a part of Gen. John H. Morgan's command. It is said that he became separated from his command and never could rejoin it. He became a guerilla, and was in and about Anderson County with other guerillas. A favorite place for them was in the Reddin neighborhood (known as the "Indian Territory"), now owned by the heirs of John C. McBrayer, and is located near and just below Clifton on Kentucky river. These men had many friends in that neighborhood, in fact all over the county. They attended the dances and other "parties" given in the county, and had been present at several dances given in a cabin which stood in a Kentucky river bottom just below the mouth of "Turkey Run," a creek emptying into Kentucky river. On one of these occasions the dance was raided by the "Home Guards" stationed at Lawrenceburg. Some one had "informed" on them. The soldiers surrounded the house and demanded surrender. The guerillas did not surrender, but made a break to escape as did every body else. Albert McClure was shot through the body as he ran down the bottom. The soldiers made no pursuit that night but returned to their quarters in town. The next morning they returned to Turkey Run to learn the result of their shooting, and found Albert McClure wounded. He had crawled to the lower end of the bottom and up the cliff to the more level ground, near the residence of John P. Reddin. Being unable to walk he had crawled the entire distance. He was put on a slide, a yoke of oxen hitched to it and carried into the court house and up the stairs into the court room, and put in a chair. His mother was sent for and came in before he died, which happened about eleven o'clock, in the northeast corner of this room as he sat in the chair. He was said to have been very popular with all who knew him. He was an only son.

Other guerillas of the county were Ben Frohman and Zay Colter, called by his friends "Big" Zay Colter. On one occasion Colter was in Nelson County, just across the line from Anderson, when he and some guerilla companions had a fight with the Home Guards, who hid in a large log barn. Shooting continued when the guerillas charged on the barn, Colter was killed in the charge. He was a son of Rowan Colter, and lived on the Colter farm on the south side of Salt river, near the Colter ford. He had a brother John Colter, who was a soldier in the Co. G, sixth Kentucky Infantry, and served with his company throughout the War Between the States. After the war he removed to Louisville and went into a successful business and after some years of success there, died in 1893. Other guerillas in the county were Dick Taylor and —— Smith. Dick Taylor was a son of Grayson B. Taylor and was born in Anderson County and was a man grown when the Civil War began. He enlisted in a company of cavalry in the Confederate army, but, as it was said, grew tired of army life and failed to rejoin his command on some occasion and became a guerilla. He operated principally in Anderson County. On the last occasion of his operations in Anderson County, he and some of his guerilla friends went to his father's house, and this Smith was one of the party. They left very early next day, going down

Hammonds creek road. An order had been published by the Federal authorities, requiring persons who knew of the whereabouts of guerillas, to report them to the nearest military post. Immediately after these young men had left his house, Grayson Taylor, the father of Dick, rode to town and reported that guerillas had spent the night at his house. The company of soldiers (Home Guards) under command of Capt. Lorenzi Brown, which was stationed at Lawrenceburg, pursued. A slight skift of snow had fallen during the night and pursuit was easy. They overtook the guerillas near Hammonds creek on the farm of a Mr. Cole. It had commenced raining and the guerillas had taken shelter under a pile of fence rails. Taylor and Smith were captured, and put in charge of Sam Shouse and another soldier, Shouse taking Taylor on the horse behind him and the other soldier taking Smith on his steed. The other soldiers went on in pursuit of the guerillas who had not been captured. Shouse and his companion started to town with the two prisoners. They had reached a point about half a mile northwest of the house now owned by Mrs. Rinehart, when upon some signal between Taylor and Smith they grabbed the pistols of their captors. In the scramble Shouse's horse became frightened and ran about a hundred yards in front of the soldier and Smith, when Shouse got possession of the pistol and killed Taylor. He then rode back to the others who were still struggling, and killed Smith. This is the tale as told by the two soldiers. The bodies of Taylor and Smith were brought to town and carried to the house of W. R. Taylor, a brother of Dick, and from there they were buried in the family graveyard on the Taylor farm. The killing as told by the soldiers was believed by their friends and sympathizers. It was not believed by any one else, but was called murder. The Taylor family had many friends and the sympathy for them was widespread.

Another Anderson County guerilla was Ben Froman. He enlisted in Co. "I," 2nd Kentucky Infantry, CSA, at the beginning of the Civil War. How long he served with this company and regiment is not known. The historian of the regiment, Capt. Ed Porter Thompson, says: "He transferred himself to the cavalry; how long he served with it is not known." But he certainly served with the guerillas in Anderson County in 1864-65, probably serving with them in all their raids. All of them in Anderson served with Quantrell at times. It is known that the James "boys," and Cole and Younger were in this county a number of times, and after one of their train robberies, were concealed by their friends in this county. Froman, it is said, never took more than one meal in the same house in succession, and never remained in the same house more than one night at a time. He was constantly hunted by the Home Guards, and on several occasions a house was searched the night after he had been there. At one time he had taken supper at a house, and had crossed the road in front of it on his way to turn in for the night, when the Home Guard company which had been further west searching for him, came riding past on their way to town. Froman is said to have been well armed on all occasions, and having reached the bushes after crossing the road, he turned loose on them with two pistols. The horses of the cavalry took fright and ran. The informer who was with the company searching for him, was thrown from his horse and crawled behind a log and remained there until morning, while the horse went home. Many tales were told of Froman's prowess with pistols. He was not looked upon by the community in which he spent much of his time, as a bad man, but was regarded affectionately, and is so spoken of at this time by sons and daughters of his friends. After the close of the war, he removed to another county in Western Kentucky and for some years very little is known of him. It seems that Anderson County was one of the stopping places for the nefarious Sue Munday, "One Arm" Berry and many other guerillas.

ASIATIC CHOLERA

Asiatic cholera appeared in Lawrenceburg and Anderson County in 1833, from May 30th to August 1st, and in this time eighty-nine persons died in the town and county. It had appeared in a number of towns in the state, particularly in central Kentucky in 1832, but there were only a few deaths. In 1833, however, it again invaded central Kentucky, and beginning on May 30th to August 1st there were eighty-nine deaths in the town of Lawrenceburg and the county. In some instances a whole family was wiped out; in others the parents would die, leaving a family of children. No one seemed to be safe. The town and county were in a panic, except two or three families, Lawrenceburg was deserted, and the population did not return till after the first of August. It was claimed by people returning that when they reached the Turner Hanks hill south of Lawrenceburg, they could smell the cholera. (Conversation with W. S. McBrayer.) It was said that even the doctors deserted the town, except one. It was equally fatal in other communities of the state. In Maysville there were sixty-seven deaths and about sixty in Mason County. In fact it first appeared in the state that year (1833) in Maysville. It spread very rapidly to other parts of the state. In Flemingsburg there were sixty-six deaths, and in Fleming County some whole families died, ten in one and twelve in another, within forty-eight hours. (Collins History.) In Paris, seventy-three deaths; in Millersburg, seventy-eight. In Lexington, June 1st to August 1st, 502 deaths, of which twenty-five were in the lunatic asylum. Only a few of the towns which suffered the scourge during the year are given, although more than twenty towns suffered. Cholera invaded the state many times after 1933, and from that time it appeared in some part of Kentucky for many years until 1873, although toward the latter date it seemed to attack fewer people, until it disappeared from the state entirely. Cholera did not appear in Lawrenceburg or Anderson County again until 1855, when it came in June, and there were many deaths, but not so many as in 1833, probably for the reason that after a few days, and after the trial and failure of all the remedies that had been discussed, the population abandoned the town, except one doctor and two or three families. There is no record of the number who died, but there were many deaths before the population dispersed. After 1833 the people thought they knew many remedies for the disease and tried them, but they all failed. One remedy that was thought to be a sure prevention was tried by a citizen named —— Duncan (an uncle of Asa Duncan). This remedy consisted of tar mixed with many other ingredients to be burned in many places at the same time, so that the fumes would fill the air of the whole town. As soon as the first case of cholera appeared, Duncan went industriously to work burning his preparation, until the disease overtook him on the second day and he died after a few hours.

County Court Day in Lawrenceburg in 1900.

CHAPTER V

BOND'S MILL ESTABLISHED BY J. F. HUDGINS

(Order book "A," page 236, January 10, 1831. January term.)

John F. Hudgins came into court and stated that he desired to erect a water grist mill on Salt river at, or near, the mouth of a branch from Winston Ryan's. It was shown that he owned the lane on both sides of the river at the place where the mill was to be erected and the dam made, also owning the beds of the stream. It was ordered that he be, and is awarded a writ of ad quod damnum, and the sheriff commanded to summons and empanel and charge a jury of twelve fit persons, freeholders, to meet on the land proposed, on the 20th day of January, to examine the lands above and below of the property of others which may overflow and say what the damage may be to the several proprietors, and whether the mansion house, offices, gardens, tenements or orchard will be overflowed; to inquire whether and in what degree fish of passage or ordinary navigation will be obstructed. On the 14th day of February, 1831, deputy sheriff returned the writ. The jury found that the land on both sides of the river for some distance up was owned by Hudgins, but that John Griffin owned the bed of the river and the lands above to the mouth of Hickorynut creek, also John McGinnis, Clement Lillard, an infant, Wm. James. That none of it would be obstructed except a spring of Wm. James would be overflowed, and assessed his damage at $11.41. The court ordered summons issued for all those whose land was affected, to the next term of court. March 14, 1831.

All the parties for whom summons was issued being called failed to appear or answer. It was ordered by the court, that leave by the court be granted to J. F. Hudgins to build a dam and install a water grist mill, and that he pay Wm. James $11.41 damages.

John F. Hudgins conveyed this mill property to Thomas J. Sellers on the 9th of July, 1841. Thos. W. Sellers operated the grist mill and saw mill until March, 1852, when he sold it to Philip Mosely. Philip Mosely owned and operated it until May, 1859, when he sold it to David Bond. Bond owned and operated it until his death, when his estate was divided this mill property was alloted his son, John W. Bond. The latter continued to own and operate it from the time it was conveyed to him (24th of January, 1870) until his death in 1901. By his will it was devised to his wife, Mrs. Louisa Bond, for life, with remainder in fee to his children. They owned and operated it until August, 1903, when they conveyed it to A. J. Rice. Rice continued to own and operate it until June, 1917, when he conveyed it to the Eagle Roll Mills Co., a corporation which still owns it in 1927. A covered bridge was built across Salt river at this millsite.

An Act, May 26, 1890, to change the line between Mercer and Anderson counties. That the line between Mercer and Anderson counties be so changed that hereafter said line shall run as follows, to-wit: Beginning at the point on the Harrodsburg and Crab Orchard turnpike, where the old Delaney road crosses said pike; thence with said road in a westerly direction to the Anderson County line on the lands of S. V. Hawkins; thence with the Anderson County line to Wheat's corner; thence on the line between Hawkins and Wheat to the Luckto road; thence crossing said road; thence with road to the Birdwhistle and Wheat line; thence with said line to Salt river, and thence with the river to the Anderson County line, including in Anderson County the farms of W. N. Birdwhistle, H. J. Miller and Wm. H. Nevins.

Delaney's road was a very early road and said to have been laid out or marked by a man named Delaney. It was said to have started at Crab Orchard, thence through Lincoln, Boyle and Mercer counties. The part in Anderson passed just beyond Berryman Chiltons. It went by Joe Morris, J. B. Case on across to, and up the Wash hill on to the Joe Hughes house; thence to Johnsonville and through the county by Wardsville; thence ultimately to Bullitts Lick. It was used by people getting salt for this part of the county. (J. B. Case is my authority.)

COVERED BRIDGES

On December 12, 1853, it was ordered that a bridge be built at Camdenville, and that Seneca Gregory and Lefair Routt report a draft of a bridge at the next term of court, with the probable cost of building according to draft. At the February term in 1854 it was ordered that the bidders of a bridge at Camdenville file with the clerk their sealed plans of a bridge and for what amount they will build according to draft, and the sheriff is ordered to advertise such fact forthwith at five of the most public places in the county. At the March term Senaca Gregory filed his proposal for building a bridge at Camdenville, and continued till the next term. At the July term commissioners to receive plans of bridges reported the plans of S. Stone and Son. At the August term the reported plan of S. Stone and Son was accepted by the commissioners and their bond and obligation executed for the building, and Catlett and Orr were ordered to superintend the building agreeable to the contract, and report. In January, 1855, the sheriff was ordered to pay Stephen Stone and Son $600, in pursuance of a bond to be accounted for on a settlement, with 6 per cent until first payment is due. And in June the sheriff was ordered to pay over to S. Stone and Son $400, as an advancement for building the Camdenville bridge to bear 6 per cent until first payment is due. In November Stone and Son were allowed $527.20 for extra work. There are no further orders relative to the completion or cost of this bridge. As a matter of fact it was completed and paid for in 1856, but the record as to this is silent. This was one of the old covered bridges built on piers. It stood for sixty-seven years practically without repair until within a year of its replacement, and it was thought at the time that with an expenditure of two or three thousand dollars it could have been made good for another sixty-seven years. There were a number of causes which induced the fiscal court to build a new bridge, which it is not necessary to mention here. The minutes book of the fiscal court of May, 1923, on motion of Esq. Goins, seconded by Esq. Champion, all of the justices voting in the appropriation except Esq. Pete Disponett. It is ordered that a bridge built across Salt river at Glensboro (Camdenville) to take the place of the bridge now at that point, which is unsafe and dangerous, be paid for out of the levy of 1924. The concrete work on this bridge is to be separate from the building of the bridge, is to be paid out of the levy of 1923. A building committee is now appointed, viz.: Esqs. Champion, Goins and Burgin. Concrete work awarded to Matt Ellis and J. H. Robinson at $15 per cubic yard. Motion, Esq. Goin, seconded by Esq. Champion, all the justices voting in the affirmative except

Pete Desponett who votes no, it is ordered that the bridge be purchased from the Champion Bridge Co. at $7,050 according to specifications and plans herewith submitted. In October, 1923, the bridge was reported complete and it was ordered by the court that it be accepted and paid for, which was done. The money paid out of the levy of 1923.

SELLERS BRIDGE, LATER BOND'S MILL BRIDGE

In the October term, 1847, on motion of Thomas J. Sellers to build a bridge at his mill across Salt river. Ordered that Elisha Beasley, Alvin Herndon and Reuben Holman be appointed commissioners to examine the proposed plan, draw a draft of the same, and the probable amount of costs and terms for which same can be built. In the January term, 1848, motion that County Attorney, Elisha Beasley, appointed commissioner to let out to lowest bidder in writing under seal from each bidder for the stone work and woodwork of a bridge across Salt river at Sellers Mill. The stone and woodwork to be let out to different individuals, upon the plan as represented by the commissioners at the January term, or such other plans as he may think proper. The undertakers to be paid out of the levies of 1849-'50. The Sellers bridge, afterwards Bonds, was completed in 1849.

EARLY FACTORIES IN LAWRENCEBURG

There was quite a number of factories in Lawrenceburg in the early days of its existence, and even before. Hats were made here, and wagons and plows. There were tan yards in several places in what is now the town limits; rope walks, where rope and twine were made; bagging factories where much bagging and twine were manufactured; candle wicks, candle molds, trace chains, plow shares, bolts, staples, poy hooks, hoes, barrels, kegs and in families, jeans, blankets, linsey, flour meal and saddles. It is not contended that there were large plants, except the rope walks and bagging factories, and these factories were either in the dwelling houses, or separate buildings on the residence lots. Shoes also were manufactured. The rope walks and bagging factories were considerable establishments, and had a market other than local. The owners of these factories placed their output with commission merchants in Louisville. Whiskey had not been mentioned, but from the earlier settlements of the county whiskey was made for local consumption, and finally became the leading industry in the county, and an industry in which millions of dollars were invested, and the market for the product of the distilleries became world-wide. The fact of the growth of this industry is not at all marvelous when we consider that there is an abundance of pure limestone water flowing from numerous springs, as pure as any water on earth. This matter of pure water was early realized, for in 1783 distilleries were built south of Kentucky river (Collins' History, Vol. 1, page 20), and on the waters of Gilberts creek, and Baileys run, where they remained until the laws of general prohibition were enacted and put into effect.

In 1870, three years before the great fire, the population of Lawrenceburg was only 393. The town was to have a future, however. During the whole time from the erection of the county in 1827 and the incorporation of the town in 1818, there were probably fifty distilleries in the county, all small—

a barrel of whiskey a day was a large output, and a short run during a season. These small distilleries supplied the local demand until 1870. During the War Between the States an internal revenue tax was put on the output of these distilleries and the warehouses were made bonded warehouses. Many of the distilleries went out of business, but the others increased their capacities. The output of these once small plants increased as the demand for it increased. Anderson County whiskey gradually became known and celebrated. Liquor men from the large cities became interested and bought all, or almost all, stocks in the bonded warehouses. They finally began to purchase the output of these distilleries and new markets were opened. The names of different brands of Anderson County whiskey became known throughout all of the states, and in many foreign countries. New and larger distilleries were built, larger bonded warehouses were constructed, and many thousands of barrels of whiskey were made and stored in these warehouses. Three banks did a large banking business, distillers became wealthy, merchants did a large business, payrolls amounted to many thousands of dollars weekly. Where local farmers formerly supplied the grain they ceased to furnish any, and grain was purchased and shipped in from the great grain centers of Chicago and Kansas City. Thousands of cattle and hogs were fattened from the by-products of these distilleries. It was estimated that more than five thousand people of Anderson County were directly living on the output of these distilleries in some way or other. There was collected as taxes on whiskey for county purposes, in one year, more than fifty thousand dollars. More than two hundred miles of new turnpikes were constructed, which couldn't have been done at that time except for these taxes on whiskey.

With such an industry within the borders of Anderson County, naturally the town took on a new growth. Such an increase of business required shipping facilities. Grain was shipped by water, and railroad people became interested. Such an enormous quantity of goods and wares as went from and to Anderson County by water or wheeled vehicles, hence a railroad was needed, it could not be ignored, hence a railroad was built and completed in 1888, from Louisville to Burgin, with a branch from Lawrenceburg to Lexington. Did Lawrenceburg thrive and grow fat? Yes, new and expensive residences were built by distillers, bankers, merchants and other business men. Large business houses were erected; new streets opened and sidewalks constructed until it became the most complete sidewalked town in Kentucky of its size. As one county representative from Anderson expressed it to a fellow-representative in Frankfort, "In some places it was more than a mile and in one, it was two miles."

EARLY INDUSTRIES BRIEFLY REVIEWED

While the population of Lawrenceburg in 1830 was only 320, there had been for some years three taverns in the town. One, known first as Lawrence tavern, afterwards as Whip's tavern, and to those of the present generation, the Anderson House. Another, the second one built, was on the corner north of the court house, operated for many years by Mary May. Then, after the town had been laid off in 1818, a brick tavern erected by William Lawrence, where the post office is situated, rented by Lawrence to Mathew Galt, and afterwards purchased by Galt and known as the Galt House. These were large taverns for a town with a population of only 320. The smallest of these taverns contained eight rooms and the largest eighteen. Lawrence had established a brick yard on the lot known as the cooper shop lot, (where whiskey barrels later were made), the property now of Mrs. Mary Dowling. Brick from this yard had been built into a two-story hotel, the Galt House, a two-story brick at Ballard's drug store, the Pierian Club house, a two-story brick dwelling near the depot, and a two-story brick residence where the Christian church, corner Main and Chatauqua stands. There were a few other brick buildings. Now it is pertinent to ask what supported this population? We presume the question was alive in that day as to what could be done to maintain the population.

Edward C. Miller bought from William B. Wallace an acre of ground just west of and adjoining lots 26 and 28.* He also purchased from John Story just north of and adjoining the first two lots, back of lots 30 and 32, another acre and a quarter; he also bought from Ann Harris, the lot 26 where the Presbyterian church stands. Upon the two back lots he erected a rope walk and bagging factory. He operated this for some years, when he sold the rope walk and bagging factory to C. H. Fenwick and Benjamin F. Hickman for ten thousand dollars, five thousand of which was cash. Fenwick sold his interest after a time, and it continued to be operated until about 1837, when John F. Hudgins got the first two lots, those just west of lots 26 and 28, and on these he erected a carding factory and steam mill. A steam mill is still there. The carding factory remained there until it was sold and removed to Glensborough, and it is still there, although it has not been operated for some years. This factory was operated for sometime by Elisha Beasley, and some idea may be gained as to its proportions when he mortgaged it, and the mortgaged property consisted of the hire of fifty-one negro men, and his stock on hand for eight thousand dollars, and this mortgage he paid off. The lots back of T. J. Ballard's and Mrs. Hughes were bought by Fielding L. Connor, and he built a rope walk and bagging factory, and while there is no mortgage to show the extent of the property on these lots, it seems to have been as successful as the Edward C. Miller factory. This was sold to R. W. Sea and Tarlton Railey.

In the sales on mortgages on these properties, they always included stocks of ropes, twines and bagging in the hands of commission merchants in Louisville. These properties went out of existence very gradually and as competition became too keen at more convenient markets, although there is no record of failure. The north end of town in those days was the center of business, and there is little definite by which to fix the value of merchants' stocks of goods. But Joel Medley operated a store on the corner of Main street and White's alley, where Mrs. Hughes now lives, and in order to secure new stock, mortgaged his stock to Brenan and Marshall, Philadelphia merchants, for $5,688. All merchants here traded at Philadelphia, and this Philadelphia firm, at one time, owned in Lawrenceburg the old Lawrence tavern and the houses and lots upon which the Christian church is situated.

The following recorded mortgage of a rope walk factory may be of interest:

---

*See plat of Lawrence.

Elisha Beasley
   to John F. Hudgins, Jacob Elliston, James B. Wallace, Delancey Egbert, and C. H. Fenwick.

(Mortgage, June 7th, 1837.)

In consideration second parties being bound on sundry notes as sureties for first party for $1200 or $1400 payable to John Bond, and $1100 or $1200 payable to Turner Hanks. Also $300 payable to John Bond and $400 payable to John Bond; $150 to Thomas McCall, and one $4000 or $5000 payable to Thos. A. Withers, and will be due 1838. One house and lot in Lawrenceburg conveyed to Beasley by Simon Gregory and one-half of Rope Walk, purchased by Bain and Marrs, and machinery laying on southwest side of Main street, and which I have in occupancy and also stoves, also hired interest in following negroes now employed in the Rope Walk until 25th of December next; Harry, Jerry, Lige, Peter, Green, Sip, Lewis, John, Charles, Frank, George, Tom, Bob, Stephen, Jim, Simeon, Jane, Charlotte, Jack, Bettie, George, Charles, Arther, Charlie, Tom, Jacob, Dick, Henry, Amos, Willis, Nelson, Noel, Louis, Bill, Everett, Smith, and Nelson and Tom Calomore waggoner; also wagons and 6 horses and 6 pair of gear; also all the rope and bagging I have on hand in the town of Lawrenceburg, or in the hands of my commission merchants in the city of Louisville, between five and seven hundred pieces, besides all the hired negroes not mentioned, not recollected in this mortgage, together with all the interest I have in the Rope Walk rented from John S. Egbert and Joshua Saffell.

TAVERNS

September 3, 1827, Mark Lillard was granted license to keep tavern at his home in Anderson County, the former residence of Thomas Lillard (afterwards the McCall home). On the same date William McClure was granted license to keep tavern in the house formerly occupied by Lewis Hyatt in town. During the same year license was granted to the following: Thomas Phillips, Mary May, William Lawrence, Lewis Hyatt and John Whip. In 1830 license for tavern keeping in the town were granted George Morris, Matthew Galt, and John Busey for tavern in the county. In 1834 license was granted Izzard B. Bush and William Withers, to keep tavern in the county. Those granted license in 1840-'41 were Smallwood Maddox, Howe Maddox, Jacob Saffell and James Ripy. In 1860 Joshua Saffell had tavern license. The same year William Tindall operated a tavern at Lick Skillet, and William Searcy at Johnsonville. Many of these licenses were renewed from year to year, not merely for the profit that accrued therefrom, but for the hospitality the taverns could proffer friends and the traveling public.

The record shows that ninety-three men lived in Lawrenceburg in 1854. Witherspoon and Saffell operated stage coaches through here in 1860. The same year merchants license was granted B. F. Caldwell.

The Pierian Club House. Oldest house in Lawrenceburg. Built in 1818.

OLD FIELDS

In December, 1859 (Order Book "D"), the first five miles of the Lawrenceburg and Camden turnpike was completed. In a depression in this road about one mile west of Lawrenceburg, in front of the residence of Grayson B. Taylor (the residence a large brick, one and a half-story, since destroyed by fire, the farm now, 1927, owned by Holly Witherspoon), a very considerable fill was made. The culvert crossing this pike at this place was made near the level of the pike, so that a large and deep pond was made. Strother Taylor, a son of G. B. Taylor, on his way home from some part of the farm, was accidentally drowned in this pond. After this accident many people in passing at night, claimed to see ghosts. From description given of the ghosts by these persons, they never appeared in the same manner to any two persons, and always appeared in some wild, fantastic shape. For instance, George Mitchell, in returning home from the western part of the county on horseback on a dark, misty night, surprised his wife by asking her to "smell his breath." After this formality he related to her a tale to this effect: "Now you see I am not drunk. I was riding along the Camden pike a while ago, and when I got to a place near where the old pond was located, I noticed a man walking by the side of me; his head and body was on a level with me, and I looked for a horse but could see none. I listened and could hear no horse-hoof beats. I put my horse into a faster pace, but this thing seemed to keep even with me—there was no noise save that made by my own horse. By the time I reached the grade towards Lawrenceburg, my horse was doing his best, but this man or beast, whatever it was, was still even with me. As I started up the grade, I looked again and he had disappeared. No words were passed between us, except when he first appeared at my side, I said, 'How do you do?' No answer. Thinking he might not have heard me, I raised my voice and said, 'What are you doing out so late at night?' No answer, then I knew the ghost was with me."

There were many tales such as this. These things occurred when no one else was along and on very dark nights.

The writer passing this place with Judge J. M. Posey one night mentioned that this was the ghost place. He said, "Yes, but they had been told long before Strother Taylor had been drowned; that the land to the south of the road at this place had always been called the 'Old Fields,' and the place had evidences of cultivation when first settled. The timber showed that it was a new growth, and vastly younger than the surrounding forests; that there had been evidence of a tract, or trace down this branch to Hammonds creek." Afterwards the writer mentioned the "Old Fields" to Mr. W. S. McBrayer, and he said the place went by the name of "Old Fields" when he was a boy; that it was supposed a tribe of Indians had at one time lived there, but the name had been gradually supplanted by the name, the "Grayson Taylor place." In connection with these "Old Fields" John Howard and his wife, Mary Howard, appointed one George Bain their attorney to prosecute claims for land in Green Briar County, Virginia, supposed to have been owned by John Arbuckle, that John Arbuckle owned the farm on which the "Old Fields" were located, and died there in 1796 or 1797. Bain, in the prosecution of these claims, was permitted to introduce deposition by the Anderson County Court (Order Book B, April term, 1843). The depositions were copied on the order book and were given by Margaret Jett, Berry Searcy, Thomas Bunton and Benjamin Wash, Sr. It appears from these depositions that John Arbuckle had come to Kentucky from Green Briar County, Virginia, that he was a large man about six feet high, with black hair, grayish blue eyes, coarse but regular features, swarthy, large head, square forehead tapering to the chin with the tip of his nose bitten off in a fight in Lincoln County, Kentucky, at which Benjamin Wash, Sr., was present; and that he frequently spoke of owning a great deal of land in Green Briar County, Virginia.

At the time of his death he had one daughter, Elizabeth, who married a man named Stephens. They left, and the witnesses knew nothing more about them. Another daughter, Mary, who married John Howard, was born about six months after his death; that he lived at a place called the "Old Fields," about three-fourths of a mile west of Lawrenceburg, at this time known as the Grayson Taylor farm, afterwards owned by R. H. Lillard and today owned by Holly Witherspoon. These fields were sometimes called Young's Old Fields and constituted the greater part of Coffman's western boundary.

Benjamin Wash, Sr., came to this county in 1791, and in his deposition he testified that he knew John Arbuckle from the time he came here until his death in 1797.

NOTED SPRINGS IN ANDERSON COUNTY

A part of Anderson County forms the dividing ridge between Kentucky river and Salt river. Here are the headwaters of Hammonds creek, Indian creek and other creeks flowing into Salt river, and Gilberts Creek, Baileys Run and Little Benson flowing to Kentucky river. This ridge, or rather it should be called a plateau, is the location of many springs, some of them particularly celebrated. The McAfee party, the first whites to pass through what is now Anderson County, are said to have passed just east of Lawrenceburg, and stopped for the night at a remarkable spring, at that time called Cave spring, afterward known as Lillard's spring. This is the spring located on the Harrodsburg pike at McCalls. The McAfee diary says that they left the spring the next morning and went down Salt river, which they called Crooked creek, to the mouth of Hammonds creek, above which they surveyed 400 acres of land for each of the party. The writer has never believed this spring was the McCalls or Lillard's spring, for the reason that this spring is located on Gilberts creek which flows in Kentucky river, and the party would have had to travel eight or ten miles to get to the mouth of Hammonds creek, which flows into Salt river. Another reason is that the McAfee party called it a "Cave" spring, when there is no cave near it. It is an unusual spring and has had a fine flow of water at all times, and during long dry spells has furnished water for a whole neighborhood. Another good reason for the belief that the McCalls' or Lillard's spring is not the spring mentioned by the McAfee party—there is another remarkable spring east of Lawrenceburg and about four miles from the mouth of Hammonds creek, and it IS a "Cave" spring. It is located southeast of Lawrenceburg, about three-quarters of a mile therefrom. It rises in a depression of the ground, about fifteen feet deep, probably seventy-five feet wide and seventy-five or a hundred yards long. It is a very large spring, formerly there was a great flow of water and a considerable flow now. It came out of the ground at the north end of this depression, flowed south to the end and disappeared in the ground near the mouth of a cave; it passed under the earth into the cave and appeared on a hillside beyond, and its abundant supply of water operated the Bond and Lillard distillery for many years. This spring is on the farm now owned by W. Tom Bond (1928), inherited from his father, W. F. Bond. There was no "cave" near the McCalls or Lillard spring; it came out from under a large ledge of rock on the north bank of Gilbert's creek and runs into Gilberts creek a few yards away.

There is a spring called Boiling Spring, probably a mile above the mouth of Hammonds creek, on the creek. It was sufficient to operate a distillery, the Hoffman plant, for many years, and has a decided sulphur flavor which it lent to the whiskey made there. It is now covered with concrete and is pumped out.

There is a spring on Salt river near the Goodnight bridge called Buffalo Lick. It has no large flow of water, but the water is impregnated with sulphur and was generally used as a tonic in former years. There are many springs in and around Lawrenceburg in addition to those mentioned. There is a spring at the Eagle Roller Mills, which for many years has been walled up and made into a pond, which now supplies water to operate the mill, but formerly and before being walled, operated two tan yards, two bagging factories and a carding machine. There were quite a number of other springs in the vacinity of this mill spring.

What is believed to have been the last deer killed in this county was killed at the spring known as the Brumfield spring (now owned by Wade H. Morgan, 1928) in 1854. The farm on which this spring is located was owned at the time by Peter Shely, the grandfather of Judge J. B. Shely. Peter Shely cut off one of the horns of the deer and made it into a powder measure for his gun. He lost it and did not find it again during his life. He died in the early seventies, but continued to bewail the loss of his powder horn during the balance of his life. Years after his death, in plowing the garden where he lived, this powder measure was turned up with the initials "P. S." which he had cut on it. It was given to Judge Shely who prizes it as an heirloom. The spring where this deer was killed, while not a large one, has never ceased its ordinary flow at any time.

Brock's spring is the Blakemore distillery spring between Alton and Frankfort. Thomas Collins lived at the crossing of the Shelbyville and Lawrenceburg road, where the line between Anderson and Franklin counties is located, that house being left in Franklin. The creek at this place is Knob Fork or Big Benson.

The old Bardstown road (1860) crosses Kentucky river at Shryock's ferry, runs through Stringtown by the J. W. Rice farm, through the Samuel Saffell place, through the Jordon farm, crossing Salt river near the Kavanaugh (now Wallace) farm, through Fox creek.

Christopher and Brook's Ferry, now Clifton, was opened August 13, 1832. Scott's Ferry, Booze Ferry and Sword's Ferry, all the same at the mouth of Gilbert's creek.

In November, 1834, John Dawson, who was appointed by a former order of the Court a surveyor to cut open the new road leading from Lawrenceburg to White's Ferry, this day returned his report which was received and filed by the Court.

In October, 1834, on motion of Izzard Bacon Bush, it was ordered that Josh Buckley, Samuel McGuire, Christopher Lillard and Green Hawkins, any three of whom being first sworn, to act as viewers to view and make an alteration in the Buckley Ferry road and make a report to the Court. Near here was the town of Buckleyville. In deed book "G," page 211, there is a record of the sale of two lots in Buckleyville in 1847, on the waters of the Kentucky river in Anderson County, at the ferry called Miller's Ferry, the latter having been established in 1845. One Armsted Miller and wife, Polly, sold and conveyed lots 13 and 26 in the town of Buckleyville. It is possible that the name was later changed to "California," as the latter village was near this vicinity. This place called California in Anderson County was opposite Clifton, and in 1857 was referred to in a deed by the Matthews family to Armsted Miller. Another deed on August 16, 1858, states: "In consideration of $600 paid me by Samuel D. Williamson, I have sold and hereby convey him with general warranty, five lots of land in California, Anderson County, on Kentucky river, and known in plat of the town as lots No. 6, 7, 8, 11 ad 12, and also the land on the river commencing with Second street, and running with the river down the same, down to S. B. Williamson's line, including the two warehouses thereon with the appurtenances, etc." (Signed) John H. McBrayer, Sarah McBrayer. Jas. A. McBrayer, Clerk A. C. C.

Miller's Ferry was established on June 9, 1845. In Order Book "C" the record states that Miller's Ferry was established according to law, and further ordered that the ferry rates be established as follows, to-wit: for man and horse 6¼ cents; for every coach wagon and driver, 25 cents; for every two-wheeled carriage, 12½ cents; for meat cattle per head 6¼ cents; for every shoat, goat or lamb, 1½ cents. Miller's Ferry was formerly Christopher and Brooks Ferry at Clifton.

The only mounds in Anderson County is one below the Bond's Mill site on the land of Mrs. Mary Jones, now the home of Col. Davis Brown, about a hundred yards below the mill, near a high bank. Another mound is on the farm of John W. Dawson, about three miles north of Lawrenceburg, and there is another mound on top of a cliff on the south side of Gilbert's creek.

UNKNOWN CONFEDERATE SOLDIERS

After the organization of the local chapter of the Daughters of the Confederacy at Lawrenceburg, they went out into the county on what was called the Mitchell or Ridge road, between Fox creek and Johnsonville, and disinterred the bodies, or what was left of them, of three Confederate soldiers. They brought the remains of these soldiers to the Lawrenceburg cemetery and buried them there in one grave, marking them unknown. The circumstances of the death of these soldiers follows: Early in 1862, Kentucky was completely occupied by Federal soldiers, and became the base of supply for them and the soldiers further south. Confederate soldiers from the south also entered the state from the south and occupied a great part of the state. Lawrenceburg being located on the main road between Louisville and Cumberland Gap, saw thousands of soldiers of both sides pass. Gen. Kirby Smith invaded from the south in 1862, and fought several battles and skirmishes in the state. Federal armies passing through Lawrenceburg on October 7th, 8th and 9th, 1862, passed through the county by way of Fox creek and the Ridge road on out of the county through Nelson County. Gen. Kirby Smith's army followed from south passing out the same road on October the 9th, certain units of the two armies clashed in a very severe skirmish, at what is called in the records at Washington, indiscriminately, Dog Walk, Chesher's store and Salt river. The actual place of contact was on the Ridge

In 1796 this log house (now weatherboarded) was built by Thomas Coke. A continuous line of the Coke family for six generations have lived here. An original land grant from the second Governor of Kentucky.

road, at a point on the Henry Wilson farm, now owned by Wilson's grandsons, and in a skirt of woods on the opposite side of the Mitchell road. In the Kerr history of Kentucky is found a list of battles and skirmishes fought in Kentucky during the Civil War, and in Vol. 2 is an account of the skirmish called "Dog Walk." The writer had known of this skirmish since it occurred in his small boyhood. Recently he brought the subject up with John T. Buntain, whose father, J. T. Buntain, lived in the immediate neighborhood at time of its occurrance, October 9th, 1862. Three Confederate and seven Federal soldiers were killed in the skirmish. This was close to Dog Walk, which was a store with two or three residences about it, and also being at that time a voting place. One of the Confederates was killed on the Wilson farm at the entrance gate to his residence. He was said to have been a very young man, probably in his teens. It was said that he was a sharp shooter and killed all the seven Federals. He was buried by the gate where he was killed, and a picket fence was erected around his grave, and was a subject of curiosity to all strangers passing. His name and the place he came from are unknown. The second of the Confederates was killed in a skirt of woods on the opposite side of the Mitchell road, about three or four hundred yards in front of the Wilson house; a rail pen was built around his grave by the neighbors. The third Confederate was wounded and afterwards died. He was on the opposite of a deep ravine, or small creek in front of the Wilson house and on that farm. After being hit, he walked down this little ravine or creek to Indian Gap, as the place is called, where it opens on Salt river. He then went on down the river to the Neddy Sherwood house, which stands on the opposite side of the river. The river was crossed and he went to the Sherwood home where he was taken in and cared for by that family. After a few days he died and was buried in the Sherwood family grave yard. At the time of this writing (1928) his name is not remembered. The Federals killed in this skirmish were seven in number, and as they were discovered by the neighbors after the troops had left the neighborhood, their bodies were not lying very far apart from each other. The neighbors testified that they were all killed by the one Confederate sharp-shooter, who was himself killed at the Wilson gate. The seven were buried in the skirt of the woods where they fell, by people of the neighborhood, and a rail fence was built around their burial place. Their names were unknown. (These facts were given the writer by John T. Buntain, son of J. T. Buntain, Sr.) It is probable that three or more of the Confederate soldiers were buried in the same grave. At any rate a number of soldiers' bones were dug up at that place and removed to the Lawrenceburg cemetery by the Daughters of the Confederacy.

There were three skirmishes near Lawrenceburg, fought October 8th, 11th and 25th, 1862. Two of these fought near the railroad crossing south of Lawrenceburg in fields owned now by W. T. Bond and L. W. McKee, near the intersection of the Louisville and Crab Orchard turnpike with the Bond and Lillard pike. At least two Confederate soldiers were killed, and a number of Federal, and they were buried where they fell, their graves unmarked. The two Confederates were interred on the Bond farm and the Federals on the back of the lot of L. W. McKee.

CHAPTER VI

REMINISCENCES

The writer as a small boy lived within two or three hundred yards of the Hardinsville and Crab Orchard turnpike, which was a direct road to Cumberland Gap, although not piked all the way, also a road further to the west. He saw many thousands of troops pass along this road, and in 1862, saw a large body of General Bragg's Confederate army pass by. Meeting Gen. Kirby Smith at an inter-state drill in 1883, which took place at Nashville, I was told by him that he was in command of thirty thousand men when he passed through Anderson County.

In 1886, the writer met Governor Charles Anderson, a former governor of Ohio, at Kuttawa, Lyon County, Kentucky. After the usual greetings he said, "Well how is Dog Walk?" He had been a colonel in the Federal army, commanding the 93rd or 98th Ohio Infantry (the writer has forgotten which), and his regiment passed with the division of which it was a part, through the county in 1862. The county having been named for his brother, Richard Clough Anderson, he probably took special notice of things as he passed through. His was a regiment of the division which had the brush with a part of Gen. Kirby Smith's army at "Dog Walk" or "Salt River" or "Chesher Store" or "Fox Creek"—called indiscriminately in one of the histories of Kentucky. It occurred two or three miles west of Fox Creek in the Chesher neighborhood.

There was considerable friction between certain elements of Southern and Federal, among the survivors just before and after the Civil War; wounded men and some not wounded had returned. Amongst the ex-Confederates was James Hanks, who had lost a leg and had been wounded through the body from which he never recovered. He had a brother, Dick, also an ex-Confederate, who had also returned. On one occasion Jim was at the Williams' tavern, about three miles south of town, when a quarrel occurred between him and some home guardsmen in which he got the worst of it. Dick, who was some distance away at the time, when he was told of the trouble, put spurs to his horse, rode to the Williams tavern, and without a word, shot and killed Green Cardwell. In the excitement Bone Cardwell got away, riding south along the pike. Thinking he might be pursued, he left his horse and crawled into a culvert under the pike. He was pursued by Hanks, who passed on, hunting him, when he crawled out and made his way back to town.

Battle of Lawrenceburg, October 6th, 1862, saw a hand to hand fight between Col. Scott's Confederate Cavalry and Col. R. T. Jacob's 9th Ky. Cavalry. Heavy firing throughout most of the day. There were many more troops both Confederate and Federal in the county at the time, but no general engagements. The Federal troops, I do not know whether this regiment or not, retreated out the Fox Creek pike through Johnsonville, Chaplin and on, followed by all or a part of Gen. Kirby Smith's command. There was skirmishing through the county between rear and advance guards and quite a number killed. The Battle of Perryville was fought two days afterwards, October the 8th. Many troops of both armies passed through the county at different times during the war. There was a company in this county raised in 1858 for service in Utah. This company was commanded by Capt. —— Hanks.

"Forest Hill," the W. F. Bond home, built 1850.

HISTORY OF ANDERSON COUNTY 79

On April 1st, 1858, Gov. Morehead tendered a regiment to the War Department for that service. The Anderson County company was one of the ten companies that composed that regiment. Twenty-three companies were enlisted in Kentucky for this service, and ten of them were chosen by Gov. Morehead by lot. The Anderson County company was one of these ten. They were accepted in the event they were needed, but were never mustered into U. S. service and never left the state. (Collins' History Kentucky, Vol. 1.)

ROSTERS OF CONFEDERATE SOLDIERS IN ANDERSON COUNTY

The following is a list of the names that appear on the Confederate monument that was erected in the courthouse yard prior to 1900:

COMPANY C, 6TH KENTUCKY INFANTRY

Killed

Capt. Gran Utterback	Geo. W. Williams	Robert Baugh
Lieut. Samuel M. Orr	Thomas Abbott	T. S. Gillis
Chas. H. Dawson	William Griffy	William Lyons
John W. Hackley	E. Lonaker	Lloyd Redmond
A. Murray	John Phillips	Riley Jackson
	Adelbert Walker	

Wounded

John Abbott	W. L. Routt	John Colter
J. F. Matthews	Ben F. Bond	G. T. Shely
J. Hal Williams	Jas. T. Prather	Jas. Searcy
Wm. T. Knight	William Clark	W. W. White
T. H. Bowles	Jesse F. Sweasy	

Died

J. W. Allen	Jos. Searcy	P. Thurman
W. P. Routt	Thos. Gibboney	W. W. Penny
T. J. Dyer	Z. W. Shely	W. N. Waterfill
R. G. Routt	D. H. Prather	George Peach
E. Floyd	Shith Sherwood	J. P. Waterfill
	D. C. Prather	

Returned Not Injured

Capt. Wm. Stanley	Geo. W. Hume	William Young
Charles Dawson	G. M. Walker	Jos. Moore
F. M. Sullivan	Geo. Harrison	D. W. Bond
William Gudgel	Euclid Walker	O. Martin
John Wilson	Lieut. Joe J. Waterfill	B. F. Dickerson
Lieut. J. H. Cole	Wm. T. Johnson	H. Oliver

CO. F, 5TH KENTUCKY CAVALRY

Killed

Capt. James P. Jordon	Zay Colter	Richard Taylor
John Ash	A. J. Boggess	Alex. Hockersmith

Wounded

Lieut. M. Van Gudgel	Jno. Swisher	A. N. York
E. O. Hawkins	James E. Carlton	Fielding Watts

Died

James Coke	C. C. Crumbaugh	John McKee
James Tipton	N. H. Johnson	Thomas Penney
J. W. Dewitt	A. G. Herndon	James Watson
	John Martin	

Returned Not Injured

Lieut. Thos. H. Munday	W. G. Stucker	Joe Richards
R. Calvert	Riley Williams	Thos. Shelburn
John B. Mason	T. J. Crossfield	A. B. Wash
Jno. B. Parker	J. W. McDonald	Henry Brooks
Frank Stevens	Chris Perry	D. W. Herndon
J. E. Thacker	J. H. Stucker	Van Morgan
Jas. B. Catlett	J. W. Utterback	A. G. Sherwood
B. L. Mundy	Andy Ackins	James Thacker
Asa Oliver	Wm. H. Glass	Wm. S. Bond
Richard Stevens	N. S. Mitchell	Jas. P. Gee
Jno. P. Thomas	J. G. Shely	W. B. Mitchell
Lieut. P. H. Oliver	Pres. H. Thomas	J. W. Shely
William Cummings	B. A. Wash	Al Thacker
George Martin	Sam Coke	H. L. Stucker
David M. Roach	H. C. MeLear	

COMPANY H, 5TH KENTUCKY CAVALRY

Killed

Leonidas Gaines	Edw. Jordon	W. O. Reddin
	Albert G. McClure	

Wounded

Sam Edwards	Henry Smith	Randal Walker
	William Hardy	

Returned Not Injured

Capt. E. S. Dawson	Jack Burge	Richard Cumins
Lieut. Wilkerson Fenwick	David Froman	Joe M. Hanks
	Lieut. L. W. Chambers	Joe. T. Hughes
John Crossfield	W. T. Burrus	Joe Lane
Green Harris	Ben Froman	S. O. McGuire
Elijah Mothershead	A. B. Jordon	Jeptha Vaughters
William Robinson	Cabel Maddox	A. B. Jones
N. Holly Witherspoon	Milton Parrish	John Moffitt
Jasper Frazier	S. P. Davidson	Jas. P. Ripy
J. Dick Johnson	J. S. Coke	John F. Wills
Lieut. J. F. Witherspoon	Wm. H. Hughes	Thos. Jordon
E. P. Austin	William Black	Jordon W. Mizner
Phil Dean	Elijah Gudgel	Jno. Reddin
Dan Hankins	Minner Jones	William F. Leathers
Jno. G. Leathers	Dudley Moore	Noel Moore
H. H. Maddox	Tom Rice	Jas. M. Searcy
Jno. C. Thompson	Chas. Ash	William York

COMPANY I, 2ND KENTUCKY INFANTRY

Killed

Capt. James G. Redmon	Jas. O. Egbert	Perry Turpin
A. O. Hornbacker	John D. Sale	Oscar Hackley
Chas. H. Bowen	Edward J. Collins	John L. Street
Fount Peach	John S. Penny	Geo. W. Jamerson
John Miller	W. O. Hardester	

Wounded

Capt. W. E. Bell	William Jett	William Brown
Chas. Appleton	F. M. Robinson	Pat H. Jones
Dick O. Hanks	Frank Lane	J. W. Speer
Jas. A. McGuire	S. G. Hagerman	Robert Woolridge
Jno. P. Vaughn	Richard Mothershead	S. O. Hackley
Geo. W. Chaney	Thos. Tindall	Chas. J. Klem
D. P. Lane	Lieut. Jordon M. Frazier	Sam Tindall
Geo. H. Taylor		John Jett
Lieut. S. James Hanks	John H. Crain	J. H. Kinkton
Ben F. Brown	John Kelly	Mark P. Rucker
	J. W. Smith	

Died

Ben H. Hackley	Robert Johnson	N. H. Penny
Morton Watts	Sam S. Moore	James Paxton
H. C. McMichael	Jno. McGuire	Wm. Street

Returned Not Injured

Lieut. C. C. Lillard	Jno. M. Hanks	Jordon Fidler
Jos. Ford	John Farrell	F. Kinkton
Lieut. S. S. Collins	Ben F. Taylor	R. R. Stephenson
John R. Mothershead	Joe A. Frazier	Thos. Coke
Jno. Aubrey	Thos. Tolls	Chas. R. Tolls

ANDERSON COUNTY MEXICAN WAR VOLUNTEERS

Company "C," Second Regiment, Foot Volunteers, enrolled at Frankfort. Ky., May 23rd, 1846. Mustered in June 9th, 1846, at Louisville, Ky.: G. W. Kavanaugh, Captain. Resigned September 9th, 1846.

John H. McBrayer, Captain; Andrew J. Galt, 1st Lieut.; John M. McBrayer, 2nd Lieut., resigned September 9th, 1846. John H. Lillard, 2nd Lieut.; Alva C. Threlkeld, 2nd Lieut.; W. S. Galt, 1st Serg.; John S. Petty, Sergt.; Wm. W. Lillard, Sergt. (wounded); Joseph Warren, Sergt.; John Buttersworth, Corporal; Thomas Munday, Corporal; James B. Oliver, Corporal; Wm. F. Bond, Corporal. Privates were:

Hugh H. Brown	Wm. F. Haslett	Joseph Montgomery
James Brown	Frederic Hoffman	(wounded)
John Banfield	Jefferson Leathers	Hezekiah Neely
Jackson Catlett	Larkin Leathers	Berry Perry
Francis Catlett	James McGuahey	(wounded)
John Cardwell	George Morgan	Geo. W. Reed
Francis M. Cummings	Hamilton G. Moore	(wounded)
William Craig	John Huffman	Thos. Searcy
Jno. R. Craig	John Watson	George Searcy
Thos. R. Davis	Thomas Gudgel	(wounded)
Travis H. Davis	Henderson Wise	Beverly Searcy
Jno. G. Davis	Wm. P. Reynolds	Leonard Shouse
Geo. W. Gilpin	Auther Thacker	Joseph Siers
William Howard	James Layton	Thos. Siers
Sam'l Howard	Carter Bryant	John Siers
Joseph Hanks	Samuel Martin	John Tindal
James Hewlitt		Henry Taylor

Discharged—Peter Bradshaw, Sanford Brown, Lawkin Breckinridge, Jordon Frazier, privates, discharged for sickness at Camargo, September 28th, 1846.

Henry Driskell, William McGaughey, Newman Moischel, John Montgomery, Wilkerson Palmer, A. D. Patterson, Frederic Roach, discharged for sickness at Matamoras, September 30th, 1846; Smith Fitzgerald, Samuel Silvey, James Paxton, Robert Garvey, James Norton, discharged at Camp Belknap, August 10th to 15th; George McCormack, discharged at Ceralvo, December 18th, 1846; James Petty, Chesney Hamlet, William Warford, died; Daniel Morgan deserted at Louisville, Ky., June 30th, 1846; John Johnson, Davis David, James Layton, Wm. P. Reynolds, Arthur Thacker, John W.

HISTORY OF ANDERSON COUNTY 83

Watson and William Board. Mark Leathers died at Matamoras; Wise Henderson died at camp opposite Camargo, 1846; Brown Peyton, Thomas L. Driskell died at Camp Belknap; Bryant Carter died at Buena Vista, and John Hoffman at Camargo.

A monument has been erected to the dead and wounded of this company by the people of Anderson County, and stands in the yard of the courthouse in Lawrenceburg. It is surmounted by a copper cannon ball, picked up on the battlefield of Buena Vista, and brought home by Thomas Munday, one of the survivors of that battle. It was the last solid shot by the Mexicans down the Gorge, and stopped near Tom Munday's feet. In 1890 there was a union of the Mexican War veterans at Stanford, Ky. A picture taken of this group and published in the Courier-Journal shows twenty-four of the veterans and a Mexican servant that returned with one of them. The photo reveals them as tall sturdy old gentlemen, grey bearded and stalwart, even under the weight of many winters that have passed since they repulsed Santa Anna and saved the day at Buena Vista. Those in the picture from Anderson County were W. F. Bond, Capt. John H. McBrayer, Edward Arthur and Jackson Holmes. On September 25th, 1894, the Mexican War veterans, forty-four in number, met in Lawrenceburg, Ky. James McGuahey, ninety-one years of age, the oldest, and W. J. Roark, sixty-two, the youngest at the meeting. The latter enlisted when only fifteen years of age. Major L. W. McKee gave the address of welcome, and the daughters of the veterans served a sumptuous noon-day meal for the distinguished guests.

REVOLUTIONARY SOLDIERS OF ANDERSON COUNTY

Edward Atkins	Benjamin Haley	John Payne
William Alexander	Samuel Hutton	James Robinson
John E. Ashford	George Jordon	David J. Roach
Reuben Boston	William Hill	Francis S. Slaughter
Samuel Britton	William McIntire	Richard Searcy
John Butler	James McGinnis	Jeremiah Searcy
William Bond, 1st In. Ky.	Merian Mills	Bartlett Searcy
William Butts	Alexander McClure	John Satterwhite
Matthew Cummings	John Oliver	John Story
Stephen Franklin	John Penney	John Watson
Thos. Hedger	Rodham Petty	Wm. B. Wallace, Lieut.
James Hutton	John Piper	William Warford
James Hawkins	James McGuire	Benjamin Warford
	Thos. McQuiddy	Nathaniel Wills
	Daniel Plough	

Soldiers from the territory of Anderson County who served in the War 1812 were, John Penny, Jr., Chichester Hanks, Christopher Lillard, Joseph Allin, William Cummings, John M. Jordon, Thompson Thomas, Jordon H. Walker, Reuben Holman, W. W. Penny, Henry Huffman, Dudley George, Lewis McBrayer, James McBrayer, William Nelson, Newman Barnes, Bartlett York and Bartlett Searcy.

DISASTROUS FIRE IN LAWRENCEBURG IN 1873

The most disastrous fire that ever occurred in Lawrenceburg, occurred on the 15th of March, 1873, in the forenoon. On the east side of Main street all houses were destroyed from Court street to the little red brick cottage on White's alley, now the property of the Pierian Club, except the court house on the east side, from the Boston residence (now vacant lot next to Ford Garage) to the house opposite the little red cottage. While Woodford street did not have many houses at this time, there were quite a number of residence there, and all but two of them were consumed. A very strong wind from the southwest prevailed throughout the day. The fire originated in a frame house occupied as a store and residence on the corner where the Lawrenceburg Bank now stands and spread rapidly. There was no fire apparatus of any kind in the town, not even a "bucket brigade," except a little fire extinguisher owned by Mr. J. E. Collins, which would probably hold five or six gallons of fire extinguisher fluid, and the writer well recollects seeing Mr. Collins after the alarm, as he trotted along the street with his extinguisher strapped on his back. He reached the fire, but was overcome by the heat and smoke and had to be assisted out. He went to the place in the house under the roof where the fire originated, and used up his material in a brave attempt to stop the conflagration. The fire spread rapidly and within a few minutes all attention was turned to the saving of household effects. Much of this, which had been dropped too near burning buildings, was consumed. Very little was saved by any one, and the night following was a night of woe for all. The few remaining houses were thrown open for those who had lost their all. Whole families would occupy a single room, with probably a cat or dog. People could not starve in a land of plenty and this is about all that could be said for many of them, who had lost all they possessed, except a smoking lot where a home had stood. There was little insurance. A list of sixty-six of the sufferers at the time showed a loss of $191,100, with an insurance of only $36,250. Sixty stores, groceries, residences, besides all outbuildings, were destroyed, and sixty-three families rendered homeless. Only fifteen houses were left standing in the town. People of the county gave what aid they could, but was a difficult matter to replace what had been lost. Very few people had any insurance at all. The Legislature was in session at Frankfort and there was a great deal of sympathetic speech making. The Senate by a vote of twenty-three to two voted a subscription from the state treasury of $5,000 for the sufferers in Lawrenceburg, and $2,500 for those suffering from the Carlisle fire in January before, but the house refused to pass a similar bill by a vote of thirty-six to thirty, and did not act upon the Senate bill. But the Legislature did pass an Act authorizing the Fiscal Court to subscribe, not exceeding $20,000 for the sufferers and to refund it by taxation. The citizens of Frankfort subscribed $1,092, and the city council subscribed $1,000. Louisville merchants and the Board of Trade contributed $1,015 to the Lawrenceburg sufferers. The home people did what they could but no account is in existence of how much was raised. While these subscriptions were very liberal, they necessarily could not go very far with the people who had lost everything they possessed. Many old residents left the county and never returned. Within a week many merchants had put up shacks and continued their business in these temporary places with small stocks which they purchased, but there were many who were not able to renew business. During the summer and fall following,

HISTORY OF ANDERSON COUNTY 85

several houses were rebuilt and during the succeeding two or three years others were erected, but many who were not able to rebuild moved away, and these lots were not built upon until sold. All rebuilt places were more substantial than those that had been destroyed.

CHURCHES IN LAWRENCEBURG

The principal religious denominations represented in Anderson County are, Christian, Methodist, Baptist and Presbyterian, although there are others. These denominations were active even before Anderson County was erected, worshippers meeting at private homes, and, in the summer time in woods, where shade was always convenient. Probably the most active of the early preachers in what is now Anderson County was Rev. John Penny, who came from Virginia and had been a soldier in the War of the Revolution, a member of the second Virginia State Regiment, from which he was discharged on the 1st of March, 1780. He established Baptist churches at Goshen, Salt River, Fox Creek and Little Flock, and with Dr. Lewis J. Witherspoon and Epraim Lillard, was instrumental in establishing the Baptist church at Lawrenceburg. The beginning of a church building in Lawrenceburg was on the 22nd of November, 1833. William Hudgins sold to Dr. Lewis J. Witherspoon, Ephraim Lillard and John Penny the land now owned and occupied by the Lawrenceburg graded and high schools (1926), for which the trustees paid $250. In the southwest corner of this lot a Baptist church was built, sometime after its purchase and prior to June, 1835, for on June 12th, 1835, two of the trustees, Lewis J. Witherspoon and Ephraim Lillard and Eli and James Penney acting as trustees—John Penney having died since the purchase of the lot—sold this lot to William S. Hickman, reserving the church and lot upon which it was situated, also the spring near the southwest corner of the present school building and fifteen feet east of the church building and twenty feet south of the building. This part of the lot was sold to Hickman for $256 cash. This was a small brick church, and what became of it county records do not disclose, but it was still standing April 1, 1851, when for some reason Dr. Lewis J. Witherspoon, the only surviving trustee of those who purchased the lot from Wm. Hudgins, made conveyance of the church and lot, with covenant of general warranty, to Christopher Lillard, Lemuel W. Chambers and Wm. S. Hickman, "Trustees appointed by the United Baptist Church" (deed book G, April 1, 1851). By this deed it appears that the church, itself including fifteen feet on the east and twenty feet on the south, was a lot 109 feet six inches long on the alley, and seventy-six feet on Woodford street. The church disappears before 1870, the manner of its disappearance is not known, whether by fire or otherwise, but the lot was vacant for some years, and during that time the Baptist congregation used the Methodist church. On the 9th of December, 1870 (deed book N, page 53) the trustees of this church, Newton H. Witherspoon, C. M. Lillard and James M. Posey, conveyed this lot to F. M. Bourne, the deed reciting the consideration of $186.50 paid by L. J. Witherspoon and the assignment of his purchase to Bourne. On the 31st day of May, 1873 (deed book O, page 26), the trustees of the church, C. M. Lillard, J. M. Posey and J. A. Witherspoon, without the church having been reinvested with the title, conveyed this lot to L. J. Witherspoon without any mention of F. M. Bourne, reciting the consideration of $186.50 which had been paid by Witherspoon originally. At this time the dimentions of the lot were given as seventy-six feet front along Woodford street, and 109 feet and six inches along the back alley.

On the 21st day of November, 1870 (deed book N, page 176), Christopher M. Lillard and his wife, Frances A. Lillard, conveyed to Newton H. Witherspoon, Christopher M. Lillard and James M. Posey, as "Trustees of the Baptist Church of Jesus Christ commonly known as the United Baptist," a certain lot in Lawrenceburg, bounded on the east by Main, or Madison street; north by the alley running between said lot and the property of W. H. Witherspoon (White's alley); west by the back lot of James E. Collins, and south by the lot of C. Hagermen, containing about half an acre. (Lot No. 30 on the plot of the town.) The consideration of this lot, as shown by the deed, was $100 paid, and was evidently a gift of Christopher M. Lillard and his wife to the Baptist church. Upon this lot a large and commodious church was erected within a short time, but without much effort at beauty. This church was damaged by high winds several times, the roof having been blown off, and at least once, by part of the wall having been blown in. It was always repaired after these blows, and remained on the same lines as built until later when it was improved and modernized, and afterwards destroyed by fire. It was rebuilt on modern lines within the succeeding year with the idea of a beautiful appearance and all the necessities of a model church.

[This disastrious fire occurred in January, 1924, and it all but destroyed the building. The handsome pipe organ was totally ruined. The church was completed and dedicated on November 31, 1924, by the Rev. R. Q. Levell. The new pipe organ was a gift from Mr. Lewis J. Witherspoon and the music was under the direction of Mrs. Wilkes Morgan, who has been organist of the church for fifty-one years. Some of the pastors who have served the Lawrenceburg Baptist church are F. M. Noel, who preached the first sermon in 1836; Duval, Vaughn, Frost, Harvey, Simons, Williams, Hungerford, Gwatkins, Petty, Amis, McCarty, Ray, Cox, Binns, Levill, Stallings and others. The present pastor is Dr. E. N. Perry.—L. K. B.]

CHURCHES—PRESBYTERIAN

Of the early settlers in Lawrenceburg, probably the greater number who sympathized with a church, were Presbyterians, at any rate, a Presbyterian was the first church built in the town. On the 25th of September, 1826, William Hudgins purchased from Nellie Coffman between two and three acres of ground which was west of the town of Lawrenceburg, and adjoined lots 14, 16, 18, 20 and 22 and 24, as numbered on the original plat of the town. This lot lies east of the lot of Mrs. Stanley Trent, and is that part of the lot which lies east of a small creek, or drain, which runs diagonally through the lot from northeast to southwest. On the 20th of July, 1833, Wm. Hudgins and his wife for a consideration of $25 sold a quarter of an acre of this lot to Fielding L. Conner. This lot is described as "A piece of land lying near and adjoining the boundary line of the town of Lawrenceburg, containing one-quarter of a acre, and on which the Presbyterian church is situated. It begins fifteen feet from Edward C. Miller's dwelling." This lot was in the northwest corner of the lot, located at the intersection of the long alley west of town with West Woodford street, although there was no alley there at the time the deed was made. This lot fronted on Woodford road, 5, 64 poles, and extended back along where the alley is now, 7, 15 poles.

This alley was the fifteen feet which was between the residence of Edward C. Miller and the church. The church was built of brick. It fronted on Woodford street, and there were two doors entering from the front. On the 22nd of January, 1834, this lot was conveyed by Fielding L. Conner to Dixon G. Dedman, James B. Wallace and Robert McMichael, trustees for the benefit and use of the Presbyterian church. This church was destroyed by fire sometime before 1860, and was never rebuilt. The empty walls stood there except for the brick carried off a few at a time, until March 25, 1879, when it was sold to L. J. Witherspoon, who cleared off the rubbish. On the same day, March 25, 1879, L. J. Witherspoon sold to James A. McBrayer, Jasper W. Lyons, Monroe Walker and Wm. H. McBrayer, trustees of the Presbyterian church, a lot on the southwest corner of Main and Woodford, opposite the Galt House (now the post office) a lot fronting fifty feet on Main street, and seventy-five feet Woodford street. A brick church was built on this lot and it is still standing (burnt in 1905). This lot extended west on Woodford street to within ten feet of a wall of a brick warehouse. Afterwards Mrs. Onie Witherspoon Moore, donated twenty-three feet further west on Woodford street to the church and after her death, her husband, D. L. Moore, Jr., the chief beneficiary of her will, donated seventy-seven feet further west along Woodford street, making the church lot 175 feet on Woodford street, including a brick building used for general church purposes. Names of some of the pastors who have served this church are: J. S. Lyons —— Watson, J. W. Tyler, L. Humphreys, Dr. William Lindsay, W. Y. Davis, Tyler Davis, J. E. Parks, D. T. Brandenburg, William McKay, J. J. Rice and others.

METHODIST

It will be remembered that one of the first orders made by the Anderson court, after the completion of the first court house, June, 1830, was an order permitting the use of that building for religious services. This was not confined to any particular denomination. At that time there was no church standing in Lawrenceburg. Upon the making of this order, any denomination might use the court house for religious purposes at any time during the day, when it was not being used for court purposes. All denominations which were represented in the county, used it under this order. In 1833, a Presbyterian church had been built, and a Baptist church within one year thereafter. Both of these were brick churches and had disappeared before 1844, the Presbyterian church by fire and the Baptist church probably the same way. On the 21st of March, 1844, Jefferson Searcy and his wife, Amanda, for the consideration of sixty dollars, conveyed to Jefferson Searcy, Allen Rowland, J. Wood, Thomas Dawson, John Howard, Thomas McGinnis and James Cole, trustees in trust, for the use and benefit of the Methodist Episcopal church of the United States of America, a lot 40 by 60 feet lying on the east side of Main street in Lawrenceburg, Kentucky, being a part of lot 5 on the original plot of the town. Upon this lot the Methodist church was built in 1844. It was built of brick, flush with the street, and was entered from the street by two doors, one on each side of the front, having a partition from front to rear down the middle, separating the men from the women and small children. Few men had the temerity to sit on the women's side with their wives or families; no resident did, but when a man did occupy a seat on the female side, he was not turned out, but was looked on askance, and with criticism by the rest of the congregation. This church was used by all denominations regularly until other churches were built. The church stood until 1892, when its trustees, whose names are not given, purchased ten additional feet back the same width, from Mrs. Harriet C. Hanks, for fifty dollars, and built a new frame, or wooden church, which, while not so costly as some of the others, is neat in design and appearance and a credit to the denomination which constructed it.

Dr. Poynter, President of Science Hill College, was the leading spirit in building the new Methodist church. He encountered many difficulties, as the membership was small, but he was sanguine, and with the liberality of other Christian people in town the church was completed and dedicated the 3rd of April, 1892. The auditorium was thirty-six feet wide by fifty-six long with hardwood finish. It was built by Bowen and Crawford, local contractors, at a cost of $3,200. The dedicatory sermon was preached by Dr. T. J. Dodd, whose ministerial work was in Lawrenceburg thirty years before. Dr. Poynter was present and thanked the public for the generous help which made possible the new edifice. The first Methodist church in town was dedicated in January, 1844, by Rev. Bascomb, who was later ordained a Bishop. [Some of the pastors who served this brotherhood were, Andrew M. Bailey, who was first pastor when all communions worshipped in the court house; Preston Bond, Minor, Allen, Dodd, Lewis, Johnson, Vaughan, Scott, Young, Baker, Vanderpool, Ragland, Jordon, and others. The present pastor is E. C. Watts.—L. K. B.]

ROMAN CATHOLIC

Numerically the Roman Catholic church has never been very strong in Lawrenceburg, but there have always been faithful members of this church. The church purchased a lot from J. B. Miller on the 28th of April, 1873, only a few days after the disastrous fire in March which had destroyed the dwelling on this lot. A small neat building was erected on this plot and used by the church until it was sold on the 2nd of March, 1894. On March 31st, 1894, for the price of $1,650 this church purchased the Lawrenceburg Public Common School building from H. B. Carpenter, J. M. Johnson, C. E. Bond, W. C. Shryock, T. B. Ripy and Thomas McGinnis, the school trustees. This building was of brick and was remodeled by the church and made suitable for church purposes. It is situated on the west side of Gatewood street on a large lot. [This article was evidently written by Major McKee before 1900, for this church building has not been used by the Catholics as a place of worship for many years, and now stands in partial ruin and dilapidation. The communicants of this faith have fitted up a room in the Odd Fellows Hall over the Blue Grass grocery where they meet twice a month for worship. The Rev. Father Lubrecht from Versailles is the pastor of this flock.— L. K. B.]

THE EPISCOPAL CHURCH

The Episcopal membership has never been strong in Lawrenceburg and never had a church building here. There was a pastor regularly in charge of this congregation beginning in 1866 and for three or four years succeeding, but no church established, although in 1916 the church purchased a lot in the

Christian Church

Lillard subdivision of town on the southside of Broadway, which it still owns. The Bishop of the diocese comes at times and holds services with the parishioners at the home of Mrs. Martha McKee. [Since the death of Mrs. McKee, the Episcopal services are sometimes held at the Presbyterian church.—L. K. B.]

CHRISTIAN

A little more than three years after the building of the Methodist church on the 18th day of October, 1847, Thomas T. Ellison conveyed to Delaney Egbert, Joseph Hickman, Will Marrs and Madison Searcy, agents and trustees of the Christian church of Lawrenceburg, a lot beginning at the northeast corner of said lot where Allen (Court) street runs to the town limits, south from where the jail stands, thence running southwardly, and with the line of said town limits, 108 feet and a half to Ashford's lot, thence westwardly with Ashford's line, seventy-five feet to corner of a lot belonging to Madison Searcy, thence northwestwardly with Searcy's line 108 feet and a half to Allen street, then with Allen street seventy-five feet to be beginning. The church people erected a frame building upon this lot, with the inevitable two front doors. This church was built at once and used by the church until the 7th of June, 1869, when it was sold to James Medley, Noah Hawkins, Simeon Cabill and James Hayden, trustees of the free colored Christian church; the purchase price was $1,200 of which $600 was cash, and balance payable later. The trustees of the Free Christian church failed to pay for it, and it was sold under judgment of the Anderson Circuit Court, for the balance of the debt, to Peter Ellison, Lewis Harris, Ben Pleasant, John Penny and Lewis Coleman, trustees of the Free Colored schools of Anderson County, in December, 1871. The members of the Christian church immediately upon the sale of this lot began taking subscriptions for a new church. Amongst other subscriptions, W. H. (Horace) Witherspoon in a writing donated the lot on the northeast corner of Main and Court street, with a front of forty feet, five inches on Main street, and running back seventy-nine feet, two inches on Court. While this donation was made in writing, no deed was made. The church was built without a deed having been made, and it appears that the church authorities took little interest in the matter. At any rate Mrs. Lizzie Witherspoon, widow of Horace Witherspoon, made a deed conveying all her interest in the lot to the trustees, R. I. McQuiddy, C. C. Lillard and John W. Hickman, in 1878. In the meantime a suit was instituted against the heirs of Horace Witherspoon in the Anderson Circuit Court, by the trustees of the church, and on the 8th of June, 1878, W. E. Bell, commissioner, conveyed the interests of the infant heirs of Horace Witherspoon, to the trustees of the church. The building was occupied by the Christian church until 1899, when it was destroyed by fire. Before rebuilding there was conveyed to J. R. York, J. M. B. Birdwhistle and R. H. Lillard, trustees, a small lot, fifteen feet along Court street, immediately east of, and adjoining the church. Upon the old lot as enlarged, the church erected a beautiful and well appointed church, which it occupied until a new church on a new lot, on the southwest corner of Main and Chatauqua streets, was erected. This lot was conveyed by J. W. Shouse to the trustees of the church, on the first of January, 1920, the lot fronting on Main street 116 feet one inch, and 223 feet and four inches on Chatauqua. The church erected on this lot is modern in all respects, a church auditorium, assembly room, gymnasium, pastor's study, Sunday School rooms and all modern church improvements. The old church and lot was sold in 1922, and shortly after the old church building was destroyed by fire. A new building with numerous offices has since been erected on this lot by F. R. Feland.

[The new Christian church was built at a cost of $100,000 and has a $5,400 Pilcher organ. It was dedicated August 28, 1921, by the pastor, the Rev. Carl Agee, using for his subject, "The Best Samaritan." There are twelve departmental Sunday School rooms over the large gymnasium, dining room, kitchen, toilets and showers in the basement and a large reading room that has been the meeting place for the Boy Scouts for many years.

Among the names of the pastors who have served this Brotherhood are Hastings, Haley, Lloyd, South, Polk, Stafford, Ranshaw, Lampkin, Reubelt, Gibbs, Bourland, Grimm, Agee, Bowen and others. The pastor today is W. G. Eldred, who has been with the church for twelve years.—L. K. B.]

MARRIAGES IN ANDERSON COUNTY, 1830 TO 1835

November 2, 1831, Samuel Saffell to Sara Woods, daughter of Joseph Woods.
December 5, 1831, Jas. W. Whittington, Martha A. Lillard, daughter of John Lillard.
December 12, 1831, Randall Walker, Sarah Boggess.
March 5, 1832, David Blackwell to Susan Mountjoy.
April 23, 1832, Sheridan B. Hawkins, Mary Ann White.
June 2, 1832, Isaac Prather to Maria Prather.
June 22, 1832, Jefferson Searcy, Amanda Zimmerman.
August 13, 1832, Merritt M. Breckinridge to Eleanor Paxton.
September 18, 1832, Steven Lillard to Rose Hudgins, daughter of Wm. Hudgins.
November 13, 1832, Joseph Griffy, Ann McMichael.
November 14, 1832, Geo. Catlett to Nancy Cole, daughter of Elijah Cole.
December 24, 1832, John Dawson to Lydia Bond, daughter of Anthony Bond.
April 23, 1833, Yelverton Adkins to widow, Lydia Ann Finch.
June 4, 1833, Basil O. Carlisle, Margaret Robinson.
September 3, 1833, Leroy Mountjoy, Louisiana Cardwell.
July, 1833, Madison Searcy to Susan Mountjoy.
October 17, 1833, Jesse C. Waterfill to Rena Routt.
November 4, 1833, Wm. Vardeman to Lucrecia Middleton.
November 14, 1833, Jno. Draffen to Mary Robertson, daughter of Jos. Robertson.
December 19, 1833, Wilford Cheser to America Hackley.
February 3, 1834, James Bond to Melinda Frazier.
February 10, 1834, Jno. L. McGinnis to Mildred Mountjoy.
February 25, 1834, Delaney Egbert to Jane Ashford.
April 24, 1834, Elijah Mothershead to Kathrine McGraw.
May 20, 1834, Jno. R. Hedger to Stacy Ann Dawson.
July 26, 1834, Benj. Catlett to Elizabeth Spears.
August 11, 1834, John C. Lillard to Frances Buckley.
August 18, 1834, Robert Elliott to Polly McBrayer.
September 10, 1834, Wm. Mothershead to Elizabeth Reddin.

September 12, 1834, John Mothershead to Ailcy Boggess.
September 25, 1834, Jas. Saffell to Martha T. Hazlette.
November 29, 1834, Jas. B. Oliver to Mary Ann Hiatt.
December 16, 1834, Randol Walker, Jr., to Eliza Matthews.
January 12, 1835, Obadiah Martin to Mary Prather.
January 14, 1835, Richard B. Bickers to Elizabeth Walker.
February 14, 1835, Samuel Burgin to Philadelphia Moore.
March 17, 1835, Jas. M. Bell to Martha A. Penney.
April 23, 1825, Elisha Beasley to Almeda Penney.
May 20, 1835, James Egbert to Mary Smith.
June 3, 1835, John G. Holman to Sarah Vandyke.
June 8, 1835, Robert Moore to Margaret Moore.
July 27, 1835, Delaney Egbert to Rebecca Carter.
July 3, 1835, Patrick O'Brien to Sarah Hiatt.
September 3, 1835, Robert W. Sea to Mary McBrayer.
October 6, 1835, John Walker to Elizabeth Lillard.
October 14, 1835, Wm. R. Marrs to Lydia Ann Parker.
October 27, 1835, Tarlton Railey to Sarah McBrayer.
October 3, 1835, Michael Goodnight to Elizabeth Smith.
November 12, 1835, James McFadden to Dianna Smith.
December 14, 1835, Samuel Robertson to Caroline Williams.
December 22, 1835, William Thomas to Elizabeth Herndon.
April 8, 1836, Spencer Tinsley to Katherine Mizner.
April 21, 1836, Robert Carlton to Elizabeth Morning.
June 21, 1836, John A. McKee to Narcissa Boston.

CHAPTER VII

FIRST ANDERSON COUNTY SCHOOLS

At the time the city was incorporated under the name of Lawrence in 1818, and at the time the county was erected in 1827, and the name of the city changed to Lawrenceburg, it could hardly be said that there had been any effort at education of the children of the town and county. Once in a long time an itinerant teacher would wander in, get up a subscription school, teach it for a few weeks or months, and go on to some other place. The school would be taught under the shade of trees, or in the room of some vacant cabin or dwelling house. As soon as the court house was completed to the extent that the court room, which was on the lower floor could be used for holding courts, the county court at its September term in 1830, granted permission to one W. Benedict and his partner, not named, to use the lower room of the court house for the next thirty days, court days excepted, for a school house. To this permission, two of the justices, James McBrayer and Thompson Thomas, seriously objected, and required the court to note their objection on the order book. The permission was granted and a thirty-day school was taught.

One of the first schools, if not the first, was a log school house located where Ninevah is now located, and for a longer or for a shorter time, the children living where Lawrence was afterward incorporated, attended there when there was a school taught. But there was no deeded school lot for some years afterwards. The Ninevah neighborhood was one of the first settled in the county, and this was probably the first school. That neighborhood was always noted for its high class citizens. School teaching had not then become a calling, or profession as it has since, and the schools were taught by persons passing through, and could read and write and cipher, and wanted a small stake to pass on to another place. Lawrenceburg and Anderson County, having gotten into their swaddling clothes, early began to think about their children. At the December term, 1827 (Order Book "A," 51) of the Anderson County Court, the court memorialized the Senator and Representative of this county, relative to the Anderson Academy, which was only another name for the Anderson County Seminary. "On motion it is ordered by this court that the clerk of this court do forthwith make out and transmit to the Senator and Representatives representing this county in part, a respectful memorial to the General Assembly, requesting that Honorable body to pass a law appointing David White, James McBrayer, Wm. K. Vanarsdell, Ephraim Lillard, Jordon H. Walker, Alvin Herndon and William Hudgins, trustees of the Anderson Academy, and providing that the said trustees, or their successors in office, may and shall have power to locate and carry into grant a due portion of the waste and unappropriated lands of the Commonwealth for the use of a Seminary of learning for said county, with power to said trustees and their successors, to lease for a term of years, or to climate the same at their pleasure, so as to promote the education of the youth of said county."

Nothing seems to have been done about the above memorial, but the matter was agitated from time to time in the county court, and on the 11th of July, 1831, the county court entered an order appointing Nelson C. Johnson, who at the time was clerk of the county court, to cause to be entered, surveyed and carried into grant so much of the vacant land of the Commonwealth as this county is entitled to, for a seminary of learning (Order Book A, page 262), the said survey, grant, etc., to be entirely at the expense of the said Johnson, and for his trouble and expense in causing said land to be located and carried into grant, he shall be entitled to, and receive one-half thereof according to quality. Nothing having been done by N. C. Johnson about this matter, and he having died in May, 1833, the court at its September term in 1834, Basil O. Carlisle was appointed in the place of N. C. Johnson, and he, also, failed of any accomplishment, at least the records fail to show any.

On 3rd of February, 1839, the Kentucky Legislature passed an act for the benefit of the Anderson County Seminary, provided, however, that a majority of the legal voters requested it by petition. It is needless to say there is no evidence that it was requested. It was never levied. On February 3, 1839 (Acts 1839, page 268) the Legislature gave all vacant and unappropriated lands in Anderson County to the Anderson County Seminary. All that was realized from this Act was about three acres and twenty poles of land lying between the lands of Ephraim Lillard and Abraham Sharp, which was sold by Wm. S. Hickman, Lewis J. Witherspoon and L. W. Chambers, trustees of the Anderson County Seminary, to Ephraim Lillard, for fifteen dollars (Deed Book "G," page 603) June 7, 1851.

On November 22, 1833, Dr. Lewis J. Witherspoon, Ephraim Lillard and John Penny (Revolutionary soldier and Baptist preacher), bought from William Hudgins (see deed book B) for church purposes all the land which is now Lawrenceburg graded and high school (1927). The church was built before 1835 and probably as soon as the lot was bought. On 12th of June, 1835 (deed book C, page 144), L. J. Witherspoon and Ephraim Lillard, two of the trustees of the Baptist church, together with Eli and James Penny, executors of the will of John Penny, who died in the meantime, conveyed all of this lot, except the Baptist church with fifteen feet east of it, and twenty feet south of it, to William S. Hickman. He owned it until the first of April, 1839, when he conveyed it to Lemuel W. Chambers, Delaney Egbert, John Howard, Dixon G. Dedman, William S. Hickman and Lewis J. Witherspoon, trustees of the Anderson County Seminary. The purchase price being $200 paid.

This is the boundary of this school lot. Adjoining on the east side of the town of Lawrenceburg, beginning twenty feet from the southwest corner of the Baptist church on the alley, and running with said alley to John Davis' corner on Jackson alley; thence at right angles with said Davis line eastwardly 224 feet and two inches; thence northwardly 325 feet to Woodford street, westwardly down Woodford street to a stone in the edge of Woodford street; thence with a line running parallel with said church wall on the east side, so as to leave fifteen feet on the east side between this land and said church; thence at right angles with the last named line to the beginning so as to include the spring. Upon this lot a two-story brick school house was erected, with two large rooms, one above the other. The stairway was in a rather large room, and off of the west side of this stairway room, two small rooms were made, one above the other. This brick house was used for the school house from the time it was built until it was destroyed by fire in March, 1873. This was not a public school, and was never a public school until the Lawrenceburg public graded school was established. The Anderson County Academy never owned the Baptist church lot which was in the northwest corner of the present graded school lot. But remained the Baptist church lot for some years after the Baptist church on it disappeared.

On the 9th of December, 1870, the trustees of the church, Newton H. Witherspoon, C. M. Lillard and James M. Posey, sold it to L. J. Witherspoon who paid the trustees $186.50 for it. The deed was not made to Witherspoon, but to F. M. Bourne, and recited the fact that Witherspoon had assigned his purchase to Bourne. (Deed book N, page 53.) Bourne evidently did not pay Witherspoon for it, for on the 31st day of May, 1873, the trustees of the church, without a reconveyance to them by Bourne, or so much as a "by your leave," conveyed the lot to L. J. Witherspoon. (Deed book "O," page 26.) After the destruction by fire in 1873 of this two-story brick school house, the trustees erected a one-story, two-room brick house which was used for some years on the same spot. Sometime after this second brick school house was built, Prof. John C. Willis and some associates came into control of this school and by considerable advertising, and much personal work, built it up until there came a necessity for four or five teachers and much more room than the small brick house afforded; and there was added to this brick house a two-story, four-room frame building connected with it in front. This was the condition of the building when the Lawrenceburg graded common school was voted and organized. In order to perfect the title to this Anderson County Seminary property, so that the graded school might draw its proportion of state school funds, and also improve buildings, a local tax was voted. The trustees of the Anderson County Seminary, W. E. Bell, J. I. Felix, J. M. Johnson, J. B. Ripy, T. B. Ripy and G. W. Walker, on the 25th of June, 1894 (Deed book "W"), conveyed all the original Anderson County Seminary lot and the buildings on it, to T. B. Ripy, C. E. Bond, J. M. Johnson, W. C. Shryock, Thomas McGinnis and H. B. Carpenter, trustees of the Lawrenceburg graded school.

The Lawrenceburg graded school, in 1903, instituted condemnation proceedings against L. J. Witherspoon (Deed book 3, page 449), to condemn his lot on the northwest corner of the old Anderson County Seminary lot, the same which he had purchased from the trustees of the Baptist church. The commissions appointed in the suit awarded him $512. He accepted to this award, and a jury awarded the same amount to him. On an appeal a jury in the Circuit Court awarded him the same amount, $512 on the 21st of December, 1903. H. S. Wise, special commissioner of Anderson County Court, conveyed this old Baptist church lot to G. W. Huchinson, W. P. Marsh, T. J. Ballard, J. P. McWilliams, W. T. Bond and H. B. Carpenter, trustees of Lawrenceburg graded school. The dimentions of the lot in this deed were given in the deed as sixty-four feet on Woodford street, by eighty-five on the alley, now College street. In 1904 a creditable and quite a beautiful graded and high school building was erected on this lot, and still stands, and while there has come a need for additional rooms in this school, it is, and has been for sometime, in the discussion state. This building is two stories, of brick, convenient, with all modern improvements, a credit to the trustees, and a very desirable addition to the town.

Kavanaugh High School, Mrs. Rhoda C. Kavanaugh, Principal.

CAPTAIN JAMES GUSTAVUS DEDMAN

Was Captain of Company "I," Second Kentucky Infantry C. A., which he organized at Lawrenceburg, Ky., in the spring of 1861. He was killed in action at the battle of Chickamauga on the 20th day of September, 1863, and was buried on the battlefield. About the year 1880 his remains were removed from Chickamauga and burried in the cemetery at Lawrenceburg. He was the third son of Dr. Dixon G. Dedman, who practiced his profession at Lawrenceburg and vicinity for many years. His oldest brother, Dr. Will Dedman, removed to Missouri before the Civil War; he was driven out from his residence by Federal sympathizers, and came to Lawrenceburg and remained until the war was over, then returned to his home in Missouri where he died. Another brother, Henry Dedman, went to St. Louis to live, and died there a short time after the war. A half brother, C. M. Dedman, was a druggist at Harrodsburg, Ky., and died in 1917. Capt. Dedman was married to Miss Josephine Hickman in 1855. There were born to this marriage three children, two girls and one boy; the girls died in infancy; the son, Will Dedman, is now living with his mother in the west.

Capt. Dedman was School Commissioner of Anderson County (an office corresponding to the present County Superintendent of Schools) for several terms. He was elected to this office in October, 1859, for a term of two years. The last payment of his salary was in October, 1861, probably paid to his wife as he was never here after his company left. There is quite a romance connected with Captain Dedman's marriage. William S. Hickman removed with his family to Missouri. His daughter, Miss Josephine Hickman, returned to Georgetown College to attend school. Captain Dedman found means to persuade her to run away with him and they were married at Ohio Gretna Green, Aberdeen, she being too young to be married in this state. Capt. Dedman was about twenty-eight years of age at his death. The following personal characteristics were given the writer by Captain W. E. Bell, Orderly Sergeant of the Company, who was wounded at the time Dedman was killed: "Captain Dedman was a small man. He was spoken of in those days of badly dressed men as a 'dandy,' meaning he was always clean, well dressed and of good appearance. He was genial in his disposition and quite popular. He was a good comrade, and held the respect and confidence of his friends, as well as the affection of his company. All mourned his death. He was a school teacher before he became a soldier. He was teaching in the C. M. Lillard, or Ninevah, neighborhood at the outburst of war, and with his family was boarding at Lillard's home."

At the November term of Court in 1832, John Draffen, Esquire, produced in court a license to practice as an attorney and counselor at law in the Superior and Inferior Courts of this Commonwealth, and on his motion leave is given him to practice as such in this County Court. He thereupon took the several oaths required by the Constitution and laws of this state, including the oaths against duelling as required by law. Major John Draffen was State Senator from 1845 to 1849. He was Representative from 1839 to 1840; Succeeded Vincent Ash as a Representative in 1862-'63 after Ash had been expelled on August 19, 1862, "for joining Morgan's rebel band." Draffen was also Representative from 1865 to 1867. He was County Attorney elected to serve six months in November, 1832, immediately after qualified to practice law. The County Attorney was appointed by the County Court (now Fiscal Court), until the office became a constitutional office. John Draffen was elected County Attorney continuously from his first election in 1832 to 1845, except the year of 1843. He also occupied this office from 1862 to '65, and from 1872 to '78. Major Draffen's first wife was Mary Robertson, a sister of Governor Letcher's wife. Six children were born to this union. His second wife was Mary Lillard, daughter of Christopher Lillard and granddaughter of Captain John Lillard of Revolutionary fame. To this union was born three children: Edward W. Draffen, Mrs. Lou Lyons and Mrs. Maude Colter. Major Draffen came to Anderson County from Charlottsville, Virginia.

PIONEER SKETCHES AND EARLY HISTORY

Hammonds creek in Anderson County got its name from Nathan Hammond, one of the early settlers. Hammonds was first at Harrodsburg with James Harrod. He was a member of the House of Delegates of the Colony of Transylvania, begun 23rd of May, 1775. (Collin's History of Kentucky.) By a treaty of the heads of the Cherokee nation, Col. Richard Henderson and his associates became the proprietors of all that country which comprises more than half the state of Kentucky. This was in 1775. A propriety government of which Henderson became the President, was established and had its seat at Boonesborough. The new country received the name of Transylvania. The first Legislature assembled at Boonesborough and held its sittings under the shade of a large elm tree near the walls of the fort. It was composed of Squire Boone, Daniel Boone, William Coke, Samuel Henderson, Richard Moore, Richard Calloway, Thomas Slaughter, John Lythe, Valentine Harmond, James Douglas, James Harrod, Nathan Hammond, Isaac Hite, John Todd, Azariah Davis, Alexander Dandridge, John Floyd and Samuel Wood. A beautiful description of the elm tree is found in Col. Henderson's Journal: "About fifty yards from Kentucky river behind my camp, and a fine spring a little to the west, stands one of the finest elms that perhaps nature has ever produced. The tree is on a beautiful plain, surrounded by a turf of beautiful white clover. The trunk is about four feet through to the first branches which are about nine feet from the ground. From thence it regularly extends its large branches on every side, at such equal distances as to form the most perfect tree the imagination can suggest. The diameter of the branches from the extreme end is 100 feet, and every fair day it describes a semi-circle on the heavenly green around it, of upwards of 400 feet in circuit. At any time between the hours of 10 to 2, one hundred persons may commodiously seat themselves under the branches. This divine tree—or, rather one of the many proofs of the existence from all eternity of its divine author—is to be our church, council chamber, etc. Having many things on our hands we have not had time to erect a pulpit, seats, etc., but hope by Sunday night to perform divine service in a public manner, and that to a set of scoundrels who scarcely believe in God or fear the devil, if we may judge from most of their looks, words or actions." Early settlers in Anderson County who were first in Harrodstown (Harrodsburg), between the years of 1775-'77, were Richard Benson, Garret Jordon, Patrick Jordon, William McBrayer, James McCown, John McCown and Nathan Hammond. These men did not come into this county until after Jacob Coffman built the first settlement here in 1780.

The Alexanders, the Odells, the Fidlers, the Adams and others came here about the year 1800. Prior to that time came Benjamin Wash, Thomas Buntain, Bartlett Searcy and William McBrayer. Collins' History of Kentucky records that Bartlett Searcy was of the party that rescued Jermima Boone, 14; Betsy Calloway, 16, and Fannie Calloway, 14, from the Indians.

The pioneer Utterbacks originally came from Siegen, Germany. Benjamin Utterback was a Revolutionary soldier and served as a gunner of Virginia artillery. His son, Charles, was the father of Sarah Utterback, who married John Bond of Anderson County, September 25, 1825. The Utterbacks came here in 1797, and Charles died in Anderson County in 1843.

MATHEW GALT AND THE GALT HOUSE

It may prove of interest to give the history of some of the best known of the lots and buildings in the early town of Lawrence, afterwards Lawrenceburg. One of these buildings from a time shortly after its erection and until the new United States post office was erected in 1910, was known as the Galt House. On the 24th of February, 1814, Nellie Coffman conveyed twenty-nine acres of land to William Lawrence, which was all of the land she owned lying on the east side of the Harrodsburg road, now Main street. On the 18th of February, 1818, William Lawrence conveyed to the trustees of Lawrence six acres and eighty-eight and one-half poles. This land was laid off into town lots and streets and alleys. The lots fronted on Main street 104 and a third feet, and were 208 and two-thirds feet deep. Lots on the east side of Main street bore odd numbers, and those on the west, even numbers. Lots one and two were in south part of town, and were opposite each other. The trustees of the town made all deeds. The lot upon which the hotel building was erected afterwards known as the Galt House, was lot No. 25, and was situated on the northeast angle formed by the intersection of Main street, then Madison street, and Woodford street. On May 21, 1821, the trustees of Lawrence conveyed lot No. 25 to William Lawrence for the consideration of $1.00 (Deed book "I," Franklin County Court); this lot was a part of land and lots conveyed by Lawrence to the trustees of Lawrence, and the purchase money was due to Lawrence. William Lawrence immediately built a hotel on the lot. This house was a two-story brick house, a hall running through the middle from Madison street. There were two rooms above and below on each side of the hall, adjoining from the front and back. The front room, fronting on Madison and Woodford streets, was the office; the room back or east of the office was the bar room, the family room next east along Woodford street, dining room next, then the kitchen. There were guest rooms above all of these. Lawrence operated this hostelry for a time, then he conveyed it to his brother-in-law, Thomas Phillips. Some years later Lawrence sold to Phillips (July, 1827), twenty-eight feet of lot 27, fronting on Madison (Main) street running back to an alley. Upon this lot Phillips erected a two-story frame building fronting two rooms on Madison street. Thomas Phillips operated the hotel until he sold it to Mathew Galt for $1,600 (Deed book A).

It was operated by Galt until his death in 1833. His family continued to run it as a hotel until they sold it to James Saffell in 1852 for $2,400. (Deed book H.) James Saffell and his wife, Martha, sold the hotel to William Terry in 1855 for $6,000. This included all the Galt House property, stables and the lots east of the stables north of Woodford street, except the sixteen foot alley and the graveyard. The Galt House occupied the site of the present post office and the grave yard was in the graded school yard.

CAPT. E. SCOTT DAWSON

Capt. E. Scott Dawson was captain of Co. H, Regt. Cavalry, C. S. A., and his company as well as that of Capt. Jordon, composed a part of the command of Gen. John H. Morgan. Capt. Dawson's company was the first of the two cavalry companies organized in the county. E. Scott Dawson was a son of John Dawson, Esq., and a brother of Charles, William and Wade H. Dawson.

CAPT. W. E. BELL

History of the Orphan Brigade, by Ed. Porter Thompson, second edition, page 1050, Company I, Second Regiment, to-wit:

"W. E. Bell, Anderson County, was elected Second Lieutenant, July 28, 1861, promoted to First Lieutenant February 15, 1863, and to Captain October 1, 1863. He fought at Donelson, Huntsville, Stone River, Jackson and Chicamauga. He was Acting Adjutant of the Second Regiment from the battle of Stone River to that of Chicamauga, and at the latter place was wounded and disabled for further duty during the war. After having despaired of recovery, for efficient service he was placed on the list of retired officers October 24, 1864."

Capt. Bell was an honored and esteemed citizen of Lawrenceburg. Several of his children married and moved to other states. Two daughters, Mrs. Wilkes Morgan and Mrs. Morris Case still reside in Anderson County.

His only son, Walter Bell, lives in California, and another daughter, Mrs. Annie Lockridge, resides in Dallas, Texas.

JAMES F. WITHERSPOON, LIEUTENANT IN GEN. MORGAN'S COMMAND

James F. Witherspoon was a son of Dr. Lewis J. Witherspoon, and in a division of the land of the latter, a farm on Salt River containing 304 acres was set aside to James as his one-seventh share of his father's land, exclusive of the dower. This division of land was made in 1855. The War Between the States began in 1861, and James F. Witherspoon became a First Lieutenant in Co. H, Fifth Kentucky Cavalry, which was commanded by Capt. E. Scott Dawson. The regiment was a part of the command of Gen. John H. Morgan. In 1864, Gen. Morgan's command invaded Kentucky, and on the 8th day of June, 1864, captured the city of Mount Sterling and the Federal forces stationed there to defend it. On the 8th day of the capture and immediately after the surrender, one of Gen. Morgan's subaltern officers and a small band of his soldiers forcibly entered the vaults of the Farmers Bank of Kentucky and took about $60,000 which was kept, and none of which was ever restored. Whether this taking of the money was sanctioned or known to Gen. Morgan was not known at the time nor since. Lieut. Witherspoon was a member of the invading force, and aided in the capture of the city, but there was no evidence that he was present at the robbery, or aided or approved it. On the contrary so far as a negative was susceptible of proof, facts shown by several witnesses conduced strongly to the presumption that he had no part in the robbery either before or after. But for imputed participation in the robbery the Farmers Bank sued for damages in the amount of its loss, Gen. Morgan's command and Lieut. Witherspoon with it. He was proceeded against as a non-resident by warning order and without answer, procured a judgment for $59,057.33, and an order for the sale of his land and all other property which had been attached. After the sale after the war was over, but before a confirmation of the sale, Lieut. Witherspoon filed an answer denying any participation in the robbery direct or indirect, openly or covertly. On this issue the evidence above referred to was taken. On the final hearing of the case thus opened, the circuit court affirmed its former judgment and confirmed the sale. This judgment was appealed from the Court of Appeals, and is found in Duvall's Reports, and was decided on the 17th of June, 1866, Judge Robertson delivering the opinion reversing the lower court. The attorneys in the case for the appellant, Witherspoon, were T. N. Lindsay, the father of Gen. D. W. Lindsay, and Harland and Harland, one of whom was afterwards Chief Justice of the U. S. Supreme Court. It is of interest to quote some parts of the decision of the Court of Appeals: "The appellant was certainly not legally liable for this flagrant wrong unless every other soldier with him in the battle was individually responsible for it. And as no other appears or can be imagined, we may presume that the Circuit Court assumed that comprehensive ground. But according to the record this is indefensible. had it appeared that such spoilation was one of the objects of Morgan's invasion of Kentucky, then he and his whole army, jointly and severally, would have been guilty and responsible to the indignant judgment of the civilized world and to the laws of their country * * * there is no proof of such wrongful purpose. On the contrary there is some proof that on entering Kentucky an order was announced interdicting all such outrages. Nevertheless if Morgan had any such unlawful design, there is no evidence tending in the slightest degree to show that the appellant knew or approved it. It is true, as argued for the appellee, that the appellant by aiding in the capture of Mount Sterling, helped to 'pave the way' to the robbery; but it is not true, as also argued, that the capture of the town itself was, in the military sense, an unlawful act. It was not forbidden, but allowed by the laws of war between antagonistic parties, recognized as beligerents. It may be admitted that had there been no capture of the town, there would have been no robbery of the bank; and so, likewise, had there been no unconstitutional session, there would have been no rebellion, and had there been no civil war, there would have been no such plunder of the bank. Hence the assumed and perverted principle which would make the appellant responsible, would hold equally all the agitators who incited the rebellion or helped its cause in either a civil or military capacity. This is too much. But this logical argument, ex absurdo, is a satisfactory refutation of the only plea urged in support of the judgment. * * *

The outrage was great and ought to be punished; the loss was heavy and ought to be repaid; but we cannot see how or why the appellant, uncivic and reprehensible as his recreance from the Union cause may have been, should be made the victim for a wrong in which he took no more part than every other rebel in Morgan's army. Wherefore the judgment of the Circuit Court is reversed and the cause remanded with instructions to quash the sale and dismiss the appellee's petition."

EPHRAIM LILLARD AND FAMILY

The pioneer, Ephraim Lillard, who helped promote the early interests of Anderson County, married Margaret Prather. He was of rugged physique, six feet, two inches tall, slightly stooped, broad shouldered, blue eyes, light hair, nose inclined to Roman. When Margaret Prather's mother was a widow, she married a British soldier, named Freeman. When peace was made in 1815, all of the British soldiers who were prisoners at Frankfort, were sent home, but Mrs. Freeman refused to go with her husband, and they never met again. She lived and died at Ephraim Lillard's and was the first person buried at the Lillard, afterward the Witherspoon, burying ground. The manner in which the burial ground was established is this: there was a summer pippin apple tree growing on this location, and old Mrs. Freeman would sit under the shade of that apple tree in summer time with no companion except a slave boy, Harry, her body servant. As she grew older she expressed a desire to be buried there, and at her death her son-in-law, Ephraim Lillard, had her interred on this spot. Of Ephraim Lillard's children, Mary married Ed Collins; Elizabeth married John McClure; Susan married John Witherspoon; Mary Ellen married Lewis Witherspoon; Stephen married Rosannah Hudgins; Ephraim, Jr., married Martha McQuiddy; another daughter married Dickey Collins. Susan, who married John Witherspoon, lived to be over eighty years of age. Her children were L. J. Witherspoon, who married Cordelia Lillard; Eliza married W. H. Shipman; Margaret married M. W. Curry; Dr. Oran Witherspoon, who was a beloved physician of Lawrenceburg, married Miss Offutt, of Georgetown; Allie C. Witherspoon married Miss Fannie Gatewood. Mary Ellen married Dr. Lewis J. Witherspoon and their children were John A. Witherspoon, physician and banker; Martha married J. H. D. McKee; Wm. Horace married a Miss Elliott; James F. married Miss Penny.

Another daughter of Ephraim Lillard's was Martha and she was the second wife of Dr. L. J. Witherspoon. Their children were Newton Holly, a soldier in the Confederate army, and Lister, a farmer of Woodford County. Holly Witherspoon and P. H. Thomas, with several others after digging out of prison at Camp Douglas during the War Between the States, separated in order not to arouse suspicion by so many being together, and Witherspoon and Thomas walked into Chicago and were not captured. At Chicago they got on a train and went as far south as their money would take them, then they hired themselves out—Holly, as a nurse for a man's baby. They got word to Thomas' father and to J. A. Witherspoon, who finally succeeded in getting them home.

James McClure, father of John McClure, was a large man who always wore a hunting shirt. He is buried on the old McClure farm, where James A. McBrayer, Jr., lived about four miles west of Lawrenceburg. At his request his son, John, covered his grave after his death with a great many wagon loads of rock. It is a well-built cairne, such as still exists in Ireland and Scotland. John McClure married Elizabeth Lillard, and their children were Susan Williams, Lucrecia McClure and Albert, who was killed during the Civil War down on Turkey Run. He had been a regular soldier in Morgan's command, but was cut off in Kentucky and became a Guerrilla. Susan married Jackson Williams, and had a daughter who married —— Rogers in Woodford County. Mary Lillard, who married Ed Collins, had one daughter, Nancy, who married a Tinsley. Nancy Tinsley's daughter was

Lawrenceburg Post Office.

Maggie Tinsley Gividen, who was the first and only milliner in Lawrenceburg for many years.

REV. JOHN PENNY, REVOLUTIONARY SOLDIER

On the 30th of September, 1819, John Penny purchased lots 22 and 24 from the trustees of Lawrence. These lots fronted on Madison (Main) street and comprised 208 and two-thirds feet on Main, lot 24 running west on Woodford, being the southwest corner of Main and Woodford streets. (Book H, Franklin County Court.) He paid the trustees $250 for these lots. He built a two-story brick house on lot 24, and a blacksmith shop on lot 22 adjoining. The blacksmith shop was replaced with a brick residence many years later. The brick buildings remained until the destructive fire in March, 1873. John Penny lived on a farm lying between the Glensborough and Fox Creek pikes. On September 14, 1829, he produced in court the following document: (Order book D.) I do hereby certify that I served three years in the 2nd Virginia State Regiment and was discharged by an Act of Assembly on the 1st day of March, 1780, and wish to receive the pension granted to me under an Act of Congress. Given under my hand the day and date above written. (Signed) John Penny. Attest, Alvin Herndon. John Penny died June 17, 1833. His widow, Mrs. Fannie Penny, was then placed on the pension roll at the rate of $80 per annum. She died in Anderson County on the 27th of April, 1839, leaving the following children: Eli, James, Polly Freeman, Almeda Beasley, Martha Bell, John E., Thomas, William W., Susan Mary, and Frances Hackley. John Penny's Pension Certificate read as follows: "I certify that in conformity with the law of the United States, John Penny of the State of Kentucky, who was a private in the army of the Revolution is entitled to receive $80 and —— cents per annum during his natural life, commencing on the 14th of March, 1831, payable semi-annually on the 4th of March, and 4th of September in every year. Given at the War Office of the United States, this 28th day of November, 1832. (Signed) Lewis Cass, Secretary of War.

DR. RICHARD RANDOLPH STEPHENSON

The facts set out relative to this man, were obtained from the history of the Orphan Brigade, by Col. Ed Porter Thompson, and, locally from John Wash, Chief of Police of Lawrenceburg for many years, and from W. T. Johnson and W. L. Routt, both of whom were members of Company G, commanded by Capt. Grandison Utterback until he was killed at Stone river, of the 6th Kentucky Infantry, commanded by Col. Joseph H. Lewis. Johnson was a Sergeant.

Dr. Richard Randolph Stephenson became a citizen of Anderson County at least two years before the outbreak of the War Between the States in 1861. At the outbreak of that war, he had been teaching school at least two years. One of these years he was employed by John Wash to teach his children. He was permitted to accept other children of the neighborhood, and for these he was permitted to receive pay outside of his contract with Wash. At least one other year he taught in a small log cabin or shack, on Beaver Creek, a short distance above the Wash residence. Whether these two or more years were immediately preceding the war, or some years prior, is not now known. It is not known where he came from, although immediately after the war was over, he went from his last place of duty at Andersonville Prison in Georgia, to North Carolina, and it may be surmised that he had been a native of that state before coming to Anderson County. At any rate, there was no family of Stephensons living in this county prior to 1860. He was a physician, and besides practicing his profession in the county, taught the two or more years, as stated above. Except for the foregoing facts relative to his residence in this county, all of the following information is taken from Capt. Thompson's History of the Orphan Brigade. Dr. Stephenson was practicing his profession in Anderson County in the Wash neighborhood (now the village of Sinai) at the outbreak of the war, and in 1861 he offered his services as a surgeon. He was recommended for appointment as a surgeon to the Richmond authorities, and pending appointment, was attached to the Staff of the 6th Kentucky Infantry. He was finally commissioned surgeon December 18, 1861, and assigned to that regiment and served it for a year with this rank, when he was promoted to surgeon in December, 1862. He continued to do field duty until January, 1864, when he was assigned to duty at Andersonville prison in the prison hospitals. It is said that in the discharge of his duties at that prison, he did a great deal to relieve the suffering of the prisoners. From all accounts there was great suffering, and it was claimed that medicines and proper food could not be obtained. He is said to have kept a record of all deaths, and to have had all graves marked by a number, which corresponded with numbers given prisoners, so that all graves and numbers could identify the dead, of whom there were about 13,000. Dr. Stephenson, with others, including Capt. Henry Wirtz, were indicted for the murder of prisoners at this prison and Capt. Wirtz was actually tried, convicted and executed by hanging, but Dr. Stephenson, being at Newburn, N. C., when he heard of the indictments, made good his escape. He left Newburn in disguise, passed through Washington, Philadelphia, New York and Portland, and thence by sea to Halifax, Novia Scotia, where he is said to have been hospitably received by the medical fraternity. When he fled he left his family at High Point, N. C., where they remained until he secured a home in Upper Stewiacke, Colchester County, Novia Scotia. He remained here practicing his profession for about ten years. In 1875 he removed to Worsham, Va., and thence to Farmville and probably to some other location in that section. He lost his second wife while in Virginia and soon after returned to Novia Scotia, where he married his third wife and where, a few years later, he died. It was written of him by Dr. James B. Read, a prominent physician of Sherman, Texas, "Dr. Richard Randolph Stephenson was my warm personal friend, and for five years my preceptor in medicine. I first knew him early in 1864, when he was surgeon of the 6th Kentucky Infantry. * * * He was sent shortly to Andersonville, Ga. * * * It was my good fortune to know him intimately. He married my cousin, Miss Frances Ilsley in 1864, to whom was born five children. * * * He was a gentleman of the old school, brave, chivalrous, hospitable, true to his friends and magnanimous to his foes."

But what should be remembered by every ex-Confederate, and every southern man, woman and child, is the fact that he used his pen in vindication of the south in reference to the treatment and exchange of prisoners. He was the author of a book entitled, "The Southern Side, or Andersonville Prison," published in 1876. In this book he gives a full account of the Wirtz trial and a great deal of valuable information in regard to the mortality in northern and southern prisons, exchange of prisoners, etc. At this time

(1927) W. L. Routt and W. T. Johnson think they are the only survivors of Company G, Sixth Kentucky Infantry. The writer has talked today (December 30, 1927) with W. L. Routt, and his recollection of Dr. Stephenson is particularly vivid. He does not know the exact place in the county where Dr. Stephenson lived and practiced, but mentioned Camden, Anderson City and "somewhere below." He remembers him as being first with Company G, then with the regiment as Regimental Surgeon, and thinks he was Brigade Surgeon. He remembered at an inspection and dress parade, at Marietta, Georgia, the doctor made him take his shirt off and discovered smallpox and sent him to a hospital. While he remembered that the Dr. was detached, he does not remember for what purpose.

Captain Grandison Utterback was Captain of Company C, Sixth Kentucky Vol., Infantry, C. S. A. He had a brother, Russell Utterback, who married a Miss Bond. They were born and raised in a house that stood on a prong of Bailey's Run back of the Chichester Hanks farm, two and one-half miles south of Lawrenceburg. At the beginning of the War Between the States. Capt. Utterback lived in the neighborhood of Tyrone on what was afterward the C. C. Lillard and W. F. Lillard farm above Tyrone. Russell Utterback moved to Texas before the war and nothing heard of him since. Capt. Utterback was killed at the battle of Murphreesboro. He, with his company, was out in front on skirmish line where he was wounded. He was brought back of the line where he died. Capt. Utterback was married to Elizabeth Frazier, daughter of Thompson Frazier, on the 12th of August, 1853. She was a sister of Holman and Geoff Frazier.

MEMUCAN ALLIN

Memucan Allin, born in North Carolina in 1753; died in Anderson County, Ky., in 1833, of cholera. His wife, Mary White, born in Virginia in 1758, died in Anderson County at the age of ninety-five years. She was a sister of Philip White whose name appears in the early history of the county.

Memucan Allin came to Anderson County and settled on Hammonds Creek in 1790, where the pike leading from Camden (Glensboro) crops the creek.

There he built a mill and distillery. There were two other small distilleries on this creek above his. One of them built by Archibald Elliott. Allin sold his place and removed to the farm which was afterwards sold by Allin's family to L. W. Chambers, and by him to Dr. L. J. Witherspoon. In the division of Dr. Witherspoon's estate, this farm was allotted to Mrs. Martha E. McKee, and the exact location of the Allin house and outbuildings was allotted to L. W. McKee (forty-six acres) in the division of Mrs. McKee's land. The house is many years gone, but it was a two-story log house, a very excellent one of that day. The logs were poplar and very large and smooth. The stairway was lined with very wide dressed poplar planks. Memucan Allin died at this house and was buried on this forty-six acres. His son, Joseph Allin, was born in 1792, and was a soldier of the War of 1812, and pensioner of that war. He served at the battle of New Orleans where he was wounded by having the iron ramrod of his gun run through his hand. Memucan Allin was the son of Joseph Allin of North Carolina, who served from July 3, 1777 to 1780 as Sergeant under Capt. Griffith, as appears from the Muster Roll of Regiment of Continental line, as appears in the

Colonial and Revolutionary records of soldiers in North Carolina, in office of State Auditors Research and Certificate of Service. He also had a son, Joseph.

Record: "Colonial and Revolutionary Records. Soldiers in North Carolina line. T. Palmer, Jr., Chief Clerk State. Auditors Research and Certificate of Service, Raleigh North Carolina, June 3, 1896. This certifies that there appears on Muster Roll of the First Regiment of the Continental line the name of Joseph Allin. The said Muster Roll which is on file in the State Auditor's Department of North Carolina, shows the First Regiment to have been under appointment of Joseph Allin, a Sergeant to date from July, 1777, and under command of Captain Griffith. The service of said Joseph Allin is recorded from 1777 to 1780. (Signed) T. P. Jarman, Jr., Chief Clerk State Auditors Department. This is a true copy of certificate concerning Joseph Allin. Given under my hand and seal this 25th day of November, 1813. (Signed) A. H. McArdelly, Notary Public, Fayette County, Kentucky. Memucan Allen's children were Elizabeth, who first married Penney, and her daughter was Mrs. Sallie Penney Carpenter; then the widow Elizabeth Penney's second husband was Chichester Hanks and they were the parents of Joseph M. Hanks, William Hanks, Susan Mary Hanks, who married William F. Bond, and Fannie Hanks who married Holman Frazier, and Keturah Hanks who married Henderson Hanks.

RICHARD CLOUGH ANDERSON, JR.

It is fitting that a short history of the life of Richard C. Anderson, Jr., be given, as he is the man for whom Anderson County was named. After the close of the War of the Revolution, in the latter part of 1782, or early in 1783, the Virginia Legislature enacted into a law a Military Bounty Law, by which all officers and enlisted men of the Continental Line of Virginia were granted Bounty Land, to be located between the Green and Cumberland rivers in Kentucky, and between the Scioto and Miami rivers to the north of the Ohio river. These soldiers were also granted the privilege of naming the chief of the military land office. Richard C. Anderson, Sr., was named by these soldiers to open and conduct their Military Land office at "The Falls," now Louisville. In 1784 he came to Louisville and opened this office. He had served throughout the Revolutionary War, and attained the rank of a Lieutenant in the Continental line of Virginia. He married Elizabeth Clark, a sister of Gen. George Rogers Clark, who was celebrated as a pioneer and commander, and whose reputation as a soldier was conspicuous at the time.

Col. Anderson built his residence about nine miles out of Louisville, almost in the city now, and called it Soldier's Retreat. There he lived and died. A close neighbor was Col. Richard Taylor, the father of Gen. Zachary Taylor, afterwards President of the United States.

There were born to Col. Anderson and his wife four sons. They were, Gov. Charles Anderson, afterwards a colonel in the Federal army in the War between the States, and Governor of Ohio; Gen. Robert Anderson, who with his garrison defended Fort Sumpter until it was blown down by artillery, and did not surrender it until word came from President Lincoln to abandon the fort; another son, Larz Anderson, who afterwards became a capitalist of Cincinnati, and a descendant of his named Larz, now has a residence in Washington and Boston. Another son of the senior Anderson, was Richard Clough Anderson, Jr., who was born at Soldiers Retreat on August 4, 1788. When of a proper age he was sent to William and Mary College in Virginia, where in the course of time he was graduated. He studied law with Judge Tucker, a celebrated lawyer of Virginia, afterwards returning to Kentucky, he began the practice of law in Louisville. After a time he became a member of the Kentucky Legislature, and was re-elected several times. In 1817 he was elected to Congress and served four years, and declined re-election in 1822, but became a candidate and was elected to the Legislature of Kentucky and became speaker of the House. One might think it strange that a man would decline a re-election to Congress and become a candidate for the Legislature; but it must be remembered that at that time Kentucky was passing through the greatest crisis in her history, and that all the greatest men were members of the Legislature, or were the advisors of those who were members; when the State had two courts of appeals, with some circuit judges obeying the mandates of one of these courts, and some, of the other, a greater crisis than the Civil War or the killing of Goebel. In January, 1823, Richard C. Anderson was appointed Minister to the Republic of Columbia in South America, where, in 1824, he negotiated the first treaty between the United States and Columbia which was ratified by the United States Senate in 1825. At this time his wife died and he returned to the United States and placed his two children, a girl and a boy, in school and returned to Bogota. He remained here until July, 1826. His brother, Capt. Robert Anderson, returned with him. In 1826 he was directed by President Adams to join Mr. Sergent, both of whom had been appointed Ministers Extraordinary and Plenepotentiaries to attend a Congress of Central and South American states. On his way to Carthagena to meet Mr. Sergent and take shipping for Panama, he was taken sick at a village, Turbaco, twelve miles out, and after a few days illness he died on July, 1826.

In January, 1827, the Kentucky Legislature erected a new county. The great successes and the eloquence of Richard C. Anderson were still house-talk in Kentucky, and to do him honor and to perpetuate his name to all Kentuckians, the Legislature named the new county Anderson, for Richard Clough Anderson, Jr. He was thirty-eight years of age when he died.

Lewis Collins, in his History of Kentucky, in speaking of Richard C. Anderson, said: "His death alone, in all probability, prevented his reaching the highest office in the Union," and also stated that "while in private life he was without a vice, in his public career he was equally without a reproach."

Col. Anthony Crockett was born in Prince Edward County, Va., where he resided during the Revolutionary War, in which he saw active service. History records that he was in fifty-seven battles during the war. He died at his home in Franklin County in 1838, and was buried in the church yard of the old Franklin church near Bridgeport. In 1916 what was left of him, consisting of some dirt and the sole of one shoe, was removed by the D. A. R. to the D. A. R. lot in the cemetery at Frankfort, Kentucky. In 1790, at the age of thirty-four, Col. Crockett married Margaret Robertson, sister of Alexander Robertson, who was the father of Chief Justice George Robertson, one of Kentucky's greatest lawyers. His daughter, Elizabeth Crockett, was married to John McKee, December 12, 1812. John McKee, Elizabeth's husband, was born in Rockbridge County, Va., October, 1787, and was brought to Kentucky by his father, Robert McKee, in 1790, and died February, 1875.

John McKee and Elizabeth Crockett McKee were the parents of J. H. D. McKee, who died in Anderson County, July 8, 1889.

WILLIAM B. WALLACE

William B. Wallace came to Kentucky from Augusta County, Virginia, at a very early date, and before Anderson County was erected. His wife's name, as shown by deeds, was Barbara, but what her name before marriage was there is no proof. He was a member of the first Board of Trustees of Lawrence (burg) when the town was incorporated by Act of the Legislature in 1818. He was a large real estate owner, owning some of the most valuable houses and lots in the town. He owned the house and lots where the Christian church and parsonage now stand, having purchased it from Joseph Benham of Louisville. Wallace died less than a month after he became owner of this house. By his will he gave it to trustees for his daughter, Eliza Dedman, wife of Dr. Dixon G. Dedman. She, with her husband and children, occupied it until her death. Dr. Dedman continued to occupy it until his death in 1850. Wm. B. Wallace died on the 21st of June, 1833, and was buried in a country graveyard on the farm he sold to Thomas Phillips. He presumably died from cholera, since that disease appeared that year on the 30th of May and continued until the 1st of August, and Wallace, as shown by his purchase of the Burnham house, and his mortgage of it (mortgage, Deed book B) to secure a part of the purchase money, was continuing in active business. In Order book B in the Anderson Circuit Court appears the following: September 16th, 1833; Dixon G. Dedman produced in court this day, a certificate from the Secretary of the Treasury Department of the United States, showing that Wm. B. Wallace, of Lawrenceburg, Anderson County, Ky., was a Lieutenant of Artillery in the Revolutionary War, and entitled to a pension. The said Dixon G. Dedman then proved in court that the said Wm. B. Wallace departed this life on June 21, 1833, leaving no widow but the following legitimate children: Fannie Hudgins, wife of John F. Hudgins; Eliza Dedman, wife of Dixon G. Dedman; William B. Wallace; Ann Daviess, wife of John T. Daviess, and James B. Wallace, all above the age of twenty-one years, which proof being satisfactory to the court, it is ordered that the same be certified.

The children of Dixon G. Dedman and his first wife, Eliza Wallace, were, William Wallace Dedman, Henry Nathan Dedman, James Gustavus Dedman and Ann Davis Dedman. Dr. Dedman's second wife was Mrs. Mary McBrayer Sea, daughter of Andrew McBrayer, and sister of the late Judge W. H. McBrayer. Their son, the late Charles M. Dedman, a druggist and representative citizen of Harrodsburg, Ky., died in 1917. Mrs. Dedman (the widow Sea), owned the Parker farm formerly owned by Judge McBrayer, and now a part of the W. T. Bond farm. Mrs. Sea-Dedman was the mother of Andrew and R. W. Sea.

[A double log cabin was built on the Parker farm about the year 1818. This was later added to and weatherboarded. In 1934, the old weatherboarding was torn away, the logs numbered and moved by B. R. Bond on the Harrodsburg road, a mile south of Lawrenceburg, and erected as in the early days of its construction. There was not a nail in the original structure, wooden pegs were used throughout the cabin. The same stone was used in the reconstruction of the chimney, the broad hearth and wide fireplace.—L. K. B.]

ANTHONY BOND

The subject of this sketch was the son of William Bond, Revolutionary soldier, and his first wife, Frances Ballou. He was born in 1782 and died in 1847. He was an early settler who took active part in molding Anderson County history. He was married to Jane Boggess in 1805. There were thirteen children born to this union, nine boys and four girls. Four of the boys bore the names of Henry Harrison Bond, Andrew Jackson Bond, George Washington Bond and Benjamin Franklin Bond. This family record is in the old family Bible in the possession of Anthony Bond's grandson, James W. Bond, at Sinai, Anderson County.

JORDON H. WALKER

On June 4, 1827, Jordon H. Walker was appointed deputy sheriff by John F. Blackwell, sheriff of Anderson County, and from this date until the day of his death, he held some office in the county, which was over a period of thirty-five years. He was deputy of John Walker, who was sheriff of Franklin County in 1824, and it had been commonly said that he tied the rope around Beauchamp's neck on the 7th of July, 1827, when he was hung for the murder of Soloman P. Sharp, who was assassinated in November, 1826. In May, 1833, when Nelson C. Johnson, clerk of the county court died, Jordon H. Walker was elected clerk pro tem. In May, 1844, he renewed his bond as county clerk and continued in this office until the resignation of Judge W. H. McBrayer, who was the first county judge, when he became McBrayer's successor, and was elected to the office in 1851, and again in 1858. He died in office in 1862.

It may be mentioned here that Order Book D was destroyed by fire with the court house in 1859, and in the new book D there is a blank from page 91 to 250.

SHERIDAN HAWKINS

Sheridan Hawkins lived on a level of the top of the cliff on the opposite side of Gilbert's Creek above the residence and distillery of M. S. Bond, later the Wiley Searcy distillery, "Old Joe." Names of his sons were Granville Bourbon, Eromulus Remus, Ferdinand Erastus, Ballard DeWilton, Onecrinus DeKalb; his daughters were named Alvi Revi, Florella Hervie, and Auterior Rosaline. Mr. Hawkins was a highly respected citizen, recognized for his true worth and left many descendants, in fact they are among the prominent families of the county.

WILSONS AND RIPYS

From the years 1850 to 1860, a number of aliens from Ireland and one from Prussia, took the oath of allegiance to the United States, and were invested with the privileges of natural-born citizens of Anderson County. The children and grandchildren of some of these early settlers are recognized as most exemplary and valued citizens of the community today. In Order Book "B" Anderson County Court appears the following: This day Henry

Wilson, Jr., an alien and free white person showed that he had on the 2nd of May, 1856, in court made the necessary declaration of his intention to become a citizen of the United States, and having declared on oath that he will support the Constitution of the United States, that he doth absolutely and entirely renounce and adjure all allegience and fidelity to any foreign prince, potentate state or sovereignty whatsoever, particularly Victoria, Queen of Great Britain and Ireland, where he was before a citizen or subject, and having produced to the court satisfactory evidence of his having resided in the United States five years at least, and in this state one year at least, and that during that time he has behaved as a man of good moral character, attached to the principles of the Constitution of the United States and well disposed to the good order and happiness of the same; whereupon the said Henry Wilson, Jr., is hereby admitted and declared to be a citizen of the United States.

On November 13, 1850, the following record appears in Order Book "B:" On motion of John Ripy, who personally appeared in open court and exhibited satisfactory proof that he came to the United States when he was under eighteen years of age and that he is now twenty-seven years old and has been residing in the state of Kentucky ten years and in Anderson County nine years, and upon the oath of Randall Walker and Wm. W. Penny proved that he had resided in Anderson County five years, and having declared on oath that it was bona fide his intention to become a citizen of the United States, and that he has forever renounced all allegiance to any foreign prince, potentate, state or sovereignty whatever, particularly Victoria, Queen of Great Britain and Ireland, and having further applied to be a citizen of the United States, and taking the oath to support the Constitution of the U. S. and to be true and faithful to the Commonwealth of Kentucky so long as he shall be a citizen thereof, and having taken again the oath of renunciation aforesaid, it is now ordered that he be a citizen of the United States, all of which is ordered to be certified.

Signed, M. D. McHenry, Judge.

Other citizens subscribing to the oath in Anderson County were, Henry Koch, Patrick O'Connell, Moritz Flexner, Hugh Dougherty, James Oakley, Daniel Parks, James Beywood, and Morris Vale.

CHAPTER VIII

SHERIFFS OF ANDERSON COUNTY

February 5, 1827, John F. Blackwell; Sandford McBrayer and Jordon Walker, deputy sheriffs.
February, 1929, Jesse Guess; Jordon Walker, deputy sheriff.
January, 1831, James McBrayer; Jordon Walker, deputy sheriff.
January, 1833, John Wash; Jordon Walker and Randall Walker, deputies.
January, 1835, Andrew McBrayer; Randall Walker and Thos. Coombs, deputies.
January, 1837, John Busey; Randall Walker and Lewis Walker, deputies.
January, 1839, Christopher Lillard; Silas Myers and Randall Walker, deputies.
January, 1841, Reuben Boston; Randall Walker and Lewis Walker, deputies.
January, 1843, Thompson Thomas; Lewis Walker and John Walker, deputies.
January, 1845, John Morgan; John Baker, deputy sheriff.
Last order in Book B. Order Book C lost.
September 12, 1853, I C. Oliver, sheriff; S. R. Franklin, deputy sheriff.
February, 1860, J. M. Hanks; L. W. Chambers, deputy sheriff.
January, 1863, R. M. Kerchival; B. L. Boston and L. J. Witherspoon, deputies.
January, 1867, Martin V. Gudgel. Resigned February, 1868, J. G. Hawkins.
January, 1868, Pleasant H. Oliver.
January, 1870, John Colter; 1872, Ambrose Portwood, resigned 1874.
R. H. Crossfield appointed to fill unexpired term.
July, 1875, James Stinnett; resigned in November, W. S. Morgan.
December, 1876 to 1878, M. M. Crossfield.
January, 1881 to 1882, R. H. Crossfield. December, 1884 to 1886, J. W. Baxter.
December, 1888 to 1890, H. B. Carpenter; 1892 to 1894, I. C. Oliver.
December, 1897 to 1899, W. J. Hyatt.
Later sheriffs were J. R. Paxton, R. S. Collins, Sam Mitchell, Oscar Walker, Oscar Mayes and Tom Jeffries.

ANDERSON COUNTY JAILERS

1827 to 1833, George Morris.
1833, John Whip. Resigned and John Story appointed; elected in 1837. Story died in office and John Whip appointed to 1840.
(Order Book C lost.)
September, 1854, Bartlett Searcy, elected and died in office.
1855, William Brown. (Blank in Order Book D until 1859.)
1860, S. H. Crane, elected and died in office.
1860, H. H. Maddox.
1862, Lemuel Hammond, was elected and removed (incapacity) in 1864.
1864, George S. Hammonds appointed, and the same year Lemuel Hammonds reinstated. May, 1865, Lemuel Hammond having been convicted of a

110 HISTORY OF ANDERSON COUNTY

felony, and sentenced to the penitentiary for a year, vacated his office; having been reprieved is hereby appointed jailer until next regular election.
1866, Wade Dawson; resigned in 1868. George Bain appointed.
1870, H. H. Maddox, elected jailer and died in office March 10, 1875.
1875 to 1878, E. W. Mitchell.
1878, Henry Wilson elected and died in 1880.
1880, W. J. Bickers to 1886.
1886, L. Kinkton. August, 1890, C. J. Klem. 1894, L. Kinkton; resigned in 1897.
1897, L. H. Boggess elected and died in 1900 and P. H. Farley appointed jailer.
1900 P. H. Farley; resigned and W. J. Hyatt appointed.
1901, W. A. Sparrow elected; 1905, C. L. Scearce; 1909, J. W. Siers.
Others following as jailer were John Cottrell, Smith Lancaster, Hardin Baxter and J. D. Thompson, the present jailer.

COMMON SCHOOL COMMISSIONERS

On December 1, 1850, the court ordered that Lemuel W. Chambers and James M. Bell be appointed commissioners to district the county into school districts. September, 1851, and October, 1852, Lemuel W. Chambers, School Commissioner, made settlement and applied for term of two years. October 1, 1859, Gustavus Dedman was Commissioner of common schools, allowed salary of $100. In 1862-'63, J. M. Posey was Commissioner, and paid out at this time amount received from Auditor, $1,191.35. He was allowed $100 salary. October, 1864, William Sherman, Commissioner. In 1866 and '67 Robert Draffen was Commissioner and resigned to become Postmaster. L. W. Chambers elected Commissioner from 1867 to '70, salary $143. 1872 to '74, A. M. Portwood, Commissioner. 1876, F. M. Robinson; 1878, John F. Morgan; 1880 to '84, R. B. Sweeney; 1886, John W. Gudgel; 1890 to '92, John W. Gudgel; 1882 to 1897, W. D. Moore; 1901 to 1905, M. L. Chowning; 1910, J. Will Baxter.

COMMONWEALTH ATTORNEYS

1827, Charles S. Bibb; 1868-'74, J. W. Schooling; 1874-'76, P. B. Thompson, Jr.; 1876-'92, J. S. Morris; 1893-1904, R. Frank Peak; 1904, Charles H. Sandford; 1922, H. B. Kingsolving, Jr.; 1928, Chas. Sandford; 1932, H. B. Kingsolving, Jr.

ASSESSORS

1851, Jas. G. Hawkins; 1862-'66, Allen Wash; 1866-'70, Jas. A. McGuire; 1871-'78, J. E. Paxton; 1879-'85, H. S. Wise; 1885-'89, A. S. Mountjoy; 1890-'94, J. W. Baxter; 1895-'97, W. P. Hammond; 1898-1901, J. L. Crossfield; 1902-1905, J. S. Long; 1906, L. B. Young.

HISTORY OF ANDERSON COUNTY

REPRESENTATIVES OF ANDERSON COUNTY

When Anderson County was a part of Franklin County, it was represented by the following men: 1816, Philip White; 1824, James McBrayer; 1826, David White.

Representatives after the county was erected in 1827: 1828 to 1832, David White; 1829 to 1832, Andrew McBrayer; 1833, Thomas White; 1834, John G. Jordon; 1835, Robert Blackwell; 1836 to 1837, Benj. F. Hickman; 1839 to 1840, John Draffen; 1841 to 1842-'47, Keeling C. Gaines; 1843 to 1850, George W. Kavanaugh; 1844, Robert W. Sea; 1845, Randall Walker; 1848, Edward Sherwood; 1849, Thos. H. Hanks; 1851 and 1853, Alvin Herndon; 1853 and 1855, Thos. Moring; 1855 and 1857, James S. Littlepage; 1857, 1859 Wm. F. Leathers; 1859, 1861, Joseph H. D. McKee; 1861, 1863, Vincent Ash (expelled for "joining Morgan's rebel band"); 1862, 1863, Jno. Draffen, succeeded Vincent Ash; 1863-'65, John L. McGinnis; 1865, 1867, John Draffen; 1869-'71, Dr. Landon Carter; 1871-'73, William F. Bond; 1873-'75, William Neal; 1879, John S. Odell; 1881, Thos. H. Hanks; 1883, John S. Odell; 1885, John H. Crain; 1887, Thos. H. Hanks; 1889, R. H. Crossfield; 1891, Thos. H. Hanks, served two terms; 1895, J. T. Stout; 1897, Wm. H. McKee; 1900, W. P. Cox; 1902, Dr. C. M. Paynter; 1904, M. C. Champion; 1906, Dr. C. M. Paynter; 1908, Wm. E. Dowling; 1910, L. H. Carter; 1912, J. R. Paxton; 1914, B. L. Cox; 1916, Wm. E. Dowling; 1918, H. V. Bell; 1920, B. L. Cox; 1922, Emery L. Frazier; 1924, Wm. E. Duncan; 1926, Jas. Doyle Cox; 1928, Wm. M. Duncan; 1930, B. L. Cox; 1932, Grover C. Springate; 1934, Ollie J. Bowen.

Senators from Anderson County from 1884: L. W. McKee, 1884-'88; Lillard Carter, 1898-1900; Wm. E. Dowling, 1910-1912; H. V. Bell, 1922-1924; E. B. Miller (Mercer County), 1934-1936.

ANDERSON COUNTY CLERKS

February 25, 1827, David White; J. T. Daviess, D. C.

August 27, 1827, to January, 1831, Nelson C. Johnson. (White resigned.)

July, 1833 to 1850, Jordon Walker, Caleb Fenwick, deputy; 1854, J. A. McBrayer; 1862 to 1866, C. W. Matthews; deputies, J. M. Bell, A. W. Wash, Robert Draffen; 1866 to 1870, J. M. Posey; deputies, W. E. Bell, John F. Wills; 1874 to 1878, Francis M. Robinson; 1882 to 1894, P. H. Thomas; 1897 to 1905, Hary Wise; 1909 to 1913, J. H. Crook; 1917 to 1925, Robert Goodlett; William Routt, Clerk today (1936).

Clerks of the Anderson Circuit Court from 1874 to 1889, W. E. Bell; 1889 Bell resigned and J. A. McGuire appointed; 1890 to 1891, W. C. Brown; 1891 to 1905, G. W. Walker; 1905 to 1909, J. Walker Crossfield. Others were W. R. Johnson and John Graham Bond; 1924 Miss Loulie Walker was appointed Circuit Clerk.

CORONERS OF ANDERSON COUNTY

February 5, 1827, Ephraim Lillard, commissioned Coroner by the Governor (Joseph Desha), but refused to accept. Everard White appointed and resigned October 1; December 3, 1827, Webb Harris appointed. December 12, 1831, John B. White appointed; 1836 to 1842, Jeremiah Mizner; 1842, Allen Rowland; 1853 to 1854, Samuel Coke; 1854 to 1862, R. H. Paxton; 1862 to 1864, Y. C. Atkins, elected and resigned and in 1864 Thomas Freeman appointed; 1866 to 1870, Joshua Hardy; 1874 to 1875, C. H. Johnson elected and resigned; 1875 to '78, John Whitehouse; 1878 to '79, Joseph Simpson; 1879 to '83, W. A. Hungate; 1891, J. P. Morton; 1894, J. B. Oliver; 1897, C. M. Paynter; 1901, G. D. Lillard; 1910, E. M. Leathers.

SURVEYORS OF ANDERSON COUNTY

Surveyors of Anderson County were: April 2, 1827, Lewis J. Witherspoon; April, 1828, Basil O. Carlisle: Wm. Vanarsdall and Lewis Madison, deputies; August, 1831, Lewis Madison, Surveyor; 1832, Joshua McMichael; 1833 to 1836, Joshua Routt; 1836 to 1854, James M. Bell; 1861 to 1862, W. E. Bell; 1863 to 1866, A. W. Wash; 1870 to 1874, F. M. Hanks; 1878, A. W. Wash; 1882 to 1886, John J. Gregory; 1894 to 1901, T. J. Leathers.

EARLY ATTORNEYS

Early Attorneys at Law were: 1827, Lewis Sanders, Nelson Cole Johnson, Chas. S. Bibb, Washington Dorrell, John Stutt Greathouse, Preston Samuel Longbourough, Thomas Triplett, and William Bailey. In 1828, Wm. K. Vanarsdall, Crawford W. Hall and Frederic Augustus Olds qualified. In 1829, Charles F. Marshall. In 1830, Basil O. Carlisle and Caleb Fenwick admitted to practice. In 1831, Nimrod E. Martin. In 1832, John Draffen qualified. In 1833, William Agin and Victor Monroe. In 1838, William Payne. In 1840, Keeling C. Gaines and John W. Huett. In 1873, W. E. Bell. In 1880, W. H. Posey. In 1882, F. R. Feland and Wilkes Morgan.

COUNTY ATTORNEYS OF ANDERSON COUNTY

September 3, 1827, David White appointed County Clerk, salary $50 per year.

December, 1827, David White resigned; John S. Greathouse appointed Attorney.

November, 1828, Wm. K. Vanarsdall; June, 1829, Charles F. Marshall; April, 1830, Basil O. Carlisle; November, 1832, John Draffen (salary $80); November, 1835, John Draffen. He served until 1843, salary increased to $100; December, 1845, Jomes D. Harland; 1847-'8, John Draffen appointed; 1849-'54, W. W. Penney. Blank in Order Book D from page 91 to 250; 1865, Thomas H. Hanks; August, 1866, John I. Felix, salary $175; 1871, John F. Wills, County Attorney, sued for more salary, won his suit and the court allowed him $300 salary; 1874, John Draffen elected; 1878, George Cohen, County Attorney; 1886, Wilkes Morgan; 1890, W. H. McKee; January, 1895 to December, 1905, Wilkes Morgan, salary $450; January, 1910, George Williams; October, 1910, F. R. Feland in absence of Geo. Williams; November, 1911 to 1917, Frank L. Ripy.

On June 9, 1851, W. W. Penney was the first County Attorney elected. Prior to that time the county attorneys were appointed.

CONSTABLES

Constables in Lawrenceburg from February, 1827, to December, 1830, were: James Hackley, James J. Morgan, Joshua W. McMichael, Randall Walker, James Twyman, Richard D. Phillips, James M. Hawkins, Samuel Lawrence, John G. Holman, John M. Pulliam and Andrew Gudgel.

ANDERSON COUNTY JUDGES

June 9, 1851, William H. McBrayer, qualified first County Judge. Resigned; 1856-'58, Jordon H. Walker. Salary $175; 1862, J. H. Hickman. Salary allowed, $204.50; 1865, J. H. Hickman, resigned; 1865, G. W. Catlett elected by majority of magistrates over James M. Bell; 1866, James M. Bell, salary $225; 1868, James M. Bell, resigned; 1868, Wade H. Morgan; 1870, Isaac C. Oliver; 1874, James M. Posey; 1878, J. M. Posey; 1882, Lewis W. McKee; 1885, L. W. McKee, resigned, elected to Kentucky State Senate; 1885, R. H. Crossfield; 1886, C. M. Lillard; 1890, J. M. Posey; 1893, J. M. Posey. Resigned, appointed Stamp Deputy; 1893, E. H. Brown; 1895, John I. Felix, served three terms; 1901, J. S. Odell; 1904, J. B. Shely; 1905, Judge's salary fixed at $600; 1909, Wilkes H. Morgan; 1913, J. S. Odell; 1917 to 1925, Powell Taylor; 1926, John T. Cox.

BOOK II

LYDIA KENNEDY BOND

Anderson County History

By

Lydia Kennedy Bond

By research and interview it has been my privilege to supplement and bring Major L. W. McKee's History of Anderson County down to date. I wish to acknowledge with gratitude the following who have helped me place in durable form some of the events in the succeeding pages: J. M. B. Birdwhistle, W. G. Eldred, Ezra Sparrow, H. S. Milton, Morton Green, W. E. Dowling, Mrs. Morris Case, Mrs. Leslie Sale, Mrs. Nannie Nichols, Mrs. J. C. Cantrill, and Judge F. R. Feland and Mr. R. E. Garrison for the use of the Anderson News files.

My contribution to Major McKee's valuable history is dedicated to the present and future sons and daughters of the courageous pioneers who settled and formed Anderson County.

—Lydia K. Bond.

November, 1936.

CHAPTER I

RESUME OF THE HISTORY OF ANDERSON COUNTY

It is a deplorable fact that much interesting history has been lost by the death of our ancestors who figured in the dawn of the county's early settlement. We search for material that will lift the veil and show us how those folk lived and wrought. In Book 1 of this history, Major McKee made copious citations of many things of value to the annals of Anderson County early history. He gathered material which the present writer has gone over carefully and arranged in the order which seems to have relation to the subject under treatment. Much of the past is secure. In a few more decades our grandchildren will ask, "Who was who, what was what and where, in Anderson County in the early part of the 20th century?" We are anticipating these questions by supplementing the first book with facts that are as historically accurate as possible. Some errors may inadvertently creep in, and it may not be a comprehensive county history but it may assist a future historiographer to elaborate on a fuller account of our place and people.

It is mere conjecture how our first settler came to this neck o' the woods. History records that a great number of emigrants from Maryland and Pennsylvania from 1780 to 1800, who were seeking any part of the west, came by the Ohio river. The principal point of embarkation was Redstone Old Fort, at Brownsville, Pennsylvania. This route was also accessible to Virginia, but, as a rule, pioneers from the latter state came through Cumberland Gap, thence by Braddock's Road to Kentucky. The roads were impracticable for wheeled vehicles, and overland transportation was on pack-horses.

The probability is that Jacob Coffman, with a few household effects, a small stock of supplies, a wife and five children, was a member of a cavalcade of pioneers with cows, hogs, and horses that was led by men and boys on foot, following deer and buffalo trails and seeking new homes in an unbroken forest.

There were no friendly tourist camps on the way to provide food and shelter. Their meager meals were prepared under Heaven's blue canopy, and repose was wrapped in a blanket by a sheltering tree. All Kentucky histories record the privations to which the early settlers were subjected, and we can contribute little to the thrilling word pictures. Suffice it to say, the intrepid backwoodsman from Pennsylvania, Jacob Coffman, "arrived," and in February, 1780, made a clearing, built a cabin and planted the embryonic seed for the future town of Lawrenceburg. The Coffman family neighbored with snakes, hoot-owls, wild turkey, deer, buffalo and painted savages. At this time, "Kentucky was in her primeval beauty; the hand of man had not been laid upon her forests, nor the wild grandeur of nature succeeded by the arts of a civilized people." While our first settlers were wresting Kentucky from the Indians from 1774 to 1784, and protecting the Old Dominion from more savage hordes, the Colonists were fighting and defeating the British and Indians along the Atlantic seaboard. Verily our pioneers were filled with the spirit of adventure and devoid of fear. When Jacob Coffman indicated that he was going to "stay put," the Virginia Legislature allowed him a pre-emption right to another thousand acres adjoining the 400 he first acquired. In six months time he owned 1,400 acres, and this embraced the entire boundary of Lawrenceburg. (See drawing of division of the Coffman land). Coffman lived only twelve years to enjoy these possessions as he was killed by the Indians in 1792, the year Kentucky was admitted into the Union.

Collins' History of Kentucky says he was the last of three or four victims of savage treachery in Anderson (then Mercer) County. Other undaunted pioneers were coming across the mountains of Virginia conquering the virgin soil with primitive tools, building schools and churches, and savage war dances and massacres were superceded by good will and thrift. Today we are the descendants of those sturdy builders who trained their large families to industry and morality. The mills of the gods grind slowly and generation after generation "pass into the shadows," and we pause to wonder if the old days before the present feverishness didn't produce a sturdier civilization than we'll pass on to our posterity. A small voice whispers, "Do justly, love mercy and walk humbly with thy God."

"The air for the wing of the sparrow, the bush for the robin and wren;
But always the path that is narrow and straight for the children of men."

In 1822, in an almanac published by William Worsley, in Lexington, Ky., Lawrenceburg was given a population of seventy-one. At that time there were 109 towns in Kentucky and sixty-seven counties. Lexington was the largest town with 5,279 population; Louisville next with 4,012, and Frankfort had 1,669. When Anderson County was erected in 1827, it was the 82nd county formed in the state and its population was about 4,000. It is interesting to note that the present site of Lawrenceburg has been in five counties, counting Kentucky County, which was established when the Virginia Legislature passed an Act on December 31, 1776, erecting Kentucky County, which embraced the present state. When our first settler, Jacob Coffman, came in 1780, Kentucky County had been divided into three counties: Jefferson, Fayette and Lincoln. Then Coffman's Settlement was in Lincoln County. In 1792 when Kentucky was admitted into the Union, she had nine counties, the three mentioned, and Mercer, Madison, Mason, Bourbon, Nelson and Woodford. In that carving Lawrenceburg was placed in Mercer. In 1794 Franklin County was formed out of Mercer, Woodford and Shelby and Lawrenceburg found herself in Franklin and here she remained for thirty-three years. History tells us that some counties were not generous in the partition of territory. 1798 was the banner year for the creation of new counties, as thirteen were formed that year. In 1827, when Anderson was erected out of parts of Mercer, Franklin and Washington, Joseph Desha was the seventh Governor of Kentucky. This was the last slice taken from Franklin. The boundary line of Anderson has been changed once and we got another sliver out of Mercer. Today the county embraces 200 square miles, and the assessed value of its property is $4,128,249.

LAWRENCEBURG TODAY

Lawrenceburg lies at the cross roads of the nation. Down Main street comes the Taft Highway (once a deer trail), starting at the northern point of Michigan and continuing to the southern tip of Florida to Key West, the last ravellings of that state. Route 62, which unites the Atlantic and Pacific, comes into town along Woodford street, turns south on Main and west again at Broadway. The Midland Trail from Cumberland Gap to Louisville, is straight through the town. License plates from every state are daily seen as the touring cars pass through, many of them stopping. Over the Tyrone bridge will one day be routed the air course from Lexington to Louisville.

The town itself presents an inviting appearance to the stranger. Main street is as clean, neat and presentable as any principal street of any town in the state. From whatever direction Lawrenceburg is approached, no slums or unkempt buildings are encountered.

The public works administration has been busy the past year with projects which have immeasurably improved the streets. West Woodford has been paved with rock asphalt and concrete gutters and curbing built from Main street to the city limits. Broadway has had the same treatment, and Main street, south of the business section, is now undergoing these repairs. The water mains have been cleaned, new dams built along Salt river to insure an adequate water supply, and plans are on foot for the erection of a new brick school building in "The Grove" for the colored school children.

Lawrenceburg without any "boom" methods, has enjoyed a steady and healthy growth. Houses are generally in demand, seldom a vacant one in town and building is constantly going forward. No town of the same size in Kentucky has more beautiful homes.

Most of the recent building has gone out Broadway, which is now built up almost solid to the city limits. The population of the town has remained at about two thousand, through good years and bad. Almost one-fourth of the people in Anderson County live in Lawrenceburg. This is not excessive and shows a well-settled country side. Through the years of depression, which began at the close of 1929, and has not entirely abated, Lawrenceburg has suffered in silence and without any financial catastrophies. The two banks have never closed their doors or been subject to reorganization in the interest of the depositors. There has never been any wild wave of speculation in the county.

The merchants of Lawrenceburg are rated as the best of credit risks by the commercial agencies. Main street is solidly occupied from Ballard's corner to Court street, with several stores overflowing to the south. Five butcher shops, eight drygoods and department stores and a half-dozen groceries assure a service which supplies every want. The Kroger Grocery Co. and The A. and P. Co. both have branches in Lawrenceburg. Compton's Food Market supplies and combines all services. R. C. Trent & Co., managed by Raymond C. Trent (who is the oldest merchant born and reared in Lawrenceburg), is one of the oldest department stores in town, having been established by C. C. Trent more than a half century ago, and is stocked with a merchandise which could not be bettered in cities the size of Lexington. The Louisville store, the Lincoln store and the Rozen emporium offer ranges of value and prices which satisfy the most discriminating.

The firm of J. W. Shouse & Co. has enjoyed a large patronage since 1892. White's Bargain Center, C. A. Routt & Son and The Fashion Shop, lately acquired by Miss Ada Corn and Mrs. Bruce Crook, all handle special lines of ready-to-wear clothing. Lloyd's Hotel, operated by Connie Lloyd, and the Lawrenceburg Hotel by Archie Moore, offer the weary traveler rest and refreshment.

Lawrenceburg is well provided with restaurants. Taylor Bros., Dick's Place, Warren's and Paul's serve everything from soft drinks to a complete meal. Four beauty parlors for women and four barber shops for men are indisputable evidence that her women are not neglecting their charms and her men are not unmindful of their appearance. Ballard's Drug Store, founded by the late T. J. Ballard, is one of Lawrenceburg's institutions and is now under the management of "Speed" Woods. Jas. L. Hughes operates the drug store formerly owned by the late Park Smith. Brunk Brothers, jewelers, have been in Lawrenceburg almost from the beginning of the century. Newberry's Five and Ten Cent Store has a branch in Lawrenceburg. Squire Gordon is the only mortician in Lawrenceburg. Connie Lloyd has recently opened a furniture store under the management of Hiram Marrs. An automobile accessory store and radio store have both opened this autumn of 1936. Lyle Bond, on Court street, sells labor saving machines for the household. R. H. Marrs & Co, and Vanarsdall's Hardware Store, handle seeds and farm implements, under the management respectively of John Ed. Sweeney and Major McBrayer. The Anderson News, owned and published by R. E. Garrison, with Frank Swift as editor, details all the news of the town and county once every week. Carter's Furniture Store handles furniture and fixtures for the home. Six garages offer every facility for repairs and some display the lower priced lines of new cars. The Standard Oil Company operates a service station under the management of Tom Renfro, Robert Hanks and Jasper Martin.

C. D. Lyen operates a hardware store and offers plumbing service. For amusement, the Lyric Theatre under the management of Chas. Humston, shows a line of first-run pictures. Mrs. Nell Marrs is the specialist on ladies' hats. The Lawrenceburg Supply Company, owned and managed by Chas. E. McGinnis, sells everything in the way of fuel and building supplies. George Burford handles coal. Wilkes Bond, Mac Crain and H. H. Hobbs, not forgetting Mrs. Harry Carpenter, are the insurance agents. Lawrenceburg also has a wholesale gasoline distributor, the Camp Oil Co., and several large trucking operators.

John T. Cox is County Judge; Ed Jeffries, Sheriff, with Ernest Stinnett as Deputy; Dud Thompson, Jailer; Wm. M. Routt, County Clerk; William E. Dowling, County Attorney; T. C. Ward, County School Superintendent, and Lindsay Baxter, Tax Commissioner with Mrs. Harry Carpenter as Deputy.

Dr. J. L. Toll is Mayor of Lawrenceburg, and O. C. McKay is the City Treasurer. The members of the City Council are: J. M. B. Birdwhistle, J. W. Gaines, J. W. Gilbert, Lister Gaines, J. E. Sweeney and E. W. Ripy. Frank Baxter serves in the capacity of city business manager, having charge of the water works, the street cleaning and oiling and the fire department. Oscar Mayes is Chief of Police, and has an efficient force. At the head of the health work in Anderson County is Dr. Lee Dare, who succeeded the late Dr. S. R. Boggess, who made for himself at this work a national reputation. George Insco, specially educated in the science of agriculture, is the County Farm Agent, and has handled the various programs of the Agricultural Department with efficiency and skill.

The business affairs of the county is handled by the Fiscal Court, composed on the 1st of January, 1936, as follows: First District, Hurd Hawkins; Second District, Joe Young; Third District, Hubert Tinsley; Fourth District, Earldy Champion; Fifth District, Otha Lawrence; Sixth District, Lige Drury.

Lawrenceburg has always been noted for good physicians. The tradition is carried on by Drs. J. L. Toll, J. W. Gilbert, J. B. Lyen, C. A. Overall and R. N. Lawson. Dental surgery is practiced by Drs. T. H. Posey, G. B. Claxon and Robert Hensley.

Western High School, Ezra Sparrow, Principal.

Lawrenceburg is represented in the Legislature by Ollie Bowen, and in the Senate by Edmund Miller, of Salvisa, Ky. Circuit Judge, Charles C. Marshall, holds court here once every four months and oftener if the docket demands it. H. B. Kinsolving, of Shelby County, is Commonwealth Attorney. Mrs. William E. Dowling and Mrs. E. W. Ripy are the newly elected members of the school board, assisting C. E. McGinnis, Ed Brown, Lewis Sherwood and Howard Birdwhistle. The relief work carried on by the National Government is handled in Anderson County from the Danville Area office and is supervised by Mrs. Oneita S. Smith, assisted by J. A. Cooper, Paul York and Mildred Roberts. Mrs. Stanley Johnson has charge of the Old Age Pension distribution.

Miss Lulie Walker is City Tax Collector and Circuit Court Clerk, ably assisted by Mrs. Lizzie Witherspoon.

For the convenience of all planes flying over the town, Lawrenceburg has an airway marker. On the big roof at the fair ground, the name of the town is painted in letters seven feet tall and two feet wide, with huge arrows pointing north and south.

TOWNS IN ANDERSON COUNTY

ALTON, FORMERLY "ROUGH-AND-READY"

More than four score years ago, during the administration of President Tyler (1840-'44), a post office was established four miles north of Lawrenceburg and named "Rough-and-Ready" in compliment to the President who established it. About the year 1880 the name of the town was changed to Alton. In the year 1854 the town of Rough-and-Ready was incorporated with Robert Hollis, Judge, and G. H. Gaines, Marshal. In 1878 the population of Rough-and-Ready was 160. Time was when this little hamlet was very busy and prosperous. It afforded a large hotel run by William Tracy which was widely patronized by the traveling public. Drygoods stores drew customers from Lawrenceburg and the surrounding county. Names associated in the mercantile business of the village were Horace Ragan, James Wilson, Richard Parent, J. B. Catlett, R. K. McClure, G. H. Gaines, John T. Stout, Ed Thomas and others. Alton has always had good teachers in her schools. Prof. Isaac McAfee, an educator of note, taught here in the public school for more than thirty years. Miss Mary Fidler, another well known teacher, conducted a school at this place. In years gone by most of the business portion of the town was destroyed by fire, and after the Southern railroad was built about two miles from the place where the station was called "New Alton," the business seemed to drift from the old town and it did not teem with the activities of former days. Alton has always been a religious community. Churches have been within her confines and pulpits filled by ministers of ability. Dr. J. W. Speer, who died a few years ago, was perhaps the only permanent physician who ever lived in the town. He was an esteemed citizen and an Allopathist of ability, and had a wide practice in the county.

Anderson City is a hamlet in the exact center of Anderson County, and on that account was strongly indorsed for the location of the "Seat of Justice" after the formation of the county. At one time this place had some semblance of future growth, as there was a large water-power mill operated here, and other enterprises in business were pending, but a post office was never established and today only a few families remain in the neighborhood, while an old covered bridge has survived the picturesque water mill.

In 1862 a round school house was built in Anderson City according to the plans of a Mr. Crook, who taught, what he termed a blab school, having the pupils seated in a circle, he seated in the center while the children studied aloud. When a voice ceased to hum, Crook would point out the youngster and reprimand him until the intoning of the lesson was resumed.

In the early days two other little towns sprung up in the county and bore the droll names of "Lick Skillet" and "Pinchem." Law abiding and respected citizens lived in these vicinities, but the development of the hamlets was arrested and not much lingers but the names. Judge J. T. Cox vouches for the fact that Lick Skillet got its name when a political rally was held at this point in the county and burgoo was served, but the crowd was underestimated, and a disappointed soup taster said "They ate up all the burgoo and licked the skillet." Another town in the county is Sparrow (formerly Wardsville), named for the number of Sparrow families residing in that section. In fact it has been dubbed the "Sparrow's Nest." Mitchell's store is the chief place of business. Johnsonville, near the Washington County line, is in the western portion of Anderson County. It was incorporated by the General Assembly of Kentucky in 1856, and was named in honor of David Johnson, the pioneer settler, who, about one hundred years ago, built a log house on the site of the residence that was afterwards occupied by his son, W. T. Johnson. Judge Wade H. Morgan, father of Judge Wilkes Morgan, moved to the town in the early '60s and established a large general store which he successfully conducted until a short time before his death in 1893. Mr. J. W. Shouse conducted a store at this point before opening a store in Lawrenceburg in 1890. B. W. Ash kept a grocery and tavern here for several years. Another merchant of Johnsonsville was Lloyd Simpson, who was also a member of the Fiscal Court of Anderson County. The trustees of the town in 1886 were David Johnson, Sr., Lafayette Hughes, B. W. Ash, Judge W. H. Morgan and J. W. Shouse, and James Elder, Police Judge.

VANBUREN

On September 14, 1835, Edward Harris was granted a right to lay out a town on his land at the mouth of Crooked creek on Salt river, and introduced a plat and survey which was ordered filed and recorded. John Busey, John Morgan, Thomas Harris and Bryce Ray were appointed trustees. Harris executed bonds for the deeds, but died before he had a chance to make the deeds. The town was rechartered some years after, with one main street running through the center and three side streets. This town is eighteen miles from Lawrenceburg. It was laid out during the presidency of Martin VanBuren and named for him. In 1878 the population of VanBuren was seventy. Today the little village has a population of fifty-eight. The lure of the larger towns and cities has a tendency to depopulate the smaller hamlets. Ashby & Co., in business for forty years in VanBuren, is the only old-time country store in the entire county. A small grocery store, two blacksmith shops, Dadisman's truck line and the VanBuren bank constitute the other business enterprises of the place. C. F. Adkins, son of Rev. B. F. Adkins, is cashier of the bank.

GLENSBOROUGH

From the time this hamlet was settled until about 1880, it was known as Camden or Camdenville. After the establishment of the post office, the name was changed to Orr, in honor of an early settler. In 1904 the name of the place and post office was changed to Glensborough. In 1847 there were only three residences in the place, occupied by Elijah Orr, Brook Miller, and Mrs. Edith Harris, with her sons, John, Nat and Green. Other families residing near here were W. A. Stephens, John Sherwood, James Minor, the Moores, Browns, Jewels and others. All the early settlers lived in log cabins, which was no reflection on their thrift for that was the style of architecture in that period.

Dr. J. C. Gibbs laid claim to having built the first frame house between Lawrenceburg and VanBuren, for which the lumber was sawed by hand. This house was still standing in 1910. The early settlers were quick to appreciate the power supplied by nature by the waters of Salt river, and a mill was one o fthe first public enterprises promoted and erected at Camdenville. The first mill was operated by an undershot wheel, and the water supply was so abundant that grinding could be continued almost throughout the entire year. In 1853, the Christian church was erected and the first officers were W. A. Stephens, R. J. Milton, Silas Jones, and Elijah Orr. Later a school house was built by popular subscription and one of the first teachers was Fountain Crook. Glensborough points with pride to the fact that Champ Clark, represented in the Congress of the United States from Missouri, was a teacher in this little town in the early '70s. His school was near the old covered bridge which was erected over Salt river in 1855. This structure was 140 feet long and cost $5,000. In 1868 a carding factory was erected by Thomas Montgomery and operated by himself and heirs until 1892 when it was acquired by the Franklin brothers. In 1893 this building was razed and the Glensborough Bank built on the site. In 1883 the Baptist church was built by W. H. Bell, B. F. Franklin, Warren Peters and others. A roller mill was built in 1896 by Franklin Bros. The Farmers Bank began business in February, 1904, with a capital stock of $15,000. Dr. O. L. Townsend, President; W. L. Franklin, Cashier. Other prominent citizens of the town were T. N. Calvert, who ran a large drygoods store; Dr. J. C. Gibbs, who hung out his shingle in 1847, and Simpson and Elder, who ran a large milling industry near the confines of the town. The population of "Camdenville" in 1878 was seventy-five, according to Collins' History of Kentucky published that year.

TYRONE

"In 1847, where the little town of Tyrone now stands was a dense forest extending from Shryock's Ferry to the present site of the railroad bridge, and over a half mile in width. There were only three houses in all this wilderness, two of which stood back on the hill quite a distance from the river, one of which was occupied by John Cobb, the other by Robert Woolridge. Near the site of the present post office stood a lone cabin of the Daniel Boone type, of round logs, mud chinks, stick and clay chimney, board roof held down by poles. Such was the beginning of the little hamlet nestling among the beautiful Kentucky river hills. In 1868, and prior to that time, Tyrone was a wayside landing called "Streamville" by the steamboat men. In 1857 the first mile of pike, which is now Main street leading to Lawrenceburg, was built by Martin and Utterback, the whole road being finished next year just before the completion of the road leading to Versailles. In 1868 the first distillery was built in the town by S. P. Martin, and after a few years passed into the hands of Walker, Martin & Co., and was capable of mashing 110 bushels of grain daily, which was a large enterprise for that day and time. A few years later when T. B. Ripy became the sole owner of this plant, it was enlarged and the capacity of the house was raised to the mashing of 4,000 bushels of grain a day, and was the largest "mash tub" distillery in the world. An average of 125 workmen in the various departments were employed, nearly all of whom were residents of the little village of Tyrone. In 1879 the town was incorporated with T. B. Ripy, S. P. Martin, J. T. Coke, G. M. Walker, W. M. Edmonson and H. M. Carter as trustees, N. T. Watson as Police Judge, J. A. Wash, attorney, and John W. Wash as marshal.

"In 1885 the voting precinct was established. In 1880 the first public school was established in the town, Judge Martin building the school house gratis. Later, under contract, he built another which had a capacity of 200 pupils, and was opened in 1906 as a graded school, with the following board: J. J. Lancaster, W. P. Frazier, W. T. Patterson, L. R. Carter and C. C. Toll.

"In 1882 the post office was established and J. T. Coke appointed postmaster. In 1880 S. P. Martin, J. M. Scearce and T. B. Ripy built the Methodist church. This was later destroyed by fire, but later rebuilt. In 1890 J. N. Butts, R. S. Taylor and W. M. Carr and others built the Christian church. In the '90s Tyrone had a population of 600 people, good streets and pavements, splendid water supply, excellent lights, commodious school house, six lodges, two churches, two good Sunday schools, six complete stores, two blacksmith shops, two hotels, two barber shops, one physician, two teachers, bookkeepers, stenographers, etc. About this time Gov. Lillard Carter, a graduate of Vanderbilt University, and a lawyer of superior qualifications, with residence in Lawrenceburg, was attorney for the little town of Tyrone. The village gets its name from Tyrone County in Ireland, and was named for the pioneer Ripys who came here from that county shortly after Anderson was erected from parts of Franklin, Mercer and Washington counties."—Notes from the Souvenir Supplement of the Anderson News of 1906.

SINAI AND SHILOH

To the uninitiated, Sinai and Shiloh may be thought to be two separate places or localities. The post office has always been Sinai; the church, Shiloh. The first location of the post office was at what is now Ed. Baxter's place. Matt Wash was the first postmaster and Matt Crossfield was the first carrier. The office was next moved to Cal Dewitt's store, but on the securing of a rural route, it was again moved to the building of Robert Sallee's place. Miss Mamie Forsham became postmistress at this time. The next move was down opposite the church with Miss Green Searcy in charge. This arrangement still continues. The Shiloh Christian church was organized at Brown's school house about 1870. The present building was erected about 1906. The Baxters, Tolls, Champions and Washs were among the early members, and descendents of these families are present leaders of this church. The following had their religious training in the Shilo church: Dr. J. L. Toll, Lawrenceburg, Ky.; Dr. C. W. Sweeney, Bohon, Ky.; Dr. H. M. Baxter, Harrodsburg, Ky.; Supt. W. R. Champion, Mt. Vernon, Ky.; Prof. M. C. Brown,

Presbyterian Church.

University of Kentucky, Lexington, Ky.; Prof. Marshall Hahn, University of Kentucky, Lexington, Ky.

Mr. William Mullins, grandfather of Rachel Baxter, who has taught twenty years in the Shiloh community, taught forty years in the same community. Miss Greene Searcy taught for more than twenty years.

In February, 1886, a bill was offered in the Legislature incorporating the town of Dowling in Anderson County. It referred to a space opposite Clifton where Captain John Wills hoped to found a city. The city did not materialize and the town is obsolete today.

The following history of Ripyville is taken from the Souvenir Edition of the Anderson News of 1906, and was written by Rev. Dudley Moore, who was a resident of that town:

"Our little village is situated about four miles south of Lawrenceburg on the Louisville and Crab Orchard turnpike, and while she is small and unpretentious she sits among her sister towns and has a history. In 1830, two brothers, young men at the time, left their home in Tyrone, Ireland, seeking their fortunes in the New World. They were James and John Ripy. James embarked in the grocery business and John in the dry-goods business in Lawrenceburg. In 1855 John Ripy bought the "Bright" farm, where R. E. Thacker now lives, and in connection with John McMichael, engaged in the mercantile business. This partnership continued about two years, during which Mr. Ripy resided in Lawrenceburg and McMichael lived in the storehouse. Our village therefore gets its name from its first merchant, John Ripy. After their dissolution, Mr. McMichael sold goods for several years at the same place. Other merchants who sold goods at this point were James McFadden, D. G. McMichael, E. H. Rice, W. H. Morton, A. H. Boggess, C. W. Sanders and H. H. Houchin. Mr. McFadden came from Clark County, Ky. He was a jolly old bachelor, kind to all, especially children, talked in a loud voice, kept his shirt collar unbuttoned all the time and persisted in going in his shirt sleeves winter and summer. He was a low fleshy old man, wore a beegum hat, and seemed to suffer a great deal with heat. All the older folks remember good old "Uncle" Jimmy McFadden. Among the early industries of the town, two must not be omitted. One, an oldtime bark tannery, operated by George Bright which turned out good leather, no doubt; the other, a cooper shop, conducted by Joseph Hedger, Sr., and his sons, William and Joseph. They made many a barrel, keg and churn, some of which are still in existence. The most important house for entertainment was the tavern, kept by Samuel D. Williams, where H. S. Wise, our County Clerk, now lives, and known as the 'Williams Stand.' Hundreds of people made that their stopping place, and it is said that the pike on each side of the house would often be lined with oldfashioned covered wagons. Religious meetings were held at Salem, on L. W. Routt's place, old Hebron, Salt river and at Abbott's school house. Rev. Laban Jones, the Pennys, Jordon Walker, Dr. R. A. Nelson and others preached at these places. Among the early farmers in the neighborhood were William and Stephen Houchin, William Hunt, Reuben Morton, Joseph and Lewis Abbott, Allen McAllister, Matthew Duncan, John Burford, D. W. Bond, James and John McCall. James McCall was born in Virginia in 1828, and was brought the next year by his father to the place where he lived and died. He was the owner of the Famous spring that still bears his name."

Collins' History of Kentucky, in 1878, gave Ripyville a population of thirty.

FOX CREEK

Fox Creek has been recognized as a thrifty and desirable little hamlet for a century. Some of the most public spirited citizens, who put private interests secondary to local benefit, have lived in this locality, and others have gone out beyond its confines to shed a wholesome influence in other communities. The first merchant in the village was Douglas Zimmerman. The first church was a Primitive Baptist, organized by Rev. John Penny. Other merchants have been Ottenheimer, Melear, Gudgel, Calvert and Crossfield. In 1847 the new Christian church was built to replace the log "meetinghouse" of 1841. This church has a large and substantial membership here today.

In May, 1886, the new post office at Fox Creek was called "Hawkins," and many of the citizens considered it "nonsensical" for the village to wear one name and its post office another. This post office was eventually discontinued.

For more than a quarter of a century R. Calvert & Son conducted a store of general merchandise at Fox Creek. Mr. Calvert was a Confederate soldier and bore himself with bravery and distinction. Some of the splendid farm homes were owned by R. H. Crossfield, R. Calvert, J. R. York, C. K. Crossfield, and Dr. R. L. Milton. Thomas P. Mullins, born 1824, died 1907, owned a substantial farm adjoining the York acres. Other well-to-do citizens occupied pleasant and well-appointed homes around the village and hospitality graced every board and visitors were kindly entertained. In 1906 the estimated value of property of Fox creek was $200,000.

The little town of Mt. Eden, generally supposed to be in Anderson County but is just across the line in Spencer. In 1885 a writer in speaking of the place faceciously observed that "Mt. Eden has 200 inhabitants, three churches, two stores, a mill and a fair amount of intelligence."

ST. CHARLES PARK

St. Charles Park lies on the north of town on the east side of the Southern railroad. This part of Lawrenceburg was developed and lots sold October 10, and 11, 1909. Bond street runs parallel with North Main street, north and south, while Center and Diamond streets run east and west. This new addition was laid off by C. E. Bond in sixty-five building lots, and many neat homes have been erected here. The land was originally owned by Dr. J. A. Witherspoon and was conveyed to C. E. Bond by Clarence A. Witherspoon on December 7, 1904.

The Lillard subdivision of the city of Lawrenceburg, on Broadway, was sold in 1916 by Roger H. Lillard, executor of the will of his father, C. C. Lillard, who died in 1896 at his home on the corner of South Main and Broadway. This handsome home was built by C. E. Bond in 1886, and occupied by him until he sold it to C. C. Lillard in the early '90s. Broadway is one of the most desirable residential streets in Lawrenceburg, and many attractive homes have been built here in the last ten years.

"The Highlands" addition to the town was land formerly owned by W. B. Saffell. This tract was acquired by the Wakefield-Davis Realty Company that laid off lots and sold them on April 17, 1920. "The Highlands" comprise four streets: Saffell Ave., Bond street; Marrs and Johnson streets, which run parallel north and south; Ripy avenue in the rear, runs full length of the other streets east and west. This valuable addition is the highest elevation in the city and affords some very desirable building lots.

In 1886 a Real Estate and Investment Association was formed in Lawrenceburg with George A. Cohen, President; Capt. W. E. Bell, Secretary-Treasurer and Survey for the company. The directors were W. H. Bickers, T. B. Ripy, Isaac Hoffman, J. M. Johnson, John Dowling and C. E. Bond, with capital stock of $25,000. Through this association C. E. Bond bought the farm lying next to town limits on the north and opened up the new suburb called Lanawee. This property was laid off in building lots and Judge F. R. Feland was one of the first to erect a handsome home in this part of town. The spacious home occupied by J. L. Sherwood today was built for G. G. Frazier in 1894.

LAWRENCEBURG CEMETERY

On February 29, 1856, John W. Mizner, administrator of the estate of Spencer Tinsley, conveyed two acres of ground on the northeast corner of the present cemetery to the trustees of the town of Lawrenceburg, Ky., for a cemetery. The deed reads: In consideration of $275 paid me as administrator of Spencer Tinsley, I hereby sell and convey as his administrator to the Board of Trustees of the town of Lawrenceburg, Anderson County, Ky., a certain lot of ground bounded as follows: beginning at a stake 25 feet from the center of the turnpike, thence a parallel line with said road S 24 E 25 poles to a stake 25 feet from the center of said pike, thence S 36 W 10 poles to a stake in Tinsley's field, thence N 24 W 25 poles to a stake in Witherspoon's line, thence N 36 E 10 poles to the beginning, it being the lot of land known as the Lawrenceburg Cemetery. Given under my hand this February 29, 1856. (Signed) John W. Mizner. James A. McBrayer, Clerk A. C. C.

A part of this plot of ground had been used as the Tinsley family grave yard, as two tomb stones show that Spencer Tinsley, born 1798, died 1854; Kathrine Tinsley, his wife, born 1798, died 1855. A great number of old land owners had private burial grounds on their home plots, and a few of the early settlers were buried here as the following dates found on the old stones show: Rev. Howard Williams, born 1795, died 1859. Miss Ann Chambers, 1798-1872. Eliza McBride, 1796-1863. Turner Hanks, 1795-1858; his wife, Nancy, 1801-1864. Dennis Driskell, 1785-1851. Thompson Frazier, 1807-1868. Urias Randall, 1806-1856. Lucrecia Armstrong, 1809-1855. Harrison Hackley, 1815-1858. Joshua Saffell, 1820-1861. After this plot was incorporated for the Lawrenceburg Cemetery in 1856, Mrs. Clark, mother of the Hon. Champ Clark, was the first person buried here, and her grave is marked by the pine tree, which tradition says her husband planted. Today it is one of the handsomest evergreens in the cemetery. After a quarter of a century the old cemetery was enlarged. On June 15, 1880, J. H. D. McKee sold to the Lawrenceburg Cemetery Co. six acres, two rods and thirty-five poles of land lying south and west adjoining the two acres of the Tinsley land for the consideration of $403.12½. J. H. D. McKee and W. F. Bond laid off the lots and planted many of the evergreens that makes this a beautiful City of the Dead. The cemetery was again enlarged in 1933, when a tract of land adjoining was sold by the heirs of the late L. W. McKee to the cemetery company and incorporated in this burial ground.

According to Dr. W. D. Funkhouser, Professor of Anthropology at the University of Kentucky, there are some prehistoric sites in Anderson County. A number of mounds have been inspected that are strewn with interesting artifacts that are now on display at the university, including knives, pipes, highly polished stone and metal celts, and other types of flint. The largest mound is on the Bond's Mill pike, on the farm of Mrs. Agnes F. Laurie. This mound has not as yet been excavated. There are a number of old springs in the county, one called "Treaty Spring" spoken of in old writings. Around these springs are evidences of struggles that took place between early tribes of men and animals.

Anderson National Bank.

CHAPTER II

THE ANDERSON NATIONAL BANK

In the Souvenir Supplement of the Anderson News of 1906 we find the following: "In 1866, at a time when the people were struggling to repair the damages done during the long drawn out War Between the States, when business transactions were such that the centralization of capital was necessary for the promotion of legitimate enterprises, a private bank sprang into existence under the name of J. and J. A. Witherspoon, two of Anderson County's best and wealthiest citizens. With the management in the hands of these financiers, and James A. McBrayer, a man of strong moral character, as cashier, this institution grew and soon became necessary to incorporate as the Anderson County National Bank, with many of the leading business men as stockholders. During the long and successful period that this bank has been in business, it has had as directors such worthy gentlemen and able financiers as William F. Bond, Gabriel H. Gaines, James R. York, Sr., A. C. Witherspoon, Dr. John A. Witherspoon, Dr. J. W. Gilbert, Sr., Dr. O. H. Witherspoon and many others."

The officers today are J. W. Gaines, President; Frank Routt, Vice-President; L. W. McBrayer, Cashier; B. S. Griffy, Assistant Cashier; Misses Mary Searcy and Euith Crossfield, bookkeepers; Miss Aileen Houchin, stenographer. Directors, J. R. York, John W. Dawson, B. S. Griffy, W. B. Morgan, J. W. Gaines, L. W. McBrayer and Frank Routt. Capital stock, $100,000.00; surplus, $50,000.00; deposits, $891,169.68.

THE LAWRENCEBURG NATIONAL BANK

Was organized as a state institution and opened for business on the 2nd of July, 1885, with William F. Bond, President; Christopher C. Lillard, Vice-President, and J. M. Johnson, Cashier. W. F. Bond was President until he retired from all active business pursuits, and when he resigned was succeeded by his son, C. E. Bond, who was President until his death in 1917. C. C. Lillard served as Vice-President until his death in 1896, when he was succeeded by W. B. Saffell. The bank passed through the panic of 1893 with strong resources unimpaired and was able to take care of all its customers and tide them over the hard times. The charter having expired in 1905, the management after careful consideration, reorganized under a national charter, being convinced this is the best system of banking yet devised. In 1906 the bank was managed by the following directors and officials: C. E. Bond, W. B. Saffell, J. W. Rice, T. J. Ballard and A. B. McAfee, Directors; President, C. E. Bond; Vice-President, W. B. Saffell; J. M. Johnson, Cashier; E. V. Johnson, Assistant Cashier, and Joe W. Waterfill and Herbert Crossfield, bookkeepers. At that time the United States Government collected at this point nearly $2,000,000 for internal revenue and this bank was the temporary custodian and handled all this immense fund. Another son of W. F. Bond who organized this bank, W. T. Bond, became President in 1917 after the death of C. E. Bond. In 1926 J. M. Johnson died and his son, Robert E. Johnson, became Cashier of the bank, and resigned after two years to enter the insurance business. In 1927 W. T. Bond resigned as President and became

Chairman of the Board; he was succeeded by J. L. Sherwood as President, who acts in that capacity today, with Ollie C. Calvert as Cashier, J. M. B. Birdwhistle and Dr. S. R. Boggess, Vice-Presidents; William McGurk and Julian Cole bookkeepers. The bank has a capital stock of $125,000.00; surplus fund of $150,000.00, and deposits of $904,360.78. Directors of the bank today are A. B. McAfee, Chairman of the Board; Ollie C. Calvert, J. L. Sherwood, James C. Bond and James Sherwood. After a disasterous fire in 1894 the bank was rebuilt by C. E. Bond as it stands today.

THE LAWRENCEBURG FAIR

Prior to 1872 the Fair Association was known as the Anderson, Franklin and Salvisa Agricultural and Mechanical Association, and for many years had been held in a large woodland a mile south of Salvisa on the state highway.

An old certificate of stock preserved in a scrap book belonging to Mrs. Annie Bond Cole reads as follows: This is to certify that John Wicks Bond has paid me the sum of ten dollars, the first installment of stock in the Anderson, Franklin and Salvisa Agricultural and Mechanical Association. Given under my hand this 19th day of August, 1872. (Signed) W. C. Nelson, Secretary A., F. and S. A. and M. Association.

Later it was recognized as the Lawrenceburg Fair Association and in 1874 a woodland owned by Mr. J. H. D. McKee was rented and an ampitheater built and every thing put into shape for the new adventure, and soon the fair became one of the most substantial and enjoyable institutions of the county. It was a public enterprise and reflected credit on those who worked unceasingly for the good of the community. It was an incentive for the citizens to raise and exhibit fine stock, pure bred poultry, produce from the garden and manufacture from the home, competing for awards given by experienced judges. Some of the finest stock in the state competed for the liberal premiums at the Lawrenceburg fair, while record breaking crowds surged through the gates, and friends, relatives and acquaintances experienced and proffered the old-time hospitality for which Kentucky is proverbial.

In the course of time the old buildings in the rented woodland proved inadequate and were disintegrating and it was deemed advisable for the association to own and improve its own property. Thirty-three acres of land adjoining the McKee woodland was purchased from J. M. Johnson in 1911, and more modern and commodious buildings were erected, and the fair association had an unbroken chain of meetings annually until August, 1929, when it was deemed expedient not to open the gates on account of the serious drouth, as the water supply was too low to be piped to the grounds to quench the thirst of man and beast. Streams were low and all vegetation seared, cutting short the various resources of the county that helped make exhibits for a successful fair. The sprinkling of lawns had been prohibited and for a while the town was on water-rations for a few hours through the day. Among those who worked indefatigably without thought of acclaim for the success of the old fair association were the names of Cole, Moore, Moffitt, McAfee, Johnson, Bond, Dowling, Morgan, Witherspoon, Major, Birdwhistle, Lillard, Marrs, McKee, Thomas, Gaines, Speer, Booth, Crossfield, Sherwood and others. Among those who bred and trained fine horseflesh, and whose names extended beyond the confines of the state were R. H. Lillard, W. D. Mountjoy, J. M. Johnson, Eli Shelburn, McAfee and Cole.

It seemed for a while that the old fashioned fair was to be relegated to the past with the obsolete hitching posts and oil street lamps, for the grounds and all buildings thereon were put up at public auction on February 13, 1931, and the property passed into the hands of Mr. J. L. Sherwood, who was the highest bidder. But, like the sacred bird of Egyptian mythology, the old fair institution arose again young and vigorous, when the property was purchased from Mr. Sherwood by the Anderson County Post of the American Legion, on September 1, 1933. The following August, 1934, the gates were again opened with all the eclat of the old days and a most successful three days meeting was held. The officers were: President, Ben Young; Vice-Presidents, Lester Rucker and Frank Routt; Secretary and Treasurer, William Ripy; Assistant Secretary, Stanley Johnson.

The Anderson Post No. 34 has the co-operation and appreciation of the public in conducting a fair that will prove educational and profitable, and perpetuate the hospitality for which the Lawrenceburg fair has been proverbial for more than sixty years.

GREAT FIRES IN LAWRENCEBURG

The disastrous fire of 1873 has been noted elsewhere in this book, but the heroism of one man should be recorded in connection with that calamity. P. D. Brown was a carpenter and undertaker, who stayed on top of the courthouse while his own dwelling was destroyed. His efforts saved all the priceless records of the town and county from going up in smoke. In 1892 the town suffered another fire which broke out in the city work-house and consumed more than a dozen buildings and a man by the name of King perished in the flames. Since then almost all buildings on Main and Court streets have been burned. Our last destructive fire was in 1898, which started in a livery stable and consumed about twenty buildings including the Christian church which stood where the Feland building is today. Since that time a fire started in a grocery store opposite the depot and burned a number of dwellings and most of the property of the Dowling Cooperage Company. It is said that every fire improved the town, for better and larger buildings and homes were erected than stood on the sites prior to the conflagrations. Fires in town were declared to be "as sure and regular as the seasons," and the Anderson News of February, 1886, denounced the authorities who refused to take any precaution whatsoever, leaving the town helpless and exposed to fire with nothing but insurance companies between it and utter loss. This seemed to awaken the authorities from lethergy, and that year the trustees of the town purchased a "hook and ladder" layout at a cost of $350 for the purpose of fighting fire. A house was built for the fire department on the old jail lot, about where the city hall stands today.

It was claimed that the wells and pumps in town did not furnish adequate water supply for fighting fires, and the house and equipment was sold at a loss. In August, 1894, a fire department was organized and the first equipment was a hand pump. At the regular meeting in October, 1894, Mr. D. E. Hooper addressed the Council upon the practicability of using the Eagle Roller Mills pond as fire protection for the city. In 1905 a hose and ladder wagon was purchased and a team of horses held in readiness at Morgan's livery stable to answer the fire alarm. W. B. Morgan was the first fire chief. The city council meeting of March, 1913, appointed Chairman Hawkins to investigate and buy an auto fire truck, and the report showed that one was purchased from the Lehman Motor Company, of Louisville, for the sum of $2,000. In June, 1922, two thirty-five gallon tanks, mounted on a Ford chasis, was bought for the sum of $2,750. The last fire truck, a Ford V-8, was bought March, 1935. Today the members of the fire company are S. F. Baxter, Matt Utterback, Morris Hoffield, George Gortney, Blakemore McBrayer, Kennedy Parker and Earl Gordon. This is an efficient force and destructive fires have been unknown for more than two decades in Lawrenceburg.

THE LAWRENCEBURG GRADED AND HIGH SCHOOLS

The building of the Lawrenceburg Graded School in 1904 was mentioned in the Souvenir Supplement of the Anderson News in 1906, as follows: "When the old school building would not accommodate the pupils, an agitation was begun for a new building which resulted in an election held in 1903 for the purpose of voting bonds for building purposes. After a short but vigorous canvas, the election resulted in a vote of 161 to 17 in favor of the bond issue. The Board of Trustees then consisted of G. W. Hutcheson, J. P. McWilliams, W. T. Bond, J. T. Ballard, H. B. Carpenter and W. P. Marsh, and they employed Mr. Martin Gertz, an architect from Lexington, to prepare plans, which were adopted; then bonds were issued in the sum of $12,500, bearing interest at 5 per cent to run not less than two nor more than fifteen years. These were sold to the Lawrenceburg Bank and accrued interest. The contract was let to Mr. Charles E. Bond for $12,500. He agreed to take the old building in part payment for $1,000. Immediately after closing the school the following summer of 1904, the old school house was torn down and within four months a splendid two-story brick building with basement and slate roof and heated from furnaces, was completed and ready for use. The tax levy for general purposes was only 30 cents on each $100 worth of property in the district, and an additional levy of 15 cents has been found amply sufficient to take care of the bonds and their interest, and a thousand dollars of the principal has been paid."

Prof. Horace V. Bell was elected first principal of the new graded school, and he served continuously for twenty years. He was recognized as a very successful teacher, and won a reputation as an instructor of teachers institutes. Prof. Bell and his estimable wife, Mrs. Bettie McCall Bell, began teaching in Lawrenceburg September, 1891. For two years they taught a private school, the Anderson Seminary. The graded school was organized in 1893, with eight grades and four teachers: Prof. H. V. Bell, Mrs. Bell, Miss Dovie Burton and Prof. Houchin. Later a two-year high school was added, and when the new building was completed, a four-year high school course was added. Other teachers associated with Prof. Bell throughout his encumbency were Mrs. Lee M. Campbell, Misses Gertrude Crowder, Flora Lillard, Martha Bell, Fay Walker, Zula Holmes, Mattie Adams, Lois Williams, Verna Toll, Mary Searcy, Elvie Bickers, Bessie Flippin, Sarah Marshall, Bess Crain, Etta Calhoun, Ophelia Carr, Olive Tanner. Prof. Dudley Johnson taught drawing and oil painting, and Miss Blandelia Frost was teacher of physical culture.

City School and Gymnasium, Chas. O. Ryan, Superintendent.

Prof. Bell was educated in the schools of the county and a graduate of Georgetown College. Mrs. Bettie McCall Bell, a graduate of old Daughters College, whose halls were proverbial for turning out women of refinement and culture, was a daughter of James McCall, who owned one of the finest old homesteads in Anderson County, and the historic McCall spring, which is perpetuated in Kentucky history. It was a favorite sentiment of Carlisle, the Apostle of Heroism that "when a hardy good stock of humanity once takes root in a land it never dies out, remaining always, sometimes obscured it may be, yet always capable of bearing good and sound fruit." The good seed that Prof. and Mrs. Bell sowed as educators and Christian citizens, greatly enriched the county and they left the imprint of their fine influence and personality upon students and host of friends with whom they came in contact. After resigning from school work, Prof. Bell was editor of the Anderson News for a number of years. He finally retired from active business and he and Mrs. Bell moved to Louisville in 1928, where the latter died in 1935, and her body was brought back to Anderson County, and laid to rest with three generations of her ancestors.

Prof. Charles O. Ryan, the present Superintendent of the City Schools, came to Lawrenceburg in August, 1918, and education has been signally marked under his efficient leadership. On account of the town's growing population, the City High School built in 1904 was not adequate to house the pupils and furnish proper facilities for instruction. The Witherspoon home on North Main street was sold to the County Board of Education in 1925. This property was resold to the City High School Board in 1929 for the sum of $10,750. This spacious old home was remodeled for school purposes and a large gymnasium built in the rear for the sum of $30,000. There is a tract of land that furnishes a football and baseball field for athletics. Drives built through the grounds and all necessary school equipment installed to make this institution a credit to a prosperous town. The indebtedness on the property is fast being liquidated, as Edward Brown, Secretary of the School Board, has been able to pay off the bonds as they fall due.

Members of the faculty of the High School are C. O. Ryan, Superintendent; Edward Adams, Principal; H. S. Milton, Mrs. Morris Case and Mrs. Fannie Bailey, teachers. Teachers of the grades are Miss Zula Holmes, Principal; Misses Rayma Frazier, Daphne Hedden, Loraina Young, Kathrine Moffitt, Virginia Goodlett, Mrs. Frances Trotter and Mrs. Margaret Martin, teachers. Mrs. Reichert Bottom, teacher of music. In passing it is interesting to note that the remodeled home occupied by the graded school today was built in 1829 by Dr. Lewis J. Witherspoon, and four generations of this family have lived in this old brick mansion, whose walls stand today as straight and true as when they were built. Dr. A. H. Witherspoon, who was the last to reside in the ancestral home with his family, was educated at Georgetown College and graduated from the Jefferson Medical College in Philadelphia. In 1894 he was married to Miss Frankie Lillard, whose ancestors were among the first settlers in the county. They have two daughters, Mrs. June Givens and Mrs. Dowling Stewart.

A few years ago there were forty schools in Anderson County, but, with the establishment of Western High School, several of the small schools have consolidated and today there are thirty-four country schools. These have been comfortably built. The number of children in schools in the county are 1,858. At present the County Superintendent is Prof. C. T. Ward, who succeeded Judge J. B. Shely. The four schools which consolidated are

Wardsville, Tanner, Johnsonville and Klondike. This year a much-needed school bus was purchased at a cost of $1,500. This bus will operate in the territory around Western High School and prove a convenience for the children who live at various distances from the school.

Lawrenceburg has a good colored school, with a four years high school course. This year there are eighty elementary pupils enrolled, and thirty in the advanced department of the school. The principal is William Colerain; teachers, William and Mary Coleman.

Old records show that the fall term of the Anderson Seminary opened the first Monday in September, 1887, with Prof. E. A. Cheek, Principal and John Parrent, Assistant. J. M. B. Birdwhistle had been Principal of this Seminary from 1882 until 1887, when he opened a select school in his home called the Birdwhistle Academy. The public school taught by Prof. Joel Lyen and Miss Emma Gilroy, of Lexington, opened in 1887 with eighty in attendance. At the close of the next term this school conducted "an exciting spelling match of one and one-half hours, which was won by Miss Emma Crain." Just at this time the following problem was rampant in the schools: "If a hen and a half lay an egg and a half in a day and a half, how many eggs will six hens lay in seven days?" The answers given ranged from twenty-eight to forty-two.

In September, 1888, a new school, called the Kentucky Normal College and Commercial Institute, housed in new buildings, opened with eight departments, and fifteen professors and instructors. John C. Willis was President. This institution stood on the present site of the Lawrenceburg City High School. J. W. Gaines, President of the Anderson National Bank, was one of the teachers in this college.

KAVANAUGH ACADEMY AND THE ANDERSON COUNTY HIGH SCHOOL

Kavanaugh Academy, organized in 1903 by Mrs. Rhoda C. Kavanaugh, ran successfully until 1909, when the Anderson County High School was put under Mrs. Kavanaugh's supervision, and the merger of these institutions has placed Anderson County in the limelight as an educational center. The members of the first graduating class of the Academy were: Freeman Gilbert, Loena Huffaker, Earl Lindsay, Emma Young and Mollie Whitenack. The faculty, Dr. Wm. C. Lindsay, Ph.D., of Harvard; Miss Lucile Sharp, graduate of Ward-Belmont; Mrs. Rhoda C. Kavanaugh, University of Kentucky. The State Department of Education at the request of the Anderson County Board of Education, located the first County High School at Lawrenceburg in the Kavanaugh building, and the school was officially named the Anderson County High School. The first corps of teachers, Mrs. Kavanaugh, Principal; Miss Lucile Sharp and Judge J. B. Shely.

Training and coaching teachers for county and state certificate examination became a distinct factor in this school, and continued as long as examinations were given for certification of teachers.

The first basketball teams were organized and coached by Miss Susan B. Bond (Rutherford), graduate of Hamilton College, Lexington, Ky., who also taught expression and drawing at the Kavanaugh High School in 1912-13.

These two outstanding teams, the "Green and Gold" and the "Red and White," were the pioneers in Lawrenceburg and Anderson County in central Kentucky. The gym suits for girls at that time were middy blouses and baggy bloomers that buckled below the knee, and were considered quite blase by a few patrons who looked askance at the girls appearing in public thus attired, but only one irate father forbade his daughter indulging in this healthy sport "wearing pants." By and by the sport became more popular and the "pants" more abreviated.

The Kavanaugh boy's basketball teams have been rated among the best in the state, ranking high in the tournament tests, and have been coached by the following men: H. C. Vannatta, graduate of Purdue University, Indiana; Rice Mountjoy, of Centre College, Danville, Ky.; H. H. Chidsey, East Haven, Conn.; Earl Jones, University of Kentucky, and "All Southern Guard," and Forest (Aggie) Sale, graduate of University of Kentucky, and twice "All American." As this school grew in attendance, extra teachers were provided and all educational facilities increased. A few years ago a large and commodious gymnasium was erected on the grounds at a cost of $14,000. Owing to the enthusiasm of the alumnae, the work of the faculty and students and the executive ability of Mrs. Kavanaugh this building today is practically out of debt.

Oratory is stressed in the school, and many state, county and national medals have been won by students of this institution. Coaching for entrance examinations to West Point and Annapolis, the United States Military and Naval Academies, has been the individual and outstanding work of Mrs. Kavanaugh. Her first student for an entrance examination was Andrew Irwin McKee in 1913, son of Major L. W. McKee, and today he is a Commander in the Navy. From that beginning, boys from twenty-one states in the Union have been coached by Mrs. Kavanaugh for these rigid and far-reaching examinations. All these boys, with hardly an exception, have been honor students who have reflected great credit on their preceptress. It was declared by an instructor at the Naval Academy that some of their brightest students received their basic education from Mrs. Rhoda C. Kavanaugh. Her work has been lauded and endorsed by governors, senators and congressmen. It is a conceded fact that more credit is due her than any other person for the educational progress made in Anderson County. The Western High School was her dream for which she worked indefatigably to make a possibility, that the children in a remote part of the county could have better educational advantages. Mrs. Kavanaugh has striven to make these high schools places where each student may plot his course with a definite object in view, demonstrating that money spent on an education is not a cost, but a fine investment. The advancement made by many of her students shows the worth of her teaching. It has been said that "the sun never sets on the Kavanaugh alumni," for some of her pupils are scattered far beyond the borders of their native heath.

WESTERN HIGH

It was eighteen years after the passage of the Kentucky High School Law that something was finally done to provide high school facilities for the boys and girls of the western part of the county. In the fall of 1925, a little group of eight pupils assembled in a vacant store building belonging to Lloyd Simpson, in Johnsonsville. Ezra Sparrow was the teacher. Neither teacher nor pupils anticipated that this very humble beginning would have any far-reaching results. However, the class had grown to such proportions in ten weeks time, that their efforts received recognition from the Board of Education. A high school was authorized and C. T. Ward was made its first principal. Mr. Ward held this position until June, 1933, when he became Superintendent of Public Schools for the county. At the time of the establishment of Western there were only eight high school graduates in the western half of the county. Since Western has brought high school advantages to that section, more than seventy boys and girls have been graduated from this school. A number of these have gone on to college, and eight are now teaching in this and adjoining counties.

At the present time a program of expansion is in progress at this school. A WPA project calls for the erection of a gymnasium and the improvement of the grounds. Also the first attempt of the county at consolidation will be undertaken at this place. Next year will see the five-teacher organization with Junior High and grade rooms taking the place of the regular three-teacher high school. C. T. Ward was Principal of this institution from 1925 until 1933, after which Ezra Sparrow was elected to the position. The latter is devoting his life to pastoral duties and teaching. These two young men are the type that lifts a community to higher levels, and whose Christian influence will fit pupils for places of prominence and good citizenship. Some of the teachers in Western High are Misses Rhea Franklin, Frances Eldred, Grace Brumley, Alta Frazier, Mrs. J. B. Sweeney and Mr. Wyatt Shely. Mr. Stanley McGowm, first coach.

The following school announcement was found in a scrap-book belonging to Mrs. Annie Bond Cole:

Lawrenceburg Seminary, Lawrenceburg, Anderson County, Kentucky.

The Fourth Annual Session of this Institution under the Supervision of the Undersigned will open for the education of males and females on the first Monday in September, 1871, and continue two terms of twenty weeks each. Curriculum thorough, embracing the branches of an English and Classical Education. To its former patrons, it is sufficient to say that the Institution shall, as heretofore, have the undivided attention of its Instructors. No labor or care shall be wanting to maintain still the high character the Institution has acquired within the last few years.

Tuition per term of twenty weeks: (One-half payable in advance, the other half at the end of ten weeks), Primary Department $15. Intermediate $20. Advanced Department $25. Incidental Fee $1.00. Pupils will be charged from the time of entrance until the close of the term. No deduction except in protracted illness. Competent assistance will be had according to the patronage and requirements of the school. Music under the care of a competent teacher. For further particulars apply to A. B. Jones, or J. A. Nooe.

WINDSOR FEMALE INSTITUTE

One of the schools established in Lawrenceburg just after the War Between the States, was the Windsor Female Institute, of which J. H. D. McKee was Superintendent. This school was in the building once known as the old Lawrence Tavern, which occupied the entire lot that contains the homes of Mrs. Lucien McBrayer, Mrs. Kinkton and Mrs. Mary Jane Cox today. This old land-mark was destroyed by fire in the early '90s. The institution of learning only ran three or four years, as it was too confining for Mr. McKee's health and he resigned and resumed the practice of law. Members of the

Baptist Church

Board of Instructors in the Windsor Female Institute were: Teachers in Scientific Department, Miss Annie Fiquet and Robert B. McKee; teachers of Music, Mrs. Martha McKee and Mrs. Fannie Alexander. Board of Visitors, William S. Hickman, James A. McBrayer, John A. Witherspoon, John Draffen, William H. McBrayer, William F. Bond, Monroe Walker, B. L. Boston, C. M. Lillard, James G. Hawkins and John Witherspoon. In the first record of 1866 appears the following: "It is proposed and hereby ordered that three annual scholarships in this institute, free of charge for tuition, and the appointments made to them from the county of Anderson in the following manner, viz: One to be appointed by Anderson Lodge No. 90 (Masonic); one by the Board of Visitors of the Institute, and one by the Superintendent. The appointments to be made for the school year of such young ladies as will attend regularly for the time of their appointment, and if by reason of death removal, or any other cause the beneficiary should fail to fill out said term."

At a meeting of the Board of Visitors of Windsor Female Institute at Lawrenceburg, October 3, 1868, William S. Hickman was elected President and Robert B. McKee, Secretary. On motion it was resolved that Miss Mary E. McMichael be appointed by the Board to a scholarship in the Institute for the school year, and resolved that the Board concur in the appointment of teachers as made by the Superintendent. (Signed) J. A. McBrayer, Secretary pro tem. The record chronicled the fact that other scholarships were conferred on Miss Sallie Alexander (Mrs. Porter Walker) and Miss Lou Maddox (Mrs. Ed Mitchell). The following two of the members of Board of Visitors resigned and the vacancies were supplied by James M. Posey and L. H. Penny. For the year 1868 the following pupils matriculated in this school: Tibbs Taylor, Wm. H. Posey, Mary Posey, Lewis McKee, Wm. H. McKee, John J. McKee, Henry Hickman, Laura Witherspoon, Clarence Witherspoon, Lily Myers, Susan Shipman, Randolph Walker, Porter C. Walker, John B. Walker, Maggy Penny, Mary Woods, Lizzie Woods, Alice Fidler, Jos. A. Penny, Lou Phurl, Maude Phurl, Mary C. Whittington, Lou Maddox, Annie Maddox, John Dunegan, Thompson Dunegan, Emma Baker, Mattie McKee, Ella McKee, William Witherspoon, Frank Witherspoon, Sallie Alexander, Nanie Alexander, Laura Walker, Joseph Walker, Mary E. McMichael, Susan McMichael, John F. Alexander, Mary Maddox, James Hawkins, William Gibson, Kate Paxton, J. H. McBrayer, George Walker, Eliza Horne, Kate Horne, Jeremiah Horne, Druarm Holmes, Sallie Fidler, Sallie Burrus. While this institute was primarily for females the record shows many males in attendance.

The commencement program of this institution on Thursday evening, June 17, 1869, was as follows:

Song—"Can You Sing"..............................By the Whole School
Declamation, "Graves of the Household"..................John H. McBrayer
Essay, "Duty to Parents"...................................Miss Sallie Fidler
Music, "Ocean Wave Waltz"............................Miss Lizzie Woods
Song, "Ye Mariners of Spain"..........................Miss Mattie McKee
Essay, "Amusements"..................................Miss Annie Maddox
Music, Duet, "Flores Waltz".......Miss Laura Walker and Miss Sallie Fidler
Essay, "Music"...Miss Maude Furl
Speech, "The Bird's Sorrow, a true tale of a broken heart"
                                                        Miss Mary Maddox
Song, "I Am Dying, Egypt, Dying"..................Miss Russell Alexander
Essay, "Soul, Fearful is Thy Power"....................Miss Maggie Penny

Song, "In the Starlight"....Misses Susie Penny, Sallie Fidler, Annie Maddox
Declamation, "Napoleon"...............................John F. Alexander
Duet, "Home, as a Waltz"............Susie Shipman and Ellen Witherspoon
Essay, "Silent Cities"...............................Miss Russell Alexander
Song, "Summer Sweets"...............Misses Lou Maddox and Mattie McKee
Essay, "The Darkest Hour is Just Before Day"............Miss Lou Maddox
Duet, "German Gallopade"...Misses Laura Witherspoon and Susie Shipman
Essay, "Peter the Great of Russia"...................Miss Sallie Alexander
Speech, "Which is the Greatest Evil, a Scolding Wife or a Smoking Chimney?"
John B. Walker
Music, Song, "Home of My Heart"...Misses Penny, Walker, Fidler, Alexander
Music, "The Whistling Farmer Boy"...................By the Whole School

Many of the students mentioned in this sketch have long since paid nature's last debt, but there are some still living whose grandchildren will enjoy these reminiscences.

THE OLD SALT RIVER PRIMITIVE BAPTIST CHURCH

This is one of the oldest churches organized in this county. It was "constituted" in 1798, nearly thirty years before Anderson County was erected. The record of the first meeting reads as follows: We, the Baptist Church of Christ on Salt River in Franklin County, constituted (on the Philadelphia Confession of Faith with its exceptions) on the 3rd of February, 1798, by Elder William Taylor of the Salem Association, with seven members, to-wit: John Penny, Raleigh Stott, Lucy Stott, Ann Tracy, Albert Plough, Benjamin Elliston and Stott's Nanny.

Bro. William Taylor was chosen moderator and then proceeded to form rules of decorum, to-wit: (1st). We, the Baptist Church of Christ on Salt River, constituted on the Philadelphia Confession of Faith with its exceptions, do agree that our meeting for business be on the second Saturday in each month, and that all matters of dealing be done privately that the church may deem to be of a private nature. (2) Resolved, that no member shall be received into fellowship without a unanimous voice of the church, and that the method of secluding members shall be done by a majority of the church present. (3) Resolved, that we meet at eleven o'clock on each day to do the business that may come before us. (4) Resolved, that any member holding and believing in a general redemption from hell (if they cannot be reclaimed), shall be excluded. (5) Resolved, that all free male members shall pay an equal portion of church expenses according to their abilities. (6) Resolved, that no member shall withdraw himself in time of business, without leave of the moderator, and that but one person speak at a time, and that he arise from his seat and address himself to the moderator. (7) Resolved, that any member reflecting on the judgment of the church shall be dealt with for such conduct. (8) Resolved, that no member shall speak more than once without leave of the moderator. (9) Resolved, that any member suffering their children to go to dancing school while under their attention, shall be excluded. (10) Resolved, that any member failing to vote in any matter as respects fellowship, shall assign their reasons. (11) Resolved, that any member of this church who shall attach himself to the Masonic Lodge shall be excluded.

The minutes of April, 1799, record the fact that Bro. and Sister Stott were admonished to give up the manner of their living, which was, they had left their farm and taken up the occupation of tavern keeping, which caused general dissatisfaction to the brethren, who enjoined it on them to return to their former place of residence. In April, 1800, the church still continued to be dissatisfied with Brother and Sister Stott for running a tavern, and appointed Bro. Woolfork to "cite them to attend the June meeting," and the church further determined to call for help from the sister churches, to-wit: Clear Creek and Beech Creek to sit with them in council on this occasion. These churches sent representatives to the meeting of August, 1800, and "Bro. and Sister Stott came forward and informed the church their intention to quit tavern keeping the following December, which gave satisfaction."

At a meeting in February, 1801, the following were received in the church by experience: Sallie Hanks, Betsy Hanks, Anthony Bond, Betsy Walker, Turner Hanks, Pitman Hanks, James Bond, Henry Shouse, Ephriam Lillard, Randolph Walker, Fanny Barnes, William Barnes and others. On second Saturday in August, 1801, the church met and having raised a subscription for building a meeting house, appointed Joseph Boggess, Ephraim Lillard, Edmond Waller and George Hanks to let the building of same. At this meeting Amos Coffman was reprimanded for going to a horse race, and as an apology was not forthcoming, he was excluded from the church. At a business meeting on Saturday, December 16, 1801, one of the sisters came forward and charged another sister with having told a falsehood. This was carried over to a subsequent meeting when the record states that "from the testimony and face of things, the church is of the opinion that both sisters are possessed of a spirit of hardness." The controversy waxed warm and one sister withdrew from the church. At a meeting in 1803, a brother was commissioned to "cite Sister Nellie Frazier to attend church next meeting and answer for her conduct in dancing." At the next meeting the brother reported that he "had labored with said sister and she refused to give up her dancing." She was excluded. In July, 1804, the following question was brought before the church: "Is it right for members of society to wear earrings?" Answer, "We think not." At a subsequent meeting two of the brothren were "cited to labor with a sister for wearing earrings and make report." Another sister was cited for using "hard and unchristian-like language," while others were importuned to appear and "state why they had been out of their seats so long at church." Another brother was reprimanded for "stripping to fight unjustly." At a meeting in 1811, Bro. Penny was to "cite a brother to the next meeting to answer for his conduct in jumping at a log rolling." In August, 1815, several members were reprimanded for attending a barbeque on July 4th of that year. The question was put, "Is it right or wrong to attend a barbeque?" Answer by the church, "It is wrong." The laws of the church were as rigid in 1820, as, at a meeting that year "Brother Anderson Allen had been betting on an election and is no more one of us." In 1836 several of the brethren joined the Masonic Order and were dismissed from the church. In March, 1842, David, George and P. C. Walker were appointed to "draw up and circulate a subscription for the purpose of building a new church at this place and make due return thereof when enough money is subscribed." In 1842 they appointed Turner Hanks, Dudley George, Robert Lock and Wilson Coke to "let the building of the new meeting house to the lowest bidder, to be erected on the spot of ground on which the old church now stands." Joshua Cummings got the contract and the church was completed in December, 1842. It is standing today (1936) in a fair state of preservation, and in the graveyard around it lie sleeping many of the early pioneers and parishioners. On the 29th of January, 1863, the churches of Salt River and Goshen called the Rev. J. F. Johnson to minister to them. He was the father of Lawrenceburg's esteemed citizen, Jesse M. Johnson, for many years cashier of the Lawrenceburg National Bank. After 1863 cases of censure against the erring parishioners for drunkenness, dancing, etc., were conspicuously absent from the minutes of the meetings. Rev. John Penny who organized the church in 1798, was pastor for thirty-five years. J. H. Walker was ordained in 1833 and served for twenty-nine years. J. F. Johnson, called in 1863, served eighteen years. Other pastors were N. T. Watson, G. P. Lester, Smith Hawkins, C. W. Bond, and L. B. Ragan.

CORINTH CHRISTIAN CHURCH

The Corinth Christian Church is next to the oldest church of this brotherhood in the county. It was organized in 1870 by Rev. Levin Merritt. After its organization the congregation worshipped at the Gordon school house for a number of years. In 1882 the seat of worship was moved to Fellowship church until the first church was built in 1886 at Corinth, and the pastor was Rev. Jackson Simms. Officers were Dawson Redmond, W. H. Glass, I. B. Peak, Jordon Warford, Dawson Grace, Marion Cox and A. J. Sherwood. The Rev. Merritt also organized churches at Antioch and Shilo. This pioneer preacher is buried at Antioch The new church building at Corinth was dedicated in August, 1923, by T. Hassell Bowen; $355.70 was raised on that occasion to wipe out the debt on the new building.

THE NEW LIBERTY CHURCH

A familiar old landmark in the county is the New Liberty Christian Church which has been standing since 1881. This church has been visited by a number of celebrities and nationally known persons. William Barton and William Townsend, both outstanding Lincoln authorities who have written books on the famous Emancipator, have worshipped in this old church. The first New Liberty Church was founded years before the present old building was erected but no records can be found to determine the date. The church was organized by Henry Sparrow in an old log building near where the present church stands. Plans now are being made to erect a new church building within the next year.

OLD GOSHEN PRIMITIVE BAPTIST CHURCH

One of the oldest churches in Anderson County today is Old Goshen, built in 1812. It is on the Bond's Mill and Ballard turnpike, near the John Case property. The ground on which it is built was donated by James Hendrix, one of the early pioneers, and a trustee of the church. Hendrix was "keeper of the meeting house" for several years for the sum of $3.50 per year. Later the janitor fee was raised to $5. The rules of Decorum were similar to those of the Salt River Baptist church organized in 1798, except nothing was said about prohibiting the members from uniting with the Masonic Order. The Constitution was as follows: "Constituted on the Scriptures of Truth; holding and believing in the imputed Righteousness of Christ; to believers, baptism by immersion; the final perseverance of the Saints; the resurrection of the body, and the happiness of the saints and the torment of the wicked shall be eternal. We, the Baptist church of Goshen, constituted the 4th of January, 1812, by brethren John Penny, Sr., and William Hickman, Jr., consisting of 29 members whose names shall be herein written, to-wit: Burrus, Riley, Egbert, Downey, Phillips, Slaughter, (and others) and a dozen slaves belonging to some of the members." For many years the church was very strict in discipline. Members were brought before the tribunal for "the sin of dancing, profane swearing, public rioting, absence from their seats in church," etc., and if an apology, when taken in a fault wasn't forthcoming, the offender was declared "no more one of us," and was excluded from the fellowship. Suffice it to say, many members repented and were reinstated. In more recent years the churches have swung away from the former extremity in discipline. Probably the modern church points to the parable of the Tares, the Wheat and the Dragnet, and leaves the erring members alone. In 1846 a committee was appointed to repair the Goshen church. John Nevins, J. Munday, J. H. Smith and J. M. Bell served on this committee. In 1869 a meeting was held to select a site for a new church, and "it was agreed to build a partnership house with the Methodist," but a later record states that the Methodist brethren failed to meet with the committee and steps were taken to build a Baptist church on the corner of Bro. F. M. Morris' land on the Bardstown road." At the next meeting it was reported that the old meeting house was sold conditionally for $30 to Bro. F. M. Morris and "his note shall bear interest at the rate of 10 per cent per annum and the interest be given the pastor, Bro. S. S. Perry." There was a rift in the church ranks in 1839, when part of the membership was enrolled in the "General Union," while others declared for non-fellowship in said Union. This course was strongly remonstrated against, as "contrary to Baptist Order, and departure from the principles upon which she was constituted." However, those who withdrew from, and declared a non-fellowship for the General Union of Baptist, were given letters of dismission, stating that "they were in fellowship with us as Christian, but not in relation to the General Union." In 1874 a new Bible was bought for the pulpit. In 1887 $360 was subscribed to build a new meeting house, the dimensions to be 32 feet by 46, with 14 foot ceiling. The foundation was built gratis by some of the members and $10 was contributed for another half acre for a burial plot near the church. The house was completed and dedicated September, 1889, by Bro. B. F. Hungerford. The record shows that "sisters Nannie Case, Maggie Sales and Mattie Morris were appointed a committee to raise money for chandeliers and stove for the new house." A Sunday School was organized in 1883 with J. A. Morris, Superintendent. Bro. W. D. Moore, who was killed in an automobile accident two years ago, was pastor of this church many years. The record states that "Bro. Moore began his labors with this church in November, 1886, and the text for his first sermon of the new pastorate was John 3rd chapter and 16th verse."

Some of the early pastors were Penny, Walker, Perry, Watkins and Dean. W. D. Moore was the son of Hamilton Moore, and he was one of the most widely known citizens of Anderson County. It is conceded that Bro. Moore performed more marriage ceremonies, and officiated at more funerals than any other minister in Kentucky. His home on the Harrodsburg road, two miles south of Lawrenceburg, was the Gretna Green where numerous couples treked to plight their troth, and receive the blessing of this good man.

THE FOX CREEK CHRISTIAN CHURCH

The old record of the organization of the Fox Creek Christian church is in the custody of Mr. J. R. York, and the first official record states: "The Congregation of Disciples of Jesus Christ at Fox Creek in the county of Anderson and State of Kentucky, constituted at Fox Creek meeting house, on the fourth Lord's day in July, 1841. We, the members of this congregation, having been immersed upon a confession of our faith in the Messiah as the only begotten son of God, declare it to be our full purpose and determination to acknowledge no leader but Christ, no infallible teachers but the Apostles and Prophets, holding no other articles of belief but the Old and New Testaments, and the latter as containing our faith and the rules of our behaviour as Christians." The following names of the first members of this congregation are, in many instances, perpetuated in the county today: William and America Cheshire, Edward Sherwood, Legrand Sterling, Susan Freeman, Hulda Stephens, Margaret Searcy, Elizabeth Baxter, William Kavanaugh, Elizabeth Kavanaugh, Margaret Sherwood, Elmira Cooms, Richard and Nancy Mullins, Zerelda Grace, Henry McKee, James Buntain, Julia Birdwhistle and others. A few years later we find the names of Cox, Utterback, Bond, Perry, Patterson, Sweeney, Major, York, Driskell, Crossfield, Gillis, Baker, Hawkins, Cole, Morris, Herndon and others who have been among the representative citizens of the county, and whose lives measured up to the necessities of the days in which they lived. In this early church the paths were straight and narrow, and when a brother or sister was taken in a misdemeanor, they were admonished to repent and mend their ways, or else were excluded from membership in the church. The minutes of the meeting on October 14, 1843, states: The congregation of Fox Creek met according to a former appointment, and after prayer proceeded to business. Whereas it is the opinion of the congregation, after taking the proper steps of the gospel, that we exclude Brother Thomas Smith for drinking ardent spirits to excess, and playing the fiddle for dancing. (Signed) R. H. Mullins, Clerk. Occasionally other backsliders were cited and remonstrated with, and often the erring members confessed their sins and were re-instated in full fellowship. The record shows that one sister was reprimanded for "swearing and outrageous profanity," but she grew penitent and promised to bridle her tongue in the future. In a number of instances slaves in the church families were baptised into the fellowship of the church. The minutes of this congregation of nearly a century ago, show that the members comforted the sick, helped the needy, and tried to restore the outcast, reclaim the wanderer and instruct the young in the fear and admonition of the Lord. The new church was built in 1847, the deed to the lot reads as follows: "Know all men by these presents that we, Madison M. Mullins and Albert G. Mullins, each of the county of Anderson and the State of Kentucky, have this day bargained and sold to Elwood Sherwood, William Kavanaugh, Dennis C. Driskell, Zachariah Fortune, Bartlett Searcy and Albert Mullins, Trustees of Fox Creek meeting house, a certain tract of land, near the waters of Fox Creek, containing one-half acre bounded as follows: commencing at the S E corner of a lot of land given by Yancy Freeman to the old Fox Creek meeting house, running in the same direction with said lot about N E far enough to make one-half acre, thence straight to the road, thence with the road to the lot belonging to the old meeting house, thence with said lot to the beginning, for and in consideration of one dollar we give said lot of land to the above Trus-

tees to build a meeting house on, dedicated to the worship of Almighty God. When said house shall have been builded, we bind ourselves to make to the said Trustees a warranty deed to the same, for and in consideration of the above amount for the above purpose. Given under our hands and seals, August 23rd, 1847."
(Signed) Madison M. Mullins, Albert Mullins.

Elder Samuel Street, of Mercer County, first organized this church in 1841 in an old log building formerly used by the Primitive Baptist. There were fourteen charter members. The first elders of the church were, William Kavanaugh, Edward Sherwood and A. J. Mullins. Five years later the old log building was replaced by the new building. This served the congregation until 1904, when the church that stands today was dedicated. This building cost $2,000. In 1916 the membership was 300. Pastors who served this church were, Everett Merritt, Lewis, Hume, Yancy, Corn, Case, Walden, Darnell, Miley, Wilson, Parrish, Harrison, Hightower and others.

When the early churches were established in the county, there was no training in sacred music and hymn books were scarce. A few old favorite songs were memorized and copied in manuscript by some of the members and these were sung with "hearts full of praise and throats full of noise." The scarcity of song books was often supplied by the preacher's help in lining out the words from the pulpit, a couplet at a time, then the congregation joined in singing regardless of key or tempo, but it was minstrelsy from the skies for there was melody in their hearts for the Lord's worship. In the course of time, a song leader could vibrate a tuning fork, which saved the high and low voices from getting too far away from the tune. After the forming of singing schools in the rural, the church choir made its debut, and for a time this innovation was frowned on and censured by some of the older saints in Israel, and when the first organ was placed in the Christian Church in Lawrenceburg, "discord was created by harmony," as some of the members withdrew to an organless church in another hamlet. But harmony prevailed and the organ became a necessary instrument and today three fine pipe organs peal their harmonies over Lawrenceburg worshippers.

Before the Fox Creek cemetery was laid out in 1885 many old families had been laid to rest in the church burial ground. One tomb stone record shows that J. Bartlett, consort of Agnes Bartlett, was born 1792, died 1853. Agnes, the wife, died in 1887 in her 91st year. Garland Cox, born 1773, died 1861. George W. Baxter, born 1824, died 1883.

METHODIST*

Col. R. T. P. Allen, who for many years was in charge of the Kentucky Military Institute (at present Stewart Home), was a member of the Kentucky Conference M. E. Church. He was appointed as president of the school and preached in the neighboring community. He introduced Methodism at Rough-and-Ready (Alton). On September 23, 1871, James A. Reed and wife, Mary, conveyed to John Draffen, Wm. J. Hughes and James A. Reed, Trustees," a lot in the town of Rough-and-Ready for $1. on which a house of worship was then in process of erection." About 1892 the congregation disbanded, the members uniting at Lawrenceburg. The building was sold and torn down.

*Contributed by Rev. E. C. Watts.

The Pleasant Valley Methodist church was first in the old log cabin building known as Pleasant Ridge. Later a new building was erected at Glensborough, then Camdenville. On March 23, 1889, Mary Edwards and husband, James, conveyed to John B. Shely, James C. Shely, Ben Franklin, Thomas N. Vaughn and James T. Edwards, Trustees of the Methodist church, a lot for a new church building. This was erected and called Pleasant Valley. The Edwards, Franklins and Shelys were prominent in this church. Four sons of Mr. Ben Franklin became Methodist preachers. At present it is an appointment of the Salt River Circuit. Among the early Methodist families locating in the southwestern portion of Anderson County, were the Washes, Leathers, Yocums and others. The early Circuit Riders visited their homes, held meetings in the community and organized a society or church. Leathers' Store was the business center. Near this point a Mr. Penny built a log building for religious purposes. The Primitive Baptist had charge for many years. It appears that the Methodist later used the building. About 1893, during the pastorate of Rev. F. M. Hill, the poplar log building was torn down and the logs sawed into building material for a new church which is in use. At present the membership is weak and it is connected with the Salt River Circuit.

THE HEBRON CHURCH

"The Hebron Church of Anderson County was organized in the year 1827, in a log house on the farm of Thomas McCall on Gilbert's Creek, as a Cumberland Presbyterian church by Rev. Laban Jones, an itinerant minister, whose circuit was from Perryville through Danville, Harrodsburg, McAfee, Winchester, Mt. Sterling to Jeffersontown, Ky. About every six months he visited these preaching places on horseback, according to his biography. The elders of the early church were John McBride, Mark Duncan, Benjamin Peyton, and Daniel Hockersmith. The organization worshipped in the log house until 1844, when the church built a new house on the hill overlooking the Louisville and Crab Orchard turnpike, and opposite the famous McCall Springs. The church, since its organization, has received 317 members, of this number seventy-one are still living, some in other states, but thirty-three active at home. Within the century the church has had thirty-five pastors, among them being R. H. Caldwell, who was pastor for twenty-three years. The names among others were, Gilliam, Bonta, Oakley, Turner, King, Trimble and McKay. It has had eighteen elders, the four mentioned above and others in the order named as follows: John Hutton, J. W. Fletcher, Gran Utterback, John Griffy, John McMichael, B. L. Boston, D. G. McMichael, Jas McCall, Thos. Coke, Holman Frazier, Jas. Coke, Thomas Gilliam, Hamilton Coke and Louis Routt. There were seven colored people, servants of Bacon Meaux, John Jordon and Willis Fletcher, who were members of this church. Hebron was formerly a Cumberland Presbyterian church, but in 1906 in the union of the two churches, the Cumberland went with the U. S. A. Church. Then after a lapse of twenty years, being isolated from all U. S. A. churches, Hebron by petition was transferred to Transylvania Presbytery of the U. S. Church. This being the one hundredth year since the organization of the church, an all-day meeting will be held June 19, 1927, with dinner on the grounds."—J. S. Coke, Clerk. (Christian Observer, 1927.)

*On June 24, 1901, a number of Missionary Baptists met at the Salt River school house for the purpose of organizing a church. B. F. Adkins acted as Moderator and W. D. Moore as Clerk. After reading of the third chapter of first Timothy by the Moderator, and prayer by the Clerk, an opportunity was given to all those who wished to go into the organization to do so. Thirty-seven presented themselves. Forrest Moore was elected Clerk and B. F. Adkins was called as pastor.

W. D. Moore, H. S. Wise and D. F. Hanks were selected as the building committee. George W. Fallis, G. C. Burford and H. S. Wise were elected trustees. H. S. Wise was chosen as Treasurer and was requested to collect as rapidly as possible the subscriptions for the new church. Sand Spring was chosen as the name of the church. George Fallis and wife made the deed for the ground on which the church is built August 13, 1901.

The church was dedicated June 29, 1902, sermon by Dr. J. G. Bow, Louisville, Psalms 127:1—"Except the Lord build the house they labor in vain that build it."

Pastors—B. F. Adkins, W. D. Moore, E. W. Summers, Garrett Reed, C. T. Ricks, Zell Shaw, J. E. Darter, Bert Gould, H. H. McGinty, M. D. Morton.

The present membership is 545. This church is on the Harrodsburg road, two miles south of Lawrenceburg.

---

*Contributed by Mrs. H. S. Wise.

CHAPTER III

THE THREAD FACTORY

Some of our enterprising citizens interested in bringing industrial plants to Lawrenceburg, were instrumental in locating the Dean and Sherk Thread Factory from Detroit on Anderson County soil. In the eastern part of town on Lincoln street the building of the thread mills was begun July 7, 1926, and the whir of machinery was set in motion the following January, 1927. The space occupied by the plant is forty thousand square feet, and more than a million pounds of the product a year is shipped throughout the United States and some foreign countries. The firm has its own formulas for dyes and there are huge vats where the thread is treated to every color of the rainbow. The thread is used for industrial purposes, as upholstering furniture and automobiles; sewing coarse merchandise, as overalls, shirts, shoes and knitting cotton dresses and sweaters, etc. The plant employs 125 workers, about equally divided between men and women.

Thomas Sherk is President of the company; G. W. Krentler, Vice-President-Treasurer and General Manager; H. Dewey McBrayer, Secretary.

* * * * * * * * * * * * * * * *

The Broom Factory was first opened by Mr. John Parlin, of Cincinnati, father-in-law of Wm. F. Lillard, on the latter's farm on the hill above Tyrone, and was known as the Riverside Broom Works. In 1920 Mr. Parlin sold the business to Frank Simpson and Carl Cooper, and they moved it to Lawrenceburg. At one time 15,000 brooms were turned out every year by this plant. Later the industry was bought by Mrs. Fannie C. Gaines, who owns it today and the output is thirty dozens brooms per day.

CHEESE

After the closing of the distilleries in the county it was highly expedient that a move should be made to get other sources of revenue in Anderson, and the effort was launched to bring in a Kraft Cheese factory. In 1927 W. T. Bond, President of the Lawrenceburg National Bank, in company with C. A. Routt, S. V. Gordon and Charles McGinnis, went to Paoli, Indiana, to inspect a Kraft plant and ascertain the requirements to procure this industry for our county. The first demand was a pledge for the milking of 2,000 cows and furnishing of the building for the enterprise. The 2,000 cows were the stock to be subscribed by the local people, and later, if the project proved a success the cheese company would take over the plant. Workers were sent through the county to lay the proposition before the people, and get them to pledge so many cows to milk. It was enthusiastically received by the citizens and in a short time the required number of cows was pledged. The two banks in town loaned money with which to buy the stock, and soon several loads of fine Jersey and Guernsey cows were shipped in.

The plant was erected and opened in 1928, and it has brought a revenue of much value to the citizens of the county. Truck lines are run through all the hamlets and villages in the farming communities bringing in the great cans of milk to the factory on Lincoln street. This plant has been enlarged twice since it was opened, and a Kraft inspector declared that the

Ripy Bros. Distillery at Tyrone and Young's High Bridge over Kentucky river.

best plain cheese this firm makes was turned out by the Anderson County factory. Approximately 4,000 pounds of cheese a day is the output of this industry, and twenty-six workmen are employed in the plant. Mr. A. H. Paasch, whose home was in Wisconsin, has been the very efficient manager since 1929.

DISTILLERIES

While Anderson is not rated as strictly a blue grass county, it is on the edge of the famed blue grass section and embraces many rich and desirable farms. Most of the land in the western part of the county is hilly and broken but fine for grazing purposes. A few years ago the average value per acre for taxation purposes was computed at $32.11, which was but a few cents over the Kentucky average of $30.89, while her neighbor, Woodford County, a very choice farming county, was valued at $111.59 per acre, which shows where Anderson stands. Much of her land is rolling and underlaid with limestone, rock and clay sub-soil, hence erosion of a serious nature follows too much cultivation. Anderson county is bound on the north by Franklin and Shelby, on the south by Mercer and Washington, on the west by Nelson, Spencer and Shelby, on east by Kentucky river. It is fifty-five miles from Louisville and twenty-eight from Lexington. On one boundary of the county flows the picturesque Kentucky river, which for sheer grandeur and savage beauty, world travelers have pronounced superior to the Hudson. All long the other boundary runs Salt river, a smaller stream, where there are some fine river bottom lands. On the ridge which separates the two rivers, now straight, now winding, lies the old Wilderness Trail over which the pack-horses and bands of pioneers made their way from the Cumberland mountains to the Falls of the Ohio. Since the early settlement of the state, the reputation of Anderson County for fine whiskey was a by-word far beyond the confines of the Blue Grass. Those who are qualified to pass as experts, assert that the best beverage whiskies of the world originated in regions affording limestone springs, in which Anderson County abounds.

For years Anderson's rare whiskies had an international reputation. "Cedar Brook," "Waterfill and Frazier," "Bond & Lillard," "Old Hoffman," "Old Joe," "Old Prentice," "T. B. Ripy,'" "Belle of Anderson," "Dowling Brothers" are a few that filtered from Anderson's pure limestone springs and were shipped to every port in the world.

The Ripy distillery at Tyrone had one warehouse alone that held 50,000 barrels. This was the largest "sour mash" plant in the world. The "sour-mash" method of distillation has always been used in the manufacture of Anderson County whiskey. In the spirit provision of the Pure Food laws originated the bottling of whiskey in bond under that Act. The method of maturing the beverage in wooden barrels stored in dry warehouses gives richness of flavor and aroma to the product. At one time a large part of the population of Anderson County was directly, or indirectly, engaged in the business of distilling. Hundreds were employed at the large plants, while here farmers sold their corn, rye and barley to the distillers.

In fact, Anderson County's economic fabric was so closely interwoven with this industry that she became a pauper county when the wheels of the business ceased to turn after the passing of the Volstead Act and the Constitutional Amendment. Thousands of head of cattle were fed in the pens at the distilleries on the by-product known as "slop," which is a fine cattle food. This is the rich, hot mash left after the white whiskey, or "foreshots" has been run off. It is high in protein content, well-cooked and fed warm, being piped to barns or troughs in pens in which cattle are fed during the period the distillery runs. This business gave employment to scores of men designated as "cattle-feeders." Hay and cotton seed meal were mixed with the slop and the cattle thus fattened commanded the best market prices.

After the Volstead Act was passed all the distilleries in the county were closed and dismantled, the warehouses razed and sold for old lumber, and many of the employees migrated to other factory towns and cities seeking work.

Legend has it that the War Between the States was the cause of Anderson County's reputation for fine whiskey becoming a national one. Both armies skirmished over its soil, and the men of the North sampled its product. When peace came and they returned to their cold wintry homes in the northland, they remembered the excellence of the Kentucky product and ordered some. Supply kept pace with the demand, and small private distilleries became huge plants, and for three generations Anderson County was converting corn, rye and barley into Bourbon whiskey. The oldest brand of whiskey in Kentucky was first made in what was later Anderson County, and it is fitting that we give a resume of its history: During the spring of 1818 there emigrated to this section of the country a man who became the pioneer of distillation of corn whiskey in Kentucky. This early settler, "Old Joe" Peyton, reached the mouth of Gilbert's Creek in his canoe, tied his boat, and soon found a suitable place for his habitation. In following the windings of this peaceful stream, he discovered a spring which, for its pure and salient qualities, he had known no equal. Here he erected a small still-house of rough hewn logs, and with the nucleus of a two-bushel tub, he began the manufacture of this primitive brand "Old Joe." Eventually this little plant was enlarged, and it passed into the ownership of the Hawkins family, who were pioneers that settled on Gilbert's Creek soon after Peyton's arrival. When Peyton operated his plant in 1818, his still was so small he could get only from two to two and a half gallons of the beverage out of a bushel of meal, where a modern distillery gets from four and a half to five gallons. In pioneer days many farmers had their own still-houses which supplied "likker" for their own consumption, and it is said that many were just as careful to lay in a barrel of whiskey as they would a sack of meal or keg of molasses.

The "Old Joe" brand passed into the ownership of Sheridan Hawkins in 1840, uncle of Gratz B. Hawkins.

In 1847 the industry was owned by Granville Bourbon Hawkins, father of Gratz B. Hawkins. In 1857 it was acquired by Medley S. Bond (brother of W. F. Bond, the founder of the noted brand of Bond & Lillard). After the latter's death T. B. Ripy bought the plant and later sold it to Captain Wiley Searcy, who ran it for several years, when "Old Joe" again became the property of the Hawkins family, Gratz B. and Hurd Hawkins, who manufactured this brand until Prohibition in 1917. Today, after the passing of a century, four generations of the Hawkins family have distilled this historic brand of the first whiskey made in this county. "Old Joe" has risen, Phoenix-like, from the ashes of Prohibition with the following officers in control: Gratz B. Hawkins, President; Mrs. Agnes F. Laurie, Vice-President; Wilgus Naugher, Secretary-Treasurer, and Maurice Hawkins, Superintendent. This plant is in the heart of Anderson County, has a picturesque natural setting and in point of architecture is one of the most imposing distilleries in the state. Its

"Old Joe" Distillery

HISTORY OF ANDERSON COUNTY 151

new location is on the beautiful estate of Mrs. Laurie, at "Montrose," where her son, Mr. Naugher, resides with his family. The building of the new plant was begun in 1933 and began operating May 10, 1934, with a capacity of 900 bushels per day.

The number of cattle fed at the distilleries in Anderson County in 1892 were 4,990; hogs fed were 1,150.

The name of Ripy has been associated with the distillation of fine whiskies in Anderson County for many decades. James Ripy, father of Thomas Beebe Ripy, was born near Barney in the county of Tyrone, Ireland. He came to this country in 1838, and located in Lawrenceburg, Ky. He was a farmer, merchant and postmaster. In 1868 he was partner with S. P. Martin and Monroe Walker in the manufacture of whiskey at Tyrone, Ky. Thomas Beebe Ripy (father of Ernest W. Ripy), with Judge W. H. McBrayer, bought the distillery of Martin, Walker & Co., in 1869. The next year T. B. Ripy bought the interest of Judge McBrayer and enlarged the plant to 1,500 bushels per day. In 1882 W. J. Waterfill, Dowling Bros. and T. B. Ripy built the Clover Bottom plant at Tyrone, and in 1885 Mr. Ripy bought the interest of his partners. In the late nineties T. B. Ripy was the largest independent sourmash distiller in the world. On June 1, 1935, ground was broken for another Ripy distillery on the same location at Tyrone as it was in pre-prohibition days, and the new "Ripy Bros." plant began operations on November 28, 1935, with Ernest W. Ripy and his son, Ernest, Jr., at the head of the industry. The beverage of the Ripy Bros. plant is being made by the same formula as was used in the olden days by T. B. Ripy. It is stored in heavy, charred white oak barrels and rolled into large, well-equipped dry warehouses on the cliffs of the scenic and beautiful Kentucky river in Anderson County.

Another well-known brand of Anderson County whiskey, "Old Hoffman," is again manufactured since the relaxation of Prohibition. This plant has been reopened on the banks of Salt river, five miles west of Lawrenceburg, and has advantage of never-failing deep wells of limestone water, which keeps the concern running the year round. Originally the Hoffman plant had capacity for fifteen bushels per day; today it mashes 275 bushels. It is managed and operated by Ezra F. and Robert Ripy, sons of the late T. B. Ripy, and they are duplicating the beverage that was made famous by the pioneer Ripys.

An old covered bridge over Salt River on the Bond's Mill road was built over a hundred years ago, and is one of the few picturesque old wooden bridges still standing in Kentucky. In sight of this romantic relic, which gives a vivid impression of reality of a century past, a new distillery has been erected called the Bond's Mill Distillery, and it enjoys the distinction of being not only the smallest whiskey-making plant in the state of Kenucky, but the only water-wheel distillery in the United States. Power is furnished from Salt River by a water-wheel of the turbine type concealed under the floor of the distillery at the dam side. The original grist mill built in 1831 was of wood. It was rebuilt about 1900, and has recently been further rebuilt and iron-armored in the usual Kentucky distillery manner. Here for many years the Bond family ground grain for other nearby distilleries, and Bond's Mill has stood for more than a century as one of the historical landmarks of Anderson County. Today, after 116 years the old grist mill has been transformed into a distillery with Mr. Robert E. Johnson president of the industry. Mr. Johnson is of the fourth generation of noted distillers in the county. His great grandfather, John Bond, built a plant on Bailey's Run in 1820. His grandfather, W. F. Bond, took out distillery license in 1853, and his father, J. M. Johnson, was partner in the W. B. Saffell Distilling Company for many years. The distiller at Bond's Mill, James R. McMichael, has been associated with the Bond and Saffell families since 1892. The brand, "Bond's Mill," is one of the best known in Kentucky and has been shipped to nearly every state in the Union. The celebrated heavy-bodied sour-mash formula, carried on by experienced distillers, has made Anderson County beverages celebrated the world over.

CEDAR BROOK DISTILLERY

Cedar Brook Distillery had a world-wide reputation, having received the gold medal at Vienna in 1873, and at the Centennial in Philadelphia in 1876. It is said to have been the highest selling brand of Bourbon on the market. When Cedar Brook plant was dismantled in 1922, much interest was manifested in opening the corner stone of the new plant built in 1880. It had been said there would be found two bottles of rare old whiskey, a quantity of money and old newspapers. There were found two pint bottles but they were empty. Sealed in a glass jar was found a letter, setting forth a brief biographical account of Judge W. H. McBrayer, the founder of Cedar Brook, together with the roll of men employed at the plant. The money was there too, small silver coins, ranging from half dollars to pennies, covered with mold of the years. In the collection of newspapers, were the Louisville Courier-Journal of June 29, 1880; the Cincinnati Gazette of June 9, 1880; the Louisville Commercial and The Gavel, a Masonic magazine published at Danville. The roll of persons employed contained in the record was as follows: W. H. McBrayer, proprietor; W. B. Saffell, superintendent; J. C. Peden, draughtsman and chief mechanic; James Shields, Sam Shields, John Burford, Johnson Trimble, Henry Augustus, carpenters; George Fallis, G. McGurk, William Highbarger, John Collins, Sam Fallis, Sam Yates, stonemasons; John Gamble, rock quarryman; James Crow, John Hanley, James Carter, George Wash, Josh Mountjoy, C. Cunningham, Moret Cunningham, George Cunningham, Ed Cunningham, Josh Allin, Chap Hayden; R. V. Bishop, distiller; Ed Smith, assistant distiller; Tom Hayden, Green Kennedy, Frank Carter, John Overstreet, beer runners; Henry Avery, fireman and miller; W. T. Morrow, United States gauger; S. H. Lewis, U. S. storekeeper; Will Rice, Lewis Harris, Dud Pleasant, Will Roberts, colored wagon drivers; Sam Shackleford, blacksmith; J. B. Burford, housekeeper; J. W. Waterfill, Charles Adams and J. M. Faulkner, visitors.

From this roll it will be seen that the whiskey industry of Anderson County gave renumerative employment to a host of employees. It paid a large per cent of the local taxes, county, state and municipal. This plant has not been rebuilt.

THE ANDERSON NEWS

The Anderson News, founded in 1877 by Judge John (Jack) F. Wills in the interest of Lawrenceburg and Anderson County, has, through all the years that have elapsed, kept in touch with the public pulse, fostering worthy enterprises and supporting commendable movements. Judge Wills, the first editor, was a lawyer of considerable ability who practiced in the courts of

The Hoffman Distilling Company.

Anderson and adjoining counties. He was one of the county's first citizens to advocate free turnpikes and made the race for the Legislature on that platform. Though he was overwhelmingly defeated, the agitation started by him against the tollgates resulted in their being destroyed by irate citizens many years after his death.

Jack Wills was something of an humorist, and frequently to this day one hears recalled some of his outbursts that provoked mirth from his hearers. Back in the days when he practiced law it was told that he was in the courts at Standford regularly. At the time W. P. Walton, known by reputation to many of our older citizens, was owner and publisher of The Interior Journal. It appears that Wills had contracted a small printing bill with Walton and was a bit slow in liquidating the same. Walton met Wills in the courthouse at Standford one morning and, being turned down for the 'steenth time in payment for the account, threatened Wills with a write-up in the Journal. Whereupon Wills retorted in hot language, "Write and be damned; I'll ride out of your circulation in fifteen minutes." And that was in horse and buggy days."

Wills carried on in the newspaper business in Lawrenceburg but a short while and sold out to Charles E. Kincade, who had just graduated from Centre College. The new owner had associated with him as editor Charles Burton. Claude Buckley purchased the paper from Mr. Kincade and a few years later sold it to J. T. Boswell. Fire destroyed the Boswell plant, and when the new one was bought it was installed and operated in the court house for a short while, then moved upstairs over the business room now occupied by E. E. Spencer. Boswell disposed of the plant to F. R. Feland in 1884, who published the paper five years and sold it to J. M. B. Birdwhistle and Harry Buckley. They were publishers for a number of years and sold to Owen Hawkins. A stock company composed of J. M. B. Birdwhistle, W. D. Moore and F. R. Feland, then acquired and operated the plant a short time, then sold it to Morris W. Bartlett, who had associated with him as editor and manager W. Owen McIntyre. Mr. Bartlett took over the management of the paper after awhile, and W. C. Woods assisted him in the local news department. Mr. Bartlett sold to another stock company composed of J. R. Paxton, George Williams, Harry Wise and Dr. C. W. Kavanaugh, and The Anderson County Herald, published by Forrest Moore and Morton Green, was merged with it, the latter gentlemen becoming stockholders in the corporation. Jesse M. Alverson then purchased the paper and added to the equipment a modern Babcock newspaper press, a linotype and other needed machinery, besides buying a home for the plant which he remodeled at considerable expense. Other improvements made by him fitted the plant out as one of the best to be found in the state. Mr. Alverson sold the paper to Mr. H. V. Bell, who, after operating it for six years, sold to Keene Johnson and R. E. Garrison in November, 1921. Mr. Johnson went to Richmond a few years later as editor and part owner of the Daily Register, selling his interest in the Anderson News to Mr. Garrison, the present publisher. For forty-two years Morton Green has been associated with the paper, the greater time as manager and foreman of the mechanical department. His first employment was with Birdwhistle and Buckley, when the plant was housed in two small upstairs rooms, with a room at the rear of the building just large enough to accommodate the Country Prouty newspaper press. The Anderson News is a member of the Kentucky Press Association. In competition it has been awarded several silver loving cups in recognition of its class among weekly papers of the state. Twice it was given first honors, being judged on news and artistic makeup.

THE EAGLE ROLLER MILLS

In 1870 G. W. Forston erected on the present site of the Eagle Roller Mills a large and excellent mill of the old style, and this he operated successfully for twelve years. In 1882 he had the plant greatly enlarged and the old machinery removed and replaced with new machinery for the roller process. Shortly after this Mr. Forston died and the property was bought by T. B., J. P. Ripy and John Dowling and the firm known as Ripy, Dowling & Co. The expert miller was George Gildersleve, and it was at this time that the popular "Sifted Snow" brand of flour originated. This milling industry has passed into the hands of several companies since that time and today is owned and operated by J. Andrew Cain and son.

The Walnut Grove Stock Farm, owned by W. D. Mountjoy on the Fox Creek pike, four miles west of Lawrenceburg, is visited by buyers from far and near who are interested in aristocrats in horse flesh. For many years W. D. Mountjoy and Son (Billy) have been breeding and training thoroughbreds, and they have commanded some of the highest prices on the market. Their horses have tasted victory at many fairs, as is attested by the numerous trophies captured by this firm. When a discerning buyer wants a good saddle horse he comes to "Cordie" Mountjoy to find the "poetry of motion" for which he is looking, that has been trained to the Nth degree by Billy Mountjoy. Some of Kentucky's finest equine progeny that have been shipped to every state in the Union have grazed the succulent blue grass on the Walnut Grove Stock Farm.

There is another industry on this farm that enjoys a wide patronage, The Walnut Grove Hatcheries, in a large walnut-shaded woodland, is operated by Linn Mountjoy, and from this plant is shipped thousands of newly hatched chicks during the year. These home industries are numbered among Anderson County's assets.

LAWRENCEBURG ELECTRIC LIGHTS AND THE ICE PLANT

The water works were installed in Lawrenceburg in 1904, the water supply coming from Salt River, three miles distant. A short time after that event, the fire department was organized. Prior to that time the only defense against fire was the volunteer bucket brigade. In 1905 the electric light plant was installed. In March, 1905, the Commercial Club had called a meeting looking toward establishing a light plant to diffuse a brighter radiance than the oldtime street oil lamp. Within a month of the first call, $10,000 worth of stock was subscribed and the plant became an assured fact. Ground was broken in April on land secured from Mr. W. F. Bond near a big spring on his farm and in the following fall lights were turned on to the joy of hundreds of spectators. In May, 1906, there was issued bonded stock for the purpose of running an ice plant in connection with the electric light plant. Soon $7,000 was subscribed and the ice plant assured. Instead of ice being shipped in from other towns, Lawrenceburg now bought her cold product at home. This first ice plant had a capacity of five tons per day and the water was drawn from the same bored wells as for the light plant, and was filtered before being made into ice. J. B. Ash was superintendent of these industries. The first officers were: J. M. Johnson, President; Ernest Ripy, Vice-President; Dr. C. A. Leathers, Secretary, and J. C. Thompson, Treasurer. This electric light plant was operated until 1912 when it was taken over by the Mid-West Utility Co., and later in 1913 the Kentucky Utilities. At this time the manufacture of ice was suspended and again this commodity was shipped in to our town from other places. There was a large concrete building on the Southern railroad, not far from the depot, known as the "turkey pen." This was owned by G. B. and A. H. Hawkins and had been a large shipping center for a number of years, where great numbers of turkeys were slaughtered and shipped in car loads to distant cities. In 1923 this building was purchased by W. T. Bond, President of the Lawrenceburg National Bank, and he converted it into an ice plant. Modern machinery was installed and in a short while this new ten-ton-a-day plant was furnishing ice for the town and county.

During the serious drouth of 1929-'30 the town was, at times, put on "water rations," only allowed two hours in the morning and two in the evening to turn the water on, as Salt River was very low and water conservation was important. Stock was driven miles to rivers for water and the manufacture of ice suspended. Mr. Bond had a well drilled near the ice plant and at a depth of sixty feet struck a good stream of water which supplied the plant which was then run without interruption.

Before the manufacture of ice in the town, many of the farm homes in Anderson County had specially constructed ice houses which were round pits twelve or fifteen feet deep walled up with stone. A conical shaped roof over the pit reached to the surface of the ground with a dormer-like door at the base of the roof. When ice on ponds and rivers was four or five inches thick it was cut and hauled in, the pit filled with the frozen water and a heavy layer of sawdust thrown over the top of it to help preserve the commodity for summer consumption.

THE FIRST RAILROAD AND THE TYRONE BRIDGES

In Major McKee's history of the county we find that a road was opened to Sublett's Ferry in 1833, later known as Shryock's Ferry. The present writer is able to supplement the history of the ferry with war stories in connection with it, from a record furnished by Mrs. Carl Cooper, of Lawrenceburg, who is a great granddaughter of John Shryock, whose family owned this ferry more than fifty years. Louis Sublett, a pioneer, came from Virginia, built a log weather-boarded house at the ferry on the Woodford County side which he operated as a tavern. It had a large ball room and was a social center in the early days. He ran a quart house on the outside but did not allow drinking on the premises. He also built a stone room in the yard where grain was stored until shipped down the river. Sublett died in 1830, and the ferry was acquired by John Shryock who operated it until 1850 when he sold it to his son-in-law, Johnson Miller. After the War Between the States, Miller sold the ferry to Joe Boothe, another son-in-law of Shryock's. Two granddaughters of John Shryock reside in Lexington today, they are Mrs. Elizabeth Shryock Fields and Miss Ella Shryock, the latter is ninety years of age, and they have furnished the writer with the following interesting war stories: While Johnson Miller owned the ferry during the War Between the States, it

HISTORY OF ANDERSON COUNTY

was crossed at different times by both Rebel and Union soldiers. Hearing that General John Morgan and his men were to cross Shryock's ferry at a certain time, Union soldiers came from Lexington to the river and made Shryock sink his ferry boats, but he, with the help of a negro slave, took out just enough calking to put them below the surface of the water; then the Union soldiers returned to Lexington satisfied that Morgan and his men would have to stay on the Anderson County side of the ferry, but Cincinnatus Shryock (son of John) did not think so, for, with the help of a number of persons who had come to the river to see General Morgan across, raised the ferry boats from the water, recalked them, and when the Rebel leader arrived with his men, every thing was in readiness to bring them across. They were all day crossing. The Union soldiers had raided Mrs. Shryock's pantry but she had one chicken and a small supply of food left, so she prepared dinner for Gen. Morgan and his officers. When she went to the front of the house to call the General to dinner, one of the soldiers slipped in the side door and disappeared with the chicken. When the General was informed what had happened to the fowl he said, "Let him have it, I am not as hungry as he is."

Another time Cincinnatus Shryock found out that some of the Union soldiers from Lexington would cross the ferry on their way to Lawrenceburg to arrest some of its citizens for "talking too much." He sent his twelve-year-old son, John, in a row boat to Tyrone with the message of the impending arrests. The Union men crossed the ferry in three omnibusses and went to Lawrenceburg only to find the men they were looking for had fled.

Joe Boothe bought the ferry in 1864. His wife was Miss Kate Shryock and they were the parents of S. E. and Henry Boothe and Mrs. Lee Boothe Hill, of Lawrenceburg. Joe Boothe died in 1884, and the ferry was sold to Holman Frazier and Ezra Griffy for $7,500. In the early days the boats were propelled by oars, and Joe Boothe was the first to put an overhead wire to guide the boat during high waters. After ten years Frazier and Griffy sold the ferry to Pink Ledridge for $8,000. This was during horse and buggy days and a good price for the property at that time.

Ledridge operated the ferry many years and after his death his heirs sold it, with the farm, to J. W. Gaines, Ezra and Porter Griffy for $34,000.

This company made another step toward progress when they attached the ferry boat to a gasoline launch and the crossing was made in a fourth of the old time. John and Jane Radcliff Shryock had eleven children; eight lived to be grown; Martha Ann married Will Saffell of Lawrenceburg; they had one daughter, Jennie, who married John Frazier; Kate married Joe Boothe and their sons, Ed and Henry, lived in Lawrenceburg many years; Adelia married Joe Forsythe and they lived at VanArsdell, Mercer County, where Mr. Cal Snyder lives at the present time.

In 1932 when the new structure, named the Joe Blackburn bridge, was opened for traffic, the ferry was sold by Gaines and Griffy to the government for $35,000, and the farm for $3,500. The ferry was closed and relegated to the past with covered bridges and log cabins. This new bridge just below the ferry was opened June 11, 1932, at 12 o'clock noon. Grover C. Springate was the first toll collector on this new structure, and the first car to drive over the bridge and pay toll, was a model T Ford with a Fayette County license. The bridge was formerly dedicated the 8th of June, 1932. The setting for the exercises was nature's natural ampitheatre on a hillside near the beautiful bridge overlooking the rugged palisades of Kentucky river. Many people

Home of Judge William E. Dowling
Built in 1873 by Dr. Oran Witherspoon.

from Anderson, Woodford and adjoining counties assembled for the rites. The Lawrenceburg High School Band furnished the music, and Judge William E. Dowling was master of ceremonies, and introduced the speakers of the day: Governor Ruby Laffoon, the Hon. Ben Johnson, Chairman of the Highway Commission, Tandy Ellis and a Mr. Harris from Woodford County. The tenor of their remarks was past achievements, the march of progress in the state, and the two bridges that are the wonderful engineering feats of Kentucky and important links in the state's great system of roads. After the speaking the little daughters of Judge Dowling and Lieut. Governor Chandler, Mary Dowling and Mildred Chandler, cut the ribbons across the bridge and it was formally opened for traffic, but it was not until three days later that the toll collector was commissioned to declare the ferry obsolete and begin the collection of fares. The bridge was built at a cost of $480,000, including the price paid for the Tyrone ferry. There are 50,000 sacks of cement in the structure; it is 1,255 feet long and 170 feet from the water under the bridge, where the depth of the river is thirty-five feet. The Hon. J. C. S. Blackburn, for whom the structure was named, was born in Woodford County, October 1, 1838. He served in the Kentucky Legislature from 1871-'73; was a member of Congress for ten years and later elected U. S. Senator. He was an orator of rare gifts and powers, and one of Kentucky's illustrious sons.

In sight of the Blackburn bridge and lending grandeur to the view, is Young's High Bridge, named in honor of Col. Bennett H. Young, who built the Southern railroad through Anderson County in 1888. This is one of the great cantilever bridges of America, and has a span 200 feet longer than the one constructed at the mouth of Dix river. In 1876 when the latter bridge was built, it was the highest of the kind in America, and was considered a marvel of ingenuity. In Col. Young's notes he said that many noted engineers of the country had pronounced the work an impossibility. It was necessary to build a structure without trestling, and for that reason the cantilever principle was introduced by C. Shaler Smith, of Baltimore, an expert and skilled engineer who assumed the responsibility, and in the end his designs and calculations were found to be correct. Col. Young said: "The great cantilever arms stretched out from the piers on either side reaching the middle of the channel, and when the last bolt, which was to hold them in place was driven, it was said they did not vary 1-100th of an inch from the calculations which this man had made one day in his office in Baltimore." The railroad bridge that spans Kentucky river at Tyrone, Anderson County, is built on the same principle.

The following brief history of the building of the Southern railroad through Anderson County was gleaned from the files of the Anderson News which were loaned the writer by Judge Farris R. Feland, who was editor of the paper at that time. It was during the spring of 1886 that the prospect of a railroad through Anderson County engaged the attention of our citizens. The Judge wrote enthusiastic and convincing editorials, pointing out the many benefits that would accrue from having this means of transportation by adding value to the land, bringing the cities closer as markets for the farmer's produce, infusing new energy into the people, increasing the population, observing that other blue grass counties, with only half the trade that Anderson had in Kentucky, already had a railroad, and that "the stage coach must give way to the iron horse." The L. & N. railroad had the monopoly of the transportation of the county, it was said, to the amount of nine or ten thousand carloads per annum, which cost the county $60,000 or more to transfer this amount of traffic to and from the nearest depot. It was claimed that the L. & N. spent a large amount of money in the county to defeat voting the tax to procure the Southern road. Their hired attorney, Gen. Basil Duke, and other speakers, were sent through Anderson County speaking in opposition, and signifying the intention of the L. & N. to build a branch road through this territory. Feeling ran high. Many of our citizens spoke zealously for the building of the Southern, claiming we did not want a branch road, but a through road to open up the East and South, knowing that a short branch would still have a monopoly of the travel and traffic. Other good citizens were ardently opposed to voting the $100,000 tax, and spoke vehemently against it. It had been pointed out that the two banks of Lawrenceburg showed individual deposits of over $300,000, which was distinct from the capital stock and surplus, and that the county would not be oppressed by voting $100,000 stock in a railroad. For two weeks preceding the voting in August, Col. Bennett H. Young, Judge Hoke and many local speakers, began at ten o'clock in the morning, and spoke all day in behalf of the new enterprise, while citizens in their respective neighborhoods furnished burgoo for the crowds. An application had been made to Judge C. M. Lillard, of the Anderson County Court, by petition signed by more than twenty-five taxpayers of the county, requesting that the question of subscription to the capital stock of the Louisville Southern Railroad be submitted to the legal voters of said county. The election was held August 14, 1886, after which the count showed over 1400 against the road tax. Lawrenceburg registered 556 for and 197 against, while the county showed 827 for and 1,300 against the tax. The friends of the road were undaunted, and the question of a subscription was pushed. It was pointed out that those who were opposed to the tax, could give voluntarily a sum commensurate with benefits derived from a road. The watchword was "Don't Give Up the Road." Col. Young assured his friends the Southern would be built, and he expected Anderson County to cooperate. The editor of the News declared that "nothing but the most suicidal and senseless perversity can prevent Anderson County from getting this railroad." The sense of right and the principle of progress became prevalent, and in a short time $35,000 was subscribed. Alton had voted 65 for the tax and 186 against, but ere long her citizens subscribed $3,000 to the fund. Other subscriptions were secured and on October 21, 1886, the contract to build the Southern road from Louisville to Lawrenceburg was let, and in March, 1887, 150 men were at work on the road in Anderson County. On the "Roll of Honor" of 1887, the names of those who gave the right of way through their lands in the county were: E. H. Reddish, John B. Mason, John B. Wilson, W. W. Satterwhite, G. H. Gaines, W. H. Tracy and Wm. F. Bond. Others along the way sold the right of way at satisfactory prices.

By the first of April, 1888, crowds of people from the surrounding country congregated daily at the scene of the track laying of the railroad ties near Lawrenceburg. Some parties brought dinner and remained all day. On ten o'clock Thursday morning, April 5, 1888, the first passenger train to reach town pulled in with Judge W. H. McBrayer and family and a number of Harrodsburg people on board. The incoming and outgoing trains caused considerable commotion among the country folk in town, many of whom had never seen a train of cars before. May the 28th of that year saw the first excursion train to Louisville, and many Anderson County folk were aboard. The longest freight train of that day went through Lawrenceburg, June 28, 1888, with thirty-four cars, mostly cattle. During the last week of August,

1889, trains were run for the first time, from Louisville to Lexington, over Young's High Bridge at Tyrone. The number of passengers averaged over a 1,000 for every day, as recorded by Judge Feland in the Anderson News. A fresh boom of Lawrenceburg began, as was evidenced by the new buildings springing up, and Col. Bennett Young heartily agreed with the wag who said, "Lawrenceburg is a large town for its size," for, as the Colonel said the books of the railroad company showed that this town did more business than any place of its size on this line, than any in the state. At this date Lawrenceburg had 1,500 inhabitants, six churches, three schools, two banks, twelve business houses, three livery stables and three blacksmith shops.

The steel bridge across Bailey's Run at Tyrone was built at a cost of about $7,000, and was opened January 1, 1907. A large crowd was in attendance, burgoo served and speeches made by W. H. Morgan, F. L. Ripy, W. E. Dowling and Lillard H. Carter. Miss Gertrude Lancaster rode upon the structure on the "small Odd Fellow mule" and christened the new bridge by breaking a bottle of whiskey on the platform.

CHAPTER IV

THE CONFEDERATE MONUMENT

On June 1, 1893, the ex-Confederates of the county began preparations toward erecting a monument in the courthouse yard in memory of their comrades who fell fighting for the "Lost Cause." The committee to consider plans and raise $1,000 for the project, was composed of S. O. Hackley, P. H. Thomas, James A. McGuire, W. T. Rice and James Gee. The contract was let to William Adams & Son, of Lexington, Ky. The monument was to be placed in front of the office of the County Clerk where a large locust tree stood. It was to be seventeen feet high, including the statue of a soldier at rest parade, the statue to be made in Italy. On the base was to be the names of four companies that went from this county, numbering 300. In the course of a year the monument was ready for shipment, but the work was retarded on account of insufficient funds collected to defray all expenses. The business of receiving subscriptions was turned over to Esq. J. A. McGuire, and in the course of time the money was forthcoming and the monument was placed according to specifications. The dedicatory exercises were held in the courthouse, and the silver-tongued orator, Col. W. C. P. Breckinridge, delivered the address of the occasion, after which the crowd repaired to the yard to witness the unveiling by little granddaughters (who had been drilled for the ceremony) of two of the Confederate veterans, and it was discovered the veil had been lifted by a veteran who took high-dudgeon at a kind allusion the orator of the day had made to Abraham Lincoln. The disgrunted old soldier was seen marching up street with the "veil" trailing in the dust, while the two little girls wept copious tears over being denied their part in the show. The awkwardness of the situation was relieved by martial music floating on the tense atmosphere while patriotic songs burst from the throats of an amused audience.

THE LAWRENCEBURG ROTARY CLUB

The Lawrenceburg Rotary Club was organized October, 1925. The sixteen charter members were: Dr. J. L. Toll, Holly Witherspoon, Dr. T. H. Posey, Wilkes Bond, J. W. Gaines, Edward Taylor, Raymond Trent, W. G. Eldred, T. J. Ballard, Bernard Griffy, Roger H. Lillard, Harry McAfee, Robert Johnson, Earnest Ripy, Will Dowling and Frank Simpson. Others who have been members since are, Charles E. McGinnis. John Dowling, S. V. Gordon, Harry B. Lane, John W. Dawson, J. M. B. Birdwhistle, J. L. Sherwood, J. E. Blackburn, Charles O. Ryan, Jerome Robinson, Hugh R. Martin, George C. McWilliams, Dr. S. R. Boggess, Ed Adams, C. A. Routt, Frank Routt, J. A. Cain, C. T. Ward, Wm. M. Routt, George Insco, Thomas H. Renfro, John Ash, M. C. Crain, Maurice Hawkins and Dr. Lee Dare. Past presidents of the club are as follows: Tom Ballard, Charles McGinnis, Gay Eldred, Roger Lillard, Bill Gaines, Lewis Sherwood, Obie Ryan, James Madison "Birdie" Birdwhistle, John Dawson, Raymond Boggess, Raymond Trent and C. T. Ward. The activities of the club have been diversified and extensive. Besides its support of the international organization, it has spent some $2,000 for service activities in the local field. One of the first acts of the club was to reorganize

World War Memorial. Erected 1936.

the Commercial Club, and through it help secure the thread and cheese factories as industries in the community. Another important work of the club has been its activities in behalf of crippled children. The club not only sponsors drives for the raising of funds for the children's work, but it sought and secured medical treatment for every crippled child in the county, and wherever it was necessary bore the financial expense of medical and hospital treatment, and furnished such auxiliary needs as artificial limbs, braces, crutches and glasses. Every crippled child in the county has been helped, of which there were eighteen or twenty. This led the club to the sponsoring of the County Health Board and securing a full-time county health physician for the county. Dr. Raymond Boggess was chosen for this work, and under his leadership sanitary conditions have been greatly improved. Vaccination, testing of eyes and health instructions have been made available for every child in the county. A weekly clinic is held where mothers can bring their children for an examination, and correction if necessary. The club, the church and the community sustained a great loss in the passing of Dr. Boggess in the early part of this year.

The Rotary Club has furnished glasses for children of defective vision. All this has made the county one of the best in the state as far as its health activities are concerned. Another worthy project which the club has sponsored is the Scout work. For nearly nine years it has been supporting this work financially and in other ways. Over 110 Scouts have enrolled during this period. The club has led in scattering Christmas cheer, by giving baskets containing food, clothing and toys to the under-privileged of the community. Thus in its ten years of history, the Rotary Club has lived its motto, "Service Before Self," and has done much along the line of creating understanding and good will in the community. Of its charter members four have passed into the great beyond; the first president, Tom Ballard; past presidents, Roger Lillard, Dr. Raymond Boggess and Frank Simpson. We trust that they live again in "lives made better by their presence."

THE BOY SCOUTS OF LAWRENCEBURG

The Boy Scout troop was organized in May, 1926, with W. G. Eldred as Scoutmaster, who has served in this capacity through the ten years since its organization. The following have served one or more years during this time as Assistant Scoutmasters: Harry B. Lane, Ben Cain, John W. Nevins, David E. Adams, Paul Vaughn, Ben R. Bond and William Crossfield.

The following were charter members of the troop in 1928: Robert Baxter, J. G. Bartlett, John Robert Cook, Edward Crossfield, Wm. G. Eldred, Gilbert Franklin, Jack Gordon, Vincent Goodlet, Floyd Hahn, Raymond Hawkins, June Hiner, William Martin, W. S. Johnson, Marcus McBrayer, Stewart McBrayer, Blakemore McBrayer, William McGurk, Ernest Ripy, Lloyd Rogers, Carl Roberts, Edward Sweasy, Jess Sweasy, Jack Strange, Charles Sleeter, Marion Thacker, Waller Bailey Thacker, Dave Yocum.

The following have been admitted as members since that time: Hollis Ballow, Emmett Cartinhour, Herman Crossfield, Harold Hanks, William Leathers, Hugh Martin, Tom Posey, Robert Hansel, Billy Goodlet, Dan Satterwhite, Garnet Watts, Bob Posey, Leon Hansell, Rice Mullins, Otis Thompson, Floyd Black, Tom Ripy, Charles Ryan, Harold Martin, Shelby Williams, Clarence Black, Vernon Marlow, John F. Cannon, Jerome Tartar, Clifton

Tatum, W. J. Hughes, Edwin A. Brown, Charles K. Brown, Edwin Booker, Stewart Gordon, Paul Waddell, Ollie Searcy, Elliott Garrison, Steve Bates, Wallace Roach, Ben Smoot, Wilson Kent, Bronson Redmon, Alfred Roberts, Charles Sanders, Waller Mountjoy, Hudson Yocum.

The present troop as follows (1936): J. D. Cook, John T. Cox, Jr., John Gilbert, Billy Gorham, Jack Gorham, John C. Goodlett, Edward Houchins, Ben Lyen, Don McGinnis, Harold Watts, George McWilliams, William Yates, Willis Milton, Irvin Overall, Kenneth Perry, Bobbie Ripy, Howard Ripy, Billy Routt, Roland Roberts, Rob Roy Young, Dave Williams.

Ninety boys have received instructions in Scouting in nine years. Two officials and three Scouts have taken the highest Scout rank, that of Eagle Scout: W. G. Eldred, Ben Cain, Earnest Ripy, Ben Selby and Howard Ripy. Seven others have taken next to the highest rank, that of Life Scout. They are Robert Baxter, William Eldred, Vincent Goodlett, Wm. Crossfield, Bobby Ripy, George McWilliams and Wm. Yates. Eleven others achieved the rank of Star Scout: Ollie Searcy, Paul Waddell, Harold Martin, Charles Ryan, Robert Hansel, John R. Cook, Edward Crossfield, Wm. Martin, Marcus McBrayer and Edward Sweasy.

The Scout movement has been sponsored by the Rotary Club and the Christian church has furnished a Scout room, the place of meeting through all these years.

THE GIRL SCOUTS

The Girl Scouts of Lawrenceburg, Troop 1, was organized September, 1934, by Mrs. Eve Mooreman. In December of the same year the troop was registered at Girl Scout Headquarters and Mrs. C. O. Ryan was commissioned the first Captain. The following girls are registered: Red Wing Patrol, Mary Marrs Board, Mary Jane Ripy, Ann Dowling, Jesse May Holman, Ann Gorham, Mary Dowling, Rayme Trent and Rosalind Young. The Star Patrol, Sarah Louise Ripy, Nancy Toll, Martha J. Burford, Jane Ellen Boggess, Carlin Coke, Margaret Thacker, Ruth Royalty and Rosalind Routt. The purpose of the Girl Scout movement is to help girls realize the ideals of womanhood as a preparation for their responsibilities in the home and for service in the community. The program emphasizes the outdoor life, and gives a practical knowledge of health, home-making, first-aid work and handcraft. The Girl Scout movement is non-sectarian and non-political. The membership of the local troup is twenty-six. Miss Pauline McGurk has been commissioned as Lieutenant and assistant to the Captain.

CLUBS

The first Woman's Club was organized in Lawrenceburg in 1891, and was called the Magazine Club. The following ladies constituted the charter members: Mrs. J. W. Mahan, President; Mesdames T. B. Ripy, Sr., W. B. Saffell, C. F. Searcy, J. R. Walker, W. P. Walker, E. O. Witherspoon, W. C. Woods, John Dowling, J. W. Gilbert, J. M. Johnson, R. H. Lillard and W. T. Bond. Mrs. J. W. Mahan, the founder of the club, remained its only President the fifteen years of its existence. The number of the club never increased, but when a vacancy occurred another name was presented, and a new member elected only by a unanimous vote. Every member subscribed for a magazine, and twice each week these periodicals were delivered by a "club boy" at the doors of the club members in regular rote. Once a month, one of the members was hostess to the club in her home, and "a feast of reason and flow of soul" was enjoyed. A review of the most interesting articles and stories in the magazines were discussed, styles, fashions and the precociousness of one's children and the efficiency of cooks were reviewed, but "gossip" was strictly eschewed. Only four vacancies occurred during the duration of the club, and they were filled by Mesdames L. W. McKee, W. F. Lillard, D. L. Meriwether and H. V. Bell. The Magazine Club automatically ceased upon the organization of the Pierian Club in 1905, most of its members joining the new club.

THE BOOK CLUB

The Book Club, an informal and interesting club, was organized by Mrs. J. O. Franklin in 1934. It has a membership of about fifteen ladies who are interested in the newest literature of the day. Each member buys one new book a year and at the meetings a book review is given by one of the ladies for the interest and edification of those in attendance. The books are kept in circulation among the members until each is read and thoroughly reviewed, then it becomes the property of the purchaser. A savory plate lunch is served during the social hour.

The members are: Mesdames J. O. Franklin, T. H. Posey, William Dowling, Mary Dowling Bond, H. B. Carpenter, O. C. McKay, William Duncan, R. H. Marrs, C. O. Ryan, George McWilliams, Stanley Johnson, June Givens, J. L. Toll, Lydia K. Bond and Misses Sallie Spencer and Kathrine McKee.

THE COMMERCIAL CLUB

On January 31, 1905, Mr. J. P. McWilliams, who was Mayor of Lawrenceburg at that time, called a mass meeting at the court house of the business men of the town, as there existed a strong desire for a Commercial Club, looking toward the welfare of the community and betterment of conditions in the town and county. The call of the Mayor was answered by a large attendance of the best citizens of the town and county. On this occasion the Commercial Club was organized with William E. Dowling, President; C. E. Bond, Vice-President; J. W. Gaines, George C. Hoffman, E. W. Ripy, G. B. Hawkins and G. W. Hutcheson, directors; W. P. Marsh, Secretary, and J. C. Thompson, Treasurer. At the first meeting a movement was inaugurated which resulted in the installation of the electric light plant, and on September 1, 1905, electricity forced out kerosene as an illuminant in Lawrenceburg. At the annual meeting in February, 1906, the President, Secretary and Board of Directors were re-elected. T. J. Ballard was chosen for Vice-President; M. W. Bartlett, Treasurer, and Gus. D. Stephens, Sergeant-at-Arms. The admission fee was fixed at three dollars, and many new members added. It was pointed out that our town stood in need of manufacturing industries of various kinds, and that the Commercial Club could give prospective investors all the assistance and information possible in any line of business. Note was made of the fact that during the year 1905 more than $125,000 were expended in the city for new buildings and an era of prosperity was enjoyed. The record in the Anderson News shows that on the night of February 15, 1906, a delegation of twenty-two business men of Frankfort visited the Lawrenceburg Commercial Club to discuss the proposed trolley line from that city to our town. Mr. W. S. Farmer, a former merchant of Anderson County, spoke of the near proximity of the two cities, and that they should be brought into closer connection. The fact was cited that Anderson was close kin to Franklin, having been made from one of Franklin's ribs, like Eve of old. It was figured that the cost of the trolley line would be about $12,000 per mile to build, and the power house and installation would cost $100,000 more. The city already had a splendid power house, which could be used if a line of this kind were built. Many enthusiastic speeches were made in favor of the new project but the trolley line never materialized. No prophetic voice foretold the advent of the autos and bus lines that eventually put the trolleys out of existence. At this meeting the Frankfort delegation extended an invitation to the Commercial Club to see the laying of the corner stone of the new Capitol building, which would be held on the 16th of June, 1906.

At one time the Commercial Club offered a prize for the best slogan for Lawrenceburg. The winner was Mrs. Keene Johnson, and her slogan was, "Come in, but don't knock." At that time the Johnsons lived in Lawrenceburg, Mr. Johnson being the editor of the Anderson News. Today he is Lieutenant Governor of the State and his home is Richmond, Ky.

THE MASONIC LODGE

In the Court record of July 14, 1828, on motion of Nelson C. Johnson, leave was granted to the Masonic Fraternity in Lawrenceburg to finish off a room in the garret of the court house about to be erected and to pay for the furnishing of it, and to occupy it as a lodge room when the court house was finished. Record of October, 1870: Anderson Lodge No. 90 permitted to use upper large room of the court house for Masonic Lodge, provided they will make a partition and prepare the room at their own expense. To be occupied as long as they comply with the order, and until the county needs it.

On the 19th of September, 1828, under a dispensation of Samuel Daviess, Grand Master of the State, the Lodge was duly constituted and a charter granted with the following officers: Fielding L. Connor, W. M.; Dixon G. Dedman, S. W.; James S. Hackley, J. W.; L. J. Witherspoon, S. D.; John F. Blackwell, J. D.; John T. Daviess, Secretary, and William Hudgins, Treasurer.

When the court house burned in 1859 a room on the west side of Main street over one of the stores was equipped for the meeting of the lodge.

The new Masonic hall was built in Lawrenceburg in 1906, and at that time the officers were: George Hoffman, W. M.; J. W. Gaines, S. W.; John F. Johnson, J. W.; George Hutcheson, Treasurer, and W. C. Woods, Secretary; A. H. Witherspoon, S. D.; R. L. Frazier, J. D.; George Green, Chaplain; M. W. Bartlett, Organist; G. D. Stephens, S. S.; J. W. Sale, J. S.; James B. Willis, Tyler.

Today (1936) the officers are: C. T. Ward, W. M.; Eugene Mizner, S. W.; J. E. Sweeney, J. W.; Edward Brown, Secretary; Frank Routt, Treasurer.

The Centennial celebration of Anderson Lodge No. 90 was observed at the Masonic Temple, Friday evening, August 24, 1928. Masons from many sections of Kentucky participated in the exercises. More than 200 guests enjoyed the banquet. In 1906 the corner stone of the new building was laid with George A. Lewis, of Frankfort, acting as Grand Master. The welcome address was made by Col. Frank L. Ripy.

Dr. C. H. Hudson, of Frankfort, was the speaker of the occasion. The history of the Lodge was reviewed by J. W. Gaines, who told of its helpfulness in the progress of Lawrenceburg. In 1837 Dixon G. Dedman donated $200 toward purchasing a suitable site for a school house, and on November, 1839, the lodge laid the corner stone of the Anderson County Seminary. This school was succeeded by the Normal College established by J. C. Willis in 1888. On October 15, 1878, the lodge laid the corner stone of the memorial monument in the court house yard to the Salt River Tigers who saw service in the War with Mexico. Keeling C. Gaines, Master, presided on that occasion.

THE HAMILTON CHAPTER OF THE EASTERN STAR

The Hamilton Chapter of the Eastern Star, No. 293, the Woman's Auxiliary of the Masonic Lodge, was organized in Lawrenceburg, October 25, 1919. The first officers were: Miss Mary Paxton, Worthy Matron; Mrs. Verna Bond, Associate Matron; Mrs. Edward Brown, W. P.; Mrs. John Brunk, Secretary. There were eighteen charter members. Today the membership is seventy and the officers as follows: Mrs. J. B. Sweeney, Worthy Matron; Mrs. Mabel Baxter, Associate W. M.; J. B. Sweeney, W. P.; Andrew Cain, A. P.; Mrs. Hardin Baxter, Secretary.

UNITED DAUGHTERS OF THE CONFEDERACY

The local chapter of the U. D. C. was organized in Lawrenceburg in 1901 by Mrs. R. G. Stoner, State President of Mount Sterling, Ky. There were thirty charter members and the following officers were elected: Mrs. Harriet Hanks, President; Mrs. Thomas McMurry, First Vice-President; Mrs. J. P. Ripy, Second Vice-President; Mrs. John Dowling, Third Vice-President; Mrs. J. W. Mahan, Treasurer; Mrs. Wilkes Morgan, Corresponding Secretary; Miss Helen Ripy, Recording Secretary; Mrs. John I. Felix, Historian. The Chapter was named for Captain Gus Dedman, who had mustered a company from the steps of the old Galt House in Lawrenceburg and marched to the war never to return, for he was killed on the battlefield at Chickamauga. Today the U. D. C. has a membership of twenty-eight with the following officers: Mrs. Carelton Rice, President; Mrs. Stanley Johnson, First Vice-President; Mrs. Chas. Routt, Second Vice-President; Mrs. Alma Hackley Smith, Secretary; Mrs. Lizzie Carleton, Treasurer; Miss Minnie Shely, Registrar; Miss Emma Crain, Chaplain; Mrs. Mary Dowling Bond, Historian.

The Lawrenceburg D. A. R. Chapter was organized in 1916 at the home of Mrs. Lewis McKee. Mrs. Boone, the State Regent, from Paducah, was present and helped perfect the organization. There were fifteen charter members: Mesdames L. W. McKee, Roy Rutherford, Clide Moss, E. W. Ripy, J. S. Collins, Alma Felix, W. E. Dowling, C. C. Trent, O. C. McKay, Belle Walker, Rose Searcy, and Misses Kathrine McKee, Jessie Mae Lillard and Mollie Bond. Today the organization numbers twenty. The officers at present are: Mrs. Jerome Robinson, Regent; Mrs. Stanley Trent, Vice-Regent; Mrs. J. C. Vanarsdale, Chaplain; Mrs. R. E. Garrison, Recording Secretary; Mrs. W. E. Dowling, Corresponding Secretary; Mrs. T. H. Posey, Treasurer; Mrs. Robert Ripy, Registrar; Mrs. Morris Case, Historian; Miss Jessie Mae Lillard, Librarian.

HISTORY OF ANDERSON COUNTY

THE PIERIAN CLUB

The Pierian Club was organized November, 1905. Became member of the State Federation in 1906, and of the General Federation in 1910. Motto, Nulla Dies Sine Linea. Club colors, Purple and Gold. The charter members were Mrs. Aileen K. Gilbert, Mrs. C. C. Trent, Mrs. Mary B. Lillard, Mrs. Lydia K. Bond, Mrs. Leila T. Collins, Mrs. Mary L. Hooper, Mrs. Lee F. Paynter, Mrs. Rhoda C. Kavanaugh, Mrs. Ethyl G. Ripy, Mrs. Betty M. Bell, Mrs. Wallace M. Bartlett, Mrs. Louise P. Lillard, Mrs. Sadie W. Powers, Mrs. Pearl W. Bond, Mrs. Ophelia L. Meriwether, Mrs. Mary Dowling Bond, Mrs. Olive T. Posey, Misses Helen Ripy, Lois Williams, Bessie Flippin, Verna Toll, Fay Walker, Susie Hooper, and Emrine Gilbert. The first President appointed was Mrs. Wallace M. Bartlett, now Mrs. Madison Taylor, of New York; Vice-President, Mrs. Horace V. Bell; Recording Secretary, Mrs. Ethyl G. Ripy, now Mrs. J. C. Cantrill, of Frankfort, Ky.; Corresponding Secretary, Miss Bessie Flippin; Treasurer, Miss Susie Hooper.

Those who have served as presidents of the club are:

1905-'08, Mrs. Madison Taylor.
1908-'09, Mrs. J. C. Cantrill.
1909-'10, Mrs. W. Tom Bond.
1910-'11, Mrs. H. V. Bell.
1911-'12, Mrs. Mary Dowling Bond.
1912-'13, Mrs. C. C. Trent.
1913-'14, Mrs. L. W. McKee.
1914-'15, Mrs. John Dowling.
1915-'16, Mrs. Roger Lillard.
1916-'17, Mrs. Carleton Rice.
1917-'18, Miss Mary Paxton.
1918-'19, Mrs. E. H. Marrs.
1919-'20, Mrs. G. B. Claxon.
1920-'21, Mrs. T. H. Posey.
1921-'22, Mrs. J. Matt Birdwhistle.

1922-'23, Mrs. W. M. Duncan.
1923-'24, Mrs. H. B. Carpenter, Sr.
1924-'25, Mrs. G. B. Hawkins.
1925-'26, Mrs. C. O. Ryan.
1926-'27, Mrs. G. D. McWilliams.
1927-'28, Mrs. Harry B. Carpenter.
1928-'29, Mrs. C. T. Ward.
1929-'30, Mrs. Robert Johnson.
1930-'31, Mrs. Jerome Robinson.
1931-'32, Mrs. W. W. Wash.
1932-'33, Mrs. O. C. McKay.
1933-'34, Mrs. E. E. Spencer.
1934-'35, Mrs. J. O. Franklin.
1935-'36, Mrs. Victoria Woodward.
1936-'37, Mrs. John W. Dawson.

The first meeting of the Pierian Club was in the Holman House, formerly known as the Galt House that stood on the present site of the post office. Early in 1906, the club placed a library in the town. Two rooms, exempt from rent, were proffered by the Lawrenceburg National Bank over its place of business, as a repository for the books, and in a few weeks a very creditable neucleus of a library was presided over by members who took turn about acting as Librarian. In two years' time there were 2,000 books in circulation in the county. In 1908 the club President, Mrs. J. C. Cantrill, corresponded with Andrew Carnegie relative to giving a library to the town. At this time this generous Scotch-American was giving libraries to cities that met certain requirements to attain them. The club raised funds to buy a lot, and got the city fathers to levy a 5 per cent tax on the $100 making $500 a year to maintain a library, thereby assuring the $5,000 gift from the Laird of Skibo Castle to erect the building. Mr. Carnegie had never given furnishings for a library, but our President's appealing letters, accompanied by clippings from the Anderson News of the club's activities, prompted the benefactor to do the unprecedented thing and send the club $800 toward putting shelves, tables and chairs in the library. On Saturday evening, October 9, 1909, the new library was formerly dedicated at the Presbyterian

Carnegie Library.

church, Rev. H. N. Reubelt, of the Christian church, delivering the dedicatory address. The lot for the new library was purchased from T. J. Ballard by the club for the sum of $675. The contract to build was let to Mr. Charles E. Bond, a public spirited contractor who used all the funds in the building without recompense to himself.

In the record of 1915, the Librarian, Miss Susie Hooper, reported a circulation of 10,150 books for that year. In November, 1913, the club erected a $500 drinking fountain for man and beast on Main street in front of the court house. In 1915 the club rented a house on Fairview and opened a temporary hospital to treat patients in the county afflicted with trachoma. A Health and Welfare League, consisting of citizens of the town and county, helped make this project a possibility, by donating cots, linens and furnishings to help make the hospital adequate for this purpose. A nurse was in attendance, and more than fifty patients received treatment free of charge. Dr. McMullen, a trachoma specialist sent out by the government, came from Lexington twice a week and brought two experienced nurses to assist in the treatment and operations. A generous public responded to the club's SOS and sent in cereals, butter, eggs and other food stuffs, and for nearly five months this work was continued to check the ravages of trachoma. Dr. McMullen stated that this was the only private hospital in the United States for the treatment of this disease. Children from Mercer and Franklin counties also received the benefit of the treatment. In 1918 the club purchased an old landmark on North Main street, a little brick cottage built prior to 1825, for a club house, paying $1,500 for the property. In 1925 the house was remodeled, the grounds beautified, and the first meeting of the club was held in its new home on October 2, 1926. For many years the club held its sessions in the chapel of the city High School. During the period of prosperity, the holdings of the club consisted of $5,000, in Liberty bonds, an Argentine bond, a German bond and a $1,000 worth of stock in the Dean & Sherk thread factory. There were times when it was necessary to sell some of these holdings to liquidate indebtedness on the club property, its improvements and other civic undertakings. In 1928 the Junior Club was organized with Mrs. T. Ward as sponsor and counsellor.

Through the thirty-two years of its existence, the Pierian Club has been a potent factor in the civic and cultural life of the community. It has had the support and co-operation of the citizens, the Anderson News and the municipal authorities for the advancement of every good cause it has undertaken. The club gave two officers to the State Federation—Mrs. Madison Taylor was State President in 1914-'16, and Mrs. J. C. Cantrill Recording Secretary at the same time.

MONTROSE

One of the most beautiful country estates in Anderson County is Montrose, on the Bond's Mill pike about four miles from Lawrenceburg. It was founded by Col. Davis Brown of the firm of J. T. S. Brown & Sons Distilling Company, who owned and operated the Old Prentice distillery which was built on this estate in 1912. The attractive home was erected in 1914, on a high hill with a picturesque natural setting overlooking Salt River, commanding a view of a beautiful wooded area in the distance. The approach to the home grounds is through a tall Japanese gate built of teak wood, a replica of the torii gates in Japan that indicate the proximity of a Japanese temple. Col. Brown planted rare trees indigenous to this soil, and laid off the spacious grounds in flower gardens like paisley shawls; built pools and waterfalls; spanned a ravine with a picturesque bridge constructed of hundreds of cedar logs, covered with wistaria; built summer houses, bird cotes and winding paths bordered with rare shrubs and flowers that furnish a continuation of blossoms throughout the seasons. Before his death five years ago, Col. Brown and his wife entertained their friends here with true Kentucky hospitality.

Today the home is occupied by Mr. Wilgus Naugher and family. The estate embraces the new "Old Joe" distilling plant. It comprises 150 acres and is the property of Mrs. C. M. Laurie of Chicago.

"O beauteous spot!—of sweet repose,
Of tangled vine and climbing rose;
Of pine-girt hill and gleaming pool,
And shadowy grottoes, dark and cool;

Of sunny mead and flowery dell,
Of purling stream—historic bell—
Quaint eastern torii—rustic bridge—
Afar the dim and purple ridge

That shuts in this exquisite scene,
Of winding river—meadows green—
Old covered bridge—a water-mill
At base of this enchanting hill;
Upon whose summit sunlight glows
Of fairest gem of all—Montrose."
—Henry Cleveland Wood.

ANDERSON COUNTY IN THE WORLD WAR

In 1917 Anderson County rallied to the colors when the United States cast her lot with the allied armies, and 293 of her sons were inducted into the service, twenty-two having volunteered before the induction. Under the selective draft law there were 1,952 Anderson County men who registered. Fourteen men from this county lost their lives over seas. Jesse D. Lowen was the first man who paid the supreme sacrifice. Others were Randolph Coke, Willie Cinnamon, Forest Haydon, William Hansel, William Beasley, Delbert Riley, Charles Hilliard, Jesse R. Morris, James N. Tucker, Henry Monroe, Vernon Watts, Nelson Woodward and John Roy Carter, the latter being colored.

Eighteen were disabled or wounded during the service with the U. S. army or in the navy: Chris M. Bond, Roy E. Rose, Marion C. Brown, Howard Birdwhistle, Wade Carter, Bradley Disponett, Clarence Haskins, Grover D. Johnson, Lieut. A. I. McKee, U. S. navy; Ollie P. Montgomery, Andrew Richardson, James Satterly, Lieut. Ezra Sparrow, Earl Spencer, Bryan Warford, William R. Watts and Ira West. The boys under draft age in the S. A. T. C. in universities, were Paul Routt, William F. Bond, Frank Routt, Elmer Adkins, Mitchell Bailey, Miller McAfee, John Draffen, Wallace Wilson, Henry

"Montrose," home of Wilgus Naugher.

Crossfield, Raymond Boggess, Parlin Lillard, Nolan Carter and Howard McClure.

Private Randolph Coke was killed July 26, 1918, and interred in a cemetery furnished by the French government. In 1921 his remains were returned to the United States and buried in the Fox Creek cemetery, Anderson County, near where he spent his childhood days. On the occasion of his interment more than 3,000 people assembled at the little cemetery to honor his memory.

A bronze plated granite memorial, nine feet tall and five feet wide, has been erected to our World War dead. It occupies the place where the Pierian Club fountain stood in front of the court house, the latter having been removed to the club house grounds. The monument was erected at a cost of $1,000, raised by popular subscription, and supervised by the Anderson County Post No. 34, American Legion.

The dedication of the memorial took place on the morning of November 11, 1936. More than a 1,000 people filled the public square when the ceremonies were opened by Commander Frank Routt, Anderson Post No. 34, American Legion, and Past Commander Stanley Trent. As the court house clock struck eleven the monument was unveiled by Rosalind Young, daughter of Past Legion Commander, Ben Young, and Raymie Trent, daughter of Stanley Trent. The two girls pulled the covering from the stone by means of long white ribbons, after which taps were sounded by the Frankfort Bugle Corps. Then came three volleys from the Harrodsburg firing squad. This was followed by the singing of America by the assemblage, led by Mrs. J. L. Toll, after thirty seconds of silent tribute. Ben Young, Chairman of the Memorial Committee, expressed appreciation for the fine response of the public in making the memorial a possibility. This was followed by an address by Past State Commander, Eldon S. Dummitt, of Lexington. Judge J. T. Cox and Mayor J. L. Toll made short addresses accepting the monument for the county and city. The benediction by Post Chaplain, Ezra Sparrow, completed the exercises. On the speaker's stand built in the court house yard, were the parents of the boys to whom the memorial was dedicated. The fall weather was beautiful and the ceremonies were solemn and impressive.

Two beautiful flags, one an American flag and the other a blue and gold flag of the Legion, were dedicated with appropriate ceremonies the evening of the 9th at the City Hall at the regular meeting of the Legion of Anderson County.

It was revealed on this occasion that when the memorial to our war dead would be unveiled it would be paid for in full, and would be the property of Anderson County with no strings attached. Much credit was due the members of the Memorial Committee composed of Ben Young, Chairman; John McGinnis, Ollie Calvert, Tom Stratton, Mason Morgan and Frank Routt, also the Auxiliary ladies who helped materially in the promotion of the memorial project.

THE RED CROSS CHAPTER

Anderson County Chapter of the Red Cross was organized in the summer of 1917 with J. M. B. Birdwhistle as County Chairman; J. W. Gaines, Treasurer, and Freeman Gilbert, Secretary. There were five auxiliary chapters in the county. Auxiliary No. 1, at Lawrenceburg, had the following officers when organized: Mrs. J. C. VanArsdell, Chairman of Woman's Work;

Mrs. W. R. Hazelrigg, Secretary; Mrs. C. C. Trent, Treasurer; Mrs. Lydia K. Bond, Publicity. The second year Mrs. R. H. Lillard was Chairman of Women's Work. Auxiliary No. 2, at Fox Creek, with Mrs. W. R. Crossfield, Chairman of Women's Work. Auxiliary No. 3, at Johnsonsville, headed by Mrs. J. D. Crutcher. Auxiliary No. 4, at Glensborough, with Mrs. Joe Cook, Chairman. Auxiliary No. 5, at Goshen, headed by Mrs. Leslie V. Sale.

The Red Cross of this county completed and shipped to headquarters 332 soldier pajamas, 563 knitted sweaters and jackets, 810 pairs of sox, and over 250 miscellaneous articles, and 600 pounds of clothing for refugee relief. The Junior Auxiliary, known as the Lawrenceburg "Sister Susies," was organized as follows: Mrs. Lydia K. Bond, Director of Children's Work; Misses Lois Williams and Kitty Botts, Assistants; Rebecca Marrs, Secretary; Marzette Gudgel, Treasurer; Jessie Mae Lillard, Chairman of the knitting division. Eugenia Witherspoon (Mrs. June Givens) was Chairman of the Children's Auxiliary at Ninevah.

SONS OF ANDERSON COUNTY PIONEERS

Anderson County has a long roster of boys who have gone out from their native heath and "made good." They are descendants of those sturdy pioneers who overcame obstacles and carved a civilization out of a wilderness while guarding forts that formed a citadel of safety against savages. Such was the heritage from the ancestral background that the attributes of these brave men have been transmitted to the third and fourth generation, as is evidenced by the handicaps that have been overcome by some of their posterity in a struggle to attain a goal in their respective lines of endeavor. We give a thumbnail biography of some of them:

Thomas June Hiner, on the maternal side, came of substantial ancestry of the county. His grandfather, Joel G. Lyen, was a noted educator of Lawrenceburg and said to be the best mathematition in the county. "June" was educated in the city school, and the position he occupies today was attained by his own determined efforts. He is Assistant United States Meteorologist at the Luken Airport Weather Bureau in Cincinnati. He studied at the Cincinnati Trade School, and was ready to fly before he was old enough (21) to get a pilot's license. He entered the Weather Bureau Service in 1929, and was transferred to the airport office in 1930. He not only makes weather observations from the ground but when in doubt about conditions aloft, he takes a plane and taxis around the clouds to make certain about the weather. He was a private in the Cincinnati Automotive Squadron for three years, where he learned formation flying, stunting and cross-country work by flying with officers of the unit. During his airport work many notables have come to him for weather information. Among these have been Jimmy Doolittle, Amelia Earhart, Mrs. Franklin D. Roosevelt and others. Thomas June Hiner is referred to as the "flying weatherman" of the airport. His wife was Miss Florence McElhaney of Cincinnati.

Andrew Irwin McKee and Logan McKee, sons of Major and Mrs. Lewis W. McKee, received their training from Kavanaugh High School in Lawrenceburg, and were honor graduates of the United States Naval Academy at Annapolis, and are now serving with distinction in the navy. In 1928, the eldest son, Andrew Irwin McKee, who has rank of Lieutenant Commander, was designing and building submarines in the navy yards in Philadelphia.

The following appeared in the New York Tribune of that year: Portsmouth, N. H. (December 6, 1928)—"The United States submarine, V-4, established what navy officers said was a record for submarine diving in the U. S. Navy when it reached a depth of 318 feet during a five hour diving test off the Isle of Shoals. The submarine, the largest in the navy, was down twenty-one minutes, and officers said it handled better than any in which they had ever submerged. Lieut. Commander, Andrew Irwin McKee, of the Bureau of Construction and Repair of the Navy, was in command." Today this young Lieut. Commander is building Dreadnaughts at Mare Island, San Francisco. He married Miss Kathrine Brown, of Portsmouth, N. H., and they have three sons and a daughter. Logan McKee has likewise attained the rank of Lieutenant Commander and is with the fleet in Pacific waters. Three years ago he was commissioned to superintend the installation of a new Deisel engine in the Mayflower, the President's pleasure yacht, and redecorate the craft, for which work he received plaudits from President Roosevelt. Logan married Miss Elizabeth Millard, of Shelbyville, and they have one daughter, Jane Middleton. Their home is in Long Beach, California.

Hilliary Yocum, son of D. W. Yocum, comes of a family whose name is in the early records of Anderson County. He migrated to Miami, Florida, a number of years ago and became associated with the official life of that city and today fills the strenuous and responsible office of Chief of Police of Miami Beach.

J. Sprole and William Wallace Lyons, born in Anderson County, are sons of Dr. J. S. Lyons, an eminent Presbyterian minister, who for several years was pastor of the Lawrenceburg church of the denomination, and today is pastor Emeritus of the First Presbyterian church in Atlanta, Ga. The two sons on the maternal side, came of a patriotic and distinguished ancestry that devoted their time, talents and energy to the early interests of Anderson County. Their mother was Miss Wallace Lillard, a direct descendent of Captain John Lillard, a Revolutionary soldier. Her elder son, Sprole, born in 1888, resides with his family in Landrum, S. C., and is a minister in the Presbyterian church. William Wallace Lyons is married and lives in Atlanta, Georgia, where he is engaged in the practice of law.

Errol Draffen, attorney at law at the Harrodsburg bar, comes of a family that for years was active in the official life of Anderson County. His grandfather, Major John Draffen, was attorney for this county in 1832, and from 1845 to 1849, was State Senator from this district. The grandson, Errol Draffen, is an orator of ability and recognized as one of the most able lawyers at the Mercer County Court. He served a term as Assistant United States District Attorney under Judge Cochran, from 1928 to 1932. He married Miss Marzette Gudgel, a member of another pioneer family of Anderson County. They have one daughter, Frances.

Ford Bond, the N. B. C. radio announcer, was born in Louisville, Ky., in 1904, but his ancestors for four generations sleep under Anderson County soil. He has a brother, Billy Bond, who is announcer over WAVE. Ford Bond received a medical degree from the University of Chicago, and was with the Beebe expedition in Bermuda for broadcasting purposes. Zach Ford Bond is a minister of note in the Baptist church in Cincinnati.

Wilgus C. Fidler, whose paternal family tree for four generations has been deeply rooted in Anderson County soil, is at present State Senator of Oklahoma, and resides in Oklahoma City. He was born in Lawrenceburg in 1878, and went to Chicago in 1895, where he worked for the New England

Publishing Co. until 1899. He was Secretary for the W. H. Wheeler & Co., school book publishers for a number of years. He went to Oklahoma in 1908, and in 1924 was elected to the State Senate. Senator Fidler has served his constituency for twelve years and this year was nominated for the fourth term, the first time in the state's history any one was ever nominated and elected for sixteen years. His activity in the Senate has been in behalf of education. He wrote the bill which built the State Medical School, and made every motion which built the wonderful Crippled Children's Hospital, and passed a local bill which gives a three million dollar set of buildings in the civic center of Oklahoma City. Senator Fidler operates as an independent at all times and his integrity has never been questioned. Two years ago it was the writer's privilege to see Senator Fidler in action in the senate chamber and be escorted by him through the handsome Oklahoma capitol building and introduced to Governor Marland and other dignitaries in the legislative halls. Anderson County is proud that this son of her's has mounted to a high rung on the ladder of success by his own indomitable efforts.

Another boy who has given distinction to the county in which his ancestors lived and wrought, is Tyler Woolridge. Born with an ambition in his heart for an education, he trudged seven miles through all kinds of weather for four years to Anderson County High School, to be tutored by Mrs. Kavanaugh, the principal, who influenced her earnest and enthusiastic spirit into her aspiring students. Lives cradled in luxury are seldom heroic, and there are many of Anderson County boys who overcame handicaps and forged to the front, and today reflect credit on their native heath. Tyler Woolridge was an honor graduate of Annapolis Naval Academy in 1919, taking a four years' course in three. At one time he was recalled to the academy to serve as an instructor. He had the rank of Lieutenant Commander on the U. S. S. Mississippi, is now with the Tantalla, with headquarters in New York. He was born in 1897. A few years ago was married to Miss Marian Johnson, of Washington City.

Thomas H. Posey, Jr., son of Dr. and Mrs. T. H. Posey, was born in 1909 in Lawrenceburg. His great grandfather, Jeremiah Posey, was at one time "Captain of Patrol" after the formation of the boundary lines of Anderson County, and an outstanding citizen of that day. The first court house in the new county was partly built by popular subscription, and Jeremiah Posey was one of the subscribers to that fund. The name of Posey has always been in the county's official life.

Thomas, Jr., was educated in the county schools and the University of Kentucky. Married Miss Jane Vaughn, of Lexington, and today is an electrical engineer associated with the Commonwealth Edison Engineering Company in Chicago.

Joe H. Waterfill was born in 1878 a half mile from Lawrenceburg, and he is another son whom Anderson County delights to honor. His father was James M. Waterfill, and his mother, Flora Lee Allen, was a niece of that great statesman, Roger Q. Mills, of Texas. She died at the age of twenty-six when Joe was only three years old. The boy attended two schools in Anderson County, the little red school house at Bond's Mill, and the country school at Stringtown-on-the-Pike. He walked four miles every day to these modest seats of learning and that constituted his education. When sixteen years of age he came to town and clerked for Bond & Hyatt, general merchants. In his early 20s he became a bookkeeper in the Lawrenceburg National Bank. On October 3, 1898, he was married to Miss Ethel Routt, a member of a well-known pioneer family of Anderson County. On October, 1906, Mr. Waterfill went to Louisville and accepted a position with the Union National Bank, and was made an officer three years after connecting with it. Since that time he has served as one of the vice-presidents of this institution. When Mr. Waterfill first entered the Citizens Union National Bank, its resources were about four million dollars; today they have fifty-four million. By dint of his own ambitious efforts and integrity and an indomitable will to succeed, Joe Waterfill has attained his present position of trust and honor. He has two children, Martha Mills and Joe, Jr. Five years after his first wife's death he married her sister, Arabella Routt. Every fall season, when nature takes on the autumnal reds and browns, Joe Waterfill comes back to Anderson County with gun and bird dog to trek over the same fields of his boyhood haunts and spend a vacation with old friends and associates.

John Allen Witherspoon, son of Mr. and Mrs. Holly Witherspoon, and scion of a distinguished early family in the county, has a responsible position as head manager of a department in the largest milling industry in the south—the firm of Ballard & Ballard in Louisville, Ky.

Jasper J. McBrayer, one of Lawrenceburg's sons who comes of a prominent lineage of Anderson pioneers, is an attorney of note at the Lexington Bar. He is a graduate of Kavanaugh High School, where he developed marked talent as an orator, and of the University of Kentucky. This year Mr. McBrayer is a candidate for Congress from his District.

Hugh Trent McKay graduated from the United States Naval Academy at Annapolis in 1930, and has the rank of Lieutenant. For several years he has cruised with Uncle Sam's fleet around the world and is now taking a postgraduate course at the Naval Academy. On the maternal side his antecedents have lived in Anderson County since its erection. He comes of a distinguished family on the paternal side from Nelson County and is the 5th Hugh McKay in lineal descent.

Bennett Roach is another Anderson County boy whose family on both sides helped materially in the advancement of their native heath during pioneer days. He is the son of D. W. and Ora Cox Roach and a nephew of Judge John T. Cox. Mr. Roach is one of the reporters and political writers for the Courier-Journal and Louisville Times, and has a facile pen and a talent for the "inky trade" that affords him recognition in the literary realm.

Robert W. Waterfill is an Anderson County boy who is doing big things in a big way. On the paternal side, he comes of a family that has been interested in the general weal in Anderson annals for many decades. On the maternal side he is of the distinguished Clay extraction. His parents are J. William and Sadie Clay Waterfill. His grandfather, W. J. Waterfill, owned a handsome estate in the county on which he built a large and commodious home in 1885. Robert was born in Lawrenceburg in 1896, and educated in the city schools. He graduated from the University of Kentucky in Mechanical Engineering in 1920. For several years he was a Research Engineer for the Carrier Engineering Corporation in New Jersey. He was sent out into many states in the Union to supervise the air conditioning of the largest theatres and other buildings, including the Metropolitan in New York and the White House in Washington, D. C. The work of air conditioning Radio City, the Rockefellow Center, was under his superintendence. He is the author of many articles for refrigerating engineers magazines. His treatise on "Air Conditioning Deep Mines," which was read before the American Institute of Metallurgical Engineers, Inc., in New York, has been published in phamplet form. In 1931 he gave an address before the New York Railroad Club on "Air Conditioning on Railway Passenger Cars" in which he proved its practicability and worth, and today all the big roads are running air conditioned trains. Today Robert Waterfill is one of ten members of the Buensod, Tracy Corporation with headquarters in New York. He has been engaged to lecture a few hours a week at Columbia University this winter.

Russell (Pete) Johnson, whose ancestors on the maternal side were among the earliest settlers of the county, is a reporter on the Courier-Journal staff. Soon after graduation from school "Pete" became associated with the Louisville times as sports writer, and his picture accompanied his column in every edition of the paper. In his "ink-stained career" he has shown marked talent and versatility, having been sent out to cover many cases of wide interest, and his spicy and pungent articles enjoyed by all sports fans. Another brother, W. S. Johnson, has a special aptitude for this work and is also a reporter for the Louisville papers.

William F. Bond III, son of the late W. T. Bond, was born near Lawrenceburg, Ky., December 16, 1899. He migrated to Calhoun, Georgia, where he owns a large iceplant and coal yards. He has served as president of the Civitan Club, Commander of the Legion, and today is a member of the Board of Alderman in the city of his adoption. In 1926 he married Miss Jean Herrin, of Dalton, Georgia, and they have two little sons.

Edwin Casey, son of Mrs. Ellen Hanks Casey, can trace his ancestral line to the Hanks family of Virginia who were forebears of the great Emancipator, Abraham Lincoln, and who migrated to Kentucky with the same train of pack horses. Edwin is a graduate in law and today is connected with a legal firm in New York City.

Mr. Ezra Gillis was first called "Professor" down near Glensborough, Anderson County, where he taught school. He early acquired the habit of doing things systematically and methodically and today is one of the most efficient registras in the south. He has been serving in this capacity for a number of years at Kentucky State University.

Harry G. Boothe, son of Edward and Georgie Townsend Boothe, and a descendant of pioneers, was educated in the county schools and when young went to Birmingham, Ala., where he held a position in the Union Stock Yards in that city for four years. Under the same management he was transferred to Peoria, Ill., where he has been the manager of the Union Stock Yards in that city for fourteen years, having worked for the same company for eighteen years. He enjoys a lucrative position and the esteem of his employers.

The name of Witherspoon has been linked with the medical profession in Anderson County since its erection. Dr. Oran H. Witherspoon, over a long period of years, was recognized as a physician of more than ordinary ability. His son, Dr. Ezra Offutt Witherspoon, true to the traditions of his family, has forged to the front in the medical profession in Louisville. He received his early education in the Lawrenceburg schools and at Georgetown College, and is a graduate of the Louisville School of Medicine. He has a handsome home near Cherokee Park and ranks with the best practitioners in the city. Today he is retained as corporation physician for Armour and the Tobacco Corporation of Louisville. He was married a number of years ago to Miss Nell Newman of Louisville.

Will R. Crossfield, who left Anderson County in 1925, to try his fortune in Georgia, today owns four ice plants in that southern state, two in Griffin and two in adjacent towns. He was educated in the schools of Anderson

Officials of Lawrenceburg National Bank--Left to right: J. L. Sherwood, President; J. M. B. Birdwhistle, Vice-President; A. B. McAfee, Chairman of the Board; Ollie C. Calvert, Cashier; Julian Cole, Bookkeeper; J. C. Bond, Director. Back row: J. L. Blakemore, Bookkeeper; William McGurk, Ass't Cashier; James Sherwood, Director.

County and at Transylvania University at Lexington, Ky. Mr. Crossfield possesses the inherent qualities of his ancestry for good citizenship. He is an active member of the Christian church, president of the Rotary Club of Griffin and interested in the welfare of the town of his adoption. His wife was Miss Estelle May, of Lexington, Ky. They have a son and a daughter.

William Parlin Lillard, son of the late William F. Lillard, is a member of the fourth generation of Lillards born on Anderson County soil. He was born in 1898 in one of the old Lillard Colonial homesteads near Lawrenceburg, Ky., and was educated at Kavanaugh Academy and the University of Pennsylvania, and today is an official in the "Snow King" Baking Powder Company in Cincinnati, of which his mother, Mrs. Louise P. Lillard, is President. This industry was founded by his grandfather, John Parlin, in 1873, and is one of the six largest baking powder concerns in the United States. The output is more than ten million pounds per year. "Parlin" is one of the managers of the factory and travels extensively for it.

John Irvin Carpenter, born June, 1890, son of H. B. and Nora Lillard Carpenter, comes of an ancestry on both sides, who were useful and important citizens in the early affairs of the county. After graduating from the Lawrenceburg High School he attended the Virginia Military Institute for three years. When war was declared in 1917, John Irvin was the first to enlist and was a graduate of the First Officer's Training Camp at Fort Benjamin Harrison. He saw active service in France where he had charge of a training camp, and received commendations from General Pershing. At the close of the war, he went to Enid, Oklahoma, where he became Vice-President of the Gentry Motor Company. He married Miss Janice Reynolds. Later his firm sent him to Kansas City to manage a large motor concern in that city, and while here he contracted scarlet fever and died in 1930.

John W. Bond, whose family owned Bond's Mill for three generations, had three sons who, today, are successful business men in the west. Will is connected with one of the large hotels in Oklahoma City; Florian owns a drug store in Muskogee, Okla., and Attilla is a druggist in Los Angeles, California.

"Rob" Feland's ancestry did not settle in Anderson County proper, but his family tree grew in the same forest, having been rooted in Lincoln County when the present Anderson was embraced in that territory for a number of years after our first settler came here in 1780. He comes of prominent pioneer lineage, but needs no heraldry to brighten his escutcheon, for he has been the architect of his own success. F. R. Feland, Jr. (Rob), son of Judge F. R. Feland, was born in Lawrenceburg in 1887. He received his early education in the schools of the county, thereafter attended the State University in Lexington, Ky. After working for two years on the staff of the Anderson News, he went to East Aurora, New York, where he joined the original Elbert Hubbard's Roycrofters, where his first job was to set in type the complete works of Elbert Hubbard, which ran to some forty volumns. Showing an aptitude for the "inky-trade," he was soon transferred to the "Advertising Writing Department." In 1910 Mr. Feland joined the George Batten Advertising Company in New York City. Today he is Vice-President and Treasurer of Batten, Barton, Durstine and Osborn,. Inc. He has a wife and six children and lives in a handsome home in Nutley, N. J., a beautiful residential city. His eldest son, F. R. Feland, III, since coming of age, has held responsible positions in the organization with which his father is connected, which has plants in six of the largest cities in the United States.

George G. Speer, son of Dr. J. W. Speer, was born in the little hamlet, Alton, four miles north of Lawrenceburg, and comes of an ancestry that served its generation nobly and commendably. After completing his education in the public schools of the county and at Kentucky Military Institute, Mr. Speer read law in the office of Major L. W. McKee, and was admitted to the bar in 1893. For several years he was actively engaged in politics and held several important positions at the State Capital, at one time serving as State Auditor's Agent for the state at large. He served in the Senate from Franklin County from 1912-'16, and was State Banking Commissioner from 1916 to 1920. Today Mr. Speer is President of the People's State Bank in Frankfort, Ky. He was married to Miss Hallie Hanks in 1904, and they have one son, Wm. Carroll Speer.

Emery L. Frazier's ancestry on both sides came to this part of the country before the boundary lines of Anderson County were formed. He is the son of R. L. and Mary Routt Frazier. Was born September 24, 1896, educated at Kavanaugh High School and the University of Kentucky. Emery was admitted to the Kentucky Bar in 1921, and represented Anderson County in the state Legislature in 1922, after which he moved to Whitesburg, Letcher County, Kentucky, and opened a law office. He was appointed Mayor of that town in 1924, and served in that capacity several terms. He served as Reading Clerk in the House of Representatives of the Kentucky General Assembly in the sessions of 1928-30 and '32; was admitted to the bar of the Supreme Court of the United States in 1933. At the present time he is Legislative Clerk of the United States Senate and has served through the 73rd and 74th Congresses. He is a member of the I. O. O. F., and of the Christian church. Mr. Frazier was married to Miss Juanita Kelsey on March 1, 1923, and their home is in Washington City, D. C.

Dr. Charles N. Kavanaugh, son of the late Dr. C. W. Kavanaugh, is the sixth Charles Nichols of the House of Kavanaugh. His ancestors settled Anderson County when the Indians lurked in the shadows of the forests, and men tilled the soil with guns at their sides. His early training and association with his father, a successful physician, inclined him to the study of medicine. He received his academic education at Kavanaugh High School, after which he graduated from the University of Louisville and College of medicine. Today Dr. Kavanaugh is associated with the Lexington Clinic, and is one of the most successful practitioners of that city, his practice extending over adjoining counties. He attained the rank of Major during the World War and was cited for service in France, where he served with distinction and honor. He was married a few years ago to Miss Elizabeth Chenault, of Lexington, and they have three sons.

Allen M. Bond, son of the late C. E. Bond, and great, great grandson of William Bond, the Revolutionary soldier, who cut a clearing in Anderson County and "called it home," on the maternal side comes of the Witherspoon ancestry who, for three generations, were occupied with the material and commercial growth of the county. He is a graduate of Princeton University when Woodrow Wilson was President of that institution. Married Miss Elizabeth Willis, daughter of Judge Luther Willis, of Shelbyville, Ky. They have a son and daughter. Today Allen is owner and manager of the Central Book Supply Co., in Louisville, Ky.

Oscar T. Trent after graduation from Transylvania University at Lexington, Ky., was associated with his father in the drygoods business for a time, after which he left Lawrenceburg and made rapid progress in the business world. He organized a bank at Bardstown, Ky., and was later induced to accept a position as cashier of the Franklin Bank on Fifth street in Louisville. Today he is cashier and director in the bank of Somerset, Ky. He married Miss Marie Reynolds, of Scott County. They have one daughter.

A physician of note in the early erection of Anderson County was Dr. D. G. Dedman. Today Dr. William M. Dedman, graduate of Transylvania and Vanderbilt Medical College, is serving as Public Health Officer in Gallatin, Tenn.

Some of the most outstanding stars in athletic sports hail from Lawrenceburg and are the descendents of pioneers of brain and brawn who "poured their strength into the acres of the new-born county." Ralph Carlisle, forward, made the official All-Southeastern quintet last season. He is a graduate of Kavanaugh High School. Other famous players from the same school are Paul McBrayer, who coaches the K. U. Kittens, and Forest Sale, coach at Kavanaugh. McBrayer was chosen All-Southern guard in 1930, while Sale was chosen All-Southeastern Conference center, and also All-American center in 1932-'33.

In 1902 there appeared upon the streets of Lawrenceburg a spicy newspaper called "It." This little journal was mentally exciting and interesting on account of the popularity of its editor, Coleman Cox, one of Anderson's talented sons. Morton Green assisted in the launching of this news sheet. After a few months of this venture, Mr. Cox felt the lure to go west, where his talents as a newspaper man found a larger field. He worked for a while in Boise, Idaho, and Salt Lake City. Later he went to San Francisco, where, after many vicissitudes, he forged to the front as a salesman of advertising. Later he became an author of many clever books, titled "Listen to This," "Believe It or Not," "As I See It." "More Than Likely," "Just as I Thought," and many others with unique titles. These books attained popularity over night and met the hearty endorsement of Mr. Cox's warm personal friends, Luther Burbank, Thomas A. Edison and others. The books are delightfully witty and contain brief paragraphs of sound business maxims, and large commercial firms bought them by the thousands and distributed them among employees and customers. Mr. Cox's aphorisms are pungent and decidedly original and he has been styled the Elbert Hubbard of the Pacific coast. He has many letters of commendation of his books signed by noted personages as Calvin Coolidge, Luther Burbank, Henry Ford, Thomas A. Edison and others, who declare the author's books are "a royal banquet of business and social philosophy; great thoughts condensed to the Nth degree." Mr. Cox attained prominence as a lecturer through the west, talking before Rotary and business clubs, and made a success in radio, having broadcast for four and one-half years from studios in San Francisco, Chicago and New York. He was often listened to by his home-town folks. He is a brother of Mrs. J. L. Sherwood, of Lawrenceburg.

Anderson County has furnished four professors to the State University at Lexington, Kentucky, as follows: James William Whitehouse, born near Glensboro. Received his B.S. degree in Agriculture at the University in 1914, and M.S. in Agriculture in 1916. He was Professor of Animal Husbandry at Berea College from 1914 to 1917; Daviess County Agricultural Agent from 1917-'22; U. K. Expert Station, Assistant State Leader County Agent Work 1922-'24, and since that time has been State 4-H Club Leader at the Experiment Station at Kentucky University.

Thomas Marshall Hahn got his B.S. degree at the University in 1924, and M. S. degree in 1925. Received his Ph.D. from the University of Chicago in 1934, having attended five summer schools at that seat of learning. Today is Associate Professor in the Kentucky State University at Lexington.

Marion C. Brown taught in the secondary schools in Anderson County at Fairview and Hebron from 1914-'16. Received his A.B. degree from the University of Kentucky in 1923, and A.M. in 1925. Today is Assistant Professor in the institution in Mathematics.

Ezra L. Gillis, born in Anderson County in 1867 and taught in the public schools 1886-1899; Instructor Normal Department University of Kentucky 1907-'08; Assistant Professor Education 1908-'10; Registrar at the University since 1910. Mr. Gillis is also trustee of the Kentucky State Industrial College at Frankfort, and the College of the Bible at Lexington; was Secretary of the American Association of Collegiate Registras from 1914-'19, and President of same 1919-'20; a member of Kentucky Educational and State Historical Association and of the Mississippi Valley Historical Association.

Panoramic View of Salt River, covered bridge, "Old Joe" and Bond's Mill Distilleries.

CHAPTER V

KENTUCKY

History records that in 1767, John Finley, a hunter and woodsman from North Carolina, was the first white man to penetrate the wilderness of Kentucky sufficiently to see the Blue Grass region of the state, and it was he who returned to North Carolina and fired Daniel Boone with the desire to visit the territory described a "God's Own Country." Finley, in glowing terms, told of his journey to the "magnificent region where there would be an eternal feast for the hunter, where game was so abundant that droves of buffalo could be counted like cattle; where deer licked the hand of the intruder, and coons, 'possums and pheasants were so plentiful as to obstruct the pathway along which men would tread." Boone came in 1769, and brought his family in 1775. The glowing accounts of the beauty and salubrity of Kentucky rapidly brought a tide of emigration to the state. We read the population of the state in 1782 did not exceed 1,500, but ten years later it had grown to about 6,500 white people and twelve thousand slaves. Early in 1800 the population of the state was close to 225,000, an increase in ten years of 225 per cent. At that time Anderson County was getting her share of the sturdy adventurers. Our first settler, Coffman, arrived in 1780, the year that Lexington was built. It is regrettable that the history of all the pioneer families who came to Anderson County is not available. Names that are highly honorable, such as Baxter, Paxton, Champion, Toll, Boggess, Buntain, Franklin, Dawson, McMichael, Mullins, Philips, Young, McGinnis, and others, many of whom played their part in enduring the hardships of border life, as they laid foundations for better and more secure forms of society. By collaboration we are able to give a brief sketch of many families in the succeeding chapters who settled here prior to, or soon after, the erection of Anderson County.

BIRDWHISTLE

The name of Birdwhistle has been associated with this locality for a century and a quarter. In the year 1818, one Thomas Birdwhistle purchased a farm on Salt River in what was then Mercer County, afterwards Anderson. That same farm has been in the Birdwhistle family since that early day, and is now owned by Mr. J. M. B. Birdwhistle, Sr., of Lawrenceburg, who has an old deed executed by John Adams and wife, Polly, to Thomas Birdwhistle, September 4, 1818.

This deed was recorded in the Mercer County Court house when Thomas Allen was county clerk. The consideration was for $1,250 in payment for 92½ acres of land, which was at that time in Mercer County before the lines were changed. All the Birdwhistles of this state are descendents of Thomas Birdwhistle, who came to Kentucky from Maryland, and settled in Woodford County. He brought with him a daughter, Priscilla, who married Jerry Anderson. Mr. Anderson operated a horse mill near Clay Lick church for many years. To this marriage there was born one daughter, Elizabeth, who moved to Indiana.

To Thomas Birdwhistle and his wife, Sally, there were born the following children: James S., who married Miss Julia Buntain; William N., who married

Miss Mildred Smith; John, who married Miss Ellen Riggs; Henrietta, who married Thurston Cox. To James S. Birdwhistle and his wife, Julia, there were born the following children: Thomas, James, Frank, Porter, Thurston, Cecil, Delia, and Henrietta. To William N. Birdwhistle and his wife, Mildred, there were born Sarah Alice, William Ezra, Kathrine, Nathan and J. M. B. Birdwhistle.

To John Birdwhistle and wife, Ellen, were born Jerome, Leona, Henrietta and Ida. At this time there are only four of Thomas Birdwhistle's grandchildren living; they are Mrs. Delia Jordon, of Columbus, Ohio; Mrs. Henrietta Morris, of Mercer County; Mrs. Ida B. Oliver, of Beverly Hills, California, and J. M. B. Birdwhistle, of Lawrenceburg, Ky. Their descendants and families number about one hundred persons, living principally in Mercer and Anderson counties. Many of them have taken part in civic affairs and are recognized as useful and influential citizens in their respective communities. Mr. J. M. B. Birdwhistle, at present one of the vice-presidents of the Lawrenceburg National Bank, has long been recognized as an educator of note, having at one time been a member of the faculty of the city schools in the '80s, and afterward for six years taught a private school in his home. He is a graduate of Centre College at Danville, Ky., of the class of 1880, and today there are seven members of that class living, scattered in different states of the Union.

Mr. "Mat" Birdwhistle has exerted a beneficient influence upon material progress and educational and religious advancement in the county. He has been an elder in the Christian church for more than a half century, and has taught a Bible class for more than two score years in the same institution. His first wife was Miss Mattie Bond, a member of another pioneer family in the county. A few years after her death he was married to Miss Annie Gore, of Bloomfield, Ky. The Rotary Club, of which he is a member and past president, recently celebrated "Birdie's" eightieth birthday, and around the festal board, showered him with presents and enconiums and good wishes for many more years of usefulness in the community.

BOND FAMILY SKETCHES

William F. Bond, Sr., was born in Anderson County in September, 1826, and died July 4, 1910, aged 84 years. His grandfather, William Bond 1st, was born in Hanover County, Virginia, in 1740, and served three years in the Revolutionary War. He was engaged in the siege of Savannah and badly wounded in the battle of Stono, when his mother went for him and brought him back to Virginia on horseback and nursed him back to health. This Revolutionary soldier moved to Kentucky in the early pioneer days and died in Anderson County in 1827. His second wife, Sarah Cronson Bond, was allowed a pension for her husband's military services. Their son, John Bond, was the father of this sketch. His wife was Sarah Utterback, a daughter of pioneers. When only nineteen years of age Wm. F. Bond enlisted under Captain Kavanaugh and fought with the Salt River Tigers in the Mexican War. He was the youngest member of that famous Company. When the conflict was over he returned to Anderson County and began a prosperous business career. He succeeded to the distilling business started by his father, John Bond, in 1820, and built up through his individual efforts until the brand of whiskey manufactured by that plant, and later known as "Bond and Lillard," became famous the world over for purity and quality. His brother-in-law, C. C. Lillard, became a partner in the business in 1869. Bond and Lillard organized the Lawrenceburg Bank, one of the leading institutions of the city. No man in the county was more universally respected and loved than W. F. Bond, and his wise counsel was often sought and accepted by many. He helped many poor boys through college. This was divulged by the boys themselves, and not by their benefactor. Mr. Bond had a keen intellect, and took an active interest in politics, but was not an office seeker. At one time he listened to the strong solicitations of his friends and represented Anderson County in the Legislature in 1871-'73. In 1849 he was married to Miss Susan Mary Hanks, daughter of the pioneer, Chichester Hanks. To them eleven children were born who lived to reach maturity, and all were valuable citizens in their respective communities.

William Bond, the Revolutionary soldier, was married the first time to Frances Ballou in Cumberland County, Virginia, and she died before he migrated to Kentucky with his three sons and one daughter. His second wife was Sarah Cronson, who was the first Mrs. Bond married in Anderson County. One of the sons of William and Frances Ballou Bond was William Bond, Jr., and he was the father of the Rev. Preston Bond who was among the most prominent citizens in the first fifty years of the existence of Anderson County. He was born in 1824, and died in 1896. In 1847 he was married to Belinda Arthur of Knox County, and for many years they lived in the old Bond homestead five miles from Lawrenceburg, originally owned by his father, William Bond, Jr., who was a farmer and large slave owner. Preston Bond's influence, educationally and religiously, was felt throughout the county. He joined the Methodist Conference in early life and held pastorates in various sections. His varied interests later were so pressing that he resigned from conference but continued to preach the gospel. He served the Lawrenceburg Methodist church two sessions. For over forty years he held services for the Tyrone church once a month. During the greater part of his life he was teaching, farming and preaching every Sunday. Truly his life was an epic of service. Preston and Belinda Arthur Bond were the parents of nine children, of whom four are living: Mrs. Annie Ledridge, Mrs. B. D. Hawkins and Mrs. J. C. VanArsdell, of Lawrenceburg; Mrs. W. H. Hudson, Frankfort. A son, Boliver Bond, who recently died in Woodford County, owned and lived in one of the most beautiful homes in Versailles. He was a man of energy and a worthy and progressive citizen and recognized as one of the outstanding auctioneers of Kentucky. The Anderson County Bonds have figured in all walks of life as land owners, distillers, preachers, teachers and county and state officers.

C. E. BOND

Was born in Anderson County, January 15, 1851; died May 3, 1917, age sixty-six years. He was a descendant of two of the substantial pioneer families of Anderson County, and at the time of death was president of the Lawrenceburg National Bank. The real estate business—the building and developing of Lawrenceburg—was the one purpose of his business life. Probably no one man, since the town was laid out into lots in 1818, ever did more for the progress of the place than did Charles E. Bond. His enterprise coupled with his faith in the future of his home town, prompted him in the laying out of additions and building many of the homes in her confines. He owned many acres of land northeast of town which he opened up, made streets and built homes, and this addition is known as St. Charles Park to his memory. Mr. Bond was a man of high refinement of feeling, strictest integrity and always a friend of the humblest people. Men who had worked for him as carpenters, painters and stone masons, shed tears as they stood around his bier. It was said that any reliable person, no matter how little they had of this world's goods, if they wanted to own a home, could buy it on easy payments from C. E. Bond. He bought and built extensively in Harrodsburg, Frankfort, Lexington and Shelbyville, and had large holdings in some of these cities. Mr. Bond was married in early life to Miss Ellen Witherspoon, daughter of Dr. and Mrs. John A. Witherspoon. Their two children, who survive today, are Allen M. Bond, of Louisville, and Mrs. Herbert Hayes, of San Antonio, Texas. Mr. Bond's granddaughter, Miss Mollie Bond Hayes, was crowned Queen of Texas when Texas celebrated her centennial year during fiesta week in San Antonio in April of 1936.

BUSH

One of the early settlers on the Clifton pike, five miles from Lawrenceburg, was Mathias Bush, who owned a thousand acres of land near the Kentucky river on which he built a home about the year 1800. His wife was Miss Sarah Meux, a famous New Orleans beauty. Izzard Bacon Bush, born February 14, 1807, was the only son of this union (there were several daughters), and acquired the ancestral acres and became a wealthy planter and slave owner. In 1831 Izzard Bacon Bush married a Miss Sullivan, daughter of Archibald and Lucy Fox Sullivan, of Virginia. In 1850 he built the handsome home called "Welcome Hall," an appropriate name for this stately manor, as, for many years it was a place for social gatherings of visitors throughout the Blue Grass. Many distinguished personages were entertained within its portals. The approach to the house was through an avenue an eighth of a mile long, bordered by two rows of stately pine and cypress trees. In the early days an orchard on the estate had over a thousand fruit trees. Eight children were born to Mr. and Mrs. Bush: Daniel, Areanna, John, Sallie, Lucy, Tarmesia, Richard and Philip. The last surviving child, "Miss Lucy," died in 1923, in her 85th year. She was the last gracious hostess of "Welcome Hall," and true to family tradition, entertained her friends with proverbial Kentucky hospitality.

Mr. I. B. Bush, Jr., bachelor, son of John Bush, is the present owner of this estate, and the last survivor of this distinguished family. He lives in the old Colonial home and tills its broad acres. He has in his possession a letter written to his great grandfather, Mathias Bush, from a sister in Winchester, Virginia, dated August 5, 1817. The stationary is worn and yellow with age, but the script is distinct and beautiful. The postmark is on the upper left corner of the folded letter, which came without stamp or envelope to Frankfort, Kentucky, and Mathias Bush had to go nine miles to get his mail from that nearest post office. Envelopes were not used until after 1835, and adhesive postage stamps first used in the U. S. in 1847. The writer, upon investigation, finds the following statement in the text book of the U. S. post office: "In the early days of the postal service, before the advent of the postage stamp, the mailing of a letter was the transaction requiring the joint attention of the sender and of the postmaster. The letter was offered by the patron, examined by the postmaster, the amount of postage announced according to the number of sheets and the distance to be carried. The postage was paid in cash by the patron, or the request was made that it be transmitted 'collect,' and the postmaster marked the letter accordingly." The information was also given that letters of that early period were merely folded and post-marked in the upper left corner. Stamped envelopes were not used until 1853.

BURFORD

The name of Burford has been identified with this section of the county since 1820, and occupied with the material, moral and religious growth of the community. The first of the name, William Jones Burford and his wife, nee Miller, and their two eldest children, emigrated from Amherst County, Va., near Lynchburg, in the year 1820. They settled on a farm four miles south of Lawrenceburg near the Kentucky river, where to them were born three children, Susan, John and Elizabeth. John Burford, born in 1823, is the forebear of the Burford family in the county today. He married a Miss Thompson, and settled on Salt River, four miles from Lawrenceburg. They were the parents of eight children: Robert E. Lee Burford, who went south and became a noted physician in Brunswick, Georgia; John, Martha, James, twin boys—Joseph Calvin and Benjamin Alvin—Lillie and George. The pioneer Burfords are interred in a family grave-yard on the place where they first settled in Anderson County.

JUDGE J. M. BELL

Judge J. M. Bell was born in Anderson County on the 8th of January, 1814, consequently was one year old on the day the battle of New Orleans was fought. No citizen of the county was more favorably known or more highly respected than "Uncle Matt" Bell. He was proverbial for his honesty and Christian attributes. He was a leading teacher in the community, quite proficient in mathematics and was county surveyor for more than thirty years.

During that entire time the correctness of not one of his surveys was ever questioned. In 1866 he was elected to the office of County Judge, but resigned after serving a few months. It is said that he feared he might err in some of his decisions and could not bear the idea of doing any one an injustice. At the age of twenty-one he was married to Miss Martha Penny, whom he survived nine years. He was a member of the Baptist church at Goshen for more than sixty years. He was the father of nine children, only one of whom is living today—Prof. Horace V. Bell, who was Principal of the Lawrenceburg High School for more than twenty years. Two granddaughters, Mrs. Wilkes Morgan and Mrs. Morris Case live in the county today.

Rev. B. F. Adkins, born in 1849, joined the ranks of the Confederates when only fifteen years old, and served two years under Gen. Longstreet. He was a Baptist minister over fifty years. His first wife was Miss Eliza Leathers. His second wife was Mrs. Allie Hopgood.

BALLARD

Thomas J. Ballard, who died October 7, 1933, aged seventy years, had probably been in business in Lawrenceburg longer than any other person. He was not born in Anderson County but came here from Shelby when quite a young man. The corner where his drug store is located has been called "Ballard's Corner" since 1881. T. J. Ballard was one of the town's most influential citizens and had helped with the promotion of many projects for the advancement of the community. It was largely through his efforts that Main street was paved with brick, and he worked untiringly for the present waterworks system. He was a member of the City Council for thirty-one years. He was a Mason, a Rotarian and the first president of that organization in the town. Mr. Ballard was a member of the Christian church and contributed liberally to its support. He was deeply interested in the betterment of crippled children and gave ungrudgingly of his time and money in efforts to aid these unfortunates. He always advocated whatever would aid the town, the county and his fellowmen. With his passing the town lost one of its best citizens. Mr. Ballard is survived by his wife, Mrs. Gertrude Witherspoon Ballard, a daughter, Mrs. Jerome Robinson, and three granddaughters, Bettie Ballard Ripy, Mary Jane and Nancy Ripy.

CRAIN

Judge John H. Crain died in Lawrenceburg March 23, 1927. He had lived here since he was a small lad. July 27, 1861, he enlisted in the War Between the States, with Captain Gus Dedman's Company which went out from Anderson County.

Judge Crain was the last surviving member of that company. He was a member of Co. I, 2nd Kentucky Regiment, and belonged to the famous Orphan Brigade. He was wounded and captured at Murfreesboro, January 3, 1863. His comrades regarded Judge Crain as a very gallant soldier. He represented Anderson County in the Legislature at Frankfort in 1885-'86. He was mayor of Lawrenceburg 1924 to 1928. Several terms he held the office of County Judge. He and his son, Mack Crain, were in the insurance business at the time of his death, and the firm is still known as J. H. Crain and Son, and is managed by the son today. Judge Crain's wife was Miss Mollie Prewitt and their surviving children are Mack, Misses Emma and Bess Crain. Miss Bess was for a number of years one of the most capable teachers in the City High School.

A letter written during the War Between the States by the late Capt. W. E. Bell to L. H. Penny, of Anderson County, announced the death of his son, John S. Penny. This letter was dated March 15, 1862, written from Camp Chase, where Capt. Bell was held as prisoner of war, having been captured with his peerless leader, Gen. Simon Bolivar Buckner, and thousands of his comrades who had enlisted in the "Lost Cause." John S. Penny went out in Capt. Gus Dedman's company, was wounded at Fort Donalson and died in a St. Louis hospital. His remains were brought home for burial. He was the first Anderson County boy who had fallen in action whose body had been brought back to his native heath. The concourse of people that gathered to do honor to the heroic dead was the largest ever assembled in Lawrenceburg to attend funeral rites of friend or foe.

CHAMP CLARK

Lawrenceburg, Ky., is the birth-place of an erst-while candidate for the presidency of the United States. The Hon. Champ Clark, christened James Beauchamp Clark, first saw the light of day on March 7, 1850, near the "Seat of Justice" in this little hamlet in the old Robinson place, a home built by an old settler of that name. The Robinson house was torn down in the early '60s and a handsome colonial home built on the same location by Mr. Holly Witherspoon, who later sold it to his brother, Mr. Horace Witherspoon, whose family resided here for many years. Today it is owned by Mrs. Dick Vowels, and is the first home northwest of Lawrenceburg after crossing the railroad.

About the year 1912 when on a speaking tour through Kentucky, Mr. Clark, in company with the Hon. Ollie James, attended a political rally held in the old fair grounds near Lawrenceburg. The Governor of the State, James B. McCreary, was also in attendance. A delegation of representative citizens of the town met the distinguished visitors at the train to escort them to the place of speaking. As a kind expression of feeling Mr. Clark was first taken to the cemetery to visit his mother's grave. Mrs. Clark was the first person laid to rest in this burying ground. The exact date of her death is not known, but it was about 1856, as that was the year the Lawrenceburg cemetery was laid out and conveyed to the trustees of the town. This hallowed spot had been blanketed with flowers by a committee of ladies before it was visited by Mrs. Clark's illustrious son. No stone marks the grave, but a pine tree, planted by the husband, has grown to majestic proportions and stands sentinel at Mrs. Clark's grave today. After the pilgrimage to the cemetery it was Mr. Clark's suggestion that he be driven to see the place where he was born, and he identified the old Robinson location as the spot where he spent his first boyhood days.

John Hampton Clark, father of this sketch, was a traveling dentist and rode horse-back through the country carrying his saddle-bags containing pinchers, plyers and other requisites for practicing his trade. He was a man of ability and highly esteemed. His wife's maiden name was Jane Beauchamp McAfee. Mr. Clark was called "Jim" until he was grown, then he effected a complete Americanization of his name by leaving out the first two parts and signing himself "Champ." Before he was twenty years of age, Mr. Clark taught school in Anderson County, and preceding his speech at the political rally above mentioned, he was introduced by one of his former pupils, the Hon. Ben L. Cox, one of the county's representatives in the State Legislature. Two other citizens living in Lawrenceburg today, James S. and John W. Shouse, point with pleasure to the time when they sat under the tutelage of Champ Clark, when he taught school in the little village of Camdenville, today called Glensboro, and they have given the writer the following reminiscences: Mr. Clark boarded with "Uncle and Aunt Betsy" Stevens in Camdenville and taught a five months' free school and a three months' pay term in the years 1870-'71. He was a conscientious teacher and tried to instill high ideals in the minds of his pupils. Recitations were not merely prescribed questions and stereotyped answers, for he tried to create a background for a child's thinking, and impart to the students the importance of striving for a goal. At times he asked the children what they intended making of themselves, urging them to work toward an ideal, and asserting that he expected someday to be president of the United States! He tried to arouse the ambitions of the boys and girls who trudged over the hills to absorb the essence of his proficient tutelage. Mr. Clark never loafed on the streets, nor sat around the stoves in the stores, as was the habit of folks in the little hamlets, but was rather aloof and spent much of his spare time reading. He sometimes went to the county seat and mingled with the villagers when the stage-coach came into the town, for it was everybody's business to gather and see who was arriving at the tavern and get the news from the outside world. Mr. Clark opened the morning session of his school by lecturing to the children, and at the close in the afternoon had a song service led by one of the pupils. He always carried a tuning fork over his left ear, and gave the right pitch to the music. Ben Cox enjoyed telling of his expereince when called upon to "start the song." Just as Ben asked, "Teacher, please give me the sound," an old cow stuck her head near the open window and bawled, and Mr. Clark ejaculated, "there now, she has given you the sound, so go on with the song." The school house stood near the covered bridge that spanned Salt River. This bridge was erected in 1855, was 140 feet long and cost the county $5,000. One day a flock of sheep was being driven along the road toward the bridge, and instead of going through the structure, the sheep bolted and scattered in all directions. This quite distracted the children, who, with heads stuck out the windows were intent upon watching the herdsmen trying to corral the flock, whereupon Mr. Clark ordered them to go out and get sticks and round up the sheep and get them across the bridge.

While living in the Stevens home it was Mr. Clark's wont to go to the old well in the yard for fresh drinking water. At one time the well was out of repair and in the struggle to get the water, he used a strong epithet, which was accidentally overheard by Aunt Betsy. Mr. Clark duly apologized and told Aunt Betsy that he was sure she would not use such a word, "but if she tried to get water from that broken well, she would think damn." Aunt Betsy was honest enough to confess that before the well was repaired. "Jim's (Champ) declaration found lodgment in her sub-conscious mind when she tried to draw water!"

At this time Mr. Clark's sweetheart was a pretty little country lass named Betty Milton. But the romance ended when Champ Clark went out into the struggle of the world, and his first love became "A song that was piped between the acts." In reply to a letter written to Washington, D. C., asking Mr. Clark's son for information about the time his father left Kentucky, and some of his activities, the following was received:

April 15, 1936.

Mrs. W. T. Bond, Lawrenceburg, Ky.
My Dear Mrs. Bond:

I have your recent letter. The date of my father's birth was March 7, 1850. He moved to Missouri in 1876, having lived for a short time in Wichita, Kan. He served at a presidential election in 1880, and was, for a number of years prosecuting attorney in Pike County and a member of the State House of Representatives. He was speaker of the 62nd and 63rd Congresses. I thank you very much for your kind remarks and am sending your letter to my mother, who, I know, will appreciate it very much.

Yours very sincerely,
(Signed) BENNETT CHAMP CLARK.

Mrs. Elizabeth Clark Haley, who was born in 1852, in Anderson County, died in 1919 in Santa Cruz, California. She was Champ Clark's only sister. Her husband was the Rev. J. J. Haley, a Christian minister and lecturer and writer on religious subjects.

LEATHERS

Dr. C. A. Leathers, who died May 7, 1923, aged 63, was the oldest physician living in Lawrenceburg at the time of his death. He was the son of Valois and Rosema (Stoddard) Leathers, whose large farm home between Ashbrook and Leathers store, was proverbial for hospitality for a half century. The paternal grandfather, John Leathers, was born in Anderson County in 1802, and his son, Valois Leathers, was born in 1828. During the gold rush in 1849, Valois Leathers went to California, and while there married Rosema Stoddard, of Illinois. They returned to the old home in Anderson County in 1865, when Charles was five years of age. Other children born to this family were James V., Emma, Eugene, Rose, Frederic and Mitt. Dr. Charles Leathers graduated from K. M. I. in 1879, and from Louisville Medical School in 1882. He married Miss Alice Waterfill in 1883. They have one daughter. In 1902 Dr. Leathers engaged in the drug business as proprietor of the Lawrenceburg Drug Co. In 1905 he was honored with the presidency of the State Pharmeceutical Association. He was a Royal Arch Mason and member of the Methodist church. His wife, Alice Waterfill Leathers, and daughter and one brother, E. M. Leathers, reside in Lawrenceburg.

CROSSFIELD

R. H. Crossfield, Sr., son of John Crossfield, of Culpepper County, Va., first located in Woodford County, but came here several years before Anderson was erected, and built his cabin near Fox Creek. This home was inherited by R. H. Crossfield, his son, who was born October 5, 1821, and who died at this old home location March 15, 1908. In 1865 the pioneer home was replaced by a modern dwelling in the same yard, and it was here that "Uncle Dick" lived to the ripe age of eighty-seven, one of the most highly esteemed citizens of the county. He was married twice, the first time to Miss Mary Gudgel, member of a pioneer family. Their nine children were: George, Susan (York) Thomas, Julia (Ware), Belle (Ware), Matthew, Sarah Frances (Thacker), Ella (Bond), and Alice (Jones). These children are all dead, but they left many children who revere the name of their grandfather. In 1859 Mr. Crossfield was married the second time to Miss Elizabeth Jackson Golden. To this union were born three sons: W. H. Crossfield, born in 1861; died January 26, 1931, had been engaged in farming and live stock business in the county for forty years. His wife, who was Miss Mary Belle Cole, died in 1919. They were parents of four sons and two daughters: Messrs Raymond, H. S., W. R., Henry, Mrs. Leila Shewmaker and Mrs. A. C. Briggs, of Louisville. The second son of R. H. Crossfield, Sr., was Chas. K. Crossfield, born in 1863. His wife was Miss Ada Hackley. They were parents of seven children: Mary, Goldie, Louis, Maidie, Richie, Wallace and Julia. This family left Anderson County and went to Gadsden, Ala., where Mr. Crossfield engaged in a lucretive ice business, and was a potent factor in building the beautiful new Christian church of that city. On January 12, 1934, Mr. Cross field and his daughter, Richie, were killed in an automobile accident in which the mother was injured, but recovered. R. H. Crossfield, Jr., the third son by the last marriage, was born October 22, 1868, and at this time is pastor of the First Christian church of Birmingham, Ala. He attended the Anderson County Seminary and obtained his A.B. degree in Transylvania University in 1889. He graduated from the College of the Bible in 1892; received the M.A. and Ph.D. degrees from the University of Wooster in 1900. Received the LL.D from Georgetown College, University of Kentucky and Transylvania University. Dr. Crossfield was president of Transylvania and the College of the Bible for eight years and president of Transylvania for thirteen years. For three years he was president of William Woods College of Missouri; Executive Secretary of the Federal Council of Churches of Christ in America, New York, for one year. He is the author of "Christian Principles of Sociology and Their Application to Present Day Problems," and "Pilgimages of a Parson." This distinguished son of Anderson County has been pastor of the Birmingham Christian church for ten years; is a member of the Disciples Foundation of Vanderbilt University, Kiwanis Club, Country Club, member of Board of Y. M. C. A., and International Society of Theta Phi. He has traveled extensively in Mexico, Latin America, Alaska, Europe and Asia.

COKE

During the administration of Gov. James Garrard in 1798, one Thomas Coke was accorded a land-grant in the neighborhood known today as McBrayer. It was here he built his log cabin before 1800. This same house has been in the Coke family for four generations, and today is owned by the great granddaughter of Thomas Coke, Mrs. Nannie Coke Nichols. It has two large front rooms, one of which has been modernized by plaster, but the other room has the original whitewashed logs and beamed ceiling, the big old fashioned fireplace and the high mantle, and in a corner of the room a stairway hidden by a door. Most of the early homes of that period were simple structures of hewn logs and chinks stopped with mud or filled with stone and plastered on the outside. The doors were made of riven boards fastened together with wooden pins to wooden slabs. The Kentucky phrase of hospitality originated with the construction of the pioneer door. There was a latch on the inside and a hole was bored above the latch a few inches through which a leathern string passed and so fastened to the latch on the inside. When this string was pulled in, there was no way to open the door from the outside. Every morning the string was passed back from the inside so those who wished to enter could raise the latch, hence, "You will always find the latch-string on the outside," is proverbial for hospitality. Weatherboarding was not used until about 1815, and there are many of the old log houses in Anderson County today that have been encased in this material.

Thomas Coke had three sons and one daughter. His son, Robert, married a Miss Hawkins, and they were parents of four sons and four daughters: Virginia (Mrs. Reuben Hanks), Mary (Mrs. Holman Frazier), Sarah (Mrs. Sam Martin), Esther (Mrs. Frank Routt), Nathan, Thomas, James and Robert. Children of Holman and Mary Coke Frazier were Mrs. Ezra Griffy, Mrs. Rice, Mrs. William Hahn, Mrs. Farris Feland, Mrs. C. F. Snyder, and one son, Granville. Holman Frazier's second wife was Miss Fannie Hanks, daughter of Chichester Hanks, an early settler, and they had four daughters: Helen (Mrs. Ed McMurry), Gertrude (Mrs. Frank Searcy), Lena (Mrs. Kinne) and Zella.

Thomas Coke, the pioneer, married a Miss Esther Wright, and together they came to the McBrayer neighborhood in Anderson County and located by other substantial settlers. The home today, owned by Mrs. Fannie Bailey, belonged to Dr. John Penny, son of the Primitive Baptist minister, and Dr. Penny had his office in his home. Mrs. Esther Coke Routt, who was born in 1842, and today, at the age of ninety-four, has an alert mind, can recall many of the activities in this neighborhood where she has spent most of her life. A grist-mill and saw-mill was owned by a man named Carter who had several sons in the War Between the States. "Aunt Esther" remembers that more than four score years ago one of these little Carter boys was her sweetheart, and he went home from school one day and reported that "He tried to kiss that little Coke girl and she hit him right slap-dab in the mouth." She thinks child nature never changes, although she has seen the long transition from candle molds to electricity, hitching posts to hangars and spinning wheels to radios.

Children of Frank and Esther Coke Routt are: Louis, Holman, Susan (Mrs. Reuben Houchen), and Mary (Mrs. Robert Frazier).

Reuben and Virginia Coke Hanks had eight children: Carleton, Nancy (Mrs. Gee), Bessie (Mrs. T. C. Ledridge), Valeria (Mrs. Martin), Mary (Mrs. Forest Moore), Virginia, Thomas and Reuben. James S. Cokes' wife was Miss Mollie Hanks. Their children are Mrs. Jeff Thacker, Mrs. Frank Nichols and one son, Robert.

In the old church in Williamsburg, Virginia, there is a pew dedicated to the first family of Cokes who came to this country early in 1700. They were the forebears of the Coke family in Anderson County.

COX

William Preston Cox, born in Anderson County, January 4, 1843; died in 1917, age seventy-four. He was married on November 12th to Miss Martha Oliver, daughter of Judge I. C. Oliver, and they lived together to celebrate their golden wedding. Mr. Cox was one of Anderson's best and most progressive citizens, a man of strong convictions and sterling character. He was a member of the Lower House of the General Assembly of Kentucky during the stormy sessions of 1900-1901, and he fully reflected the sentiments of his constituency during those exciting days. Mr. and Mrs. Cox had three children: Mr. James Doyle Cox, Mrs. Elmer Gash, Mrs. Stanley Case. His sister was Mrs. Mildred Cunningham, the brothers were the Hon. B. L. Cox and James T. Cox.

CASE

The ancestors of the Case family were among the early Virginia emigrants who helped wrest our part of the country from the Indians. Many of their posterity still reside in Anderson County and possess all the qualities of good citizenship. The first representative to come from Virginia to Kentucky was Seperate Case, born May 1, 1790; died December 3, 1844. He settled on Puncheon Creek, near Mt. Pleasant church. He had five daughters and two sons, one of whom, John Case, was born in 1814 and died in 1889. John Case first settled on Beaver Creek, near Fairview, and later moved to Cheese Lick, near Goshen. He was the father of twelve children, and nearly all of them remained in Anderson County. One of the sons, Rev. D. W. Case, born in 1839, and died August 2, 1927, aged eighty-eight, had been a minister for over sixty years, at one time pastor of the Old Goshen church in the county. He had four sons: Fuller, Will, John and Morris. He passed away at the home of his son, Morris, who owns a farm on the Harrodsburg road. Mr. Morris Case was married twice. His second wife was Miss Martha Bell, daughter of the late Capt. W. E. Bell.

ELIJAH COLE

Elijah Cole was the pioneer of this family who came here during Indian depredations and helped carve a civilization out of a wilderness. His wife was Aquilla Hooker and they migrated from Maryland to Missouri in 1790, then shortly came to Kentucky and settled near Lawrenceburg. His grandson, William Cole, was a substantial citizen of the Fox Creek neighborhood. His wife was Martha Sherwood and they were the parents of seven children: James Ed., P. F., John William, Mary Belle (Crossfield), Loulie (Cox), Thomas Meritt, and Louis. J. W. Cole was born in 1860 and died in 1924. He was an upright citizen, a successful business man, a member of the Fox Creek Christian church and held in high esteem by the citizens of the county. In 1881 Mr. Cole was married to Miss Annie R. Bond, a member of the pioneer Bond family. To them was born one son, Burton Cole, who is a well to do farmer and land owner. His wife was Miss Loulie Roach, and their eldest son, Julian Cole, is an official in the Lawrenceburg National Bank.

CHAMBERS

The name of Chambers is mentioned in the early settlement of the county. An old record states that "Lemuel W. Chambers was a civil officer who met responsibilities courageously and performed his duties faithfully." He and his estimable wife were the parents of four daughters and three sons. The sons were all physicians of note: Dr. Whitfield Chambers, Dr. J. C. Chambers, of Lawrenceburg, and Dr. A. B. Chambers, of Warsaw. The daughters were Sarah (Mrs. J. H. McBrayer), Louisa (Mrs. J. W. Bond), Miss Monia, of Lawrenceburg, and Mrs. Mountjoy, of Missouri. Near the beginning of the War Between the States Dr. Whitfield Chambers joined the Confederate army. His command was with General John Morgan on his celebrated Ohio raid. Dr. Chambers married Miss Bettie Bond, a member of another pioneer family that came to Kentucky "before the blue grass felt the bite of plowshares." Their children were Abby, Louise (Mrs. George Hoffman), and Russell. The latter is Lawrenceburg's librarian today.

DOWLING

While the name of Dowling is not on the roster of settlers who came here before the boundary lines of Anderson County were formed, there is no family in the community that has made a more material contribution to the advancement of every interest of the town and county than have the Dowlings. Mr. John Dowling came to America from Ireland, and located in

Home of Judge Farris R. Feland.

Lawrenceburg in 1872. He embarked in the distilling business, and under his personal supervision three brands of Anderson County whiskey gained a national celebrity. At one time he was partner with T. B. Ripy in the Clover Bottom distillery at Tyrone, later selling out to his partner and purchased the Waterfill and Frazier plant at the same place. He bought the Walker plant near Lawrenceburg and operated it as "Old Dowling." In 1886 Mr. Dowling built one of the handsomest homes in the town, a house of lovely spaciousness and attractive interior. This home was proverbial for hospitality and Mr. and Mrs. Dowling were friends and neighbors who had no superior. It was here they reared seven children to maturity, one dying in early youth. Their eldest son, Judge William E. Dowling, was elected to the State Senate in 1912-16, and has been honored by his constituency by being elected to several offices in the county. Today he is County Attorney; was married to Miss Margaret Lillard, daughter of a pioneer family, and owns the home owned by Judge W. H. McBrayer on Southern Ave., built by Dr. Oran Witherspoon. A daughter of Mr. and Mrs. John Dowling, Mrs. Mary Dowling Bond, served as state president for the U. D. C. in 1912-'13.

Mr. Dowling died in 1902 and his wife carried on his business in a very efficient manner. Mrs. Dowling was a woman of unusual business acumen and a dominant figure in the business world. In 1919 she bought the W. B. Sullivan farm on Salt River, consisting of 233 acres for $32,000, one of the most desirable blue grass farms in Anderson County, and she stocked it with thoroughbred cattle, sheep and hogs, and it was one of the show places of the county. She named the farm "Shonraugh," the Irish name for "Big Hill," this being the name for the Dowling homestead in Ireland. Mrs. Dowling was possessed of the kind simplicity of an elegant woman, and when she died in 1930 was mourned, not only by a large circle of friends which her graces adorned, but by the less fortunate who were beneficiaries of her unstinted charity.

HANKS FAMILY

The Hanks family came from Scotland to Virginia. George Hanks was living with his family on the Potomac river when the Colonists rebelled. He joined the Continental army and lost his life at Yorktown. His sons, four sons and two daughters, left Virginia and came to Kentucky in a covered wagon. Three of the sons lived and died in what was later Anderson County, the fourth son migrated to Missouri. Nothing is said about there being a widow of George Hanks, nor is there any further mention made of his two daughters. His sons were George, Turner, Chichester and Pittman. The Hanks men were strong, robust and active, living to an advanced age. Pittman Hanks, before going to Missouri, lived on the Harrodsburg road in what was afterward known as the old Williams tavern, which was later acquired by Harry Wise. When in Missouri all six of Pittman Hanks' sons were in the Confederate service under Gen. Sterling Price. The second of the Hanks brothers living in Anderson County was Chichester Hanks. He married Mrs. Thomas Penny, a daughter of the pioneer, Memucan Allin. By her first husband she had one Penny child, Sallie, who married John Carpenter, and she was the mother of H. B. Carpenter, Mrs. Alice Lillard and Mrs. W. E. Bell. Children of Chichester and Elizabeth Penny Hanks were Thomas, Joseph, Frankie (Mrs. Holman Frazier), Susan Mary (Mrs. W. F. Bond) and Helen (Mrs. Henderson Hanks).

Turner Hanks, the third brother, married Nancy Holman. They had six children: George Hanks, the fourth of the pioneer brothers, married Lucy Mildred Mitchell. Three of their boys served in the Confederate army, one was killed, one severely wounded and lost a leg, and another was spoken of by his camrades as being a perfectly fearless man. Col. Thomas Hanks was born about a mile from Lawrenceburg in 1823. When he was twenty-four years old he was elected to the Legislature. Later he was elected Circuit Clerk and held the position six years. He studied law with Judge Kavanaugh and was again elected to the Legislature in 1881, where he was returned until he was known as the "Patriarch of the House." He married Miss Margaret Myers and built and occupied the colonial home owned today by Mr. Alvin Major. John Hanks, the forebear of Abraham Lincoln, was the great uncle of the four Hanks brothers who came to Kentucky during pioneer days. Many of the Hanks' descendants are living in the county today, and they have been identified with the growth and progress of the communities in which they reside. There are a number of old Hanks' homesteads in the county. The Reuben Hanks home about four miles from town, is a fine old place on one of the highest points in the county. Large rooms with high ceilings, great paneled doors and a beautiful old colonial stairway. The old Chichester Hanks homestead, a mile and half south of town, was torn away a few years ago to broaden the highway and make room for the railroad underpass. One of the columns of this old home had a number of bullets imbedded in it, bearing mute testimony to the beginning of the skirmish in this neighborhood which culminated in the battle of Perryville during the War Between the States. The farm on which the old home stood is owned today by James C. Bond, a grandson of Chichester Hanks. The Reuben Hanks home is owned and occupied today by Mr. Charleston Hanks and his sister, Mrs. T. C. Ledridge.

GEORGE-GAINES

One of the early settlers in Kentucky was Travis George, who, with his wife, Sarah Watkins George, and four children, located on Hammonds Creek in Anderson County. Their oldest son, Dudley, was born in 1769, and his wife was Lucrecia Major, a daughter of Littleton Major, who came from Culpepper County, Virginia, and established the Major family here when this was a part of Franklin County. Dudley George was a soldier in the War of 1812, and saw service at the battle of New Orleans. Mrs. George died in 1838, leaving four children, Mary L., William T., David and Eliza. The latter married Robert Gaines, and was the only living child to inherit her fathers' estate when he died in 1870, leaving one thousand acres of good farm land near Lawrenceburg. Robert Gaines was the son of Richard and Miranda Sanders Gaines. To Robert and Eliza Gaines were born nine children: William, David, James R., Lazarus, Martha (Mrs. Thos. Hawkins), Robert S., Ada (Mrs. W. H. Marrs), John W., and Boone B. Gaines. The Gaines' farm is owned today by John W. Gaines. His wife was Mrs. Imogene Tinsley Gaines, widow of his deceased brother, Boone, to whom one son, Bernard, was born. James R. Gaines was born January 27, 1851. His wife was Miss Mary Thomas, daughter of E. G. Thomas, and they reside on a 400-acre farm three miles north of Lawrenceburg, Ky. For many years Mr. Gaines was a director in the Lawrenceburg National Bank. The four children in this family are, Edmonia, Elbert, Lister and Raymond. Lister Gaines married

Miss Artie Ripy, daughter of the late T. B. Ripy. Today "Mr. Jim" Gaines is in his 87th year and carries the burdens of his many winters well. His mind is alert and he retains an active interest in all questions pertaining to his community and state.

The Gaines family migrated from Virginia, the state of tribal pride and presidents, in an early settlement of Kentucky, and located in Anderson County. The Revolutionary soldier, William Henry Gaines, had two sons, Thomas and Richard Gaines, who were pioneer settlers in the Alton Station neighborhood. Thomas Gaines located many acres of land here in 1815. A son of Richard Gaines was Gabriel Hansford Gaines, whose first wife was Miss Jane Wilson. Their children were Eldridge and Mary Gaines, the latter was the first wife of J. W. Major. Gabriel Gaines second wife was Miss Ann McCormick, and to this union was born four children: Bettie (Mrs. W. H. Leach), Carrie (Mrs. Henry Wilson), Stella (Mrs. John W. Dawson), and J. W. Gaines, president of the Anderson National Bank. The Gabriel Gaines' home in Alton was one of the most imposing in the little village, and was proverbial for hospitality for many years. J. W. Gaines married Miss Fannie Cannon, of Georgetown, daughter of Dr. F. M. Cannon, and they own a beautiful home on S. Main street in Lawrenceburg. Mr. and Mrs. J. W. Dawson own a farm and commodious home on the Frankfort pike that was the estate of the pioneer James Ripy, father of James B. and T. B. Ripy.

SHOUSE BROTHERS

Two Shouse brothers came to America from Germany in the early days and settled in Pennsylvania. One of them, Henry Shouse, migrated to Woodford County in 1750 and died there in 1835. His son, Henry, Jr., was the forebear of the Shouse family in Anderson County. John Shouse, born September 17, 1796, married Sarah Slaughter, a niece of Gabriel Slaughter, Governor of Kentucky from 1816 to 1820. Thomas Shouse, Jr., born in Anderson County, married a Miss Johnson, and their only son, Len B. Shouse, is manager of the Lafayette Hotel in Lexington, Ky. He married a Miss Richardson, of Lexington, and they have two sons and a daughter. John W. Shouse, Sr., married Miss Lucy Petty, and their children are John W. Shouse, Jr., married Miss Parma Klem; James S. married Miss Kathrine Cox. They are citizens of Lawrenceburg today. The latter couple recently celebrated their golden wedding.

JOSEPH GRIFFY

The name of Griffy has been synonimous with this county since its erection. The early forebear was Joseph Griffy, and he was the father of five sons and four daughters: David, Burrus, Joseph, Ben, Will, Nancy, Ann, Tilda and Polly. Joseph Griffy, Jr., married Miss Ann McMichael and Mrs. Lizzie Posey is their daughter. David Griffy was the father of five sons and four daughters: Jordon, Leroy, Will (killed in Chicamauga battle), Anthony, John Burrus, Lorana, Elvina, Sarah and Ann. The latter was married twice, the first time to Kavanaugh Cox, and Coleman Cox is their son; she then married Thomas Wells and Mrs. J. L. Sherwood is their daughter. John Burrus Griffy married Frances McMichael and to them were born five sons and four daughters: Gideon B., Ezra C., William T., James Porter, Elmer L., Adelia, Laura,

Ora and Lena. Gideon and Ezra Griffy are substantial citizens residing in Lawrenceburg today with their children and grandchildren, the latter being the sixth generation of this family to reside in this locality.

JESSE M. JOHNSON

Jesse M. Johnson, who died in Lawrenceburg, April 12, 1927, came of pioneer stock who helped materially in the promotion and advancement of the early interest of the county. His father, Rev. J. F. Johnson, was pastor of the Salt River Baptist church for twenty-eight years. Mr. Johnson first engaged in the mercantile business in Lawrenceburg, a member of the dry goods firm of Bond and Johnson until the Lawrenceburg Bank was organized in 1885, at which time he was appointed cashier, and served in that capacity for forty-two years. In 1874 he was married to Miss Sallie Bond, daughter of the Hon. W. F. Bond. To this union were born eight children, four of whom survive today: Frances, wife of Judge John A. Burton, of Lebanon, Madeline (Mrs. E. W. Ripy), E. B. Johnson, of Birmingham, and Robert E. Johnson, Lawrenceburg's postmaster and manager of the Bond's Mill distillery. J. M. Johnson was always recognized as a generous benefactor, a stimulating friend, a wise counselor and stable in all his ways. He was proverbial for his ready wit and genial smile, and his life was full of good deeds and love for his fellowmen.

KAVANAUGH

Mrs. Lucy Emrin Kavanaugh, born April 1, 1830; died June, 1916, was the last survivor of a family of two brothers and seven sisters. She was the daughter of Thomas Jefferson and Nancy Mountjoy Lillard, and a direct descendent of Capt. John Lillard, a soldier of the Revolution. Capt. Lillard had a son, John Lillard, Jr., who came from Culpepper County, Virginia, in pioneer days and settled on Salt River, a few miles below the old Bond's Mill location. He was the grandfather of Mrs. Kavanaugh. At the age of eighteen she was married to Charles Nicholas Kavanaugh. To this union was born five children. Three died in infancy, the other two, Mrs. Aileen K. Gilbert and Dr. C. W. Kavanaugh, were for many years residents of Lawrenceburg. At the outbreak of the War Between the States, Mrs. Kavanaugh's husband cast his lot with the Southern Confederacy, going out with Gen. Simon Boliver Buckner. After serving in the ranks for a year, he was compelled on account of illness to return home, and lived only a year afterwards. On his route home he passed through the mountains of eastern Kentucky where he lost his way. He simply gave the reins to "Old Grey," a horse that he had ridden from home, and she, with unerring instinct brought him safely into the open country where he reached home without further difficulty. Suffice it to say, Old Grey was tenderly cared for the rest of her life, and Mrs. Kavanaugh retained as a memento, one of Old Grey's shoes. During the war she was living on the farm which she afterward sold to the late James R. York, and came to town to live with her daughter, Mrs. J. W. Gilbert. Mrs. Kavanaugh was a consistent member of the Christian church, and a well-posted student of the Scriptures, as well as other kinds of literature, and was always abreast of the times in the world of politics. She was very versatile and a delightful conversationalist on current or historical subjects.

William Kavanaugh, a pioneer, bought 250 acres of land in Franklin County, now Anderson, in 1817, for $2,000. This land was afterwards acquired by Burton Cole. William Kavanaugh built a large imposing home on this land. His wife was Elizabeth Freeman, and they had five sons and three daughters. One son, Judge William Kavanaugh, married Miss Wills, sister of Judge J. F. Wills, a former editor of the Anderson News. Judge Kavanaugh organized the Salt River Tigers, the famous company from Anderson County in the Mexican War. The fourth son of Judge Kavanaugh was Charles Nicholas, who married Miss Lucy Emrin Lillard. Their son, Dr. C. W. Kavanaugh, was for many years one of the most successful physicians of Lawrenceburg, and took an active part in civic affairs. He was a graduate of the Louisville Medical College in 1885; was Mayor of Lawrenceburg for four years and health officer for thirty-five years. During the World War Dr. Kavanaugh was First Lieutenant in the Medical Corps at Fort Benjamin Harrison. His first wife was Miss Susie Mullins, and their son is Dr. C. N. Kavanaugh, of Lexington Ky. His second wife was Miss Rhoda Caldwell, and their daughters are Mrs. Aileen K. Boggess, widow of Lawrenceburg's beloved physician and health officer, the late Dr. Raymond Boggess, and Mrs. Jere Beam, of Bardstown.

The pioneer, John Lillard, father of Thomas Jefferson and Christopher Lillard, left an interesting will dated December 6, 1837, recorded in the Anderson County courthouse. It has many codicils. The preface of this long and interesting document is as follows: "In the name of God, Amen; I, John Lillard, being now diseased in body but sound in mind and memory, and calling to mind the mortality of human life, do make and ordain this my last will and testament, to-wit: I will that my body after my death be interred by my executors in decent Christian burial; after my death all my just debts to be paid. I bequeath to my daughter, Elizabeth Lillard McGinnis, one negro woman named Dorcas, together with $1,200." To another daughter, Alice Lillard Dawson, he left a slave named Melinda and a certain amount of money; to his other children he left a stipulated amount of money, slaves and acres of land. To his grandsons, Erastus and John McClure, sons of his daughter, Sallie McClure, he left 160 acres of land in Missouri. To two little granddaughters, he left $50 each, "in consequence of their great likeness to their deceased grandmother, Agnes Lillard, my beloved wife." "The family burying ground," John Lillard stated, "must be posted and railed in with cedar posts, or enclosed with a stone wall, my executors to have it done in like manner after my death." His sons, Thomas Jefferson and Christopher Lillard, were named as executors of the document.

Dr. John Webster Gilbert, who died in the meridian of life in 1893, was one of the outstanding physicians of Lawrenceburg. He attained a reputation of ability equal to any of his medical confreres, and was a valued and respected citizen. His forebears came to Kentucky when the state embraced the three counties of Lincoln, Jefferson and Fayette counties. They had a land grant in Lincoln County, where Gilbert Creek had its source, this stream being named for one of the brothers who explored it to its termination in Kentucky river. Dr. Gilbert's father was the Hon. James Gilbert, a prosperous farmer, and at one time represented his county in the State Legislature. When Dr. J. W. Gilbert, Sr., graduated from the Louisville Medical College in 1873, he entered upon the practice of his profession at Fox Creek in Anderson County. In 1876 he married Miss Aileen Kavanaugh, and they came to Lawrenceburg to reside, where he built up a large practice.

Children of Dr. and Mrs. Gilbert are Dr. J. W. Gilbert, one of the leading physicians of Lawrenceburg today; George Gilbert, for many years an electrical engineer with headquarters in Baltimore, Md.; Freeman Gilbert, an official in the State Auditor's Department in Frankfort, and Miss Emrine Gilbert, of Lawrenceburg.

CHRISTOPHER C. LILLARD

C. C. Lillard was born in Anderson County in 1833, and died in June, 1896. He was the son of Thomas and Nancy Mountjoy Lillard. This is a family, like many others, who can confess a shade of pride as they trace their lineage and recount their ancestry. C. C. Lillard spent his early days on the farm and was educated in the schools in the county. During the War Between the States, he went out with the famous Orphan Brigade, and was chosen First Lieutenant of Company I, Second Kentucky Infantry. He fought at Fort Donelson where he was captured and held prisoner on Johnson's Island for several months. He was finally exchanged in the transfer of prisoners, and saw active service at the battle of Murfreesboro. His health failed and, acting on the advice of physicians, he returned home. In 1869 C. C. Lillard formed a partnership with his brother-in-law, W. F. Bond, in the distilling business, the firm being the nationally known Bond & Lillard. Although one of the wealthiest citizens of the county, Mr. Lillard never forgot those who were less fortunate, and never refused substantial aid in the hour of distress. He gave liberally to the churches and every good cause. In August, 1864, he was married to Miss Margaret Bond and for years their commodious country home, on the hill above the little hamlet of Tyrone, was proverbial for hospitality. In the early '90s he moved his family from the home on the farm to the residence he purchased from C. E. Bond on the corner of Broadway and South Main, and it was here he died. C. C. and Margaret Bond Lillard had six children: Roger H. Lillard, who married Miss Mary Louise Burrus, of Mercer County; Wallace, who married Dr. J. Sproie Lyons, an eminent minister in the Presbyterian church; W. F. Lillard, who married Miss Louise Parlin, of Cincinnati; Ophelia (Mrs. D. L. Meriwether); Frankie (Mrs. A. H. Witherspoon), and Jessie (Mrs. George McLeod).

JUDGE WILLIAM H. McBRAYER

"No history of Anderson County would be complete without a mention of that man whose individual efforts did much for the upbuilding of the county—Judge Wm. H. McBrayer. He was the son of Andrew and Martha Blackwell McBrayer, sturdy, upright Scotch-Irish people, and they were among the first settlers of this county. Judge McBrayer was born at the old homestead, two and a half miles from Lawrenceburg, December 10, 1821. By every tie he was closely identified with his home county, having in 1849 married Miss Henrietta Daviess, granddaughter of Captain William Wallace. In a few years she passed away, leaving an only daughter, Henrietta, who became the wife of Col. D. L. Moore of Mercer County. Some years later Judge McBrayer married another daughter of Capt. Wallace, Miss Mary Wallace, of Madison County, although born in Anderson.

Until 1870 he was a prominent dry goods merchant of Lawrenceburg, but having in 1855 embarked in the shipping of mules to the south, he lost heavily and became deeply involved in debt. In order to recoup, he gave up the mercantile business and devoted his attention to a distillery he had started some years before on a picturesque little stream, named by his wife, "Cedar Brook." The brand of whiskey assumed the name and soon rose to a preeminent position among Bourbon brands. Judge McBrayer possessed the Irish wit and cheer, and the sturdy Scotch industry and honesty, and long after his death one frequently heard quoted some of his ready wit. God gave him a broad mind, a clear brain and a generous heart. William H. McBrayer was Judge of Anderson County from 1851 to 1856, and served in the State Senate in 1857-'61. He was a leading member of the Presbyterian church, being ruling elder for a number of years. It was largely due to his liberal munificence that a church of this denomination was built in this town. He gave $30,000 to a chair for the study of the Bible at Central University, and his silent charities were numberless. He was a member of the Masonic fraternity in Lawrenceburg for many years. Judge McBrayer worked for the building of the railroad through here with boundless zeal, as a strong prejudice existed against it, and many opposed its construction. He canvassed the county from end to end, speaking in every district, donating the right of way through much land and buying stock when confidence was at lowest ebb. He was a director up to the time of his death and the directors were honorary pallbearers at his funeral, and the Southern Road ran special draped trains from Louisville, Lexington and Harrodsburg on that occasion. The station, McBrayer, in this county, was named for him.

Judge McBrayer died December 6, 1888, leaving a large estate. The county mourned the loss of an honest, public-spirited, democratic and unostentatious citizen."—Anderson News Supplement of 1906.

LITTLETON MAJOR

Littleton Major was the name of the pioneer in this family to come from Virginia to this section of the country about the year 1800. He settled on the farm near Alton that is owned today by his grandson, Alvin Major. Littleton Major's son, John M. Major, was born in 1816, and died in 1881. His wife, Lucy Herndon Major, was born 1824, and died in 1871. Their son, Alvin, was born November 5, 1855, and is an esteemed citizen of Lawrencebury today. The second son, John W. Major, born 1858, died February 21, 1936. The daughter, Margaret Major, married James L. Cole, Sr., died November 29, 1882. To this union was born two sons, D. A. Cole and James L. Cole, Jr. To Alvin Major and his wife, Sarah L. Hedden, were born three daughters: Cora (Mrs. Wilson); Victoria (Mrs. Woodward), and Pearl (Mrs. McAfee). John W. Major's first wife was Miss Mary Gaines. Their children were Ellie and Mabel (Mrs. Cartinhour); his second wife was Miss Mattie Witherspoon; he was married the third time to Miss Florence Witherspoon and their children are Eleanor (Mrs. Johnson) and Walter W. Major.

MAJOR LEWIS WITHERSPOON McKEE

The subject of this sketch was born December 26, 1854, in Lawrenceburg, Ky., and died January 15, 1930. He was a cadet at the Kentucky Military Institute in the early '70s, and later a student at West Point. The legal rather than the military profession appealed to him, and he attended college at LaGrange, Missouri, and graduated from the Department of Law at that institution in 1875. Mr. McKee held three commissions in the Kentucky State Guards. In 1882 he was commissioned Major, 2nd Batallion, 2nd Regiment. In 1887 he was commissioned Colonel, 2nd Regiment Infantry. He served in the Kentucky State Senate from the 20th Senatorial District, from the counties of Anderson, Franklin and Mercer, during the sessions of 1885-'86-'87-'88. During these sessions he served on the following committees: Codes of Practice, Immigration and Labor, Library and Public Buildings, and was chairman on Public Affairs. The State Journal gave reference to many bills which he introduced. It was during Major McKee's tenure in office that Governor Knott sent the military arm of the government to Morehead on several occasions to quell the Tolliver-Martin and Logan feud, and suppress lawlessness in Rowan County. On these occasions 150 soldiers were under command of Major L. W. McKee. This celebrated feud was of three years' duration. From August, 1884, to June, 1887, there were twenty murders and assassinations in Rowan County, and sixteen wounded who did not die. Gov. Knott declared there was no official power to extend any relief to the citizens of Morehead, for, when the soldiers were withdrawn, lawlessness broke out afresh. Finally the best citizens of Rowan County, led by the sheriff, arose enmasse heavily armed, surrounded the town of Morehead, and in a fierce fight exterminated the five Tollivers and their henchmen. After the battle a mass meeting was held at the court house and a Citizens' Protective Association was formed. They adopted resolutions declaring "If any one is arrested for this day's work, we will reassemble and punish to the death any man who offers molestation." The possee that took the law into their own hands, and exterminated the feudists, washed and dressed the victims, ordered their coffins from Lexington and buried them.

Major McKee spoke interestingly of his regiment's encampment in Rowan County and the danger to which they were subjected while trying to preserve law and order. In 1886 several times he was taken from his seat in the Senate and sent on military duty for the State. He was, on account of merit as a soldier and officer, elected by the Second Kentucky Regiment of State Guard as colonel and on 30th of August, 1887, was commissioned by Gov. Knott. On December 20, 1886, Major McKee was married to Miss Eliza Irwin, of Dayton, Ohio, a most estimable woman of unusual mental endowments. She was a granddaughter of Rear Admiral James Schenck, and grandniece of General Robert Schenck, minister to England under President Grant. Mrs. McKee died in 1918. Children of Major and Mrs. L. W. McKee are, Kathrine, Miriam (Mrs. Gerow), Irwin, Logan, Jane (Mrs. Robert Fryer) and Robert.

CAPTAIN WILEY SEARCY

Captain Wiley Searcy's grandparents migrated to Kentucky from Virginia in the days of Daniel Boone. His parents later settled in Anderson County. When only nineteen years of age, Wiley Searcy enlisted as a private in Company E, 21st Regiment Kentucky Infantry, Col. E. L. Dudley commanding. His promotion from the ranks to that of captain was deservedly rapid, and after four years of service he was mustered out in 1865. Capt. Searcy was connected with the Internal Revenue Department from 1867 to 1884, serving in the capacity as store-keeper, gauger and deputy collector.

His first wife was a Miss Saffell, and their son, Frank Searcy, married Miss Gertrude Frazier and they live on an Anderson County farm. Captain Searcy's second wife was Miss Mollie Mountjoy. Their son, Matt Searcy, married Miss Dorothy Lindsay, and they reside in Miami, Florida.

MOUNTJOY

In the Anderson News Supplement of 1906, we read that two brothers, "Edward and William Mountjoy, nephews of Governor Garrard, came here from Virginia. Edward located near what is now the town of Alton, on the site of the home owned by Mrs. Sue Rhinehart, and his large tract of land extended almost to the limits of Lawrenceburg. He built what was then considered a fine house of logs, weatherboarded and plastered. Here he kept an old-fashioned tavern, and his stricter neighbors were often shocked by the fiddling and dancing. This love of music and dancing was probably due to his French extraction. In his youth when the whiskey rebellion occurred in Pennsylvania, he was a volunteer from Virginia. When General Washington reviewed the troops he especially complimented Edward Mountjoy upon his fine statue and soldierly bearing, a characteristic still to be observed in many of his descendants. These two brothers married and reared large families, and many of their descendants live in the county today." Edward Mountjoy's daughter, Nancy, married Thomas Lillard, and they lived on a farm two and a half miles from Lawrenceburg which was afterward known as the Hal Carpenter farm.

JOHN M. NEVINS

John M. Nevins, a well known citizen and son of pioneer parents in Anderson County, was born in 1833. He lived his eighty-seven years and died on the same farm near Nevins Station where he was born. His wife was Miss Mary Mosely. To this union was born four sons and four daughters: John T. Nevins, Rev. W. M. Nevins, a Baptist preacher, H. R. Nevins, Robert Nevins, Mrs. J. H. Hawkins, Mrs. D. F. Hanks, Mrs. C. L. Hawkins and Miss Sue Nevins.

A brother of John M. Nevins, Manlaus Nevins, was a soldier in the Union army and lost his life during the War Between the States.

McBRAYER

Captain John H. McBrayer, born 1826, and died 1910, was a colorful figure in the affairs of the county all his life. He was a very positive character, intellectual and brave and possessed all the attributes that constitute a gentleman of the old school. Capt. McBrayer was married when young to Miss Sarah Chambers. No children were born to this union. The following sketch was written by W. C. Woods in the Anderson News Supplement of 1906: "Captain McBrayer, born nearly eighty years ago of a family of fine men and women, has a mark which will live as long as history exists to record the exploits of man. It was he who led the Salt River Tigers and saved the day at Buena Vista; it was due to the mighty yell of this intrepid little band led by this gallant man, that victory perched and sat on the banner of the United States. His hair is now grey with the frost of many winters, his step not quite so active as in years gone by, yet his bearing is as manly, his bow as full of grace and dignity, his speech and utterance as clear, and his right hand clasped in true fellowship as strong as in days of yore. He has passed through many vicissitudes yet has bourne them all with the same undaunted courage as marked his life on the battlefield."

VAUGHAN

W. F. Vaughan was the son of John S. and Matilda Rhinehart Vaughan, was born August 11, 1842, below Camden, now Glensborough, on Salt River in Anderson County. Very early in life he felt the call to the ministry, and his first congregation was his schoolmates in the school building on Sunday evenings. He was licensed to preach and admitted into the Kentucky Conference within six days. His first pastoral charge was his home church on Salt River. He was afterwards Presiding Elder in the Shelbyville District. His wife was Miss Lizzie Gritton, of Mercer County. Mr. Vaughan died in 1920, and the Knight Templar Masons, of which order he was a member, attended his funeral in a body.

JAMES McCALL HOMESTEAD*

"Spring Hill," the home of the late James McCall, is, perhaps the oldest frame building in Anderson County, having been built prior to 1795. The house was built by Thomas Lillard. This property had been in the McCall family for more than seventy-eight years. Thomas McCall, the father of James McCall and Mrs. S. E. Boston, of Lawrenceburg, moved from Washington County, Virginia, in 1828, to Lincoln County, Ky., and the following year moved to this place, having purchased the farm from the Lillard heirs. To give an idea of the amount of labor necessary for the preparation of material in the building of homes then, we give details of this building: this house is fifty-five feet long by twenty-eight wide. There is a cellar the whole length of the building. The sills are twelve by twelve inches, twenty-eight feet long; the joists four by twelve inches, eighteen feet long; the studdings four by eight inches, eighteen feet long; the corner posts ar twelve by twelve inches with rabbet cut on inside to eight inches; the rafters and five by six inches at foot and three by four inches at crown. The heavy timbers are all hewn, while the other material was cut by an old-fashioned whip saw. The framing is all mortised and tenoned; the wall is eight inches thick, filled between the studs with brick and mortar, making a very strong as well as warm house. The door and window frames are eight by eight inches, with raised moulding for facing, and are all black walnut; the doors are walnut also. The doors and wainscoating are all paneled and beaded, the nails were hand forged. The chimney standing near the center of the house, was originally eight by eight feet at base, and had four fireplaces to it, but a good many years ago the house was struck by lightning and this chimney was torn down and in rebuilding was made smaller. About fifty yards south of the house is the most noted spring in Anderson County. This spring afforded water for Gen. Bragg's army, which was encamped on this farm for several days

---

*Anderson News Supplement of 1906.

when he retreated through this county during the Civil War. On the west side of the pike is the old muster field, and race track which witnessed many scenes of carnival as well as of conflict." Today this old McCall landmark is owned by Dr. J. B. Lyen, of Lawrenceburg.

McBRAYER

We find the name of McBrayer occurring often in the annals of the county's early history, many of whom assisted in bringing Anderson to its present prosperity. Alexander McBrayer and his wife, Susanna Wright McBrayer, came in the early days from Virginia, and their children were useful and progressive citizens. They were: William Stewart, John H., James A., and Georgianna McBrayer. Wm. Stewart McBrayer married Rachel M. Johnson, and their children who lived to maturity, John C., James A., Louis J. and Bettie McBrayer, who married Allen Berryman McAfee. Mrs. McAfee is the only living descendant of Wm. S. McBrayer. The children of Jas. A. McBrayer and Sophia Hardin McBrayer, are Watt Hardin McBrayer, Rachel M. McBrayer (Varble), and Mary McBrayer (McClanahan). The children of Louis J. McBrayer and Sallie Hicks McBrayer are: Major W. McBrayer and Jasper J. McBrayer.

Mrs. Rachel McBrayer Varble, niece of Mrs. Allie McAfee, has achieved distinction for her literary works. For several years she wrote as "Rachel Mack" for newspaper syndicates and magazines. Her book, The Red Cape, attained instant success.

McAFEE

The name of McAfee has been synonomous with this part of the country ever since the early explorers of the name, crossed Kentucky river seven miles above Frankfort and passed a little east of the present site of Lawrenceburg and camped at Lillard's (McCalls) spring in Anderson County. A lineal descendant of one of these McAfee brothers was Isaac Washburn McAfee, who married Sallie Miller, and lived in the Alton neighborhood, where for many years he was a successful and much loved teacher of the county. His only child, Allen Berryman McAfee, who married Bettie McBrayer, is one of Lawrenceburg's most esteemed citizens. For thirty-one years he has been director in the Lawrenceburg National Bank and for six years Chairman of the Board of that institution. Mr. McAfee was born October 12, 1870. He and his wife have three sons and three daughters and reside on a fine farm three miles from Lawrenceburg where he has been a breeder of prize winning Southdown sheep and Shetland ponies for many years.

McMURRY

Thomas McMurry, born in 1833, died in 1911, aged seventy-eight, lived a long and useful life in Anderson County and was esteemed and respected by all who knew him. He was married three times, first to Miss Leathers and next to a Mrs. Bond, and to this union five children were born: Dr. J. T. McMurry, of Shelby County; Ed McMurry, of Butte, Mont.; Mrs. Belle Walker, Mrs. C. C. Trent and Mrs. J. D. Cox, of Anderson County. His last marriage was to Miss Mollie Bell. Mr. McMurry was for many years a prominent farmer and at the time of his death owned a large tract of land in the western part of the county. He was a consistent member and officer in the Lawrenceburg Christian church.

COX

Burton Cox was born in 1856 and died in 1912. He was a member of one the early and substantial families of the county. He owned large farming interests and accumulated a neat fortune. He married Miss Mary Jane Bond, daughter of Wilkerson Bond, whose forebears helped materially in the development of the county. Mr. and Mrs. Cox were the parents of Judge John T. Cox and Mrs. W. D. Roach. Judge Cox, as a young man, was a merchant at Sparrow, formerly Wardsville, and later engaged in the mercantile business in Lawrenceburg for several years. Two years ago he threw his hat in the political arena and defeated the popular Judge, Powel Taylor, for the office of County Judge.

YOUNG

Rev. Daniel W. Young, Methodist minister, died May, 1929, aged sixty-three years. He was a son of Benjamin and Alice Carter Young. He was married in 1886 to Miss Louella Alderson, of Mercer County. Mr. Young was a preacher of the gospel for more than thirty years. He was also a business man and an exemplary citizen, held in high esteem by all who knew him. His children are William and Charles Young, of Louisville; Ben and John, of Lawrenceburg; Mrs. Alice Wilder, of Winchester; Mrs. Emma Case, Richmond; Mrs. M. S. Bond, Frankfort; Mrs. Clide Mitchell and Mrs. Marvin, of Lawrenceburg, and Miss Rosa Mae Young, of Covington.

JOSEPH H. D. McKEE

The McKee family has been identified with Anderson County for more than a century and a quarter. The subject of this sketch was born December 13, 1820, and died July 8, 1889. He was the grandson of Col. Anthony Crockett, of Revolutionary fame. In 1854 he married Martha Elizabeth, only daughter of Dr. Lewis J. Witherspoon. Mr. McKee was a lawyer of ability and a large land owner. He studied law under Judge Thomas Bell Monroe, a celebrated Kentuckian who lived in South Frankfort and taught a law class at his home from 1843-'48. After this Mr. McKee graduated from the law department of the University of Louisville. Col. Theodore O'Hara was the best man at his marriage in 1854. When war was declared with Mexico, Mr. McKee was made First Lieutenant of the First Regiment of the Volunteer Cavalry, commanded by Col. Humphrey Marshall. He participated in all the battles of this war, including that of Buena Vista. After this he located in Lawrenceburg and entered upon the practice of law. He represented Anderson County in the Legislature in 1859-61. In the fall of 1861 he went south in sympathy with the uprising of the Confederacy, taking part as a member of the Russellville Convention, and on the committee that framed the provisional constitution. His traveling companion at this time was Captain John H. McBrayer. In writing of Mr. McKee after his death, Capt. McBrayer said: "I can testify to his good qualities in every station of life; his exemplary conduct as a citizen, a husband and father, and our representative in the Legislature. He

The T. B. Ripy home.

evinced the principles of truth and honesty of the Scotch-Irish ancestry, and his courage and bravery were shown in the Mexican War." Mr. McKee and Martha Witherspoon McKee were the parents of seven children, three daughters and four sons: Major L. W. McKee, Wm. H. McKee, John McKee, Robert McKee, Misses Mary and Lizzie McKee, and Hawes (Mrs. James Thompson).

McQUIDDY

Dr. Robert I. McQuiddy was born October 12, 1830, in Anderson County; died April 14, 1917. He migrated to Kansas City where he enjoyed a lucrative practice until the death of his wife in 1904, then he returned to Kentucky and Anderson County, the home of his early days. He was a graduate in pharmacy as well as medicine, and at one time was sole owner of the drug business later acquired by his wife's nephew, Col. T. J. Ballard. He married Miss Sallie Lillard, daughter of Gen. Christopher Lillard. Four children were born to this union, but none lived to maturity. Dr. McQuiddy represented Anderson County as State Senator in the years 1877-'81. He was gifted with fluent speech, was talented as a poet and a delightful conversationalist.

C. C. TRENT

The R. C. Trent Company was organized more than fifty years ago by C. C. Trent, and for many years known as the C. C. Trent Co. The latter merchant built up a strong and profitable business by honest methods and fair dealings. Until a few years ago the Trent Company ran a large grocery and hardware business in the commodious building owned by the firm, but this department has been discontinued and the large emporium given over entirely to dry goods. Mr. Trent's children by his first wife are Oscar T. Trent, Paul, deceased, and Mrs. Ada Ragan, who for many years was principal of a school at Butler, Ky. Mr. Trent was married the second time to Miss Minnie McMurry, and their children are Raymond C. Trent, who is at the head of the business established by his father, Mr. Stanley Trent, attorney at law, and Mrs. O. C. McKay. For several years Mr. Trent was member of the City Council, and was Republican nominee for the Legislature in 1907. Mr. Stanley Trent is Commander of the Anderson Post, and this year will serve as District Commander of the Eighth District, American Legion, Department of Kentucky.

RIPY

The Ripy family has been identified with Anderson County for nearly a century. Two brothers, John and James Ripy, who came here from Tyrone County, Ireland, prior to 1840, left many descendants in this county who have been popular citizens, enterprising and prominent in affairs of the community and state. A sister, Eliza Ripy, came with her pioneer brothers, and married Thomas B. Lyons, of Shelby County, and was the mother of Jasper W., Robert and Hamilton Lyons. The sons of James and Artemesia Walker Ripy were: Col. James P. Ripy, born in 1844, and T. B. Ripy, born in 1847. At the beginning of the War Between the States, James P. Ripy entered the Confederate Army as a member of Company H, 5th Kentucky Cavalry under General John H. Morgan. He served with honor and distinction during the hostilities. After the war closed Mr. Ripy returned to his native place in Lawrenceburg, Ky., and became owner of the celebrated old Hickory Springs Distillery. Later he retired from business and sold his plant to the Kentucky Distilleries and Warehouse Co. Mr. Ripy was an honored councilman of the town for many years and helped put forth many of the improvements in the place. He was married in 1869 to Miss Helen Lillard, a member of an influential pioneer family, and they reared four sons and one daughter, who have carried on the family tradition for good citizenship. The oldest son, James B. Ripy, was a graduate of K. M. I. and Washington and Lee University. He is now located in Louisville and for some years was traveling auditor for the Courier-Journal, and assitant to the circulation department of the Louisville Times. Marion W. Ripy, the second son, graduated from the legal department of Washington and Lee in 1896. He was City Attorney of Lawrenceburg in 1898, but resigned the next year and moved to Louisville and was associated with Col. Bennett H. Young in the practice of law. Today he is an attorney in New York City. Hardy B. Ripy, the third son, is in the government employ in Washington City. The youngest son, Col. Frank L. Ripy, received his law degree at the University of Louisville, and began the practice of his profession in Lawrenceburg in 1902. He was twice chosen City Attorney and also served as County Attorney. Col. Ripy entered the U. S. Army on the Mexican border when outlaws threatened trouble for the United States. Here he had the rank of Captain. Later during the World War, he was made a Lieutenant-Colonel, stationed at Camp Shelby, Miss., and finally sent to France and saw active service during the closing days of hostilities. Col. Ripy died November, 1929. His wife was Mrs. Elizabeth Hazelrigg Hall of Frankfort. The only daughter of Mr. and Mrs. J. P. Ripy is Mrs. Helen McWhorter, of Magnolia, Texas.

Thomas Beebe Ripy, Sr., died in 1902. He was educated at K. M. I. and at Sayre Institute at Frankfort. When twenty-one years of age, he purchased an interest in the Walker, Martin & Company Distillery at Tyrone, and later built a more modern plant at this point, a notice of which is given in the history of famous distilleries of Anderson County. Mr. Ripy was recognized as one of the most capable men connected with distillation in Kentucky, and always did business in a high-toned manner. After his passing, a friend who knew him well, said, "It was never necessary to go a step beyond T. B. Ripy to find the ideal Kentucky gentleman, and a public spirited and generous citizen." In 1874 Mr. Ripy was married to Miss Sallie Fidler, whose forebears came here before 1800. The nine children in this happy family who were reared to maturity, are T. B. Ripy, Jr., Ernest W., Mrs. Pelham Johnson, Mrs. Lister Gaines, Ezra F., Catlett, Forest, Robert, Allen and William. In 1888 Mr. Ripy completed the erection of his imposing residence on Southern Avenue, the handsomest home in Lawrenceburg.

T. B. Ripy, Jr., married Miss Hallie Petty; Ernest W. Ripy's wife was Miss Madeline Johnson; Ezra F. Ripy's first wife was Miss Sadie Witherspoon; he was married the second time to Mrs. Lutie Swearingen; Robert Ripy married Miss Flora Witherspoon and William Ripy's wife was Miss Elizabeth Ballard.

ROUTT

Early records show that the Routt family were people of comfortable means, good citizens, devout, industrious and law-abiding. Peter Routt, of Faquir County, Virginia, had three daughters and two sons, William and Peter. Descendants of both sons live in Anderson County. William Routt married Malinda Parker October 26, 1810, and on their wedding day they set out to Kentucky with the Parker family. They located near Lawrence, afterwards called Lawrenceburg. In 1833 when Asiatic Cholera swept Anderson County William Parker, his wife and son-in-law, William Routt, were among the first victims. The latter's son, Peter, was nineteen years of age when his father and grandparents died, leaving him a widowed mother and four young sisters to care for. He married Rebecca Bond in 1839, a granddaughter of William Bond, the Revolutionary soldier, who established the Bond family in Anderson County. Peter Routt owned a large tract of land near Johnsonville in this county and had many slaves. His eldest sons, William and Richard, marched away with the Orphan Brigade during the War Between the States and died in less than a year. At the close of the war his negroes were freed, and only his two sons, Senaca and Claiborne, were left to carry on.

Children of Senaca and Jane Leathers Routt living in Lawrenceburg today are Mrs. Rose Routt Searcy and Charles A. Routt. Two sons, William and James, died in young manhood. Claiborn and his wife, Martha Morgan Routt, had nine children: Mary (Shely), Linna Bell, Ethel (Waterfill), Arabella (Waterfill), Grover C., Elizabeth (Shannard), Senaca C., William M., and Rose (Leonard). This large family has only one representative in Lawrenceburg today—William M. Routt, who occupies the office of County Clerk. He married Miss Lucile Witherspoon and they have three children.

RICE

James W. Rice was born July 6, 1840, and died January 31, 1917. He owned many broad acres of good farm land in the county and was a prominent and patriotic citizen. He spent his life in cultivating the soil and raising fine stock, and by honesty, economy and industry accumulated much of this world's goods. At the time of his death he possessed about two thousand acres of land. Mr. Rice was well posted on all public questions, and for a number of years wrote many articles for the home papers under the assumed name of "Salt River Tiger." He took an active interest in public and civic work and in his passing Anderson County lost one of its valued citizens. Mr. Rice was married to Miss Belle Wilson and to this union was born four sons and one daughter. The eldest son, Dr. Owen Rice, a prominent young physician, passed away in early life; Linwood Rice, of Seattle, Washington has a fine record as a civil engineer; A. J. and Carleton Rice are successful business men of Anderson County; the daughter is Mrs. W. D. Mountjoy, wife of the owner of Walnut Grove Stock Farm near Lawrenceburg.

SHERWOOD

Col. John W. Sherwood, who died in Anderson County April 30, 1933, was a prosperous farmer and dealer in live stock and an outstanding figure as an auctioneer through the Blue Grass for forty years. His wife was Miss Fannie Hyatt, whose family, like the Sherwoods, dates back to the early settlement of the county. Both names are in the early records. In his young days Mr. Sherwood was a pupil of Champ Clark's in Camdenville. His children are J. L. Sherwood, President of the Lawrenceburg National Bank; William S., of Missouri; Charles, of Louisville, and three daughters, Mrs. R. M. Elliott, Mrs. Elvina Whitenack and Mrs. C. E. Johnson.

JUDGE JOHN B. SHELY

Judge John B. Shely was born April 3, 1871. His father, John W. Shely, was born in Anderson County in 1838. His relatives, the Dewitts and Wyatts from Virginia, in the early settlement of Anderson County, have been examplary citizens. Judge Shely taught school for a number of years and enjoyed the esteem of his patrons and pupils. In 1904 he was appointed by the Governor to fill the unexpired term of Judge John Odell, resigned. After this, he made the race for county judge and won by a large majority. He creditably discharged his official duties, rating as an honest and upright judge. For a few years Judge Shely was a member of the faculty of Kavanaugh High School, where he was recognized as a capable educator. He has been a regular contributor to the Anderson News for years, writing articles on diversified subjects, many of them dealing with all phases of education, physical, mental and spiritual. Judge Shely was married in 1894 to Miss Lulie Buntain, of Mercer County. They have two sons and two daughters.

JUDGE J. M. POSEY

The subject of this sketch was born in Anderson County in 1832. His father, Jeremiah Posey, was of one of the leading families of Virginia, who migrated to Anderson County when it was a comparative wilderness, and in the early days of the formation of the county, was appointed "Captain of Patrol" in Lawrenceburg to be assisted by Jeptha Wall and Henry Boggess. Judge J. M. Posey was admitted to practice law May 3, 1855. His mother was a daughter of Randall Walker. When a young man Judge Posey taught school a number of years. He entered politics in 1867. He was deputy clerk under J. H. McBrayer, Sr., for eight years. He also served as Superintendent of Schools in the county. In 1892 he was stamp deputy under Cleveland for four years, and for ten years was County Judge. He was never defeated for any office to which he aspired. Judge Posey was the first man in the south to defeat a Confederate soldier for office, winning over Capt. W. E. Bell who was just back from the war and who had covered himself with glory during that struggle. By his first wife Judge Posey and eight children: W. H. Posey, attorney at law in Lexington; Dr. Albert Posey, of Frankfort; Dr. T. H. Posey, dentist in Lawrenceburg; Chas. Posey, of Baltimore; Mrs. Mary Reiss, Mrs. Lulie Ross and Mrs. Eloise Connelly, of California. Judge Posey's second wife was Miss Elizabeth Griffy, who survives him.

The Dean and Sherk Thread Factory.

SPARROW

The Sparrow family of the county is a connection of the family of the same name that was closely allied with the relatives of Abraham Lincoln.

The branch of the family in Anderson came from Boyle County. They are of English decent. As emigrants, some settled in Maryland and others in Virginia. In Maryland there is a place known as Sparrow's Point. Migrations of the family brought some to Kentucky. Thomas Sparrow, L. M. Sparrow and W. T. Sparrow were ancestors of Prof. Ezra Sparrow, principal of Western High School. There have been five preachers in the Sparrow family: Henry Sparrow, born 1801, died 1881; O. T. Sparrow, Raymond Sparrow, great grandson of Henry Sparrow; J. J. Whitehouse, descendant of Henry Sparrow, and Ezra Sparrow. The daughters of L. M. Sparrow married Silas Ashby, A. Mathley and Henry Crutcher. The little hamlet called Sparrow in Anderson County, was named for this family who settled in this neighborhood, and in the early days, was dubbed "The Sparrow's Nest."

THACKER

Since the erection of Anderson County there have been Thackers within her borders. E. J. Thacker, born in 1832, died in 1923 at the age of ninety-one years, was a Confederate veteran, a member of Gen. Hohn H. Morgan's command. He was a member of Company F of the 5th Ky. Cavalry under the command of Capt. James Jordon. Mr. Thacker was taken prisoner during the struggle and incarcerated in a prison in Chicago for eighteen months. He was a member of the Ben Hardin Helm camp of Confederate veterans. He was a Mason of long standing, having been a member of that order for nearly sixty years. His wife was Miss Exie, and his two children were Mr. Ike Thacker, a merchant in Lawrenceburg (married Miss Mary Coke), and Mrs. George Linder, of Indiana. At the time of Mr. Thacker's death in 1923 there were eight Confederate veterans in the county: Judge John H. Crain, Commander; J. S. Coke, Adjutant; S. O. Hackley, James Gee, Sam Coke, Rev. B. F. Adkins, Andy Aikin and W. L. Routt. Today in the good year of 1936, W. L. Routt, called "Uncle Buck," is the last surviving Rebel in Anderson County. He is past ninety-three years of age and living on his Kentucky river farm from which he marched away in August, 1861, to cast his lot with Jeff Davis and Robert E. Lee in the War Between the States. At eighteen years of age he went to Camp Boone, Tenn., where he enlisted in Co. G of the 6th Kentucky Infantry. We are told there were exactly seventy other Anderson County men in that outfit. Sixteen paid the extreme penalty on the battle field, eighteen more died in service, fifteen were wounded and only twenty-two of the lot returned home whole. "Uncle Buck" saw service at Shilo and Chicamauga, and was so badly wounded in the battle at Dallas, Georgia, that he was unfit for other service.

TOWNSEND

Dr. Oliver L. Townsend came to Glensboro, then known as Camdenville, in 1881, shortly after his graduation from medical school, and from the late '80s until shortly before his death in 1915, he was the only physician at Glensboro. There were no doctors nearer the village than those at Harrisonville and Alton on the north, Fox Creek on the east, Sinai on the south, and Mt.

Eden on the west. Dr. Townsend was one of the organizers of the Farmers Bank at Glensboro and was its President until his death. When he died he was one of the largest land owners in the county, having two farms on the Salt river bottoms two miles above the village. He was a Master Mason and a Democrat.

While Dr. Townsend was not native born, his wife's people were among the first settlers of this section of the state, who settled near Alton. He was married in 1882 to Susan Mary Brown, who lived in Camdenville and was a pupil of the late Champ Clark, who taught in the village school there. Her paternal grandfather was the pioneer settler of the county. The only son of Dr. and Mary Brown Townsend is William H. Townsend, born at Glensboro, May 31, 1890, and lived in Anderson County until he went to Lexington to study law at the University of Kentucky. Since his graduation and admittance to the Bar, Mr. Townsend has made his home in Lexington. He is said to be the foremost living authority on the history and life of Abraham Lincoln. His personal sketch appears in "Who's Who in America," and is as follows: "William H. Townsend, lawyer, author, born Glensboro, Anderson County, Ky., May 31, 1890; son of Oliver L. and Susan Mary (Brown) Townsend; early education public schools of Anderson County; LL.B. University of Kentucky; Honorary Doctor of Laws conferred by the University of Kentucky, 1930; married Genevieve Johnson of Linneus, Mo., June 16, 1915; one daughter, Mary Genevieve (student at Vassar); admitted to Kentucky Bar 1912, and since practiced at Lexington, Ky.; Corporation Counsel Lexington 1920-32; member of the law firm of Stoll, Muir, Townsend and Park; trustee Lexington Public Library; member Illinois State Historical Society, Kentucky Historical Society; Abraham Lincoln Association; author of Abraham Lincoln, Defendant, 1923; Lincoln, the Litigant, 1925; Lincoln and His Wife's Home Town, 1929; Lincoln and Liquor, 1934; Lincoln Speeches, 1935. Also author of Tribute to Nancy Hanks on the bronze tablet in Lincoln Marriage Temple at Harrodsburg, Ky. Completed and revised the late Dr. William E. Barton's "President Lincoln" in 1932; contributor of numerous magazine articles on Lincoln; owner of one of the largest collections of Lincolniana in United States, including Lincoln's first law book, "The Revised Laws of Indiana." William H. Townsend's father, Dr. O. L. Townsend, was for many years the family physician of the Sparrow-Hanks maternal kinsmen of Lincoln, and was said to have been present at more births and deaths of Lincoln relatives than any other person. This fact doubtless afforded Mr. Townsend many opportunities to acquaint himself with some of his Lincoln history. A publisher praised Mr. Townsend's work in the following vein: "A Democrat in politics, a lawyer by profession. Mr. Townsend's kinsmen during the Civil War were on the Southern side, many of them in the Confederate Army; but he writes with fearlessly clearsighted impartiality, holding the subject aloft as a jewel of complicated cut, searching keenly its many angles, revealing surprising things, some ugly, some beautiful," Anderson County is proud to count Mr. Townsend among her illustrious sons.

WASH

Synonomous with Anderson County since its erection in 1827, and with this section of the state since 1791, is the family name of Wash. The Revolutionary soldier, Benjamin Allen Wash, and his bride, Jemima Wash, came to Kentucky from northern Virginia and settled on a land-grant covering considerable acreage at a point where Hammond's Creek empties in Salt River. To this couple were born four children: Benjamin, Jr., and John P., Rebecca and Bettie. John P. Wash was one of the eight original justices which formed the first Anderson County Commission. Benjamin, Jr., stuck to farming, and was married in the early 1820's to Jane Mothershead. This young couple settled on a tract of land which encompassed many of the present farms in the Ninevah neighborhood. They were the parents of two boys and two girls: Allen, George, Mary and Martha. Benjamin Wash, Jr., was a larve slave owner and during the War Between the States took up arms in the cause of the Confederacy. Allen Wash was a member of Company F, under the command of Capt. James F. Jordon. During the campaign which carried his company into Illinois, Allen Wash was captured along with other Kentuckians and spent the last eighteen months of the conflict in a military prison at Rock Island, Illinois. At the end of the war he was discharged from this prison with James P. Ripy, a fellow Anderson Countain, and they walked from Rock Island, Illinois, to Anderson County. Allen and George Wash resumed farming on the old homestead acres. They married sisters, Susan and Sallie Redden, daughters of John and Jane Redden. Susan was a daring horseback rider and had gained renown during the War Between the States as a messenger, who was often called upon to deliver messages from one camp to another. It was this same Susan Redden who, when a company of Union soldiers under the command of Major John Draffen, made a wager with the latter when the Union men were encamped near Lawrenceburg, that she could penetrate the Union picket lines whenever she so desired. The wager was a picture of each Confederate General if she accomplished the feat, against a box of home-made candy if she did not. She did get through the picket lines with apparently little trouble, and at the close of war, Major Draffen presented the pictures of each Confederate General and they are now in the possession of Susan Redden Wash's granddaughter, Mrs. Stanley Johnson, and are in a fine state of preservation. To the Allen Wash family came seven children: Benjamin A. Wash the 3rd, now living on a portion of the ancestral acres in Anderson and Franklin counties; Mary, George, Fannie, Arthur, Martha and John P. Wash. Martha, the youngest daughter, married Stanley B. Johnson, and their two sons are Russell R. Johnson, whose pen name is "Pete" Johnson, and W. S. Johnson, who is on the staff of the Courier-Journal. Mary married T. W. Adams and is a resident of Lawrenceburg.

SALE FAMILY

In the year 1800, Samuel Sale and his wife, Elizabeth, came from Virginia and settled near the source of Buchannon's Creek, about four miles southeast of Ripyville. They had nine children: Clayton, Stephen, James, Ira, Samuel, Wm. D., Lucy, Mary and Nancy. In 1827 the pioneer, Samuel Sale, died. After the death of the father, William D., the youngest son, his mother and a sister, remained on the farm. On April 20, 1829, William D. was married to Miss Cathrine Cardwell. In 1845 the mother died at the age of eighty-five years. Wm. D. and his wife, Cathrine, had five sons and three daughters, and they continued to live on the ancestral farm until William's death in 1860. Then his son, W. C. Sale, on the death of the mother in 1878, bought all the shares in the farm but one, and he and his sister, Maggie, continued to live in the family homestead. This same farm was in possession of the

Sale family over ninety years. Two other brothers, S. T. and W. H. Sale, lived in the same neighborhood for many years; one brother, James, moved to Missouri, and another, John, died in the Confederate army. One sister married a Baker and another, a Sherwood. It is a tradition in the family that William D. Sale and his three sons, were never drunk, never chewed tobacco, nor were ever charged with any violation of the law.

William H. Sale, the father of Foster, Leslie V., Homer and Littleton Sale, died near Bond's Mill in 1926. He was a Mason for more than fifty-two years, and was the last of a family of eight children. He lived his entire life at the old homestead. His son, Homer, migrated to California several years ago; Littleton Sale lives in Covington. The other sons live in Anderson County. Foster married Miss Mary Mothershead.

Leslie V. Sale married Miss Garnett Morris and they have one daughter. Leslie lives on a part of the farm owned by his great, great grandfather, Samuel Sale. The Sale family has always been numbered among the good citizens of Anderson County and held the respect and confidence of all who knew them.

SAFFELL

In the biographical sketches in one of the histories of Kentucky, the Saffell family is mentioned among Anderson County pioneers, observing that Joshua Saffell settled here in 1790. His first wife was a Miss Baker, who died in 1804, leaving four children: John, Samuel, Baker and Elizabeth. His second wife was Miss Middleton, of Virginia, and to this union five children were born: James, Jacob, William, Nancy (Mrs. Trower), and Joshua. Mr. Saffell was a farmer and owned a thousand acres of land. His son, Samuel, born in 1804, married Miss Mary Belle Woods. He died in 1875. His wife who was born in 1804, died in 1872. They had nine children: Thomas, America, Ellen, Willia, Sarah Belle (Mrs. Montgomery), Calpernia, William Butler, James T. and Patelina. The latter sister married J. S. Searcy and was recently buried in the Lawrenceburg cemetery having reached the age of eighty-four.

Her only daughter, Mrs. Harry Gaines, lives in Topeka, Kansas. William Butler Saffell was born August 28, 1843, and was one of Lawrenceburg's representative citizens until his death in 1910. He owned 500 acres of farming land near town. In 1889 he built the W. B. Saffell Distillery on the Southern railroad near Alton, which became one of the brands of whiskey for which Anderson County was noted. In 1883 he married Miss Frankie Bond, daughter of the Hon. W. F. and Susan Mary Hanks Bond. They were the parents of six daughters and one son: Mary Belle (Mrs. Horace Bohon), Allie, Oneita (Mrs. Park Smith), Lillian (Mrs. Clive Moss), Todd (Mrs. Vincent Bartlett), Rose (Mrs. Rothwell Edwards) and Franklin, who died in infancy. W. B. Saffell was a Master Mason and for many years Vice-president and director in the Lawrenceburg National Bank.

FREEMAN

The name of Freeman is obsolete in Anderson County today. In Virginia many of the Freemans rose to distinction in politics and belles lettres, and some members of this family were among the early settlers to this county. George Freeman located his tract of land near Fox Creek, and built his log house here in 1804. He also superintended the building of a wooden bridge over Salt River, which bore the name of "Freeman's Bridge" until it was torn away five years ago to make way for a new concrete and steel structure. Dud Cornish was the builder of this old bridge in 1810. When only seventeen years of age George Freeman was a Revolutionary soldier. He enlisted just before the battle of Yorktown, so his army life was a brief one. George Freeman's daughter, Elizabeth, married William Kavanaugh, the first of the name to come to Kentucky.

Many concrete and steel structures have replaced the old wooden bridges that were erected when the first settlers were "heroes in the strife." A modern span, eighty feet long, was erected over Crooked Creek, east of VanBuren in 1903, at a cost of $1,098. The "Hawkins" bridge, on Gilbert's Creek, 140 feet in length, was erected the same year at a cost of $3,300. The "Petty" bridge, length 140 feet, built in 1905, cost $3,500. The "Goodnight" bridge, length 140 feet, built in 1890 at a cost of $5,200. These new structures lack the picturesqueness of the wooden spans, but they fill the need of the present day traffic.

COLORED PEOPLE OF ANDERSON COUNTY

According to Collin's History of Kentucky, in 1840 colored slaves in Anderson County numbered 1,059. In the year 1850 slaves numbered 1,282; in 1860 slaves numbered 1,357. Free colored people in the county in 1860 were fourteen; in 1870 there were 698.

As a rule the colored people are law abiding and thrifty and have preserved amicable relations with the whites. There is a colored settlement to the east of town called "The Grove," and another smaller settlement out of town limits called "Pinnacle" where colored families own their homes and a few land owners scattered over the county. Three churches are maintained in town, Methodist, Baptist and Christian, and seem to be liberally patronized.

Emma Washington, familiarly known as "Aunt Em," was a well known colored woman of Lawrenceburg; died July, 1929, age seventy-five. She served as a domestic in many homes of the community and was honest and loyal to her employees and faithful to every duty. Two pews in the colored Baptist church, where her funeral was preached, were reserved for her white folks who brought sprays of flowers which attested to "Aunt Em's" true worth. She left four sons and two daughters.

Dr. James W. Bond, minister, teacher, writer of note and a leader among Kentucky negroes, died in Williamsburg in 1929, aged sixty-three. He was a native of Anderson County, having been born and reared on the Preston Bond farm five miles south of Lawrenceburg. In early life he had such a zeal for an education he never let an opportunity pass to cultivate his mind. When he left Anderson he settled in Whitley County, where he studied law and was admitted to the bar. He was a son of slave parents. Tiring of law, he studied theology at Berea and Oberlin College, graduating in 1895. At time of death Dr. Bond was a member of the Interracial Commission.

Jordon Hall died in 1931, aged seventy-three; worked for more than twenty-five years for R. H. Lillard. He first came to Lillards to work for one day, and his work was so satisfactory that "Jurd's" services stretched over a long period of years. He was respected by his race and had many friends among both white and colored.

Mary Hayden, recently deceased, wife of Ezra Hayden, was a useful colored woman who, for many years prepared and served viands at social functions in Lawrenceburg. Matt Reid gives a good account of his stewardship as janitor at the city school and Lawrenceburg National Bank, places he has filled creditably for many years. Carleton Pleasant has been mortician for his race since 1909. He is assisted by his son, Raymond. They are useful and worthwhile colored citizens. Henry Harris, who has worked for the Saffell family for thirty-five years, has an umblemished record for honesty and faithfulness. We can mention Jim Shields and John Russell, who for many years have worked faithfully and efficiently for the white population in the homes, the offices, on the farms, at the fairs and many other places, evincing an intelligence that rates them as valuable servants.

An Act to incorporate the Lawrenceburg Colored Cemetery Company was approved March 9, 1888. By this Act and under it, this cemetery was organized with the following incorporators named in this Act: Thomas Burrus, Henry Harris, Matt Ellison, Henry Brown and General Carter.

"Uncle Will and Aunt Phoebe" Rice built a little home far out on Southern Ave., before Lawrenceburg expanded and imposing residences were erected on this street. But the white folks who built near "Aunt Phoebe" found her to be a valuable neighbor. She catered at the social functions, nursed the sick, laundered the delicate apparel, and in so many ways proved her worth. "Uncle Will" gardened and tended stock. After the death of this estimable couple, their home was sold and remodeled by a white purchaser.

John and Mary Gray, another worthy colored couple, were pillars in the colored Christian church. For more than a quarter of a century Mary kept house and John looked after the premises of the home of C. E. Bond and his two little sons, after the death of the wife and mother, until long after the boys attained manhood. Mary's fruit and angel food cakes were never excelled by the most experienced chef.

Christopher Columbus McKee and his wife, Sally, celebrated their golden wedding in 1917 when their nine children and twenty-five relatives were in attendance. They own a home and a plot of ground in the Fox Creek neighborhood where they have tended crops and worked for the best families of that community over a long period of years. Columbus McKee has been the official burgoo soup maker at all the political rallies and barbecues in the county for fifty years. Today, at an advanced age, he is not ready to "lay down the shovel and the hoe and go where the good darkies go," for he and his wife retain their activity to an unusual degree and are esteemed by all who know them.

Dal Talbert has been a familiar figure around town for several decades. He is a living exponent of the song, "Any rags, any bones, any bottles today," as he drives through the county behind a flea-bitten old nag hitched to a ramshackled wagon, whose wheels are at variance with the rest of the vehicle. Dal is honest and useful in his line, and as he makes his rounds, bestows a broad grin—especially at Christmas time—and "How-dum-do" on acquaintance and stranger alike.

The W. T. Bond home, "The Royal Oaks." Built 1898.

GLEANINGS FROM YESTERYEARS IN ANDERSON COUNTY

The population in Anderson County in 1830 was 4.520; in 1840, 5,452; in 1850, 6,260; in 1860, 7,440; in 1870, 5,499; in 1880, 9,361; today the population (census of 1930), 8,494. In Collin's History of Kentucky, published in 1878, the population of some of the towns in Anderson County was: Lawrenceburg, 400; Rough-and-Ready, four miles from Lawrenceburg, was 161; Camdenville, on Salt River, 75; VanBuren, eighteen miles west of Lawrenceburg, 30; Ripyville, 3½ miles south of Lawrenceburg, 30. In 1870 the number of acres of land in Anderson County was 110,549. In 1846, the value of land per acre was $5.66. In 1870 the value of land per acre was $9.37. Increase value per acre in twenty-four years was $3.71. In 1817, live stock in the county was as follows: Horses, 3,233; mules, 424; cattle, 3,603; hogs over six months, 7,096; tons of hay, 713; bushels of corn, 374,001; bushels of wheat, 34,290.

Three score years ago the country-side abounded in peddlers selling tinware, churns, pumps, lightning rods and big family Bibles. The hey-day of sports were debating clubs, singing schools, lawn fetes, buggy-riding, picnics and horse-jockying. Such recreations as basket-ball, foot-ball, moving pictures, radios, ice cream cones, hitch-hiking, electric devices, etc., were decades in the future. Spelling matches were pitted against contestants and singing schools a social feature. In the early days neighbors came in voluntarily and nursed the sick, also made coffins, dug graves and made all funeral arrangements free of cost. A half century ago citizens in Lawrenceburg, who strolled forth at night, carried lighted lanterns or ran the risk of stumbling into a mud hole, or contacting with a wandering quadruped, for animals had the right of way through the streets. The town had made rapid strides when oil street lamps were erected on posts to direct night traffic. Just before dusk, Corn Searcy, the "lamp lighter," carrying a ladder and a torch, made the rounds and lit the beacons that met the requirements of that day. Green vegetables in winter were not brought to the town market. Judge W. H. McBrayer owned a citrus grove in Florida in the early '80s and shipped grapefruit to friends in Lawrenceburg, and all who tasted the fruit declared it "was so sour and bitter it was not fit to eat." On the ground now occupied by the Anderson News plant stood the old town pump. It had a strong iron handle, and was used by the citizens of the central part of town for drinking water, and laundry purposes when the rainbarrel was empty. Another pump stood on the corner of the pavement below the Baptist church, and was the public fountain for that end of town. The churches were lighted by candles stuck in tin frames that were nailed to the wall, and meeting was announced for "early candle light." Everybody had a marbletop table in the parlor, and portraits of Ma and Pa, made by strolling artists, hung on the wall. Every back yard had an ash-hopper filled with wood aches with water poured over at intervals to drip red lye to make soap for the family wash. In the country on the back porch a washpan sat by the water bucket on a bench, and here the boys and Pa "washed up" when the farm bell called them in to dinner. Everybody believed in the ground hog and signs pertaining to the light and dark of the moon and planted potatoes and beans accordingly. The family doctor came with blue-mass pills, quinine and mustard plaster, felt the pulse, looked at the tongue, measured out the powders or lotions to be taken at intervals by the patient. He had no stethoscope to rely upon, but put his ear down on your thorax, and that trained organ of hearing registered all the sounds within the walls of that frame. There were no prescriptions to have filled, for the doctor carried his own drug store in his "saddle-bags," which were two large pockets of leather that he could sling over the back of his horse and attach to the saddle. The country stores sold everything from side meat to calico, and from salt to balmorals. The women wore hoop skirts and bustles, sang "Jaunita," and every parlor had a table on which lay a family Bible, a photograph album and a plush-handled stereoptican.

There were very few vehicles in the country prior to 1815, and the increase was limited to another decade, when there began to be an improvement in roads to accommodate wheeled conveyances. Road construction was more advanced in about the year 1840, and many of our "best families" had carriages drawn by two horses, sometimes driven by a liveried slave servant, who enjoyed wielding a whip and feeling his importance while driving for "de white folks."

Not until after the War Between the States was there all kinds of wheeled vehicles in common use. "Aunt" Sallie White Penny Carpenter was born in 1816 and died in 1907 in her 92nd year. She wore the names of her pioneer families, all of whom figured in the official life in the settlement and erection of Anderson County. She told the writer she remembered when there were only two vehicles in this county, one a barouche and the other a two-wheeled gig. For over a hundred years the old "worm fence," made of split rails, was used as division fences between the Anderson County farms. These were built V shape, were very strong and lasted many decades. Miles of stone fences were also built in the county. Today only a few of them remain, covered with litchen and wild vines, but most of them have been crushed into stone for the highways and wire fencing supersedes them. Johnson's History records that on May 9th and 10th, 1838, the first giraffe ever seen in this part of the country was on exhibition in Frankfort, and the press gave it wide notice, and that people from all surrounding counties went to see this "most wonderful living creature." Also on the evening of August 27, 1839, the beautiful Auoro Borealis was spread across the heavens brighter than was ever known before. Those here who saw it declared that "human language never had the power to describe it."

In Kerr's History of Kentucky in speaking of the stage coach he said: "What excitement prevailed in the sleepy village when a stage coach came dashing into town. The driver, handling four spirited horses at an imposing gallop, winding his horn, the bright colored coach swaying and swinging on its leathern straps, and enveloped in a cloud of dust as it came to a stand still at the tavern door! How rapidly the news of its arrival spread through the town, and how quickly the people gathered to see who was arriving and learn the latest news of the outside world. It was everybody's business to watch the stage come in and depart." Early stage drivers through Lawrenceburg were a Mr. Hastings and Ben Townsend. They drove four horses and the steeds were changed every ten or fifteen miles. The inside of the stage accommodated from eight to twelve passengers and the mail was carried under the driver's seat. The back of the coach was built high and deep to hold the baggage with an apron buckled over to shield it from the weather. The old Galt House, which stood on the post office site for three-quarters of a century, was kept for many years by Mrs. Margaret Saffell, widow of Joshua Saffell. Many notable guests stopped there in stage coach days, among them

Henry Clay and Thomas Marshall. The picturesque stage coach was succeeded by the jersey wagon in 1880. This was a three-seated vehicle that accommodated about a dozen passengers. It carried the mail and travelers from Mercer and Anderson counties to connect with trains at Frankfort, Ky.

There has been a drug store at Ballard's corner for 109 years. It was established by Dr. Lewis J. Witherspoon in 1827. His family lived over the store and it was here that his first grandchild, Lewis W. McKee, was born in 1854. One of the early postmasters in Lawrenceburg was William Hickman, who kept the office in his drygoods store about where C. A. Routt & Son have their store today. The frame work of the boxes was pushed up close to the front window and the boxes marked alphabetically. In passing up street, the pedestrian could locate his initial on a box, and if it contained mail, would call to see if there was any for him. Should the box be empty, there was no need to disturb the postmaster. Newt Edwards and Kavanaugh Cox were postmasters in the '70s. C. W. Williams occupied the office from 1881 to 1885, at which date W. P. Walker was appointed to the office and held it a number of years. Later T. J. Ballard was postmaster and the office was in his drug store. George Hutcheson was manager in the early '90s when the office was put in the third class. Walker Crossfield and Richard Paxton were later officials. Paxton was succeeded by J. Bert Searcy. Rural routes were established in the county in 1903. Route, with H. L. Hutton as carrier, was established in January, 1904; No. 2, with Joe Searcy; about the same time No. 3 with Ezra McGinnis carrier, and No. 4, with Casper Bryant in October, 1905. A rural route from Alton Station was established in 1906 with Jerome Grey as carrier. William Dick Johnson was clerk in the postoffice at this time. Today R. E. Johnson is postmaster.

Before the toll-gates were abandoned in the '90s, the rates were as follows: Vehicle drawn by one horse, ten cents; same by two horses, twenty cents; wagon drawn by three horses, oxen or mules, thirty cents; by four, forty cents. Empty wagons charged half rates. The bill stated that "any one attempting to defraud the company by going around the toll gate, or evade the payment of toll, for every offense he should be fined ten dollars; and if any toll-gate keeper charged a greater rate of toll than fixed by the law, he should be fined ten dollars for every offense."

The work on the dam across Kentucky river at Lock No. 5 was begun June 7, 1884, and completed December 8, 1885, costing the government $65,000. Mr. John Vaughn, a worthy citizen of the county, was superintendent of the work.

In 1885, Wells and Frazier had "handsome hacks and good horses to hire from their livery stable to the public." Also "horses were boarded by the day, week or month." The agitation for telephones began in Lawrenceburg prior to 1888, when W. P. Walker engineered the scheme and entered thirty subscribers. But it was not until June, 1889, that the first phones were installed in the grocery store of Ottenheimer & Bond, and the W. H. Searcy livery stable, and it was said "they worked perfectly." In 1889 two wells were bored on Woodford street to supply that part of town with water; one in front of the Birdwhistle home, the other, two blocks further up the street. The latter well was so strongly impregnated with sulphur that crowds drank the water and carried it away in jugs. The upper floor of the new A. C. Witherspoon building on Main street (today occupied by Trent's store), was opened for a skating rink on November 1, 1885, with an instructor from

Lexington in attendance. The hall was 100 feet long by 50 feet wide, and was said to be the finest hall for a rink of any town in central Kentucky. The interest in this sport at that time was wide-spread and intense. The Anderson News declared that every one in town from kiddies to mothers and fathers, were "on wheels."

In the summer of 1887 a new iron fence was put around the court house. The contract was let to a firm in Kenton, Ohio, and called for 628 feet of fencing and five gates at a cost of $656. After the completion of the fence suitable and sufficient hitching racks for horses were put up on the old jail lot at the expense of the county, with a notice that hitching to the new court house fence was subject to arrest and fine.

About this time the Witherspoon Hall, which had been in use for two years for all kinds of entertainments, was being partitioned off into small rooms for offices, which was a lamentable fact to many, as the only available place for ameteur performances was the court house, which was hardly adequate for many amusements. Feeling the need of a modern hotel and opera house combined, two enterprising citizens, W. J. Waterfill and W. A. Bottom, engaged R. C. Bradley as contractor and began the erection of the "Warbott Hotel" in 1891, the name of the hostelry being a contraction of the names of the builders. This hotel was on Main street where Taylor's restaurant stands today. It was completed in 1892 at a cost of $37,000. Five hundred and sixty chairs were put on the main floor of the opera house and 300 in the gallery. The opening performance was given by a stock company on May 3, 1892, and was witnessed by a large audience. The stage was 58 by 25 feet, with eleven sets of scenery and was pronounced a model theatre for a small town, and the hotel one of the best appointed in the state. A tower and water tank in the rear of the building supplied the entire block with water. This was a decade before Lawrenceburg had installed a system of water-works. The first lessee of the new hotel was C. Roose of Cincinnati. The Warbott Hotel was burned in 1898 and never rebuilt. The old Lawrenceburg Hotel, opposite the depot, was burned in 1905 and rebuilt by C. E. Bond and opened in 1908 with Morry Wakefield, of Shelbyville, the first lessee of this two-story brick hostelry with twenty-three rooms, conveniently located for the traveling public. In spite of the many disasterous fires that Lawrenceburg has suffered, she seems to have the resiliency and adaptibility to stage a come-back without loss of prosperity or population.

Prior to March, 1892, such a thing as a newsboy was an unknown quantity on the streets of Lawrenceburg. At that time a number of these little heralds having daily papers for sale, began crying out their sheets in the sing-song tone peculiar to the craft.

In the gay '90s a popular winter sport at night was a big farm sled, bedded with hay and hitched to two horses, filled with a dozen or more merry-makers driving around the country sides, filling the air with hilarious shouts accompanied by tin horns and cow-bells.

On the evening of November 18, 1892, the Democrats held high carnival in Lawrenceburg to celebrate the election of Grover Cleveland to the presidency of the United States. The entire town was decorated in flags, buntain and Chinese lanterns. All the surrounding hamlets in the county sent companies with torch lights to join the long parade, with H. B. Carpenter acting as chief marshal and leading the procession. The ladies had arranged special floats for the occasion. The line of march, starting at the court house going through all the streets, halted in front of Judge McBrayer's vacant lot (the McGinnis home today), witnessed a display of fire-works, that had been purchased by a special committee sent to Cincinnati to procure them. No difficulties or accidents marred the occasion. On November 16, 1892, a bid was put in by the Seth Thomas Clock Company for $670 to place a clock on top of the court house. On February 16, 1893, the big 135-poung pendulum of the town clock began to swing and the hands set in motion. Then the question arose, "Shall we go by sun or standard time?" The popular sentiment was for the time set by old Sol, but standard time used by the railroads was finally adopted.

The first jewelry store was opened in Lawrenceburg in 1892 by J. C. Thompson, of Shelby County. The Chatauqua held under a tent in the high school yard for many years during the summer season was a cultural influence and largely attended, but the motor car, movie and radio put it out of business forever.

In 1906 there was not an automobile owned in Anderson County. Today they are too thick to dodge. In 1907 Dr. C. A. Leathers drove the first home-owned automobile in town. By 1908 a number of our citizens were owners of "horseless carriages." J. M. Johnson and J. W. Gaines had the newest models in Cadillacs; Mrs. Mary Dowling, a Packard. The ladies wore a special chapeau with veil to keep their tresses from becoming disheveled, for none of the cars of that date were enclosed in glass, but had storm curtains to button on in inclement weather. Mrs. Roberta Bond Neet was the first woman to drive an automobile in Anderson or Woodford counties.

A record of 1922 states there was an automobile for every seventeen persons in Anderson County; today (1936) the estimate is an auto to every five persons.

On October 24, 1896, the "night-riders" destroyed the tollgates on the Louisville and Lawrenceburg roads. This destruction of property and sinister threats continued until the tollgates were taken down and the roads made free.

OLD RECORDS

The following paper is in possession of Mrs. Annie Bond Cole: "I have this day sold to John W. Bond a negro slave named Sadie, aged about twenty years, for the sum of $950.00 to be paid the first day of January, 1860, for which sum he has this day executed to me his note. I warrant the title to said slave, and warrant her sound in body and in mind, this September 22nd, 1859."—Signed, William H. Witherspoon.

Another statement in Mrs. Cole's scrap-book records: "I have this day sold to John W. Bond, for and in consideration of $750.00, one negro girl, Sarah, a slave for life, about seventeen years old and warrant her sound. Given under my hand this 8th day of December, 1856. (Signed) J. H. Walker. At this period the barter and sale of slaves was as active as that of any other property.

The following note, ninety-five years old, is in Mrs. Cole's possession: "We have this day hired of Stephen C. Brown for William Brown, a negro woman named Cynthiana and her two children. Now we bind ourselves to return said negroes to the said Brown on the first day of January next clothed as follows: the woman a good new linsey frock, a good new flax linen shirt, a good new pair of shoes, a good new pair of yarn stockings, a two dollar and half blanket, a bonnet, and in the spring we give to her two new linen shirts and frocks. The children are to be returned clothed with good new linsey shirts and frocks each. In the spring they are to have two good new tow linen slips each, and we are not to hire them out to any other person or take either of them out of the county. (Signed) William B. Mitchell, January 1, 1841.

The above Wm. B. Mitchell was the grandfather of Mrs. Mary E. Vowels of Lawrenceburg, and E. T. Mitchell, of Sparrow, Anderson County, Ky.

The old black "Mammy" was an institution in the southern home before and after the War Between the States. Farm owners of slaves fed and clothed the old negroes who grew too old to work. Today we have some grey heads who recall the black mammy who helped care for them in their early youth, and speak affectionately of them. While she belonged to "de white folks," the white people in the southern home belonged to her. She lived for two or three generations in the same family, and her authority on rearing "Missus'" children was respected. She was full of stories for the children and full of superstitions.

She could conjure warts off the children's hands, and ward off "rheumatiz in the jints" by carrying a buckeye in the pocket. A bag of "asfidity" tied around the children's neck made them teethe easily. The left hind foot of a rabbit "kotched" in a grave yard was carried for luck. Black mammy was the pioneer crooner of spirituals that soothed the white children to sweet slumbers.

A sale bill, eighty-six years old, is in the possession of Mrs. Annie Bond Cole, as follows: Having sold my farm in Anderson County, I, Joe Cooley, will sell on Saturday, September 26, 1850, the following, to-wit: one buck nigger 25 years old, weight 200 pounds; 4 nigger wenches, from eight to twenty four years old; 3 nigger boys six years old; 13 nigger hoes; 6 yoke oxen well broke; 10 ox yokes; 1 saddle pony 5 years old; 3 double shovel plows; 25 one gallon whiskey jugs; 100 gallons of apple cider; 1 barrel of good sorghum; 2 barrels of kraut; 1 extra good nigger whip; 2 tons of tobacco two years old; sale starts at ten o'clock sharp. Terms cash, I am going to Missouri and need the money. Col. W. H. Johnson, Auctioneer; Joe Cooley, owner.

FINALE

Major L. W. McKee did more for the preservation of the history of our county and its people than any one who ever lived in this locality. Over a period of forty-five years he was gathering notes and facts from Kentucky histories, and from old deed books, will books, order books and processional volumes in the Franklin and Anderson County court houses. He had just begun writing sketches of pioneer families when he died. It has been my pleasure to procure many more of these "thumb-nail biographies," for a sketch of them is a part of Anderson's history. We cannot estimate the true worth of the pioneer women who stood by their liege lords and endured the hardships of the frontier in rearing and training their children. They made the home in the wilderness, and had but little, but were happy and thankful. The history of their struggles is gripping and inspiring, and should challenge the present generation to noble achievements. We cannot rest upon the laurels won by the intrepid men and women who "held the fort" of the settlement known today as Lawrenceburg. Many a sturdy grandchild in the county wears the pioneer name and should be taught the sentiment spoken by Pericles to the Athenians of old: "You are bound to maintain the imperial dignity of your city in which you all take pride, for you should not covet the glory unless you will endure the toil."

LYDIA K. BOND.

www.ingramcontent.com/pod-product-compliance
Lightning Source LLC
Chambersburg PA
CBHW062005220426
43662CB00010B/1235